THE PINOCHET CASE
A LEGAL AND CONSTITUTIONAL ANALYSIS

The Pinochet Case
A Legal and
Constitutional Analysis

Edited by
PROFESSOR DIANA WOODHOUSE
Oxford Brookes University

·HART·
PUBLISHING
OXFORD – PORTLAND OREGON
2000

Hart Publishing
Oxford and Portland, Oregon

Published in North America (US and Canada) by
Hart Publishing c/o
International Specialized Book Services
5804 NE Hassalo Street
Portland, Oregon
97213-3644
USA

Distributed in the Netherlands, Belgium and Luxembourg by
Intersentia, Churchillaan 108
B2900 Schoten
Antwerpen
Belgium

Distributed in Australia and New Zealand by
Federation Press
John St
Leichhardt
NSW 2000

Hart Publishing Ltd is a specialist legal publisher based in Oxford, England.
To order further copies of this book or to request a list of other
publications please write to:

Hart Publishing Ltd, Salter's Boatyard, Folly Bridge, Abingdon Road,
Oxford OX1 4LB
Telephone: +44 (0)1865 245533 or Fax: +44 (0)1865 794882
e-mail: mail@hartpub.co.uk

British Library Cataloguing in Publication Data
Data Available
ISBN 1 84113–102–4 (Cloth)

1001830874

Typeset by Hope Services (Abingdon) Ltd.
Printed and bound in Great Britain

Contents

Foreword

THIS collection of essays had its origin in a workshop, organised by the Centre for Legal Research and Policy Studies, at Oxford Brookes University in March 1999. The workshop was a response to the general interest in the Pinochet affair and was attended by academics, from a range of disciplines, and non-academics. The papers presented at the workshop provoked lively discussion and this provided a stimulus for further work, resulting in the essays, which appear in this volume. They have taken account of subsequent developments, most notably the third House of Lords' decision on Pinochet, which was still pending when the workshop was held. Like the papers given at the workshop, the essays are aimed at those with an interest in the case, whether lawyers or non-lawyers. They are accompanied by the three House of Lords' judgments on Pinochet, which are contained in an Annex to the book.

The timescale for producing the essays was short and the time available for consultation was limited. We are therefore particularly grateful to colleagues who responded so quickly to requests for their comments on draft versions. We would also like to thank the participants at the workshop for their input and colleagues in the law department at Oxford Brookes, and elsewhere, for their support of this venture. In addition, thanks are due to Richard Hart of Hart Publishing for his encouragement, help and support. The authors alone bear responsibility for this volume.

DPW
8 November 1999

Contributors

Jonathan Black-Branch, senior lecturer in law, Oxford Brookes University
Paul Catley, principal lecturer in law, Oxford Brookes University
Ben Chigara, lecturer in law, University of Leeds
Lisa Claydon, research fellow, De Montfort University
Evadne Grant, senior lecturer in law, Oxford Brookes University
Judith Hendrick, senior lecturer in law, Oxford Brookes University
David Robertson, fellow tutor in politics, St Hugh's College, Oxford
Diana Woodhouse, professor in law, Oxford Brookes University

Table of Cases

Table of Legislation

Table of Treaties and Conventions

1

Introduction: The Extradition of Pinochet: A Calendar of Events

DIANA WOODHOUSE

THE saga of Senator[1] Augusto Pinochet's extradition from Britain to Spain began on 16 October 1998 when an application for his detention was received from Judge Baltasar Garzon in Madrid. This set in motion a series of events which, as the spotlight moved backwards and forwards between the courts and the Home Secretary, demonstrated the juxtaposition of law and politics within the extradition procedure and the relationship between national and international law. It also illustrated the pressures of working within a framework in which domestic decisions are tempered by the need to comply with international obligations, withstand international scrutiny and secure international approval. Such pressures may be familiar to politicians. However, the same is not true for judges and the Appellate Committee of the House of Lords has seldom received the international attention, lobbying and publicity that accompanied its three decisions.[2]

The *Pinochet* episode placed the House of Lords at the centre of the international stage and provided a valuable study of its operation in such a setting. The extent to which British judges operate within the context of international law is limited by the doctrine of parliamentary sovereignty and by the dualist system of law, under which international treaties have no legal effect until incorporated into national law. Nevertheless, the ruling of the House of Lords that Senator Pinochet, as a former head of state, was not entitled to claim immunity from prosecution had important implications for the development of international law, as did judicial statements about the need for a properly formulated system for the administration of international criminal justice, and, more generally, the discussion about the relationship between law and morality which surrounded the case.

---

[1] Pinochet's full title is Senator Agusto Pinochet Ugarte. Although he is still frequently styled "General", the title of Senator is used in these essays.

[2] R v. *Bow Street Metropolitan Stipendiary Magistrate and Others, ex parte Pinochet Ugarte* [1998] 3 WLR 1456; R v. *Bow Street Metropolitan Stipendiary Magistrate and Others, ex parte Pinochet Ugarte (No. 2)* [1999] 2 WLR 272; R v. *Bow Street Metropolitan Stipendiary Magistrate and Others, ex parte Pinochet Ugarte (No. 3)* [1999] 2 WLR 827. These cases are referred to in these essays as *Pinochet 1, 2 and 3*. References are to the *Weekly Law Reports* and to the page numbers in the Appendix, where the cases are reproduced.

At a national level, the House of Lords' ruling that its own decision could not stand on grounds of an appearance of bias, raised questions about its procedures and processes and had implications for its long term suitability as an appellate court for political and constitutional cases. It also provided an early indication of some of the issues that might arise under the Human Rights Act, in particular the standards of the European Convention on Human Rights on bias and their effect on the Appellate Committee of the House of Lords, as currently constituted.

Many of these issues are considered in the essays in this volume. The essays are based on papers presented at a workshop on *Pinochet* at Oxford Brookes University in March 1999. They have been updated to take account of events since that time. Although they attempt neither a detailed examination of all aspects of the House of Lords' decisions nor a full analysis of the implications of *Pinochet*, they provide a starting point for further study of the episode, and seek to stimulate discussion and debate.

THE PROCESSING OF PINOCHET THROUGH THE EXTRADITION PROCEDURE;
A CALENDAR OF EVENTS

The extradition procedure involves the courts, whose concern is the legality of the extradition request and the process of extradition, and the Home Secretary, who is responsible for the initial decision to initiate extradition proceedings in the court and, at the end of those proceedings, for the decision to extradite. His discretion, while tempered by considerations laid down by the Extradition Act 1989, is considerable. However, at all stages it is open to challenge by way of judicial review.[3] There is therefore always some degree of interaction between the courts and the Home Secretary in extradition cases. Where Senator Pinochet was concerned, this was exceptional. The brief account that follows traces that interaction, providing an outline of the key events and their relation to the extradition procedure.

The arrest of Senator Pinochet

On 16 October 1998 an international warrant for the arrest of Senator Pinochet was received from the Central Court of Criminal Proceedings in Madrid. This resulted in a provisional warrant for his arrest being issued by a metropolitan stipendiary magistrate, Mr Nicholas Evans, in accordance with the Extradition Act 1989.[4] The basis for the warrant was that there was evidence that between 11 September 1973 and 31 December 1983 Pinochet had murdered Spanish citizens in Chile, crimes for which, under Spanish law, he could be tried in Spain.

[3] Through the common law and via section 12 of the Extradition Act 1989.
[4] The Extradition Act 1989, section 8(1)(b).

The warrant was issued in haste and, as the High Court subsequently found, was defective, in that the crimes listed did not satisfy the definition of "extradition crime" given in the Extradition Act.[5] This requires the offence to have been committed in the country seeking extradition, or for the accused to be a citizen of that country, or for the offence to be one over which the United Kingdom courts have jurisdiction. None of these provisions was satisfied. The offences had not been committed in Spain, Pinochet was not a Spanish citizen and the United Kingdom courts have no jurisdiction to try cases of murder committed outside the United Kingdom, unless they have been committed by British citizens.[6]

In recognition of the first warrant's shortcomings, on 22 October a second warrant was issued by a different stipendiary magistrate, Mr Ronald Bartle, on the basis that there was evidence that "between 1 January 1988 and December 1992, being a public official, [Pinochet] intentionally inflicted severe pain or suffering on another in the performance or purported performance of his official duties within the jurisdiction of the Government of Spain" and that, within the same period, "he conspired with persons unknown to intentionally inflict severe pain or suffering on others in the performance or purported performance of his official duties".[7] He was also accused, first, of detaining and conspiring to detain individuals and, secondly, of threatening those detained with death, injury and further detention in order to compel them to act as their captors required. The dates for these other offences were January 1982 to January 1992 and January 1976 to December 1992, respectively. The warrant also alleged conspiracy to commit murder. Unlike the first warrant, this one contained offences which could be tried in the United Kingdom, namely, torture, under the Criminal Justice Act 1988, and hostage taking, under the Hostage Taking Act 1982, although, subsequently, the dates at which these pieces of legislation took effect played a major part in the decision of the House of Lords as to whether Pinochet could be extradited.

On the same day as the second warrant was issued, Pinochet's lawyers made applications to the Home Secretary and the Divisional Court. The application to the Home Secretary, Jack Straw, concerned his power to issue authority to proceed, which is required before any extradition proceeding can begin.[8] Pinochet's lawyers sought to persuade him not to issue it and also to cancel the warrant for Pinochet's arrest. Their application to the court was for an order of habeas corpus and for leave to apply for judicial review to quash the first warrant and direct the Home Secretary to cancel it.

The following day, 23 October, Pinochet was arrested under the second warrant. This resulted in a further application for judicial review, the main ground being that a warrant should not have been issued against him, because, as a

---

[5] Ibid, section 2.

[6] Section 9 of the Offences Against the Person Act 1861 (24 and 25 Vict. c. 100), as amended.

[7] *Pinochet 1*, n 2 supra, at 1461; Annex, p 136.

[8] The Extradition Act 1989, section 8(4).

former head of state, he had immunity under the State Immunity Act 1978.[9] The applications for judicial review were heard on 26 October by the Lord Chief Justice, Lord Bingham, who was accompanied by Mr Justice Collins and Mr Justice Richards. Two days later they quashed the decisions of both magistrates to issue warrants, holding that the sovereign immunity provided by the State Immunity Act meant that Pinochet was "entitled as a former head of state to immunity from civil and criminal proceedings of the English court".[10] It followed, therefore, that as extradition proceedings constituted criminal proceedings, Pinochet could not be subjected to them and so could not be extradited.

However, the decision of the Divisional Court did not result in Senator Pinochet being released. Indeed, the quashing of the second decision was stayed, pending an appeal to the House of Lords on "a point of law of general public importance", namely, "the proper interpretation and scope of immunity enjoyed by a former head of state from arrest and extradition proceedings in the United Kingdom in respect of acts committed while he was head of state".[11] Pinochet therefore remained subject to the restrictions of bail.

Appeal to the House of Lords; *Pinochet 1*

On 3 November a formal request for Pinochet's extradition was received from Spain and, coincidentally, the next day the House of Lords began to hear the appeal from the Divisional Court. The high level of interest in the case, evident outside the court in the demonstrations of those seeking Pinochet's extradition, was recognised by the House of Lords in its decision to grant leave to intervene to Amnesty International and others representing victims of the alleged activities.[12] Exceptionally, intervention by these parties was allowed not just in the form of written submissions, but also through oral contributions. Written submissions were also accepted from other interveners[13] while the court itself sought the assistance of an *amicus curiae* or legal adviser.[14]

The House of Lords gave its decision on 25 November[15] and, again in recognition of the interest in the case, took the unprecedented step of announcing it live on television. Moreover, the law lords departed from their normal practice and delivered oral summaries of their written speeches. These represented the

---

[9] Part 1.

[10] As recorded in *Pinochet 1*, n 2 supra.

[11] Ibid at 1462; Annex, p 137.

[12] i.e. the Medical Foundation for the Care of Victims of Torture, the Redress Trust, Mary Ann Beausire, Juana Francisco Beausire and Sheila Cassidy. Professor Brownlie appeared on behalf of the interveners.

[13] Human Rights Watch, Nicole Francois Droilly (representative of Association of the Relatives of the Disappeared Detainees) and Marco Antonio Enriquez Espinoza were allowed to make written submissions related to matters not raised in oral argument which related to the certified point of law.

[14] Mr David Lloyd Jones.

[15] N 2 supra.

"first judicial soundbites in English legal history"[16] and suggested a concern to be seen as more "user" friendly. The decision was split three-two, the dissenters being Lords Slynn and Lloyd. The majority, namely, Lords Nicholls, Steyn and Hoffmann, held, first, that the fact that Chile was a signatory of the Convention against Torture[17] meant it accepted that, where torture was alleged, the United Kingdom had an obligation under the Convention either to extradite or prosecute; second, that the absolute immunity afforded by the State Immunity Act 1978 did not extend to criminal proceedings and thus did not apply to extradition proceedings; third, that the crimes of torture and hostage-taking fell outside what international law would regard as functions of a head of state and thus the applicant's status as former head of state did not confer immunity from extradition proceedings in respect of the crimes charged against him; and, fourth, that no question could arise of the court declining jurisdiction on grounds of the common law doctrine of act of state, as the Taking of Hostages Act 1982 and the Criminal Justice Act 1988 made express provision for such jurisdiction.

It concluded, therefore, that, as the applicant had no claim to immunity and there were no grounds for a declaration of non-justiciability, the decision to issue the second warrant was a valid decision and should be restored. As a result, Pinochet was required to remain in Britain and await the decision of the Home Secretary whether to authorise the continuation of the proceedings for his extradition.[18]

The Home Secretary exercises his discretion

Attention and political pressure therefore switched from the courts to the Home Secretary. The Extradition Act gives him the power "to issue an authority to proceed unless it appears to him that an order for the return of the person concerned could not lawfully be made, or would not in fact be made, in accordance with the provisions of this Act".[19] Before exercising his discretion, he therefore had to satisfy himself that the request for extradition had been made by an authority which had that function, and that the basis for the request and the evidence furnished with it were in accordance with the requirements of the Act. This presented little problem as Spain is a party to the European Convention on Extradition 1957 and, as a consequence, comes within the ambit of the Extradition Act. Moreover, the Criminal Division of the Spanish National Court had confirmed on 5 November Spain's jurisdiction to try the alleged crimes, and the decision of the House of Lords had confirmed that the alleged offences were extraditable.

---

[16] J Rozenberg, Analysis [1999] *Public Law* 181.
[17] Convention against Torture and Other Cruel, Inhuman and Degrading Treatment or Punishment 1984.
[18] Under Section 7(1) of the Extradition Act.
[19] Ibid, section 7(4).

During the time taken for Straw to reach his decision, interested parties from both sides sought to persuade him of the factors he should take into account and of the way in which he should exercise his discretion. Those against extradition insisted that he should consider a wide range of factors. They argued that Pinochet's fate should be left to the Chileans and that his prosecution outside Chile would upset the country's rehabilitation as a democratic nation. They also suggested that the extradition of Pinochet was not in Britain's national interest, as it would damage diplomatic and trading relations with Chile, and, further, that the extradition of a former head of state would provide a dangerous precedent, which would have far-reaching national and international implications. In addition, they argued that Pinochet's arrest, while he was under medical supervision and recovering from an operation, together with his general state of health and his age, militated against extradition. Conversely, those seeking Pinochet's extradition argued that, at this stage, the Home Secretary should limit his considerations to those of a quasi-judicial nature. They stressed Britain's moral and legal obligations to the international community, arguing that crimes against humanity should always be prosecuted and that it was important to Britain's international reputation to be seen to support this stand. They were, however, concerned that, with a Chilean jet standing by to take the senator home, Straw would take what might seem to be the easier option and release Pinochet on humanitarian grounds, arguing that consideration for his age and state of health overrode other factors.

This concern resulted in yet another legal challenge on 9 December, the day on which the Home Secretary was due to announce his decision, with the applicants, Amnesty International, seeking leave to apply for judicial review of the pending decision and the way in which it had been made. The basis of the application was that the effect of the Convention against Torture,[20] which requires a person alleged to have committed torture to be extradited or, failing that, prosecuted by the competent authorities, was to turn the discretion of the Home Secretary into a duty. This meant, according to Amnesty, that, provided the Home Secretary was satisfied that the extradition request was lawfully made, he had to authorise extradition proceedings. Amnesty also requested an injunction or a stay in proceedings to prevent any cancellation of the warrant and the discharge of the senator. They were fearful that, if the Home Secretary decided not to issue authority to proceed, Pinochet would be out of the country before the decision could be challenged.

The application came before Lord Justice Simon Brown who thought it "novel" for the court to be asked for interim relief in relation to a decision which had yet to be taken, and which the applicants may not, in fact, wish to challenge. He was particularly concerned that to give effect to the injunction sought would mean imposing physical restraints on a person on bail, in advance of a decision which was yet to be made and which, when made, was challengable. This, he considered, "would not be appropriate, right or just".[21] He therefore refused the application.

As it happened, Amnesty's fears regarding the Home Secretary's decision were unfounded as, later that day, he issued authority to proceed, along with reasons for his decision. The Extradition Act contains no requirement for reasons. It simply states that the authority to proceed "shall specify the offence or offences under the law of the United Kingdom which it appears to the Secretary of State would be constituted by equivalent conduct in the United Kingdom".[22] The giving of reasons by Jack Straw therefore suggests an attempt to make his decision safe from judicial review, or, at least, to limit the grounds on which it could be legally challenged.

The Home Secretary stated that he had made the decision personally, thereby ruling out any possibility of a legal challenge on the basis of unlawful delegation or dictation,[23] and that, in accordance with the Act, he had satisfied himself that the extradition request was lawfully made. In addition, he said he had been advised that his discretion under the Act[24] was very wide and that, in the light of this advice, he had taken a range of factors into account, including representations made by all the parties, requests for extradition from the Swiss and French Governments, and the United Kingdom's international obligation under the European Convention on Extradition 1957. He had also considered the general restrictions regarding extradition, which are laid down in the Act, and, in particular, had decided that the offences charged were not political offences, the request was made in good faith and not as a punishment for political opinions, there were no time bars to prosecution and the passage of time would not make prosecution unjust or oppressive. Moreover, he had decided that Senator Pinochet was not unfit to stand trial. He further noted that he did not consider the United Kingdom's obligation to extradite Pinochet to Spain was outweighed by the possibility of a trial in Chile, or the possible effect of extradition on Chile's stability and democracy, or the possible consequences for the United Kingdom's national interest.

Mr Straw was clearly intent on minimising the opportunity for Pinochet to argue that he had failed to take relevant factors into account, although questions of whether there are humanitarian, political or national interest factors which outweigh extradition, and whether preference should be given to requests for extradition from other countries, are only stipulated in the Act in relation to the final decision to extradite.[25] Their consideration at this stage was therefore debatable. However, taking them into account favoured Pinochet and thus would not provide him with grounds for judicial review, while those seeking

[21] *Ex parte Amnesty International* [1998] *Times Law Reports*, 11 December.
[22] Section 7(5).
[23] See, for instance, *Lavender & Sons Ltd.* v. *Minister of Housing and Local Government* [1970] 1 WLR 1231.
[24] Section 7(4) The Extradition Act 1989, together with his residual general discretion under Section 12.
[25] Ibid, section 12.

extradition had the decision they wanted and so would not be challenging the process by which that decision had been made. In any case, it is not necessarily wrong to consider these factors at an earlier stage, provided they are reconsidered later. Straw indicated this would be the case, stressing that if, subsequent to the extradition hearing, he was required to decide whether to return Pinochet, he would consider the extradition request afresh. This would include listening to further representations.

The House of Lords considers the issue of bias; *Pinochet 2*

One factor which the Home Secretary specifically dismissed as being relevant to his decision was the charge of bias against the House of Lords. The issue of bias, or rather the appearance of bias, centred upon Lord Hoffmann's links with Amnesty International. This, as Jack Straw indicated, was not a matter for the Home Secretary but for the House of Lords itself and on 10 December Pinochet's lawyers lodged an application that its decision be set aside and the appeal reheard by a differently constituted panel. The grounds for the application centred on Lord Hoffmann's failure to disclose at the time of the appeal that he was a director of Amnesty International, which, given Amnesty's status as an intervener, and the fact that it had been represented by counsel at the appeal hearing, gave the appearance of bias. The challenge to the decision of the House of Lords was unprecedented. However, it did not delay the formal start of extradition proceedings, scheduled for the following day, which required Pinochet's appearance at Belmarsh Magistrates' Court.

On 15 December, Lord Browne-Wilkinson, the senior law lord, Lords Hutton and Hope of Craighead, currently Lords of Appeal in Ordinary, and Lords Nolan and Goff of Chieveley, who were brought out of retirement, started to hear the application. They sat not as the Appellate Committee of the House of Lords but as an Appeal Committee, the function of which is usually to consider applications for leave to appeal against a decision of a lower court. Just as the challenge itself was unprecedented, so was the amount of media coverage given to those hearing it. Their previous decisions, along with views as to their ideological inclinations, were used as a means of classifying them across the liberal/conservative spectrum and of predicting the likely outcome of the appeal, a demonstration, perhaps, of the scrutiny judges might expect when the Human Rights Act becomes operative.

Two days later, in another unusual move, the Appeal Committee reported to the Chamber of the House of Lords.[26] Lord Browne-Wilkinson gave a summary of its decision in which he stated that although there was no suggestion of actual bias, Lord Hoffmann should have declared an interest because of his links with Amnesty International. His failure to do so gave the appearance of bias and

---

[26] *Pinochet 2*, n 2 supra.

meant that the panel of law lords had not been properly constituted. As a consequence, the decision of the House of Lords in *Pinochet 1* was "vacated by Order of the House", which meant that the appeal from the Divisional Court had to be reheard. This did little for the reputation of the House of Lords. It did even less for that of Lord Hoffmann and there was speculation that he might resign, especially after the Lord Chancellor, Lord Irvine, described the need to reopen the decision as "in the highest degree unfortunate, particularly when the eyes of the world are upon us" and stipulated that the law lords must "put procedures in place to ensure that this does not happen again".[27] In fact, Lord Hoffmann remained in office.

The House of Lords rehears the appeal; *Pinochet 3*

As a result of the Hoffmann episode, a panel of seven law lords,[28] none of whom had sat on the first appeal, was convened at the beginning of 1999 to rehear the case. The pressure of other judicial business, together, no doubt, with the need for careful consideration, meant that judgment was not given until 24 March, when the House of Lords by a majority of six to one, Lord Goff dissenting, ruled that the offences of torture and conspiracy to torture were extraditable crimes and that Pinochet had no immunity from prosecution for them and thus could be made subject to extradition proceedings.[29] To this extent it followed the previous panel. However, its reasoning was very different and acted to limit the effect of its decision.

In the leading judgment, Lord Browne-Wilkinson argued that while the offences of which Pinochet was accused were extraditable crimes, they had only become so on 29 September 1988, the date at which the Criminal Justice Act, which gave effect to the International Convention of Torture, came into force. Offences which were alleged to have been committed before then, did not satisfy the Extradition Act as, when committed, they could not have been tried in the United Kingdom. This limited the crimes for which Pinochet could be extradited. Moreover, they were limited further by the House of Lords' ruling on the senator's right to claim immunity. Lord Browne-Wilkinson reasoned that to allow immunity for the organisation of state torture, on the basis that it was state business, would mean not only that a head of state could do something that international law had prohibited and criminalised, but that officials, who actually did the torturing, would also be entitled to immunity, as they too had been engaged in state business. The result would be that, unless Chile waived its right to official immunity, there could be no successful prosecutions of any of those responsible for the torture regime that was alleged to have operated under

---

[27] Interview with J Rozenberg, *Radio 4*, 25 March 1999.
[28] Lords Browne-Wilkinson, Goff of Chieveley, Hope of Craighead, Hutton, Saville of Newdigate, Millett, and Phillips of Worth Matravers.
[29] *Pinochet 3*, n 2 supra.

Senator Pinochet. This was clearly incompatible with the Torture Convention, which outlawed the conduct concerned, and sought to "provide a system under which there was no safe haven for torturers". In his view, therefore, there could be no claim to immunity. However, this only applied after 8 December 1998, the date at which the Convention had effect in Chile and on which Chile was deemed to have accepted its provisions.[30]

The different basis for the decision was justified by the law lords on the grounds that the point had not been argued in the previous appeal, a justification seen by Lord Donaldson, previously Master of the Rolls, as "surprising".[31] Certainly the fact that two different panels of the House of Lords could found their decisions on such different bases, raised fundamental questions about the way in which the court operates and its reliance on counsel.

The delay in giving judgment did not, of course, diminish public interest in the outcome of the case. In recognition of this interest and "given the obscurity of the judgments", which meant that they were "incapable of being understood without some explanation",[32] Lord Browne-Wilkinson, in a "very welcome innovation",[33] gave a layperson's summary to peers in the House of Lords and, by so doing, initiated "the first televised judicial press release".[34] The decision of the law lords was inevitably subject to considerable analysis, both informed and uninformed. Moreover, this analysis was not confined to the decision itself but extended to the personalities, interests and politics of the judges concerned. Lord Browne-Wilkinson was described as "humane, liberal and charming", Lord Hope as "quiet [with a] meticulous style [and] middle of the road politics", Lord Hutton as the "most right-leaning of the panel", Lord Saville as "friendly, affable and sporty", Lord Millett as "the highest ranking Freemason in the judiciary; very clever, popular with lawyers—a favourite on the bench", Lord Phillips as "liberal" and Lord Goff as "known for intelligence and moderation".[35] In addition, to aid identification, *The Times* took the unusual step of including photographs of the judges, alongside its report of the case, which was published the following day.

The case returns to the Home Secretary

The decision of the House of Lords reduced the number of extraditable charges from thirty-one to three, one of torture and two of conspiracy to torture, and,

---

[30] Lords Hope and Saville also cited 8 December as the date after which immunity could not be claimed. Lords Hutton and Phillips took the date as 29 September 1988, when the Convention was given effect in Britain; Lord Millett considered there was no immunity and all the alleged crimes were extraditable and Lord Goff that there was immunity for all alleged crimes.
[31] Interview with J Rozenberg, n 27 supra.
[32] Broadcast and televised, 24 March 1999.
[33] J Rozenberg [1999] *Public Law* Summer 181 at 183.
[34] Ibid.
[35] *The Times*, 25 March 1999.

in view of the reduction, the law lords considered that the decision to issue authority to proceed should be reconsidered by the Home Secretary. Some took this to be a strong hint to the Home Secretary that he should return Pinochet to Chile.[36] Certainly Lord Millett's contention, that the substantial reduction in charges transformed the position and made it "incumbent on the secretary of state to reconsider the matter in the light of the very different circumstances which now prevailed," could be viewed in that light. However, Lord Millett actually dissented from the decision that alleged crimes prior to September 1988 were not extraditable crimes, stating that he would have allowed the appeal in relation to torture and conspiracy to torture, "wherever and whenever carried out". A better interpretation of the requirement that the Home Secretary should reconsider his decision would seem to be that the House of Lords was simply confirming that, while the courts could rule on the process, in the end the decision whether or not to extradite was political. They were thus returning the matter to its rightful place.

Whatever the intention of the House of Lords, on 15 April the Home Secretary announced that, having looked at the matter afresh, he was confirming his previous decision. He had concluded that the senator was accused of extraditable crimes for which he had no immunity and that, even though the number of charges had reduced, they were still serious. Moreover, they had not been committed so long ago as to make it unjust or oppressive for Pinochet to stand trial for them. He stated that he had taken account of claims that the senator could face trial in Chile and the possible effect of proceedings on the stability of Chile and its relationship with Britain but had given "particular weight" to the United Kingdom's obligation under the European Convention on Extradition to extradite Senator Pinochet to Spain.

THE IMPLICATIONS OF THE PINOCHET EPISODE

Straw's decision meant the extradition process continued, although, predictably, interrupted, yet again, by a legal challenge in the High Court[37] and on 8 October Ronald Bartle, the magistrate who had issued the second warrant, ruled that Pinochet could be extradited to Spain to face trial on thirty five charges of torture, thirty three of which had been added by Spain since the original authority to proceed had been given. There was speculation that Straw might, at this point, allow Pinochet to return to Chile on humanitarian grounds; the Senator's health was said to be deteriorating. But the Home Secretary made

---

[36] e.g. J Rozenberg, n 27 supra.

[37] Challenge was sought on grounds that the Home Secretary had acted irrationally in authorising proceedings after the House of Lords had drastically reduced the number of offences. Leave to proceed was refused by Mr Justice Ognall on the basis that it would "needlessly disrupt the extradition process and postpone the machinery which will afford General Pinochet every proper opportunity to advance his case and protect his position" (*The Times*, June 1999).

known that he would not consider the matter until legal proceedings had ended. Pinochet's decision to appeal against the magistrate's ruling, which was announced a year to the day after the issuing of the second warrant, ensured that this would not be for some time. The Pinochet saga therefore continued with, whatever the outcome, far reaching constitutional and legal implications. These implications have international as well as domestic dimensions. The decision by the House of Lords in *Pinochet 2*, that one of its own decisions could not stand, was an indictment of its own processes and damaging to its reputation. It added to questions which were already being raised about its suitability as the final appeal court for cases of a political or constitutional nature[38] and provided a foretaste of the public scrutiny judges are likely to face when considering cases under the Human Rights Act. This in turn raises questions about the way in which judges are appointed, suggesting the need for greater openness and, at least where appointments to the House of Lords are concerned, for appointees to be required to declare any interests they may have and, perhaps, to submit to questioning by a parliamentary select committee.[39]

On the legal front, the reasoning of the law lords in reaching the decision that there had been an appearance of bias has implications for the development of both national and international law. It drew on the jurisprudence of the Scottish courts and the Australian High Court and, despite the fact that under the Human Rights Act the rulings of the European Court of Human Rights will be directly relevant, its decisions were all but ignored. Sooner, rather than later, these decisions and the principles they support will have to be absorbed into judicial thinking in the United Kingdom, not only to ensure the courts give effect to the European Convention on Human Rights, but also to enable British judges to play an active role in shaping the jurisprudence of the European Court and thus, indirectly, international law. As it happens, in this instance, the *Pinochet* case was of such international importance that the decision of the House of Lords is likely to contribute in its own right to the jurisprudence of other nations, raising questions about judicial interests and the requirements of impartiality.

The decisions in *Pinochet 1* and *Pinochet 3*, which denied the senator sovereign immunity, have more obvious international implications. The rulings provide a precedent for limiting claims of immunity by former heads of state and thus open the way for their more general prosecution. It remains to be seen how the precedent is utilised. In addition, the decisions contribute to international jurisprudence concerning crimes against humanity and to discussions about the relationship between law and morality. They also demonstrate the need for there to be a coherent system of international criminal justice.

These are matters which the following chapters will consider. The essays

---

[38] See, for instance, R Brazier, *Constitutional Reform* (2nd edn, OUP, 1998); R Hazell, *Constitutional Futures* (OUP, 1999).

[39] Post Pinochet, Lord Irvine stated that he was looking at the possibility of a Register of Interests for judges which would be similar to the Register for Members of Parliament.

have been grouped together in two parts. Part One concerns the House of Lords, as a judicial body, and the issue of bias raised by *Pinochet*. It contains three related essays. The first (Chapter Two), by David Robertson, uses the evidence provided by the *Pinochet* appeals to assess the suitability of the House of Lords as the final court of appeal for constitutional and political cases. He considers its structure, working methods and culture, with reference to the substantive judgments in *Pinochet 1* and *3* and to the "Hoffman-problem" raised in *Pinochet 2*. He also examines the unusual use of interveners and *amicus curiae*, making comparisons with other jurisdictions, most notably the United States. He concludes that the way in which the House of Lords operates prevents it from having the necessary authority where constitutional and political cases are concerned, and suggests that what is required is an overhaul of its working methods and structure, together with an acceptance that the law lords are part of the political process, not apart from it.

The second essay (Chapter Three), by Evadne Grant, centres on *Pinochet 2*. While Robertson writes from the perspective of a political scientist, Grant's perspective is that of a lawyer and it is the legal issues of jurisdiction and bias on which she concentrates. She considers whether the House of Lords has jurisdiction to correct an injustice, caused by one of its own decisions, and examines instances where judges have disqualified themselves from hearing a case, citing recent examples from Australia and South Africa. She then analyses the reasoning of the House of Lords in relation to bias, making comparisons with decisions in other jurisdictions, and concludes that while the ruling of the House of Lords may have been satisfactory in the *Pinochet* context, it failed to give sufficient guidance for future cases. She finishes with an expression of regret that the law lords failed to take account of the jurisprudence of the European Court of Human Rights.

This is the issue picked up in the third essay in this section of the book (Chapter Four), in which Paul Catley and Lisa Claydon argue that, although the Human Rights Act 1998, which incorporates the European Convention on Human Rights, has yet to be given legal effect, the law lords should, nevertheless, have considered the jurisprudence of the European Court of Human Rights, not least because when the Act becomes law, it will be necessary for all courts to take account of its decisions. Catley and Claydon examine the issue of bias, as it arose in *Pinochet 2*, in the context of that jurisprudence and suggest that although the conclusion would probably have been the same, the reasoning would have been different. This reasoning, they suggest, should have been used by the House of Lords to inform the common law and to provide guidance to the courts in the proper application of the Convention.

The second part of this volume also contains three essays. These are concerned with the impact of *Pinochet 1* and *3* on international law. The first essay (Chapter Five), by Judith Hendrick, provides a theoretical background to the substantive issues raised in these cases. Hendrick considers the concept of justice in the context of theories of punishment, in particular, retributivism, which she sees as most relevant in relation to *Pinochet*. She also examines the notion of responsibility, distinguishing the special responsibility of a head of state from his personal responsibility. She evaluates the evidence, currently offered, and concludes that, either way, the view that Pinochet is morally to blame for crimes against humanity, committed in Chile, is persuasive.

The next essay (Chapter Six), by Jonathan Black-Branch, examines the place of sovereign or state immunity in international law and the way in which it has traditionally operated. He considers the implications of *Pinochet 3* for former heads of state and also for individual states, which have generally had freedom to determine for themselves how best to come to terms with their past and to make a new beginning. He argues that while the doctrine of immunity might be outdated, its importance is such that any modification should be by international accord, through specific convention or treaty provisions, and not left to the vagaries of interpretation by any single nation. He also argues that it should not be for any one state to initiate prosecution for crimes against humanity. This should be the responsibility of the United Nations.

The essay by Ben Chigara (Chapter Seven) on the administration of international criminal justice relates closely to the previous one. Chigara examines the way in which international law has developed to regulate the rights and duties of individuals. He considers *Pinochet* in the context of the tribunals established to prosecute crimes against humanity in the former Yugoslavia and Rwanda, and he points to the adoption of the Statute of the International Criminal Court as evidence that the international community wants a legal, rather than political, mechanism for dealing with such crimes. He notes, however, the conflict between the internationalisation of criminal justice and the right of individual states to choose, as Chile has done, to grant amnesties as a way forward, rather than to seek prosecution of those responsible for human rights abuses in past administrations. He suggests that, as a way of reconciling that conflict, such amnesties might be approved by the United Nations.

The essays are accompanied by an Annex, in which the three House of Lords' decisions on *Pinochet* are reproduced. References to the cases in the essays refer to both the *Weekly Law Reports* and to the Annex.

Part 1

Pinochet, The House of Lords, and the Issue of Bias

2

The House of Lords as a Political and Constitutional Court: Lessons from the Pinochet Case

DAVID ROBERTSON

INTRODUCTION

Nothing could have been better calculated to demonstrate to the educated layman how far the English court system is from operating by any theory of mechanical jurisprudence, what some have called "slot machine jurisprudence",[1] than *Pinochet 2*.[2] The sheer chanciness of appellate decision making was demonstrated more brutally than in any case easily recalled this century. Consider some alternative outcomes. Had Lord Hoffmann realised, once Amnesty International was allowed to intervene, that he probably should not hear the case, he would have recused himself. A very likely replacement at the last minute would have been Lord Goff. Senator Pinochet would have left the country in December, and English law would have established that there was no new international law on crimes against humanity, which was sufficiently settled to overcome the historic right to immunity of a serving, or former, head of state. If not Goff, then perhaps Lord Millett would have taken his place. The senator would now be fighting the last ditches against deportation, and English law would hold that the international obligation to either punish or deport in cases of systematic torture was so strong that it probably did not even depend on recent domestic legislation on extradition. In neither case would we know the views of more than five of the dozen plus men entitled to sit as law lords.

---

[1] A very useful analysis and categorisation of judicial thinking on political matters in the House of Lords is: J Bell, *Policy Arguments in Judicial Decisions* (Clarendon Press, 1983). The leading historical study of the law lords, still very relevant to this topic, is R Stevens, *Law and Politics: The House of Lords as a Judicial Body 1800–1976* (Weidenfeldt and Nicholson, 1979). A recent collection of essays on the Lords in both its legislative and judicial functions is B Dickson and P Carmichael (eds), *The House of Lords: its Parliamentary and Judicial Roles* (Hart Publishing, 1999). The essay in that collection by P Maxwell, "The House of Lords as a Constitutional Court: The Implications of *Ex p EOC*", is particularly pertinent to this topic. I discuss the EOC case in my own study, *Judicial Discretion in the House of Lords* (Clarendon Press, 1998).

[2] *R v. Bow Street Metropolitan Stipendiary Magistrate and Others, ex parte Pinochet Ugarte (No. 2)* [1999] 2 WLR 272.

Effectively the timetable of judicial business would have settled the issue. Instead of which we have a legal decision cast in the narrowest possible terms, revolving round a highly disputable (and disputed) interpretation of a few words in domestic extradition law, a decision with which at least four, and possibly six judges disagree, and seven support. Such is not a record apt to persuade politically sophisticated non lawyers that the House of Lords is a fit institution to carve out our constitutional future, to solve intractable political conflicts by judicialising them, or to help shape an international law for the post cold war era.

This essay takes advantage of the unusual evidence provided by the *Pinochet* hearings to assess the suitability of the law lords in their more political functioning.[3] There are two overwhelming problems about the law lords, both eminently demonstrated in the *Pinochet* hearings and decisions. One is a structural matter—the size and working methods of the appellate committee. This is dealt with in Section Four below. The other is a matter of judicial culture and working methods, which surfaces in the substance of the arguments made in the two substantive judgments.[4] This is discussed in Section One. The *Pinochet* case, however, cannot be fully analysed without considering what "the Hoffmann problem" tells us about that judicial culture. This is therefore the subject of Section Two. Finally, the case was unusual also in its use of interveners and an *amicus curiae*. This raises further matters relevant to considering both the culture and structure of the House of Lords as a political/constitutional court and is discussed in Section Three.

SECTION ONE: A MULTIPLICITY OF VOICES

"POWELL, J, announced the Court's judgment and filed an opinion expressing his views of the case, in Parts I, III-A, and V-C of which WHITE, J, joined; and in Parts I and V-C of which BRENNAN, MARSHALL, and BLACKMUN, JJ, joined. BRENNAN, WHITE, MARSHALL, and BLACKMUN, JJ, filed an opinion concurring in the judgment in part and dissenting in part. WHITE, MARSHALL, and BLACKMUN

---

[3] We have no established vocabulary for discussing the situation where a court has to deal with a politically high profile case, whether it be a constitutional issue, a matter of contentious public international law or which, in some other way, touches on controversial political matters. I shall use "political" throughout as a shorthand, but it must be understood that this does not imply that judges are acting other than as judges, and does not suggest any conventional partisan role or linkage. In particular, I do not mean to touch on the overtly political role of law lords as members of the upper house of the legislature. This verbal problem is especially difficult in England, because the lay meaning of "political" is so completely taken up with what is also often referred to as "party political", a meaning which is emphatically not implied herein. American political scientists often discuss this sort of activity as "public law", but that label is pre-empted in the UK as a technical matter. This is increasingly going to be a problem of nomenclature as the courts, both via the Human Rights Act and the judicial review clause of the Scotland Act, become regularly involved in political matters.

[4] *R v. Bow Street Metropolitan Stipendiary Magistrate and Others, ex parte Pinochet Ugarte* [1998] 3 WLR 1456; *R v. Bow Street Metropolitan Stipendiary Magistrate and Others, ex parte Pinochet Ugarte (No 3)* [1999] 2 WLR 827.

JJ filed separate opinions. STEVENS J, filed an opinion concurring in the judgment in part and dissenting in part, in which BURGER, CJ, and STEWART and REHN-QUIST, JJ, joined."

The above extract is from the headnote in US Supreme Court case, *University of California Regents* v. *Bakke* (1978).[5] The case, a decision on the constitutional validity of positive discrimination, is notorious in US constitutional law as a mess, because the justices split in so many ways that no one could be very sure exactly what the court had found. As a legal basis for institutions to organise their policies on race and admission for higher education, the arguments in *Bakke* were essentially useless. All that anyone could really tell was that the University of California should have admitted Mr Bakke, or, at least, that they should not have rejected him in favour of candidates from ethnic minorities in quite the way they did. The point about the *Bakke* case is that it *is* notorious. American policy makers and lawyers are used to a much more clear cut line from the court. For that matter, and it is important, those opposed to a Supreme Court decision are used to having much more cogent arguments given to them by the dissenting minority.

The US Supreme Court functions, *inter alia*, to clarify and give coherence to both sides in major politico-legal and constitutional debates, as well as to decide the main thrust of preferred policy and to provide that thrust with a powerful rationale. The more contentious the case, the more that court is likely to behave in that way. So, for example, in what is probably the most famous case of the century, *Brown* v. *Board of Education*,[6] where the Supreme Court overturned the doctrine which allowed for segregated education, there was one "opinion of the court". Subsequent cases spelling out the detail, which were, if anything, even more controversial, followed this pattern, including the case which introduced the policy of bussing children round cities to ensure de facto racial balance in schools.[7] Such cases are not always unanimous. The case which established abortion rights and has set in train nearly thirty years of often violent political conflict, *Roe* v. *Wade*, had six opinions.[8] But because the justices work hard to form alliances and to offer broad, consensus seeking opinions, the intellectual structure is considerably more lucid than that figure might imply. There was an "opinion of the court", signed by six of the nine justices. Although three of those offered their own opinions, these are by their nature *additional* reflections, and they do not take away from the broad consensus with which the court could face a bitterly divided public. There were two dissents, but again one of the dissents, by Justice White, was concurred in by the other dissenter, Justice Renquist, who went on to add further reflections. Thus anyone trying to work out how to react to the decision in *Roe*, knew both what it meant and why, and also knew the more constitutionally fruitful way of opposing it. But US

---

[5] *University of California Regents* v. *Bakke* 438 U.S. 265 (1978).
[6] *Brown* v. *Board of Education* 347 U.S. 483 (1954).
[7] See *Swann* v. *Charlotte-Mecklenburg Board of Education* 402 U.S. 1 (1971).
[8] *Roe* v. *Wade* 410 U.S. 113 (1973).

Supreme Court justices do more than craft careful arguments of their own. Far more than in the House of Lords, they engage with each other. Thus to know White's position in *Roe* is not only to know why he thinks abortion is not a con-stitutionally protected right, it is to know what he thinks is wrong with the argu-ments of those who do perceive the right. Conversely, to read the majority opinion, is to be presented with counters to White's criticisms. This, above all, is what is regularly missing with English judicial argument. As I have argued elsewhere, English judges do not engage each other intellectually—their posi-tions largely slip past the alternative view with no comment.[9]

The same pattern can be found in almost all important United States cases. There is no question but that dissent should be permitted. Most practitioners as well as academics would feel strongly that Privy Council decisions in the United Kingdom have been far more useful since they allowed themselves to dissent, and although dissenting opinions are not usually allowed in continental courts, the most powerful of them, the German Constitutional Court, changed its orig-inal policy in the 1960s to allow them. Nor is a single voice of the court in itself always desirable. During the 1980s, when Lord Diplock persuaded the law lords of his generation to cut down the number of opinions, the decisions of the Lords were not necessarily more useful. That said, in a highly political case it is of enormous value that the number of voices should not be uselessly multiplied. By all means let a law lord, who thinks he has something to offer in addition to a broad position that he can support along with a majority of colleagues, add extra reflections. But what we lack in the United Kingdom is that first attempt to get one broad consensual statement, or to produce a rival "minority report". In part the latter may be because there is no tradition of the great dissent in English law. When law is largely a matter of crafting technical solutions to the contractual problems of commerce, or to restricting liability claims to narrow "pockets of common law" dissents have no particular role, except to indicate judicial outrage at colleagues. Yet dissents take on a different character when broad political and constitutional issues are at stake—they are there, or should be there, to mark out alternative avenues, to provide bases on which future courts can build if the majority position turns out to be mistaken or ill advised, or simply not to go far enough. However, in such a role, the dissenters, as much as the majority, need to strive for a collective voice and both majority and minority need to answer each other. What is so stark about the combined *Pinochet 1* and *3* speeches is that neither the majority nor the minority provide such visions for the future development of law in what must become an ever more urgent field.

Of course this is old hat in a sense. First year law students are taught about the difficulty of finding the exact *ratio* in a multi opinion case. But it is perni-cious old hat when it comes to politically controversial cases. Consider the dif-ficulty of summarising the positions maintained if we take *Pinochet 1* and *3* as a

[9] D Robertson, *Judicial Discretion in the House of Lords* (Clarendon Press, 1998).

combined case. And it is vital so to do, because this way we can get some inkling of how the House of Lords would behave if, as we argue in Section Four they should, they sat *en banc* for political/constitutional cases. We can treat *Pinochet 1* and *3* together as a simulated hearing by a UK Supreme Court, which happens to be staffed by, and run on the same lines as, the real House of Lords.

There are at least four propositions—there would probably be more were we to go below surface summaries of their Lordships' speeches. I will restrict consideration simply to the counts of torture:

> *Proposition 1: Pinochet can be extradited for all crimes alleged*—Lord Millett.
> *Proposition 2: Pinochet can be extradited at least for crimes committed after 1988*—Lords Nicholls, Steyn and Hoffmann.
> *Proposition 3: Pinochet can be extradited only for crimes committed after 1988*—Lords Browne-Wilkinson, Hope, Hutton, Saville, Phillips.
> *Proposition 4: Pinochet cannot be extradited for any of the crimes alleged*—Lords Slynn, Lloyd, Goff.

It would probably be safe to merge Propositions 1 and 2. The distinction depends on the fact that in *Pinochet 3* Lord Millett had specifically to deny the argument on which those in favour of Proposition 3 rested, while the only law lord who discussed the issue during *Pinochet 1*, and who dismissed it, was, in fact, in favour of Proposition 4 anyway. The argument is this. The power to extradite is contained in the Extradition Act 1988, which defines what constitutes an "extradition crime". The most important requirement for our purposes is that the conduct complained of would have to be a crime under the law of both Spain and of the United Kingdom. Everything depends on what this means. Is it enough that the offence alleged is now a crime in the United Kingdom, that is, has become criminal in the United Kingdom at least by the date of the request for extradition, or must the actions have been illegal in the United Kingdom at the time they were committed outside the United Kingdom? The reason it is problematic is that, as argued by the same group of law lords, torture was not a crime in the United Kingdom until 1988. Lord Browne-Wilkinson's speech on this point summarises it best:

> The obligations placed on the United Kingdom by [*The International Convention Against Torture and other Cruel, Inhuman or Degrading Treatment or Punishment, 1984*] (and on the other 110 or more signatory states who have adopted the Convention) were incorporated into the law of the United Kingdom by section 134 of the Criminal Justice Act 1988. That Act came into force on 29 September 1988. Section 134 created a new crime under United Kingdom law, the crime of torture. As required by the Torture Convention "all" torture wherever committed world-wide was made criminal under United Kingdom law and triable in the United Kingdom. No one has suggested that before section 134 came into effect torture committed outside the United Kingdom was a crime under United Kingdom law. Nor is it suggested that section 134 was retrospective so as to make torture committed outside the United Kingdom before 29 September 1988 a United Kingdom crime. Since torture outside the United Kingdom was not a crime under United Kingdom law until 29

September 1988, the principle of double criminality which requires an Act to be a crime under both the law of Spain and of the United Kingdom cannot be satisfied in relation to conduct before that date if the principle of double criminality requires the conduct to be criminal under United Kingdom law at the date it was committed. If, on the other hand, the double criminality rule only requires the conduct to be criminal under United Kingdom law at the date of extradition, the rule was satisfied in relation to all torture alleged against Senator Pinochet whether it took place before or after 1988. The Spanish courts have held that they have jurisdiction over all the crimes alleged.

According to the majority in *Pinochet 3*, double criminality does require the more restrictive definition. This is so even though Browne-Wilkinson quotes the Lord Chief Justice in the Divisional Court, who, in rejecting the argument, had said:

> the conduct alleged against the subject of the request need not in my judgment have been criminal here at the time the alleged crime was committed abroad. There is nothing in section 2 which so provides. What is necessary is that at the time of the extradition request the offence should be a criminal offence here and that it should then be punishable with 12 months imprisonment or more.

Lord Browne-Wilkinson also quoted Lord Lloyd, who, he noted, "took the same view" as the Lord Chief Justice and considered the restrictive definition to be "bad", on the basis that:

> It involves a misunderstanding of section 2 of the Extradition Act 1989. Section 2(1)(a) refers to conduct which would constitute an offence in the United Kingdom now. It does not refer to conduct which would have constituted an offence then.

Browne-Wilkinson thereafter constructed a complex argument, largely from Parliamentary intent, to oppose the Lord Chief Justice's interpretation.

The reason why this issue has been set out in detail is not to referee the debate, which is outside my remit,[10] but to consider whether the Browne-Wilkinson argument acts as a bar to fairly comparing their Lordships' speeches between *Pinochet 1* and *3*. It is not, in fact, a question that can be answered definitively. Either way round we are involved with a counter factual. For those who would limit the apparent conflict amongst their Lordships, it has to be thought that Lords Nicholls, Steyn and Hoffmann would have accepted the Browne-Wilkinson position had they heard it, and thus they are more properly to be seen as part of a eight man majority for a very restricted reading of the United Kingdom's international obligations against international crime. However, if they are treated as more naturally combined with Lord Millett, it has to be assumed that they, like Lord Millett, would have rejected the argument. There is absolutely nothing in the speeches of Lords Nicholls and Steyn to suggest that they would have preferred the restrictive version. Nor can it fairly be said that they were unaware of the issue, however little it bulked in argument before

---

[10] Although there are aspects on which I shall say a little more substantively in due course.

them.[11] The *Pinochet* cases can therefore be treated as really throwing up three positions. Two of them are relatively clear cut, and are well crafted to give the United Kingdom a definite position in this crucial question of obligations towards the creation of an international criminal justice system. One stands firmly in support of immunity, one, equally firmly, not only against immunity, but for a principle of universal jurisdiction. True, and it is a shortcoming arising from the multiplicity of voices, there are uncertainties. Lord Lloyd, for example, in part, grounds immunity on the "Act of State" doctrine, and it is very unclear what Lord Slynn's view on this is. Again Lord Steyn expressly says:

> Finally, I must make clear that my conclusion does not involve the expression of any view on the interesting arguments on universality of jurisdiction in respect of certain international crimes and related jurisdictional questions. Those matters do not arise for decision.

Those matters only failed to arise, however, because there was no one at that stage arguing for the restrictive Browne-Wilkinson thesis on double criminality. Neither of these positions, alas, prevailed. Instead, and as, with forty–forty hindsight any observer of the English courts might have predicted, a narrow, technical, and quintessentially *legal*, as opposed to a deliberately *politico-legal* "solution" emerged.

It can be argued that supreme courts ought to find narrowly in controversial cases. Indeed the US Supreme Court does have a tendency to find the least extensive way of solving a case, but this usually means solution through statutory construction rather than through constitutional review, where this is possible, or by distinguishing a precedent rather than overruling. Here we have a different type of narrow solution. Because the position, for which the majority opted, does not just use a narrow scope, as might be done by tying the decision to a very complete fact description of Pinochet's regime. Nor does it take a narrow view of international law. It is restrictive because, in the language of international lawyers, it is so purely dualist rather than monist.[12] The only reason that Pinochet can be extradited is because two English statutes coincide to say so. The power to extradite comes solely from the 1989 Extradition Act, and that applies only because an international convention was incorporated by the 1988 Criminal Justice Act. According to Browne-Wilkinson *et al*, torture simply was not a crime in the United Kingdom, wherever in the world it was carried out, until that Act said it was. What this means, of course, unless *Pinochet 3* is overruled someday, is that United Kingdom courts can never give aid to an international move towards international criminal law, except where and when, and in the terms that Parliament so provides. Contrast the view taken by Lord

---

[11] This point, that counsel chose not to make much of the restrictive version of double criminality, raises issues which will be discussed in Section Three on interveners.

[12] A very good commentary on the monist/dualist dichotomy and the law lords is B Fitzpatrick, "A Dualist House of Lords in a Sea of Monist Community Law" in Dickson and Carmichael (eds), *The House of Lords: its Parliamentary and Judicial Rules* (Hart Publishing, 1999).

Millett, and probably, though we cannot quite be sure, by the majority in *Pinochet 1*:

> In my opinion, the systematic use of torture on a large scale and as an instrument of state policy had joined piracy, war crimes and crimes against peace as an international crime of universal jurisdiction well before 1984. I consider that it had done so by 1973. For my own part, therefore, I would hold that the courts of this country already possessed extra-territorial jurisdiction in respect of torture and conspiracy to torture on the scale of the charges in the present case and did not require the authority of statute to exercise it.

This approach is vastly better suited to a court which takes seriously its role as the supreme judicial body of a modern democracy—not because it is "liberal" or "radical"—the position taken by Slynn, Lloyd and Goff is equally worthy of respect, but because it is firmly rooted in an understanding of the inescapably *political* nature of such adjudication. Slynn, Lloyd and Goff are not dualist; quite the opposite. It is from a well worked out conception of the nature of international law and how it changes that they reach their position that the *international* law on immunity has not been changed by any possible interpretation of a United Kingdom statute. Millett makes this conception of the role of national courts in the international system clear:

> My Lords, we have come a long way from what I earlier described as the classical theory of international law—a long way in a relatively short time. But as the Privy Council pointed out . . . [in 1934] international law has not become a crystallised code at any time, but is a living and expanding branch of the law. Glueck observed that: "unless we are prepared to abandon every principle of growth for international law, we cannot deny that our own day has its right to institute customs". In a footnote to this passage he added: "Much of the law of nations has its roots in custom. Custom must have a beginning; and customary usages of states in the matter of national and personal liability for resort to prohibited methods of warfare and to wholesale criminalism have not been petrified for all time". The law has developed still further since 1984, and continues to develop in the same direction. Further international crimes have been created. Ad hoc international criminal tribunals have been established. A permanent international criminal court is in the process of being set up. These developments could not have been foreseen by Glueck and the other jurists who proclaimed that individuals could be held individually liable for international crimes. *They envisaged prosecution before national courts, and this will necessarily remain the norm even after a permanent international tribunal is established*. In future those who commit atrocities against civilian populations must expect to be called to account if fundamental human rights are to be properly protected. In this context, the exalted rank of the accused can afford no defence". [Emphases added]

To those who would simply count heads it might seem that *Pinochet 3* simply confirmed the decision in *Pinochet 1*; rather, in all but the most literal sense, *Pinochet 3* overruled *Pinochet 1*, and, in so doing, produced a result with which no one can really be happy. Bluntly, we can judge the decision in *Pinochet 3* by saying that a political court is required to give leadership to a nation, to make its legal system something more than a technical solution mechanism. In this respect the Browne-Wilkinson coalition singularly failed. Moreover, its members would, almost certainly, reject that very notion of a duty of leadership, which is itself a reason for the inadequacy of the law lords in such cases. It is pointless to ask why the majority in *Pinochet 3* adopted their position, but we can say something about the lack of coherence and clarity of such cases in general. In a situation like this, it cannot be pretended that legal arguments force themselves on judges by some inner power. They are chosen; the mere fact that Lord Millett could choose otherwise proves this. There is no escaping the fact that the majority in *Pinochet 3 chose* this result. In so doing, they demonstrated how inadequately the law lords perform when judged against a primary function of a nation's supreme court, if that court is viewed, as political scientists must view it, as a major component of the national political system. Why they did this is probably too deeply dependent on inherited judicial role models to analyse here. That they were able so to do follows in part from structural matters, and partly from the absence of this necessary leadership ethos, a theme I now develop further.

SECTION TWO: LORD HOFFMANN AND THE PROBLEM OF BIAS

In an apparent attempt to downplay the implications of *Pinochet 2* Lord Browne-Wilkinson noted

> It is important not to overstate what is being decided. It was suggested in argument that a decision setting aside the order of 25 November 1998 would lead to a position where judges would be unable to sit on cases involving charities in whose work they are involved. It is suggested that, because of such involvement, a judge would be disqualified. That is not correct. The facts of this present case are exceptional. The critical elements are (1) that AI was a party to the appeal; (2) that AI was joined in order to argue for a particular result; (3) the judge was a Director of a charity closely allied to AI and sharing, in this respect, AI's objects. Only in cases where a judge is taking an active role as trustee or Director of a charity which is closely allied to and acting with a party to the litigation should a judge normally be concerned either to recuse himself or disclose the position to the parties.

It is similarly important for us to understand how narrowly conceived was the decision to vacate the result in *Pinochet 1* and order a re-hearing. When the second *Pinochet* decision was announced, it was widely felt that a very strong argument had prevailed. This was partly because in most of the speeches the language stressed the absolute and automatic disqualification. Typically their Lordships used phrases like "was disqualified from the start". The automaticity of the supposed bar on Lord Hoffmann's participation was, almost certainly, partly to avoid actually investigating a charge of bias.[13] Lord Browne-Wilkinson again:

---

[13] For discussion of this point, see Grant (Chapter Three in this collection).

on this aspect of the case, we were asked to state in giving judgment what had been said and done within the Appellate Committee in relation to Amnesty International during the hearing leading to the Order of 25 November. As is apparent from what I have said, such matters are irrelevant to what we have to decide: *in the absence of any disclosure to the parties of Lord Hoffmann's involvement with AI, such involvement either did or did not in law disqualify him regardless of what happened within the Appellate Committee.* We therefore did not investigate those matters and make no findings as to them. [Emphases added]

They also stressed not only the absoluteness, but the familiarity of the relevant rule, making it sound as though Lord Hoffmann had done something quite inexplicable in failing to recuse himself. Lord Hope, for example, comments that:

> In practice the application of this rule is so well understood and so consistently observed that no case has arisen in the course of this century where a decision of any of the courts exercising a civil jurisdiction in any part of the United Kingdom has had to be set aside on the ground that there was a breach of it.

We do not know why Lord Hoffmann felt it unnecessary to draw attention to his connection with Amnesty International; he has not discussed the matter in public. But without countenancing his decision, it is certainly possible to have considerable sympathy with him when his failure to recuse himself is presented as a breach of a crystal clear and obvious rule. Four of the five law lords who heard the case gave speeches, although this was surely an instance when a single *per curiam* opinion would have been better, along with, in the American style, an opinion by Lord Hutton, who alone actually had something else to say, and something which does not fit very well with the automaticity line the majority, as we might thus call the other four, pursued. The majority speeches took the line that the traditional rule developed since 1852 in *Dimes* v. *Proprietors of Grand Junction Canal*[14] to deal with someone having a direct financial interest in the outcome of a case could with no strain at all be extended (or had always in fact covered) a situation like the one Lord Hoffmann found himself in. Lord Browne-Wilkinson summarises his conception of the law early in his speech:

> The fundamental principle is that a man may not be a judge in his own cause. This principle, as developed by the courts, has two very similar but not identical implications. First it may be applied literally: if a judge is in fact a party to the litigation or has a financial or proprietary interest in its outcome then he is indeed sitting as a judge in his own cause. In that case, the mere fact that he is a party to the action or has a financial or proprietary interest in its outcome is sufficient to cause his automatic disqualification. The second application of the principle is where a judge is not a party to the suit and does not have a financial interest in its outcome, but in some other way his conduct or behaviour may give rise to a suspicion that he is not impartial, for example because of his friendship with a party. This second type of case is not strictly speaking an application of the principle that a man must not be judge in his own cause, since

---

[14] *Dimes* v. *Proprietors of Grand Junction Canal* (1852) 3 HL Cas. 759.

the judge will not normally be himself benefiting, but providing a benefit for another by failing to be impartial. In my judgment, this case falls within the first category of case, viz where the judge is disqualified because he is a judge in his own cause. In such a case, once it is shown that the judge is himself a party to the cause, or has a relevant interest in its subject matter, he is disqualified without any investigation into whether there was a likelihood or suspicion of bias. The mere fact of his interest is sufficient to disqualify him unless he has made sufficient disclosure. . . . . I will call this "automatic disqualification".

In truth, the Hoffmann problem is an example of the second type of case, if indeed this particular piece of legal history has any relevance whatsoever to the quite genuine problem of judicial bias in political/constitutional cases. It really makes no sense to equate the "interest" Amnesty International had in the case, which was to have Pinochet extradited because of its belief that all torturers should be tried and punished, to the sort of interest the civil law rule of *nemo in sua causa* involves.[15] The structure of the decision is tainted by this throughout. Effectively, it starts by making Amnesty International, because it was granted intervener status, "a party" in the same way as a civil litigant; then it makes Lord Hoffmann's chairmanship of an Amnesty International charity equivalent to that of director of a company which is a party; finally, it jumps to equating Amnesty International's desire for a particular outcome to wanting one's own side to win in civil litigation. The attraction of this analysis is very clear; it meant there was no need to discuss, even tangentially, the actual problem of whether Lord Hoffmann was likely to be biased, which would involve constructing an argument shaped by his political views. Moreover, by taking the line that they did, the law lords were able to refuse even to discuss the applicability of, what counsel for both Pinochet and the Crown Prosecution Service (CPS) thought was, the ruling precedent.

This is a particular pity, because discussing the applicability or otherwise of *R* v. *Gough*,[16] or its Commonwealth rivals such as the Australian case of *Webb* v. *The Queen*,[17] would have forced attention onto the actual meaning of bias. *R* v. *Gough* held that the relevant test was "is there in the view of the Court a real danger that the judge was biased?", while Australian and New Zealand cases have preferred to refer to public reaction, that is "do the events in question give rise to a reasonable apprehension or suspicion on the part of a fair-minded and informed member of the public that the judge was not impartial?". In *Webb* the Australian court refused to adopt *Gough* for several reasons, but one of them is particularly relevant for us, because it begins to get at the reason a layman might very well feel that Lord Hoffmann should not have heard *Pinochet 1*. The case involved a juror demonstrating public sympathy for the mother of a man whose alleged murderers were on trial. The problem was posed thus:

[15] A distinction is even drawn with other human rights charities which operate at a more abstract level and do not actively campaign against targeted individuals.

[16] *Reg.* v. *Gough* [1993] AC 646.

[17] *Webb and Hay* v. *The Queen* (1994) 181 CLR 41, (1994) 122 ALR 41, (1994) 68 ALJR 582 FC 94/030.

The gesture of the juror may have been spontaneous, but a fair-minded person might fairly apprehend that it revealed a *state of mind that was not compatible with the unemotional and impartial consideration of the case.* One can accept the juror's own explanation of her gesture without derogating from the impact of that gesture on the minds of fair-minded people. Her conduct was not a reaction to evidence that she had just heard. It occurred after the conclusion of the evidence and the addresses of two of the three counsel and after the jury had been warned about communicating with persons associated with the trial. The incident indicated that the juror felt strongly for the plight of the mother. Her sympathy, manifested as it was by disobedience of the judge's warning, *raised a serious question as to her ability to consider the evidence dispassionately and impartially.*

Lord Hutton alone picked up strands of judicial thought in previous cases which do, like the Australians, begin to get at the real problem—a judge's associations may lead the public to believe him to be ideologically predisposed to one side in a case. Being a political sociologist, I use the word *"ideological"*, which no lawyer or judge is likely to do, because that is really the issue when we consider what the Hoffmann problem may tell us about the shape of English judicial thinking, where political/constitutional cases are concerned. Lord Hutton describes his anxieties, when referring to the otherwise hardly discussed case of *R* v. *Gough*:

> Lord Goff said, agreeing with the view of Lord Woolf, that the only special category of case where there should be disqualification of a judge without the necessity to inquire whether there was any real likelihood of bias was where the judge has a direct pecuniary interest in the outcome of the proceedings. However I am of opinion that there could be cases where the interest of the judge in the subject matter of the proceedings *arising from his strong commitment to some cause or belief or his association with a person or body involved in the proceedings could shake public confidence in the administration of justice* as much as a shareholding (which might be small) in a public company involved in the litigation.

Hutton cites, *inter alia*, Lord Widgery CJ:

> the rule now covers cases in which the judge has such an interest in the parties or the matters in dispute as to make it *difficult for him to approach the trial with the impartiality and detachment which the judicial function requires.*[18]

Here is the real problem. Can a judge be so clearly and publicly committed to particular values that he ought not to hear a case which revolves around these values? One of the reasons that our law lords may have found it hard to tackle this issue, as directly as was necessary, is one of the reasons the court as a whole is ill equipped to face political/constitutional questions. It is still too frequently the case that judges act and speak, at least in public, as though some form of mechanical jurisprudence were a reality; they are far too committed to the notion that judicial discretion does not really exist, that judging is a matter of

---

[18] *R.* v. *Altrincham Justice, ex parte Pennington* [1975] 1 QB 549, 552F.

getting a technically right answer to a legal conundrum. Much quite unnecessary effort was spent insisting that Lord Hoffmann was not being judged to have
been actually biased. Much of the public discussion afterwards revolved round
his friends and many admirers in the judiciary insisting he would never have
allowed himself to let his legal sense be overcome by any connection to
Amnesty. I know of no one who ever thought otherwise.

The problem is quite different—it arises from realising that in cases as innov-
ative as *Pinochet*, judicial discretion is rife, and that the judges, consciously or
otherwise, are inevitably making value choices, are choosing to be convinced by
one, rather than another, legal argument in order to craft an opinion which gets
them where their ideological leanings prompt. There is nothing wrong with this.
It could not be otherwise, and the future role of the law lords when they come
to operate the Human Rights Act will demonstrate this day in, day out. The
Lord Chancellor has openly welcomed the fact, talking as he has about a future
in which judges make moral decisions. *Pinochet* was a moral decision, no less
than was the decision on whether Anthony Bland could be allowed to die,
another famous case where the law lords made great, and quite unconvincing,
efforts to stress that they were merely giving a "legal" answer.[19] Though he was
at that time only a Lord Justice of Appeal, Hoffmann's opinion in *Bland* was
widely admired and clearly very influential. He directly addressed philosophical
issues about the meaning and value of life. But he was not, as far as one knows,
involved with any pressure group campaigning to make termination of a
patient's life safer for doctors in hopeless cases.

Should that make a difference? If we admit that our judges are ideological
creatures, and that political/constitutional cases will turn to a large extent on a
clash of ideologies, what rules should we have to guide a judge? When should he
fear that his public commitment to an ideology may be too intense for the
appearance of Widgery's "impartiality and detachment which the judicial function requires"? When will, in Hutton's words, "his strong commitment to some
cause or belief . . . shake public confidence in the administration of justice"?
Those questions are not, in fact, quite properly phrased. What they should
really ask is "under what conditions are the judges going to deem the public to
be entitled to have such fears"? The discussion of the Australian test in *Webb* is
quite acute on this, as befits a High Court, on the whole, more attuned to the
fact of its political role. Discussing the difference between the rule in *Gough* and
their own jurisprudence, Mason CJ and McHugh J provide a strong argument
for this latter form of the question:

> In *Gough*, the House of Lords rejected the need to take account of the public percep-
> tion of an incident which raises an issue of bias except in the case of a pecuniary inter-
> est. Behind this reasoning is the assumption that public confidence in the
> administration of justice will be maintained because the public will accept the conclu-
> sions of the judge. *But the premise on which the decisions in this Court are based is*

---

[19] *Airedale NHS Trust v. Bland* [1993] 1 All ER 821.

that public confidence in the administration of justice is more likely to be maintained if the Court adopts a test that reflects the reaction of the ordinary reasonable member of the public to the irregularity in question. References to the reasonable apprehension of the "lay observer" . . . the "fair- minded observer", the "fair-minded, informed lay observer", "fair-minded people", the "reasonable or fair-minded observer" and the "reasonable person" abound in the decisions of this Court and other courts in this country. *They indicate that it is the court's view of the public's view, not the court's own view, which is determinative.* If public confidence in the administration of justice is to be maintained, the approach that is taken by fair-minded and informed members of the public cannot be ignored. *Indeed . . . in considering whether an allegation of bias on the part of a judge has been made out, the public perception of the judiciary is not advanced by attributing to a fair-minded member of the public a knowledge of the law and the judicial process which ordinary experience suggests is not the case.* [Emphases added]

It does not seem that at any stage members of the House of Lords considered this question: "in whose eyes does Lord Hoffmann have to seem innocent of bias"? And, of course, "what might indict him in those eyes"? The last emphasised sentence is, of course, making the point that even where legal professionals may genuinely think a judge had no choice but to find "X", it is pointless to expect the public to absolve him of a charge of ideological bias if they note a purely coincidental fit between his known ideological persuasion and "X". *Pinochet 2* did not resolve "the Hoffmann Problem" in any way that will be helpful to the House of Lords in facing future problems of suggested judicial bias.[20] This failure, almost inevitable given judicial conceptions of bias, is one major weakness in the system, a failure much more important than the mere fact that Lord Hoffmann clearly cannot himself have thought that his situation was covered by the simplistic and over restrictive version of the doctrine that the case has now enshrined. But more important is the reason the House of Lords failed to handle the issue well. They failed because they are, first, too wedded to a notion of mechanical jurisprudence, to seeing their role as that of legal technicians, and, secondly, because they are far too comfortable with a sense of their own standing in the public eye. In another guise the problem of judicious leadership shows up again.

The real pity of *Pinochet 2* is that one could argue that the House of Lords were very lucky to have a chance to tackle this question, which can only become more and more salient, so early in the new political career of the court. In fact, though, the problem of "bias by association" may not be soluble, and may rather require a re-thinking of what is meant by judicial neutrality. The point about associations like Hoffmann's with Amnesty is simply that they are external evidence of likely beliefs. Justice Ruth Bader Ginsberg of the US Supreme Court is widely regarded as one of the best appointments of recent decades. She has a long track record as a litigator on woman's issues and on race discrimina-

[20] See Grant (Chapter Three in this collection) for an expanded discussion on the House of Lords' decision and its implications.

tion cases. She was one of the counsel who filed an *amicus* brief, urging reversal of the lower court in *Bakke*, as a member of the American Civil Liberties Union. Although she resigned from all such bodies on appointment to the Federal Courts in 1980, there have been several cases where she has written the opinion of the Supreme Court on issues she litigated earlier in her career, at least once achieving the overturning of a crucial woman's rights ruling made in a case she had lost as counsel. Several leading justices in the past have had the same sort of history, the most famous probably being Thurgood Marshall, whose work on race relations cases culminated in winning the famous *Brown* v. *Board* schools desegregation case, referred to earlier. When he was later appointed to the Supreme Court, he made no effort, nor was one expected, to recuse himself when related cases came up to the court. We must learn to accept, and indeed to welcome, judicial "bias" if that means having a well known predisposition towards a certain goal for the legal system in political and constitutional cases. In that sense nothing at all can be done about Lord Hutton's concern that some judge's "strong commitment to some cause or belief" might "shake public confidence in the administration of justice". The solution to that problem is actually to educate the public, though the judiciary will have to educate itself first, to see that there is nothing untoward in a judge arguing from a publicly known position. But the language and approach in *Pinochet 2* do nothing at all to remove any fears the public may have. The actual solution, which is implicit both in what has been said earlier and in the following section, is to change the structure of the court to make predispositions less fatal. This will be considered more fully in the final section.

SECTION THREE: INTERVENERS, *AMICI CURIAE* AND CLERKS

The case of *University of California Regents* v. *Bakke* was used earlier as an example of a very unusual outcome to a high profile constitutional case in the United States. In one respect, however, it was quite normal; that was in the court's openness to advice and pleading from those who were not parties. The American practice of using *amicus* briefs is very extensive, and the filing of fifty-three separate briefs in *Bakke* was not exceptional. Unlike the situation in the United Kingdom where *amicus* briefs, if filed at all, are at the instigation of the court and are meant to be neutral, not pleading one side or another, the American briefs can be neutral, or intentionally partisan. American courts do not have the concept of "intervener", except in the usual sense of a joined party in a civil case. Of the fifty-three *amicus* briefs in *Bakke*, twenty-six are marked in the reports as "urging reversal", ten urged affirmation, and a further seventeen were, or at least purported to be, of general advice. The range of institutions and individuals filing was enormous, as might be expected in a case dealing with the legitimacy of racial quotas in the admissions policy of a law school. Justice can only be done to this point by listing a few in each category.

Those urging reversal included:

The State of Washington, the American Civil Liberties Union, the Antioch School of
Law, the Asian American Bar Association of the Greater Bay Area, the Association of
American Law Schools, the Association of American Medical Colleges, the Black Law
Students Assn. at California-Berkeley School of Law and the Black Law Students
Union of Yale University Law School, the Law School Admission Council, the
Lawyers' Committee for Civil Rights Under Law, the National Association for the
Advancement of Colored People, the National Council of Churches of Christ,
the Society of American Law Teachers, the American Medical Student Association,
the Council on Legal Education Opportunity.

Those opposed included:

The American Federation of Teachers, the American Jewish Committee, the
American Subcontractors Association, the Anti-Defamation League of B'nai B'rith,
the Chamber of Commerce of the United States, the Fraternal Order of Police, the
Order of Sons of Italy in America, Young Americans for Freedom.

Supposedly neutral briefs were filed, *inter alia*, by:

The American Association of University Professors, the Committee on Academic
Nondiscrimination and Integrity, the Fair Employment Practice Commission of
California, the Department of Health of California, the Mexican American Legal
Defense and Educational Fund, the National Conference of Black Lawyers, the Polish
American Congress, the UCLA Black Law Students Association, and by four named
individuals

In addition, one needs to remember that every one of the justices who heard
this case was supported by at least three law clerks, selected from the very
brightest graduating students of the very best law schools. In contrast, several of
the law lords who heard *Pinochet 3* remarked in amazement that as many as
fourteen counsel were involved in the case, although this total included those for
the interveners, of whom two were allowed to address the committee, and the
single independent *amicus curiae* appointed at their Lordships' request.[21] There
were, needless to say, no law clerks.

It can fairly be argued that many of the problems which beset the various
stages of the *Pinochet* case follow directly from this UK/US difference. At a very
obvious level, the Hoffmann problem either could not have emerged, or could
not have been dealt with as it was, had Amnesty International not been an intervener. Their Lordships' solution to the Hoffmann problem is directly predicated
on the fact that Amnesty International was an intervener, thus making Lord
Hoffmann, in their eyes, automatically disqualified *as a party to the result*. If
that is, indeed, to be the sole reason for worrying about a judge's background

---

[21] Amnesty International intervened in *Pinochet 1* and *3*, the Republic of Chile intervened in
Pinochet 3. Both were represented by counsel. Human Rights Watch was allowed to file briefs in
both *Pinochet 1* and *3*.

and connections, then, quite simply, there would have been no Hoffmann problem to solve had there been no interveners. The fact that a lay reaction could not be dependent on such a precise linkage only goes to say that had his presence still been challenged, the law lords would have had to craft a very different solution. They would then have had to cope with a broader question, one that still remains begged.

But is there any good reason why Amnesty International, or for that matter Human Rights Watch should have had this curious status in the first place? What sense does it make to suggest that an outside organisation which, as part of its general pressure group activity has a clear preference for the outcome of a case, is in any meaningful sense, a party to that case? The point is made more clearly when one notes that there was a very good reason why the Republic of Chile should be seen as a party, and therefore granted intervener status, a reason much more supportive of the analogy with interveners and joined parties in ordinary civil litigation. As a matter of international law, the immunity sought by Senator Pinochet was, in fact, a legal property of the Republic itself; the whole traditional justification for personal immunity for foreign heads of state is the identity international law draws between the head of state and the state. This is particularly important when dealing with a former head of state, the argument being that the undoubted immunity the state has would be undermined by allowing a side swipe at those who had carried out state functions once they retired from office. In this very precise sense, Chile could plausibly be regarded as a party, and, as such, entitled to intervene. Nothing like that argument applies to Amnesty International, which has no legal standing whatsoever. The question might be less apposite in a country with a very wide doctrine on *locus standi*, but the traditional behaviour of English courts has been to be restrictive on the question. Indeed it would be interesting to see what justifications the House of Lords could make for selecting, amongst various interest and cause groups, had several asked for such status. If Human Rights Watch had wished to be represented rather than only filing a brief, would this have been permitted? Why, furthermore, if either, or both, were to be allowed intervener status, should this have been made conditional, as it was, on none of the main parties objecting?

The point is simply that British courts do not usually use *amici curiae* at all, and when they do it is in a very different sense from that of the American usage. It is part of a general approach which includes the failure to provide law clerks, and the enormous reliance on counsel as suppliers of all the material the court should consider. One might also say, though there is no necessary connection, that another part of the syndrome is the reliance on oral argument. Argument in each of the *Pinochet* hearings went on for days. In *Bakke* there would have been no more than one or two hours of oral argument. Presumably in *Pinochet* the law lords realised they needed all the help available, given the novel issue before them, its political implications and the intense publicity which would inevitably surround their decision. The only way they could get some such help was to allow Amnesty International to join as an intervener, and to ask for the appointment of an *amicus*.

The logic of the common law trial is responsible for much of the problem. We are so wedded still to the idea of adversarial justice that it is hard for our courts to conceive of alternative routes for information. The neutral *amicus* fits badly into a system in which neutrality has no natural place and relations are deemed as naturally adversarial. It means that others, who wish to be heard, have to become parties as interveners, as there is no obvious way in which their arguments can otherwise be accepted. However valuable the adversarial system may be, and recent developments like the Woolf recommendations suggest its shortcomings are beginning to matter even in routine litigation, it is a peculiarly ill suited model for political and constitutional cases. There are many ways of coping with the need for argument and information on as many aspects of a case as possible, and for fulfilling the role of truth-seeking in a non-adversarial way. Other national and international courts have used a variety of methods. One example is the Advocate General model of the European Court of Justice. Another is the method of the French Conseil Constitutionel, which appoints one of its own members to act as Rapporteur, with a free ranging brief to consult whatever and whomever to produce a draft opinion for the Conseil as a whole. Or use can be made of *amicus* briefs, as in the US model. Allowing both partial and impartial briefs from all those who see themselves as having either an interest or a more general concern, ensures that no potentially relevant argument is ignored and no sector of public opinion sees itself excluded. The extracts from the list of *amicus* briefs in *Bakke*, reproduced above, help to make the point. It includes those with a highly pragmatic interest in the outcome, such as medical and law school administrations; those whose membership represents people likely to benefit or suffer as a result of the decision, namely black and Asian law student associations; those with a slightly wider chance of feeling the impact, such as the Fraternal Order of Police, who regularly fight cases where promotion prospects are affected by positive discrimination; those with a very much wider concern for the overall ethic of discrimination, for instance, Jewish, Italian and Polish groups; those who can only be seen as having a principled concern, like the Church of Christ; and many others.

The consequence of restricting information flow in the *Pinochet* case is very clear. The record is vague as to whether or not the argument, that Pinochet could not be extradited for anything he allegedly did before 1988, was raised at all, or whether, though raised, his counsel conceded in *Pinochet 1* that the argument did not work. Had there been a wide variety of briefs from *amici* representing all aspects of concerned opinion, it is unbelievable that the issue would not have been forced to the attention of the first five law lords. There may very well have been several other arguments which the restricted information flow denied to their Lordships. There was at least one argument which was nearly never made, as Lord Goff's remarks, when discussing the definition of torture, indicate. He said:

The argument now under consideration was not advanced before the Divisional Court; nor can it have been advanced before the first Appellate Committee or it would have been considered by both Lord Slynn of Hadley and Lord Lloyd of Berwick in their dissenting opinions. It was not advanced before your Lordships by the appellants and those supporting them, either in their written cases, or in their opening submissions. In fact, it was introduced into the present case as a result of interventions by members of the Appellate Committee in the course of the argument . . . when he came to make his final oral submissions on behalf of the appellants, Professor Greenwood, following the lead of Mr Lloyd Jones, and perhaps prompted by observations from the Committee to the effect that this was the main point in the case, went beyond his clients' written submissions in reply and submitted. . . . It is surprising that an important argument of this character, if valid, should previously have been overlooked by the fourteen counsel (including three distinguished Professors of International Law) acting for the appellants, and for Amnesty International and Human Rights Watch which are supporting the appellants in this litigation.

There are enough problems with judicial consideration of such cases without allowing for happenstance, at least at the final appeal stage. It is part of the very culture of English law for courts to rely on counsel. Law lords have said, in the past, that they do not need law clerks precisely because it is the function of counsel fully to inform the court. Yet such a reliance on counsel is both unnecessary and ill advised. Indeed, other law lords have suggested it is actually absurd. However honest counsel are, they are committed to taking strategic positions on which arguments will best work, and to directing much of their effort to making, not the "best case", but the "best case given the other side's case". They are at the mercy of their instructing solicitors and clients. Moreover, there are not very many of them. In fact, with the British system of barristers as independent practitioners, rather than litigating partners in huge firms, the back-up support for crafting opinions is very restricted. But the real problem of relying on counsel, who mainly represent the actual parties, is a broader one. In a political/constitutional case the parties are essentially unimportant or incidental. When such a case arises, the court's duty is to craft a solution for the core problem facing the society as a whole, and not only those who may, at some future date, find themselves in a situation akin to that of the current litigants. There is no limit to who may have a legitimate concern about when the United Kingdom will help the development of an international criminal justice system, or about the stance the United Kingdom will take on torture. In *Bakke* it was entirely appropriate that such a range of voices should be heard by the court, because there is no one in the United States unentitled to have a view about positive discrimination and to express that view, if it can be turned into legal argument.

In fact the need for greater use of supporting argumentation, whether called *amici curiae* or not, is beginning to be realised in some parts of the British judiciary, though the tendency is to see them more in the light of "expert witnesses", providers of technical information, or bearers of closely similar interests, rather than those who seek to aid the court in reaching a decision in line with the values they support. Because of our weddedness to the adversarial system, because our judges have grown up with restrictive doctrines of standing, because of a professional tendency of lawyers from a commercial or chancery background, as, after all, most law lords are, to focus on narrow pragmatic solutions to technical problems, it will be hard for the House of Lords to embrace a wide use of *amicus* briefs. However, there seems no legitimate alternative for political and constitutional cases. It will also be practically impossible without the willing use of law clerks. But again we come across the highly individualistic approach of the judge as sole practitioner, reinforced by his prior experience as sole practitioner advocate. English judges, when asked about law clerks, are typically lukewarm because they see them as low level research assistants, looking up points of law the judge does not have time to investigate. None of them, probably, could entertain the idea of the great judge of the future as a great editor of his clerks' opinion drafts, an image drawn by Richard Posner in a chapter called "What do Judges maximise". Posner as Chief Judge of the US Court of Appeals Seventh Circuit, is a very senior judge, as well as a distinguished and original legal academic.[22] He happily embraces the idea that each judicial input to the court's decision is that of leader of a team of assistants who work independently of, though helped by, the brief of counsel for the parties, at least as much helped by *amicus* briefs, and much concerned independently to construct arguments to support their judges' general orientation on the sorts of questions raised by the instant case. Acting under their judges' guidance, it is also their job, as it has always been of clerks to Supreme Court justices, to craft these opinions in cohort with clerks to other judges, in order to maximise the chance of the broadest possible coalition behind a majority, or if it must be, a minority, opinion. The answer to the question Posner poses—what do judges seek to maximise—is votes, votes to ensure victory for their views as judicial leaders of a society. Without law clerks, we cannot use *amicus* briefs, and we will always be at risk of happenstance in decisions. But without a major change in self conception of the judicial role, we will never have a judiciary who will regard that as a pressing problem anyway. The role conception must change, a message as much borne out by this part of the analysis as by that in Part One. All else will flow.

SECTION FOUR; THE NEED FOR A FULL COURT

The strangest thing about the *Pinochet* case is that it was originally thought acceptable to decide it by a panel of five law lords. No other supreme court in the common law world would have done so. The US and Canadian Supreme Courts always sit *en banc*, and the Australian High Court would always do so for so high profile a case. Even in England, though it is rare, seven member

[22] R A Posner, *Overcoming Law* (Massachusetts, Harvard UP, 1995).

courts are empanelled when the senior law lord realises a highly controversial case is to be decided. When the Privy Council, which usually does its business with a three man bench faces an undeniably crucial constitutional case from the Commonwealth, as, for example, when they overruled the death penalty in some circumstances, as "cruel and unusual", they fielded more judges. When the House of Lords decided, in *Pepper* v. *Hart*[23] to overrule one of their own rules and allow reference to *Hansard*, which did indeed amount to a change, if a minor one, in the British constitution, they did so with seven members. Very rarely even ordinary civil law cases, which clearly involve a major change in the law, will be sent to a seven member panel, as with *Murphy* v. *Brentwood*[24] which, overturning *Anns* v. *Merton*,[25] reversed an expansionist development in the law of liability. (And, of course, once the fiasco of the Hoffmann problem forced the Lords to overrule themselves, a seven member committee was created.)

This is the heart of the problem—the fact that the law lords make major policy decisions for the country by empanelling an essentially random set of five of their twelve members. If they never heard cases in any other mode, one could at least treat the practice as a very brave, if unbelievable, statement about judicial nature in the United Kingdom—(that judges really were machines devoid of predispositions, ideologies, even of judicial methodological preferences, and any two of them were, literally, interchangeable) But the fact that, sometimes, but at whim, they do accept their authority needs buttressing by number gives even that game away. A whole series of problems stems directly from this organisational factor, and only in one way does the fact that five is a rather small number matter. Above all, deciding cases by a partial empanelling creates the problem that far too often it is quite easy to see that a major decision might very well have gone the other way but for the happenstance of who heard it.[26] This is the point with which we started. We actually *know*, not just suspect, that Senator Pinochet could be a free man today, had just one pair of judges been switched—replace Hoffmann with Goff, and that is the result. As I have said, this is commonplace with ordinary cases, and hardly acceptable then. But it cannot be acceptable in political/constitutional cases. When the first case comes to the Privy Council, under the clause that allows a Scottish law officer to refer a bill of the Scottish Parliament as potentially *ultra vires*, will it really be acceptable for the degree of federalism implicit in devolution, to be decided by less than the whole judicial Privy Council? Even if we do not have the information to know that a case might have gone otherwise, constitutional matters cannot

---

[23] *Pepper (Inspector of Taxes)* v. *Hart* [1993] 1 All ER 42. There is already a large literature on this case, though most of it is more supportive of the Lords' decision than I am. A good article which also surveys the literature is K Mullan, "The Impact of Pepper v. Hart" in Dickson and Carmichael, n 12 supra.

[24] *Murphy* v. *Brentwood* [1991] 1 AC 420.

[25] *Anns* v. *Merton London Borough* [1977] AC 728.

[26] I develop this point at considerable length in *Judicial Discretion in the House of Lords*, and cannot here spare the space to argue the point properly.

be left to rest on potential luck of the draw. Only the strongest self discipline on those affected makes it possible even now.

Consider a case like *Re M*,[27] where for the first time, and against all tradition, it was decided that a Secretary of State could be held in contempt, or *Factortame*,[28] where the power to stay the implementation of a statute by injunction was confirmed. Both of these were constitutional decisions. They were, as it happens, unanimous cases, but they were still cases settled by only *some* of the law lords. Another case of potential constitutional importance, and which might have been even more controversial had the House of Lords gone just an inch or so further than they did, was the *Fire Brigades Union* case of 1995.[29] This was not unanimous but split three-two. We are left guessing as to whether this unprecedented challenge to ministerial authority would ever have happened had, for example, Lord Lloyd been replaced on the case by Lord Jauncey, who tended to share the judicial restraint orientation of the leading minority judge, Lord Keith. So divided was judicial opinion on this case, including the views of a powerful Court of Appeal, that Lord Mustill who gave the other minority speech felt forced to comment on it. Any idea that the case was not of potentially far reaching constitutional importance is shattered by Mustill's speech, which warns of the danger to the courts of forcing too hard onto executive territory.

Here is part of the problem. The very fact that only some of the Lords speak, weakens their authority. One might say, rather, as it is the normal method of hearing cases, it prevents them developing authority, and prevents them coming to see themselves as wielders of huge potential political authority. This partialness, this sense that things might have been otherwise, and, that, after all, it was only five old men who were never elected has prevented the British political culture itself from developing a respect for their Lordships, and it is a lack of respect of which the law lords themselves are sometimes guilty. *Pepper* v. *Hart* can itself be seen as largely a lack of self confidence, as I argue elsewhere.[30]

However, the five man random panel method has far more deeply rooted consequences for British constitutional/political judging. Law lords do not sit for very long, the average incumbency is less than ten years. The law lords do not hear many cases, on average, forty a year, and this covers the whole gamut of judicial business. There is almost no role specialisation within the House of Lords. Thus few law lords actually build up a private expertise, or even have a private history, in any area, least of all the crucial public law cases we are discussing. It is acceptable in English law to bewail one consequence of this, that is, the bad track record that those with greater expertise regard the law lords as having in criminal cases—a view with which many of their Lordships privately

---

[27] *Re M* [1994] 1 AC 377.
[28] *R* v. *Secretary of State for Transport, ex parte Factortame* [1990] 2 AC 85.
[29] *R* v. *Secretary of State for the Home Department, ex parte Fire Brigades Union* [1995] 2 All ER 244.
[30] Robertson, Chapter 5, n 9 supra.

concur. How much more serious is it that major constitutional cases can be decided by a small group which, almost by definition, cannot be guaranteed to include all the available expertise in the area? In fact, the problem is not at its most acute at the individual level but becomes crucially important when one considers interaction. It can easily be the case that any pair of law lords, after several years in the House of Lords, have heard only a dozen or so cases together. Thus a five man panel on a political case can easily consist of people who have virtually no shared experience of dealing with such issues. How can judges in such a setting develop shared understandings of constitutional matters? How can they co-operate in group opinions, how can coherent majorities and eloquent long term minorities grow? When one realises that the individualistic stance of English judges, the absence of frequent and regular meetings over cases, the non existence of law clerks pooling their masters' ideas would all make coherence hard to come by even if the panel problem was removed, the chance for a politically sensitive court diminishes further.

Small groups of five, who are not necessarily used to working together in an area, suffer another problem. We tend too easily to forget that there is nothing mysterious about a panel of law lords. It is just a committee. Committees world wide are subject to their own peculiar dynamics, one of which is the influence of the strong personality, or of the man who does have a clear idea of where he's going when others are unsure.[31] Such personality effects are present in larger courts, of course. But the US Supreme Court consists of nine men and women who meet, day in, day out, to hear every case in every category that comes up to them. There is far less chance of a single man or woman, or even a subset of them, overawing the unsure or less confident, no chance that someone can seem to claim an unusual technical expertise or experience. The Hoffmann problem, more generally the problem of bias, takes on a new light if we imagine the law lords sitting regularly *en banc*.[32] Lord Hoffmann could have recused himself, with no real effect, because there would have been no need to re-empanel, no problem about who to select in this special context. More to the point, he need not have recused himself. The fact that someone can be seen as representing an ideological position matters much less when he can only influence the outcome by carrying another five or so judges with him by sheer force of argument. This is even more so, given that those arguments will be exposed to criticism by a coherent minority group, one which may well have honed their own positions over many cases together. That is why Justice Ginsberg's past history does not matter, anymore than does that of the other Supreme Court justices—they interact all the time in public, and with known associates.

[31] This influence of one or two judges on five man panels is the subject of Chapter 2 of *Judicial Discretion*. The treatment of a court as a committee and its analysis via a range of group dynamics theories has been taken seriously and effectively in the American jurimetrics literature, which is too large to canvass here.

[32] I leave undiscussed how large the Lords should be, but there is no reason why the entire twelve current appointees should not sit together—both the ECJ and the ECHR are larger. What is important is that *all* the judges sit, not a sample of them.

   The law lords, in many ways, do not form a whole. One does not, because it would be meaningless, generally talk about how "The Lords" view a major issue. Even when a case comes up, guesswork on how it will emerge is just that—pure guesswork, because there is no sense of an identity, or of a set of group identities. (The point is well made by the total failure of most commentators, myself included, to begin to predict the outcome of either *Pinochet 1* or *3*.) But a supreme court which is largely anonymous and individualistic cannot develop that national leadership a political role will force on them. Such a court cannot develop the political antennae needed, whether it is going to try to reflect a national consensus, or bravely to go out against one. A court so dependent on what counsel choose to argue before it, a court incapable of speaking with one, or where needs must, two rival voices, a court which can be thrown off balance by one member misjudging how his colleagues will react to his extra curial political connections, cannot take us safely into a twenty-first century where constitutional review will become commonplace.

3

Pinochet 2: *The Questions of Jurisdiction and Bias*

EVADNE GRANT

BACKGROUND

With hindsight, it was an apparently insignificant event which changed the course of the Pinochet litigation and led to a series of events which caused, if not substantial, at least significant damage to the reputation of the House of Lords. Before the hearing of the appeal by the House of Lords in *Pinochet 1*,[1] an application was made by Amnesty International for leave to intervene. The petition was granted in an interlocutory decision by Lords Slynn, Nicholl and Steyn, subject to objections being raised by Pinochet's lawyers. No objections were lodged. This meant that Amnesty International became a party to the proceedings and was represented by counsel who made both written and oral submissions during the hearing of the appeal, supporting the argument that Pinochet was not immune from prosecution.

The appeal was successful, the House of Lords concluding that Pinochet was not entitled to immunity and that the issuing of the second warrant of arrest by Bow Street Magistrates was therefore valid. The decision was not unanimous. Lords Steyn and Nicholls each delivered speeches giving reasons for allowing the appeal, Lord Hoffmann concurring, but without giving separate reasons, and Lords Slynn and Lloyd dissenting.

By the time that judgment was given, rumours had begun to surface that Lord Hoffmann's wife had some connection with Amnesty International. Indeed, in the version of events which led to the unprecedented second *Pinochet* decision, as outlined by Lord Browne-Wilkinson in his judgment in *Pinochet 2*,[2] two members of Pinochet's legal team later recalled that they had been aware of the rumours, but did not raise the issue either during the hearing in the House of Lords or immediately afterwards. However, a decision to act was taken after a speaker in Chile repeated the allegation during the Newsnight programme on

---

[1] R v. *Bow Street Metropolitan Stipendiary Magistrate and Others, ex parte Pinochet Ugarte* [1998] 3 WLR 1456.

[2] R v. *Bow Street Metropolitan Stipendiary Magistrate and Others, ex parte Pinochet Ugarte* (No 2) [1999] 2 WLR 272 at 277–8; Annex, p 183.

BBC television on the evening after judgment was given. Based on what was, by all accounts, very limited information, representations were made to the Home Secretary that Lord Hoffmann's decision in the case was affected by bias and should therefore be disregarded. This was an extraordinary submission to make, since it enjoined the Home Secretary to disregard a decision of the highest court, the House of Lords. Such a course of action would constitute a flagrant violation of the rule of law, which enshrines a principle fundamental to our legal system, that everyone, from the Prime Minister down, is subject to the ordinary law as it is pronounced by the courts.[3] In the absence of authorisation by Parliament, a failure on the part of the Home Secretary to comply with the decision of a court, would breach this principle. In the view of Pinochet's lawyers, however, the action urged upon the Home Secretary was the only domestic protection available to Pinochet in the circumstances, the only alternative being to take the matter to the European Court of Human Rights.[4] Thus it appears that, at this stage, the lawyers did not consider it possible to take the matter back to the House of Lords.

Meanwhile, Pinochet's lawyers wrote to Amnesty International requesting clarification of Lord Hoffmann's links with the organisation. Amnesty's solicitors replied that Lady Hoffmann had been employed in various administrative positions within Amnesty's international secretariat since 1977, mainly dealing with the media . Her current position was that of programme assistant to the director of the media and audio visual programme. The letter from Amnesty also denied that she had been "consulted or otherwise involved in any substantive discussions or decisions by Amnesty International, including in relation to the Pinochet case".[5]

A week later, events took a further unexpected turn. Pinochet's solicitors received an anonymous telephone call alleging that Lord Hoffmann, himself, was a director of the Amnesty International Charitable Trust. Amnesty's solicitors subsequently confirmed that Lord Hoffmann was a director and chairperson of Amnesty International Charity Limited, a registered charity which undertook the charitable aspects of Amnesty International's work in the United Kingdom. The solicitor's letter further stated that directors were not employed or paid by Amnesty International or Amnesty International Charity Limited and that Lord Hoffmann had not been consulted or had any role in Amnesty's intervention in the Pinochet litigation. It was also pointed out that Lord Hoffmann was not a member of Amnesty International itself, and that he had only acted for the organisation on one occasion while practising at the Bar.[6]

Despite being informed of these developments by Pinochet's lawyers, on 9 December the Home Secretary decided to proceed with extradition, dismissing

---

[3] See A W Dicey, *Introduction to the Study of the Law of the Constitution* (10th edn, Macmillan, 1967) p 193.

[4] *Pinochet 2*, n 2 supra, at 277; Annex, p 183.

[5] Ibid.

[6] Ibid, at 277–8; Annex, p 184.

the allegations of apparent bias. The next day, Pinochet lodged a petition with the House of Lords requesting the setting aside of the order in the first case or, alternatively, that the opinion of Lord Hoffmann be declared to be of no effect. The only ground relied upon was that Lord Hoffmann's links with Amnesty International were such as to give the appearance of possible bias.

THE LEGAL ISSUES

From a legal perspective, the case raised two important questions: first, whether the House of Lords had jurisdiction to set aside its own earlier order, and, secondly, whether the decision should be set aside because it was tainted by the appearance of bias. In unanimously[7] answering both questions in the affirmative, the House of Lords laid down a number of new principles, with important implications for the development of the law.

The question of jurisdiction

The application was without precedent. Never before had the House of Lords been asked to set aside its own previous decision. In fact, as noted above, it appears that counsel for Pinochet had not even considered this to be an option at the time that representations were made to the Home Secretary. The argument on behalf of Pinochet was simply, that in the absence of any other court with authority to remedy impropriety in the House of Lords, it must itself, of necessity, have jurisdiction to set aside its own orders. This argument was not disputed by counsel for the Crown Prosecution Service, acting on behalf of the Spanish Government.

Only one of the five judges, Lord Browne-Wilkinson, addressed the issue directly. Agreeing with counsel for Pinochet, he stated that, in principle, the House of Lords, as the final court of appeal, must have inherent jurisdiction to correct an injustice caused by its own earlier decision and that, in the absence of legislative limitation, this jurisdiction remains intact. However, he was anxious to stress that it was limited to cases where an applicant had been subjected to an unfair procedure. The House had no power to vary or rescind a previous order simply because a differently constituted bench disagreed with a previous decision of the House on the merits of the case.[8]

---

[7] The leading judgment was given by Lord Browne-Wilkinson, with Lords Goff, Hope and Hutton giving separate reasons and Lord Nolan concurring in the judgments of Lords Browne-Wilkinson and Goff.

[8] *Pinochet 2*, n 2 supra, at 281 but see Robertson, Chapter Two in this collection, for a consideration of how a differently constituted bench might have reached a different decision in *Pinochet 1*; Annex, p 187.

His acceptance that the House of Lords has inherent jurisdiction to correct an injustice, which arises from an unfair procedure, must be correct. It is one of the central tenets of any legal system, which claims to be fair and just, that the law must be applied without favour or prejudice. Thus it is a fundamental principle of our law that a judge, "from the Lord Chancellor downwards"[9] is disqualified from determining any case in which he or she may be or may reasonably be perceived to be biased.[10] In *Dimes* v. *Grand Junction Canal*,[11] decided in 1852, the Lord Chancellor himself was held to be disqualified from sitting on a case. The issue arose over an injuction, sought by the Grand Junction Canal Company against Dimes, which was granted by the Vice Chancellor and confirmed by the Lord Chancellor. However, it transpired that the Lord Chancellor owned shares in the company. On appeal to the House of Lords, it was held that since the Lord Chancellor was disqualified, the decision should be reversed. Lord Campbell CJ said:

> No one can suppose that Lord Cotterham [the Lord Chancellor] could be, in the remotest degree, influenced by the interest that he had in this concern; but it is of the last importance that the maxim that no man is to be a judge in his own cause should be held sacred.[12]

Although the principle is well-established, its practical application is problematic. There is no formal rule prescribing the procedures to be followed when applying for a judge to disqualify himself or when challenging the decision of a judge not to disqualify himself. These matters are governed by practice, subject to the possibility of raising the matter on appeal or, in the case of the lower courts and other tribunals, seeking judicial review. The accepted practice appears to be that if a judge realises, before a hearing, that for some reason he should not sit, he disqualifies himself. If he thinks that, in spite of some real or perceived interest, disqualification is not warranted, he discloses the matter and usually steps down if any of the parties raise objections, thereby again, in effect, disqualifying himself.[13] A judge may also decline to sit in a case if one of the parties objects on the grounds of bias or perceived bias, but it is for the judge to make the decision. One of the best known instances where this happened was a case involving the Church of Scientology. The Church objected to Lord Denning hearing the matter on the grounds that his perceived antipathy to the sect meant he would not be impartial. Although he was not obliged to do so, Lord Denning stepped down from hearing the case.[14] But it has not been common in the past for such

[9] S Shetreet, *Judges on Trial* (North Holland Publishing Company, 1976) p 303.

[10] See S De Smith, H Woolf and J Jowell, *Judicial Review of Administrative Action* (5th edn, Sweet and Maxwell, 1995) p 525; H W R Wade and C F Forsyth, *Administrative Law* (7th edn, OUP, 1994) p 471; S H Smith and M J Gunn, *Smith and Bailey on the Modern English Legal System* (3rd edn, Sweet and Maxwell, 1996) p 248.

[11] *Dimes* v. *Grand Junction Canal* (1852) 3 H L Cas 759.

[12] Ibid, at 793.

[13] Shetreet, p 305 n 9 supra.

[14] *Ex parte Church of Scientology of California, The Times* 21 February 1978. Further examples are discussed by Shetreet, ibid, at 305ff.

objections to be raised. It has been argued, moreover, that judges should not accede to requests to recuse themselves too readily, because, as Pannick submits:

> Judges are there to decide cases, not to excuse themselves whenever a litigant doubts, without cause, the judicial qualities of those assigned to sit in judgment.[15]

The infrequency of applications for recusal and the view that such applications should not be granted too easily may stem from a high degree of confidence in the impartiality of the judges. However, reluctance to object may, additionally, reflect a fear of incurring the animosity of the judge or a desire to avoid the inconvenience and cost involved in transferring the matter to another court. A formal procedure to deal with objections would make it easier for genuine concerns to be raised, and help to allay fears that raising objections may stigmatise the party or counsel who raises such a matter. Placing the matter on a more formal footing may also be desirable, not only to maintain confidence in the administration of justice, but also because it is in the interests of litigants that questions regarding disqualification be dealt with before a matter goes to trial, rather than the parties having to resort to appeal or judicial review after the event.

The same informal practical arrangements and absence of formal procedures apply to the House of Lords, with the significant difference that there is no correcting mechanism in the form of an appeal or judicial review. It is this gap that *Pinochet 2* has remedied. Since the same principles regarding disqualification apply to it, it must be open to the House of Lords to set aside its own decision where one of its members was disqualified to sit.

The issue of disqualification also arose in Australia in 1998, in relation to the *Hindmarsh Island Case*.[16] Prior to the hearing of the case, the applicant made an oral application to one of the judges of the High Court, requesting that he disqualify himself from sitting. The basis of the complaint was that the judge had previously, as senior counsel, provided advice to the minister regarding the legislation being challenged in the case. His advice had been that the legislation had been validly enacted. Since he had already decided the matter in another capacity, it was argued, he could not be impartial in the case. The judge refused to disqualify himself[17] and the case went ahead. After two days of legal argument, but before judgment was given, the plaintiffs applied to the Full Court to disqualify the judge from further participation in the case. In the event the matter was not heard, the judge disqualifying himself unilaterally before the hearing.

As in the *Pinochet* case, this was an unprecedented application. Since the matter was not resolved, the legal question of whether the Full Court of the High Court of Australia, which is the final court of appeal, has the power to disqualify one of its members from participation in a case remains moot. Australian

---

[15] D Pannick, *Judges* (OUP, 1988) p 41.
[16] *Kartinyeri v. Commonwealth of Australia* (1998) 152 ALR 540.
[17] *Kartinyeri v. Commonwealth of Australia* (No 2) (1998) 156 ALR 300.

commentators suggest that one possible basis for the exercise of such a power may be the court's inherent jurisdiction to ensure that proceedings before it are conducted without bias.[18] It is also noted that the recognition of such a power would be consistent with Australia's international obligations relating to fair trials.[19]

More recently, the South African Constitutional Court was faced with a similar question. The issue was whether the Constitutional Court, the ultimate appellate court in constitutional matters, had jurisdiction to determine an application for the recusal of its own members.[20] The application was highly unusual. It involved objections by a respondent in a pending appeal, to five of the eleven judges of the Constitutional Court sitting in the case on grounds of apparent bias. The basis of the application was a number of allegations which, it was argued, resulted in the impartiality of the judges being compromised. These ranged from friendship with the President, Nelson Mandela, to personal animosity between one judge and the party's lawyer. If sustained, the application would have resulted in the court ceasing to be quorate.[21]

As in the Australian case, the question of bias related to a matter yet to be heard. It was, in this respect, different from *Pinochet 2*. However, referring to *Pinochet 2*, the court noted, without deciding the question, that as the final court of appeal in constitutional matters, it was the only court which had the power to set aside its own judgments.[22] Regarding the recusal application before it, the court unanimously held that it had jurisdiction to hear the application, its reasoning being that the right to a fair trial was guaranteed by the Bill of Rights in the Constitution[23] and, as it was bound by the Bill of Rights,[24] it had a duty under the Constitution to take the necessary steps to prevent any of its members from sitting, if disqualified by reason of bias or possible bias. To give effect to this duty, the court had to determine the issue of bias, since no other court had the power to do so.[25]

The Australian and South African cases illustrate the different contexts in which the question of the limits of the jurisdiction of the House of Lords may become an issue. It is arguable that if the matter of prior disqualification arose before the House of Lords, the inherent jurisdiction of the House of Lords

---

[18] See S Tilmouth and G Williams, "The High Court and the Disqualification of one of its own" (1999) 73 *Australian Law Journal* 72 at 75.

[19] Ibid, at 76.

[20] *The President of the Republic of South Africa and Others* v. *South African Rugby Football Union and Others* (*SARFU*) decided on 7 May 1999, reasons delivered on 4 June 1999.

[21] It is not entirely clear what the implications would have been if five of the eleven judges had indeed recused themselves. The court initially stated that the appeal would not have been able to proceed (at para 6), but subsequently pointed out that if the court ceased to be quorate due to recusal, it would be necessary for the President to appoint acting justices in accordance with the procedure prescribed in section 175(1) of the Constitution (at para 47).

[22] Ibid, at para 31.

[23] Sections 34 and 35 of the Constitution of South Africa 1996 (Act 108 of 1996).

[24] Section 8 (1) of the Constitution of South Africa 1996.

[25] At paras 30–1. The application was considered by the whole court, including the judges to whom the application for recusal related.

would be invoked in accordance with *Pinochet 2*. But the basis of the decision in the South African case also points to the future in which the Human Rights Act 1998 will begin to play a central role in determining such jurisdiction. Given that the right to a fair trial is guaranteed by the European Convention,[26] and that under the Human Rights Act the House of Lords is bound to act in compliance with its provisions,[27] the law lords may have to extend their reasoning, regarding the basis of its jurisdiction to set aside its own previous decisions, after the Act comes into operation.

The legal meaning of bias

The basis of the application on behalf of Pinochet was not that Lord Hoffmann was actually biased, but that because of his involvement with Amnesty International, which became a party to the proceedings, there was a real danger or a reasonable apprehension of bias.[28] As noted above, it is a fundamental principle of our law that actual or a reasonable suspicion of bias disqualifies a judge from participating in a case to which it relates. This is but one facet of a more general requirement of independence and impartiality in decision-making, which is a fundamental requirement for justice.[29] The principle at issue in *Pinochet* 2 is encapsulated in the rule that no person may be a judge in his own cause, usually referred to simply as the rule against bias. This, together with the rule that the parties to a dispute should be given a proper opportunity to be heard, are collectively known as the rules of natural justice. These apply to all judicial proceedings, as well as administrative decision-making, and are regularly invoked against inferior courts and administrative agencies in judicial review proceedings. But it must be clearly understood that the term "bias" in this context carries a particular meaning in law, which does not in all circumstances correspond with a layperson's understanding of the word.

The general requirement of impartiality and the more specific rule against bias, serve a number of related purposes. First, that impartiality, it is argued, promotes accuracy in decision-making. Secondly, a decision is more likely to be accepted by the parties as fair and accurate, if the decision-maker is thought to be impartial. This, in turn, promotes a third, more general, purpose of engendering public confidence in the judicial process and thus enhancing the institutional legitimacy of the legal system.[30] However, this third aim is the source of a major tension, which has produced a particular legal view of bias, and colours the application of the principle in practice. While confidence in the process is

---

[26] The European Convention on Human Rights, Article 6.

[27] The Human Rights Act 1998, section 6.

[28] But see Robertson (chapter Two in this collection) for a discussion of AI's position.

[29] For a discussion of judicial independence generally see, for example, Bailey and Gunn, *Modern English Legal System*, pp 239–49; R Stevens, *The Independence of the Judiciary* (OUP 1993).

[30] See De Smith, Woolf and Jowell, *Judicial Review of Administrative Action*, p 521.

inspired by impartiality, it is also harmed by any suggestion, or impression, that a judge may be biased. Such an impression may be created if a judge sits in a case in which he has some interest, even if he is, in fact, scrupulously impartial. Thus it is not only actual bias which could damage the legitimacy of the system, but also the appearance of bias. The rule against bias therefore has to prevent both. Because a finding, or even an allegation, of actual bias is itself damaging to confidence in the system, it is the appearance of bias which is most often relied upon in the cases and around which most of the legal developments have taken place. As Lord Hewart famously commented:

> [I]t is of fundamental importance that justice should not only be done, but should manifestly and undoubtedly be seen to be done.[31]

The case of *Gough*[32] is the leading English authority on the application of the rule against bias. The question to be decided in the case was whether a juror was disqualified because she was the neighbour of the brother of the accused. The juror had not realised that the accused's brother was her neighbour until after the appellant had been convicted and sentenced. After a detailed review of the authorities, the House of Lords concluded that the cases in which the question of bias comes into play could be divided into three categories. The first category comprises cases in which actual bias is proved. In such cases the judge is obviously disqualified.[33] Such cases are rare, for understandable reasons. Accusing a judge of bias is extremely serious, and a finding of bias equally so. Comity usually prevents counsel from making such allegations. Moreover, even if such an allegation is made, the practical difficulty of establishing the state of mind of the judge at the time, and the fear that a finding of actual bias will damage public confidence, usually results in the court resorting to the less damaging finding of apparent bias.

In the second category, judges are automatically disqualified from adjudicating in cases in which they have a financial or a proprietary interest, even if the interest is very small.[34] If it is shown that such an interest exists, it is not necessary to make any further enquiries as to actual or apparent bias. The mere existence of such an interest disqualifies the judge. This is so, according to Lord Goff in *Gough*, because "the circumstances are such that they must inevitably shake public confidence in the integrity of the administration of justice if the decision is to be allowed to stand".[35]

The third category comprises all other cases in which the allegation is not actual bias, but the appearance of bias. In such cases the central question is how the court should determine apparent bias. Different formulations of the test to be applied have been used, resulting in a standard which varies from a proba-

---

[31]   R. v. *Sussex Justices, ex parte McCarthy* [1924] 1 KB 256 at 259.
[32]   R. v. *Gough* [1993] AC 646.
[33]   Ibid, at 661.
[34]   See H H Marshall, *Natural Justice* (Sweet and Maxwell, 1959) pp 27–8.
[35]   *Gough*, n 32 supra, at 661.

bility of bias at one end of the scale to a suspicion of bias at the other. These various formulations are commonly grouped into two main lines of authority by commentators. In the one line of cases, a "real likelihood of bias" must be established in order to lead to disqualification. The formulation of the test in the other line is whether the circumstances give rise to "a reasonable suspicion or apprehension of bias".[36]

Clearly the principal difference between the two tests relates to the degree of apprehension, regarding the effect an interest may have on a judge's ability to be impartial, which is required in order to disqualify a judge. A real likelihood of bias requires a greater degree of apprehension and is more difficult to establish than a reasonable suspicion that the judge may be biased. But a simple comparison of the real likelihood and reasonable suspicion formulations tends to obscure the fact that there is another factor which is crucial to the determination of apparent bias, namely, the perspective from which the apparent bias is to be judged. Craig has identified four possible perspectives from which the question of bias may be viewed: the mind of the judge who is being challenged; the person affected by the apparent bias; the court which has to determine whether the decision was tainted by apparent bias after the event; or the reasonable person.[37] There is a lack of consistency in the cases regarding this question. The perspective of the reasonable man is most often associated with the reasonable suspicion test, but in some cases the real likelihood test is applied from the perspective of the reasonable man.[38] It is little wonder that Craig, in one of the leading administrative law textbooks, comments that "[t]he test for determining bias in cases other than those concerning pecuniary interest is, in short, in a state of confusion".[39]

Some clarification was provided by the House of Lords in *Gough* and, although the case related to a juror in a criminal trial, the House of Lords made it clear that the same standard applied in all cases of apparent bias, whether concerned with judges, jurors or administrative officials. The House of Lords endorsed a variant of the real likelihood test, preferring, however, to express it in terms of whether there was "a real danger of bias". According to Lord Goff, who gave the leading judgment, the real danger formulation was used in order to convey the idea that a possibility rather than a probability of bias was sufficient in order to disqualify a decision-maker. A real danger, it was explained in a subsequent case "involves more than a minimal risk, less than a probability".[40] *Gough* also stipulated that the perspective from which the danger of bias is to be viewed is that of the court, not the reasonable man, although, according to Lord Goff, there is little difference between the impression derived by a reasonable man, to

---

[36] De Smith, Woolf and Jowell, *Judicial Review of Administrative Action*, p 526; Wade, *Administrative Law*, pp 481–2.
[37] P P Craig, *Administrative Law* (3rd edn, Sweet and Maxwell, 1994) p 331.
[38] See *Metropolitan Properties (FGC) Ltd v. Lannon* [1969] 1 QB 577.
[39] Craig, p 330, n 37 supra.
[40] R. v. *Inner West London Coroner, ex parte Dallaglio* [1994] 4 All ER at 151.

whom knowledge of the circumstances as found by the court has been imputed, and the impression derived by the court itself, which personified the reasonable man.[41]

The real danger test formulated in *Gough* has not found favour in other jurisdictions. In Scotland, the test applied by the High Court of Justiciary is the reasonable suspicion test, viewed from the perspective of a reasonable man.[42] The difference in approach was noted by Lord Hope in *Pinochet 2*. However, the explanation that the difference is due to the fact that the House of Lords in *Gough* was principally concerned to formulate a test, which could be applied by the lower appellate court, and that the same imperative did not apply in Scotland, where the High Court of Justiciary itself hears all criminal appeals, is not very convincing. Clearly seeking to downplay the difference, Lord Hope expressed the view that in practice the application of the tests is likely to lead to results, which are all but indistinguishable.[43] This view, that the tests produce the same results in practice, is not widely shared.[44]

It was precisely because of a concern that the tests do not produce identical results, that the High Court of Australia expressly rejected the *Gough* test in the case of *Webb* v. *the Queen*.[45] In the view of the court, the *Gough* formulation placed too much emphasis on the view that the courts take of the possibility of bias, rather than the perception of the public, and thus did not reflect the fact that the maintenance of public confidence in the judicial process is one of the key purposes of disqualification for appearance of bias. It therefore preferred the reasonable suspicion or apprehension test, with the perception of such suspicion being that of "fair-minded and informed members of the public".[46] While an informed member of the public is not assumed to have detailed knowledge of the law and the legal process, such an individual is expected to be aware of the findings of fact made by the court and to evaluate the incident in the light of those facts. According to one Australian commentator, this is the crucial difference between the bias tests used in Australia and the United Kingdom:

> The English test is concerned with the court's perception of the facts, whilst the Australian test is concerned with "the court's view of the public's view".[47]

In the recent South African recusal case, discussed above, the South African Constitutional Court also opted for the reasonable suspicion test.[48] However, in line with Australian,[49] and Canadian[50] authorities, a preference was expressed

---

[41] *Gough*, n 32 supra, at 667–8.
[42] *Bradford* v. *McLeod* [1986] SLT 244 R 247.
[43] *Pinochet 2*, n 2 supra, at 290; Annex, p 196.
[44] See E I Sykes, D J Lanham, R R S Tracey, K W Esser, *General Principles of Administrative Law* (4th edn, Butterworths, 1997) p 222 who compare the application of the two tests in Australia.
[45] *Webb* v. *The Queen* (1994) 181 CLR 41.
[46] Ibid, at 52.
[47] M Aronson and B Dyer, *Judicial Review of Administrative Action* (LBC Information Services, 1996), quoting *Webb* at 52.
[48] See (*SARFU*), n 20 supra.

for formulating the test in terms of an apprehension of bias rather than a suspicion of bias to avoid any unintended connotations associated with the term "suspicion".[51] The perspective from which the apprehension of bias is to be judged is, again, that of a reasonable and informed person.[52] The court stressed that the test thus incorporated two objective elements, namely that the person from whose perspective the apprehension of bias is to be judged must be reasonable, and that the apprehension of bias itself must be reasonable in the circumstances of the case.[53] The court also identified two issues, knowledge of which is to be imputed to the mythical reasonable and informed person. First, the reasonable person will be aware of a general presumption of impartiality on the part of judges based on their training, experience and the oath of office, which they have taken. Secondly, the reasonable person will understand that absolute neutrality on the part of a judge is almost impossible to achieve, and that they quite properly rely on their background knowledge and experience in carrying out their functions. Moreover, the unanimous judgment of the Full Court emphasised that, while judges of the Constitutional Court have a duty not to sit when disqualified, they have an equally strong obligation to sit if not disqualified. Thus the court cautioned against ready accession to demands for recusal which are not properly made out.[54]

The argument and decision regarding bias

Counsel for Pinochet, clearly aware of the controversy regarding the test to be applied in order to determine apparent bias, took the lawyer's way out and declined to nail their colours firmly to the mast of either *Gough* or *Webb*. They simply argued the matter in the alternative, that *either* the links between Lord Hoffmann and Amnesty were such that there was a real danger that Lord Hoffmann was biased in favour of Amnesty (based on *Gough*) *or* that there was a reasonable suspicion of bias (based on *Webb*).

However, the House of Lords declined to apply either test. Instead, the law lords took an unexpected and novel approach to the law and the facts: they extended the second category identified in *Gough*, adding a new ground for automatic disqualification. This encompassed the particular set of facts giving rise to the objection raised by *Pinochet*, allowing the court to side-step both the invitation to reconsider the *Gough* test and the need to apply either of the tests to Lord Hoffmann.

[49] *Livesey* v. *The New South Wales Bar Association* (1983) 151 CLR 288 at 293–4. However, subsequently in *Webb*, the formulation of "reasonable apprehension or suspicion" reappears.
[50] *R* v. *S (RD)* (1997) 118 CCC (3d) 353.
[51] *SARFU*, n 20 supra, at para 38.
[52] Although it is somewhat confusing when the court subsequently refers to the reasonable *litigant*.
[53] *SARFU*, n 20 supra, at para 45.
[54] Ibid, at paras 46–7.

The House of Lords decided unanimously that, because of his particular interest in the case, Lord Hoffmann was automatically disqualified from sitting. The decision in *Pinochet 1* was thus set aside, since the court had been improperly constituted. Although the decision was unanimous, the arguments used by the different members of the court in reaching that conclusion vary in significant respects.

Lord Browne-Wilkinson's speech is the most detailed.[55] The point of departure for Lord Browne-Wilkinson is the fundamental principle that no man may be a judge in his own cause, which, in his view comes into play in two different contexts. First, applied literally, the implication of the principle is that a judge is automatically disqualified from sitting in any matter in which he was, in fact, a party, or in the outcome of which he had a financial or proprietary interest. Secondly, the principle is applied in situations where the judge is neither a party to the suit, nor has a financial interest, but where a suspicion arises from his conduct that he may be biased. In such a case the judge would not normally derive any personal benefit, but rather provide a benefit for another by not being impartial. For this reason, in his view, this second type of case did not strictly speaking involve an application of the principle that a man must not be judge in his own cause.

In the light of this analysis, Lord Browne-Wilkinson concluded that the events under consideration fell into the first category, namely cases where the judge is disqualified because he is a judge in his own cause. Once it is shown that the judge is a party, or has a relevant interest, he is automatically disqualified, rendering it unnecessary to investigate whether there was a likelihood or suspicion of bias.

Deriving authority from the case of *Dimes*, Lord Browne-Wilkinson proceeded to explain the development of the law in relation to automatic disqualification. In *Dimes* Lord Campbell set out the parameters within which automatic disqualification operates:

> [M]y Lords, it is of the last importance that the maxim that no man is to be a judge in his own cause should be held sacred. And that is not to be confined to a cause in which he is a party, but applies to a cause in which he has an interest.[56]

But, according to Lord Browne-Wilkinson, *Dimes* itself illustrated a development of the principle. Initially, the only situation in which a judge was automatically disqualified was if he purported to decide a case in which he was actually a party. In *Dimes* the principle was extended to cases in which the judge had other interests. However, as the only other interest, which had led to automatic disqualification in subsequent cases, was a financial or proprietary interest, the question was whether Lord Hoffman was nonetheless covered by the principle enunciated in *Dimes*.

---

[55] See Robertson, Chapter Two in this collection, for extracts of this speech.
[56] *Dimes*, n 11 supra, at 793.

Applying the principles to the facts, Lord Browne-Wilkinson concluded that, in spite of close links between Amnesty International and Amnesty International Charity Limited, it could not be said that Lord Hoffmann was himself a party to the proceedings, as, legally speaking, he and each of the organisations were separate entities. If Lord Hoffmann was not a party, the next question was whether he had an interest, which was sufficient to disqualify him automatically from participation in the case. On the facts, Lord Browne-Wilkinson took the view that Lord Hoffmann shared with Amnesty International, the Crown Prosecution Service, who was prosecuting the case, and the Government of Spain, on whose behalf the prosecution was being undertaken, an interest to procure the extradition and trial of Pinochet.[57] The question on which the conclusion hinged was whether this was sufficient to give rise to automatic disqualification.

It was on this point that the case broke new ground. In the view of Lord Browne-Wilkinson, there was no reason, in principle, to confine the operation of automatic disqualification to financial or proprietary interests. In his view, the main reason why it had been confined in this way was because the matter had, in the past, arisen only in civil cases, in which economic interests obviously predominate. But, according to Lord Browne-Wilkinson,

> [I]f, as in the present case, the matter at issue does not relate to money or economic advantage but is concerned with the promotion of the cause, the rationale disqualifying a judge applies just as much if the judge's decision will lead to the promotion of a cause in which the judge is involved together with one of the parties.[58]

However, Lord Browne-Wilkinson went to considerable lengths to emphasise that this conclusion was not based on a view that Lord Hoffmann supported the objectives of Amnesty International. If this were so, it would make it impossible for judges to sit on cases involving charities, which they support. The decision was based on three considerations: first, that Amnesty International was a party to the proceedings; secondly, that it was allowed to intervene in the case specifically in order to argue for a particular result; and thirdly, that Lord Hoffmann held a position in Amnesty International Charity Limited, which was closely linked to Amnesty International and shared the objectives which were being pursued by it in this case. In the words of Lord Browne-Wilkinson:

> Only in cases where a judge is taking an active role as trustee or director of a charity which is closely allied to and acting with a party to the litigation should a judge normally be concerned either to recuse himself or disclose the position to the parties.[59]

This was clearly an attempt to limit the application of the principle to the particular facts of the case. Nonetheless he left the door ajar for further

---

[57] See Catley and Claydon, Chapter Four in the collection, for further discussion on this point.
[58] *Pinochet 2*, n 2 supra, at 283; Annex, p 189.
[59] Ibid, at 284; Annex, p 190.

development, saying that there may be other exceptional cases in which a judge should disclose a possible interest.[60]

Lords Goff and Hope took a slightly different approach. Although they both proceed from the basic principle that a man shall not be a judge in his own cause, rather than seeking to identify an interest which leads to automatic disqualification, their judgments concentrated on the closeness of the relationship between Lord Hoffmann and Amnesty International, as the key disqualifying factor. However, it is arguable that the difference between their arguments and that of Lord Browne-Wilkinson is one of emphasis rather than substance. Automatic disqualification arose, in Lord Goff's view, from the relationship between judge and a party, which had an interest in the outcome of the case. The close connection meant that Amnesty's views regarding matters pertaining to the case were to be imputed to Lord Hoffmann himself, causing him to have an interest in the outcome of the proceedings, even if he had no personal view or objective regarding the extradition of Pinochet.[61] Lord Hope emphasised that it was Amnesty's close association with the position of the prosecutor, which gave it an interest in the outcome of the case, an interest shared by Lord Hoffmann, purely by virtue of his close association with Amnesty International. Both judges emphasised that this conclusion was not dependent on Lord Hoffmann himself holding any view about the extradition of Pinochet. It was the fact that Amnesty International was a party to the proceedings and had a very specific interest in the outcome of the case, together with the closeness of Hoffmann's links to the organisation, which led to automatic disqualification.

While Lord Hutton explicitly agreed with the reasoning and conclusion of Lord Browne-Wilkinson, he expressed the applicable principle in less restricted terms:

> I am of opinion that there could be cases where the interest of the judge in the subject matter of the proceedings arising from his strong commitment to some cause or belief or his association with a person or body involved in the proceedings could shake public confidence in the administration of justice.[62]

This seems to suggest that the two disqualifying factors emphasised by the other judges, could be applied in the alternative: disqualification arose from either a commitment to a cause or from a close connection with one of the parties.

Notwithstanding any difference in emphasis, the essential ingredients for automatic disqualification in all the judgments were: a close relationship between the judge and one of the parties and an interest in the outcome of the case, which interest could be imputed to the judge by virtue of the relationship. By placing this case in the category of automatic disqualification, the House of Lords was able to side-step the difficult question of whether there was a danger of bias or the appearance of bias. Moreover, the way in which the principle was

---

[60] *Pinochet 2*, n 2 supra, at 284; Annex, p 191.
[61] Ibid, at 287; Annex, p 193.
[62] Ibid, at 293; Annex, p 198.

developed and applied to the facts made it possible for the law lords to conclude that Lord Hoffmann was disqualified simply on the basis of his links with Amnesty. Thus they were able to avoid consideration of the possibility of bias or what view the ordinary person may take of Lord Hoffmann's links with Amnesty and his failure to disclose those links, which may have led to implied criticism of a fellow judge. The judges all made a point of emphasising that there was no suggestion of actual bias, and that the conclusion was not dependent on Lord Hoffmann actually holding any personal views about whether Pinochet ought to be extradited.

IMPLICATIONS FOR THE DEVELOPMENT OF THE LAW

The judgment of the House of Lords in *Pinochet 2* was unprecedented, in relation to both the question of disqualification for apparent bias, and the question of jurisdiction. But the circumstances in which these issues arose were themselves extraordinary. Lord Browne-Wilkinson described the facts as "striking and unusual".[63] The question is, whether the principles which were identified, developed and applied have any broader significance, or whether they are to be confined to the peculiar facts of this case. Moreover, in the light of the Human Rights Act 1998, the significance of the decision must be considered in the context of the relevant provisions of the European Convention on Human Rights and the decisions of the European Court of Human Rights.

Bias

Two questions arise in relation to bias. The first relates to the future of the *Gough* test. Widespread rejection of the "real danger" formulation and principled criticism in the Australian case of *Webb* of the lack of recognition in the test of the need to maintain public confidence in the administration of justice, raises doubts about the suitability and long-term viability of the test. The view that the *Gough* formulation may be ripe for reconsideration by the House of Lords was clearly shared by counsel for Pinochet. This is apparent from the terms in which the application was couched, inviting the House of Lords to apply either *Gough* or *Webb*.

The need for reconsideration is also clear from the terms of the Human Rights Act, which requires all courts, including the House of Lords, to act in compliance with the European Convention on Human Rights.[64] Indeed, the failure of the House of Lords to even mention the European Convention on Human

---

[63] Ibid, at 282; Annex, p 189.
[64] The Human Rights Act 1998, section 6.

Rights,[65] let alone consider the jurisprudence of the European Court of Human Rights on the issue, raises serious questions about its state of readiness to comply with the requirements of the Human Rights Act. Moreover, it is no defence that the obligation to consider and apply the Convention will only arise once the Act comes into operation. The need to consider the Convention prior to formal incorporation has been aptly stated by Sedley J in the case of McQuillan:

> [T]he principles and standards set out in the Convention can certainly be said to be a matter of which the law of this country now takes notice in setting its own standards. . . . Once it is accepted that the standards articulated in the European Convention are standards which both march with those of the common law and inform the jurisprudence of the European Union, it becomes unreal and potentially unjust to continue to develop English public law without reference to them.[66]

Given that the Pinochet litigation raised questions, which are fundamental to the right to a fair trial protected under the Convention,[67] it was incumbent upon the House of Lords to give some consideration to the principles applied under the Convention. Moreover, it would have been an ideal opportunity to raise awareness of the European Convention and the future role of the courts in enforcing it, given the level of interest in Pinochet.[68]

In the light of the decision that Lord Hoffmann was automatically disqualified from sitting in the case, it was unnecessary for the court to deal with the question whether the test in Gough ought to be reviewed. Although the future of the "real danger" formulation was therefore not decided, there are a number of indications that it is likely to be modified if the matter comes before the House of Lords in an appropriate case in the future. First, the judges have evidently noted the criticisms. In his judgment, Lord Browne-Wilkinson referred to rejection or modification of the Gough formulation in Canada, Australia and New Zealand and he identified some of the criticisms of the test which have been raised both in cases in the United Kingdom and abroad.[69] Secondly, it is interesting that there was no endorsement at all of the Gough formulation. In fact, whenever the matter was mentioned by the judges, the Gough and Webb formulations were used as alternatives. However, as the test was not rejected or modified in Pinochet 2, Gough remains authoritative for cases of apparent bias which are not covered by the Pinochet ruling.

The second question relating to bias, which arises in the light of the decision, is whether the category of automatic disqualification is now open, or whether it will be confined to the facts of this case. It would clearly be to the advantage of

---

[65] Lord Hope made a passing reference to Article 6(1) but said nothing of substance.

[66] R v. Secretary of State for the Home Department, ex parte Mcquillan [1995] 4 All ER 400 at 422. See also R v. Director of Public Prosecutions, ex parte Kebilene [1999] 3 WLR 175.

[67] European Convention on Human Rights, Article 6.

[68] The question of whether consideration of the jurisprudence of the European Court of Human Rights would have affected the decision is canvassed in full in Chapter Four.

[69] Pinochet 2, n 2 supra, at 284; Annex, p 190.

a party, who wishes to challenge a decision on the basis of apparent bias, to be able to argue that the judge was automatically disqualified. In order to succeed, an applicant would only need to establish that, by virtue of the interest involved and the relationship between judge and party, the matter was one which fell within the automatic disqualification category. It would not be necessary to show, in addition, that the court (or the reasonable person or even the fair-minded and informed person) perceived a real danger of bias (or had a reasonable suspicion or apprehension of bias). The task of the applicant is clearly simpler in the case of automatic disqualification than if reliance is placed on a real danger or reasonable suspicion of bias.

However, it cannot be assumed that satisfying the requirements for automatic disqualification is a simple task. There are a number of very specific requirements, which must be satisfied: the evidence must show a very close relationship between the judge and a party to the proceedings, and the party must have a clear interest in the outcome of the case, an interest which can be imputed to the judge. It is clear from the judgment of Lord Browne-Wilkinson that he considered the development of the law in the case to be limited to exceptional circumstances. Although he did not rule out the possibility that other exceptional cases may arise, he took great pains to emphasise that it was a singular series of events which gave rise to the application, and that this would not necessarily mean that judges are disqualified from sitting in cases involving charities in whose work they may be involved.[70]

Lord Goff appeared to accept a wider application of the category of automatic disqualification. This may be so because his reasoning placed more emphasis on the relationship between the judge and one of the parties, and rather less on the nature of the interest which they share, appearing to assume that a party naturally has an interest in the outcome of the case. He therefore mentioned as a clear possibility that a judge who is a senior executive of a charity will be disqualified from sitting in cases involving the charity, since:

> [h]e will by reason of his position be committed to the well-being of the charity and to the fulfilment by the charity of its charitable objects. He may for that reason properly be said to have an interest in the outcome of the litigation . . . and so be disqualified from sitting as a judge in the proceedings.[71]

Since the discussion in the judgments was limited to cases in which charities are involved, it is not clear whether or not the principles involved can be extended to interests other than those involved in the *Pinochet* litigation.

---

[70] Ibid, at 282; Annex, p 190. See also Lord Hope who emphasises the unique approach of Amnesty International at 290; Annex, p 196.
[71] Ibid, at 287; Annex, p 193.

Disqualification

The second area for which the decision in *Pinochet 2* has implications is the law and practice in relation to disqualification. I have argued above that the House of Lords correctly accepted that it must have jurisdiction to set aside its own previous decision because of apparent bias. To have ruled otherwise would have been seen as condoning the irregularity. Such a ruling would also have failed to provide proper protection to the individual and may have compromised the integrity of the legal process. Whether or not the House of Lords was in fact equipped to exercise this jurisdiction, and whether a case can be made for the establishment of a higher court to hear matters of a constitutional nature, are questions which are canvassed elsewhere in this volume.[72] The point made here is limited to the correctness of the decision relating to jurisdiction in the context of the current judicial system.

The judgment draws attention to a number of different issues regarding the question of disqualification, which are raised more pertinently by the recent recusal litigation in South Africa and Australia. It is perhaps no mere coincidence that applications for disqualification have been made in such a short space of time in the highest courts of three Commonwealth jurisdictions. One Australian commentator has detected a marked increase in recent years in the number of cases in which objections have been raised to judges sitting in a case on the basis of apparent bias.[73] There is evidence to suggest that the issue of bias has moved closer to the surface of public consciousness in the United Kingdom too, and it is not unreasonable to speculate that such high-profile cases in the three jurisdictions will inevitably draw attention to the issue of judicial independence and impartiality and that the number of applications for recusal might well increase because of them.[*]

It would therefore seem timely to examine the law and procedures relating to judicial disqualification and to question whether they are able to withstand scrutiny and the increasing demands that may be placed upon them. Such a project is beyond the scope of this paper and comment will therefore be limited to two questions, which arise from the litigation here and abroad. The first is whether there is a need for clearer guidance to judges regarding the circumstances in which they should disqualify themselves; the second is whether there is a need for a more formal procedure for recusal applications. The decision in *Pinochet 2* is obviously itself of some assistance in providing guidance on the circumstances in which judges are disqualified from sitting. And by drawing attention to the question of judicial disqualification in such a dramatic and public way, it is likely to ensure that judges err on the side of caution in disqualifying themselves, at least until the issue fades from public attention.[74] There is also a

[72] See Robertson, Chapter Two.
[73] Aronson and Dyer, p 259, n 47 supra.
[74] In August 1999 Judge Hootton disqualified himself from hearing an appeal on the grounds, *inter alia*, of his membership of the Countryside Alliance (*The Times*, 6 August 1999).
[*] See postscript below.

wealth of cases dealing with the question of bias in administrative law, which
apply to judges as well as administrative bodies.[75] But a large number of sometimes conflicting authorities do not necessarily provide practical assistance and
judges who do not regularly deal with judicial review cases will not necessarily
be familiar with the detailed application of the rule against bias. The matter
does receive attention during the training of judges. Moreover, in the wake of
the decision in *Pinochet 2*, the Judges Council issued advice to part-time judges
(deputy High Court judges, recorders and assistant recorders) to disclose their
involvement in organisations, which have a campaigning agenda, before sitting
in cases where this may be an issue,[76] while the Lord Chancellor wrote to the
law lords requiring them "to put procedures in place to ensure that this does not
happen again".[77] Nevertheless, it is arguable that there is a need for guidance in
a form which is clear and accessible not only to judges, but also to barristers and
solicitors and the general public who have an interest in the proper administration of justice. One option is to introduce legislation, which would clarify the
rules. It is unlikely, however, that the Government will find time in its legislative
programme, or, indeed, have the inclination, to pass such legislation in the
immediate future. Other, less formal, forms of guidance, such as practice directions, may be made equally accessible and would have the advantage of greater
flexibility to permit modification in the light of changing circumstances.

With regard to the procedure for applying for disqualification of a judge, it
has been argued in the past that there is a need for a formal procedure to make
it easier and more acceptable for such applications to be brought.[78] In the light
of the provisions of the Human Rights Act, it is arguable that the need for such
a procedure has become more acute. Section 7 of the Act provides that proceedings may be brought against public authorities, which includes all courts,[79] by
persons who claim that such an authority "has acted (or proposes) to act" in a
way which is incompatible with the Convention. Since the right to a fair trial is
one of the rights protected under the Convention, a party who wishes to apply
for disqualification of a judge on the basis of an apprehension of bias must have
the right to do so under the Act.[80] But the Act itself does not create any specific
procedures for bringing applications in such circumstances. Instead, section 8
provides the courts with wide powers to "grant such relief or remedy, or make
such order, within its powers as it considers just and appropriate" in relation to
actual or potential violations by a public authority. But in the case of violations,
or potential violations, by judicial authorities, the availability of remedies is limited by section 9, which specifies that the only remedies available to victims of

[75] *Gough*, n 32 supra, at 670.
[76] *The Daily Telegraph*, 10 April 1999.
[77] Quoted by D Pannick, *The Times*, 12 January 1999.
[78] Shetreet, p 306, n 9 supra.
[79] Section 6 (3) defines "public authorities" as including courts and tribunals. It is clear from sub-section (4) that the House of Lords in its judicial capacity is included as a court.
[80] See A Olowofoyeku, "State Liability for the Exercise of Judicial Power" [1999] *Public Law* 444 at 459.

rights violations (or prospective violations) by a judicial act, are appeal, judicial review, or another procedure which may be prescribed by the rules of court.[81]

There is, therefore, no provision in the Act itself for prospective applications for the disqualification of judges. If, as argued above, the right to a fair trial includes the right to apply for the disqualification of a judge who may be biased, it is arguable that a procedure for doing so must be made available. If an informal procedure exists, as appears to be the case in relation to recusal, it must be asked whether this constitutes an effective remedy in the light of Article 13 of the Convention,[82] or whether a formal procedure for such applications needs to be created to ensure compliance with the United Kingdom's international obligations in respect of the European Convention on Human Rights.

CONCLUSION

While the decision in *Pinochet 2* is generally regarded as being satisfactory, in the sense that justice had been done and had been seen to have been done, the case raises a number of important questions about the development of the law and practice in relation to bias and the disqualification of judges. With regard to bias, the decision may prove to have a limited impact, since the circumstances in which automatic disqualification may arise in terms of the principles laid down in the case, appear to be limited to facts which are very close to those surrounding the *Pinochet* litigation. However, there is scope for the broader application of the principles enunciated and further litigation on this question will almost certainly follow. With regard to disqualification for apparent bias, there is a clear indication in the case that clarification of the "real danger" test is necessary, if it is to be sustainable. The events surrounding the case, and subsequent litigation elsewhere, raises the question whether clearer and more accessible guidance is called for regarding the circumstances in which judges are disqualified from sitting.

On the question of its jurisdiction to set aside one of its own previous decisions, the ruling of the House of Lords pre-empted a conclusion it would have had to reach if the Human Rights Act had been effective. The right to a fair trial, protected under the European Convention on Human Rights, clearly includes the right to be tried by an independent and impartial tribunal and the absence of any mechanism to challenge apparent bias in the House of Lords would have breached this right. But the lack of a formal procedure for applying for the recusal of a judge before, or during, the trial, may equally breach the Convention, and consideration should be given to providing clear guidance and a formal procedure for making such applications.

[81] See D Feldman, "The Human Rights Act 1998 and constitutional principles" (1999) 19 *Legal Studies* 165 at 203.
[82] See D Feldman, "Remedies for Violations of Convention Rights under the Human Rights Act" [1998] *European Human Rights Law Review* 691.

The case also exposed an unfortunate lack of recognition on the part of the House of Lords of the relevance of the European Convention for the development of the common law, prior to the Human Rights Act having effect. It is regrettable that the House of Lords did not make any reference to the right to a fair trial under the Convention, or the jurisprudence developed by the European Court of Human Rights. The lower courts have recognised the need to take cognisance of the principles and standard of conduct required under the Convention prior to incorporation, and it is a matter of great concern that the House of Lords has not endorsed this approach in the course of a case which has received so much attention both in this country and abroad.

Whatever the eventual outcome of the Pinochet saga the unprecedented raising of apparent bias in the highest court has led to a number of important innovations in our law. But perhaps more importantly, it has focused attention on some of the possible deficiencies of a system which relies heavily on informal processes and which lack clarity and transparency. In the light of the imminent advent of the Human Rights Act, the time may be ripe for a thorough overhaul of the system.

Postscript

On 17 November 1999, the Court of Appeal gave judgment in five cases[83] in which the grounds of appeal related to alleged danger of bias. All but one of the appeals were dismissed by a unanimous court consisting of the three most senior judges in the English courts, the Lord Chief Justice, Lord Bingham, the Master of the Rolls, Lord Woolf and the Vice Chancellor, Sir Richard Scott. Clearly aware of the expectation that it should provide clear guidance regarding the circumstance which may give rise to a real danger of bias, the court was reluctant to be too specific, saying that "it would be dangerous and futile to attempt to define or list [such] factors". The court nonetheless proceeded to enumerate a number of factors which, in its view, should not in the normal course of events lead to disqualification. These include national origin, gender, sexual orientation and educational background. The court also drew attention to a number of circumstances in which a real danger may arise, including personal friendship or animosity between a judge and a party to the proceedings in question and the expression of views by the judge "in such extreme and unbalanced terms as to throw doubt on his ability to try the issue with an objective judicial mind". The only applicant to succeed had relied upon this final ground

---

[83] *Locabail (UK) Ltd v Bayfield Properties Ltd and Another, Locabail (UK) Ltd and Another v Waldorf Investment Corporation and Others, Timmins v Gormley, Williams v Inspector of Taxes, R v Bristol Betting and Gaming Licensing Committee, ex parte O'Callaghan* (*The Times*, 19 November 1999.)

4

Pinochet, Bias and the European Convention on Human Rights

PAUL CATLEY and LISA CLAYDON

INTRODUCTION

On 17 December 1998 in an oral judgment[1] the House of Lords granted the petition of Senator Pinochet and set aside the court's previous decision[2] on the basis that Lord Hoffmann's links with Amnesty International gave an appearance of bias. In the written opinions that followed reference was made to the case law of both Australia and Scotland.[3] However, only one law lord referred to the European Convention on Human Rights and Fundamental Freedoms ("the Convention") and this reference was solely to the applicability of Article 6 to both civil and criminal cases.[4] No reference was made to the extensive jurisprudence of the Strasbourg Court on the impartiality and independence of courts and tribunals.

This was surprising, first, because the *Pinochet* case concerned human rights and raised issues of international importance[5] and, secondly, because the Human Rights Act, which incorporates the Convention, had received the royal assent a month earlier.[6] Although its main provisions have not yet taken effect

---

[1] Reasons were subsequently given on 15 January 1999. Reported as *R* v. *Bow Street Metropolitan Stipendiary Magistrate and Others ex parte Pinochet Ugarte* (No 2) [1999] 2 WLR 272.

[2] *R* v. *Bow Street Stipendiary Magistrate and Others, ex parte Pinochet Ugarte* [1998] 3 WLR 1456.

[3] Lords Browne-Wilkinson and Hope both referred to the Australian case of *Webb* v. *The Queen* (1994) 181 CLR 41. Lord Hope considered two cases from Scotland: *Bradford* v. *McLeod* 1986 SLT 244 and *Doherty* v. *McGlennan* 1997 SLT 444. In addition, Lord Browne-Wilkinson mentioned the attitude of the courts in Canada, Australia and New Zealand to *Reg.* v. *Gough* [1993] AC 646.

[4] Lord Hope stated: "Article 6 (1) of the European Convention on Fundamental Rights and Freedoms makes no distinction between civil and criminal cases in its expression of the right of everyone to a fair and public hearing within a reasonable time by an independent and impartial tribunal established by law". *Pinochet 2*, n 1 supra, at 289; Annex, p 195.

[5] Lord Browne-Wilkinson made reference to this latter aspect in his opinion: "The hearing of this case, both before the Divisional Court and in your Lordships' House, produced an unprecedented degree of public interest not only in this country but worldwide. The case raises fundamental issues of public international law and their interaction with the domestic law of this country". *Pinochet 2*, n 1 supra, at 276; Annex, p 182.

[6] The Human Rights Act received royal assent on 9 November 1998.

in England,[7] the impending incorporation of the European Convention on Human Rights and Fundamental Freedoms and its case law might be expected to influence judicial thinking in the interim. The House of Lords was also aware that Senator Pinochet's solicitors had written to the Home Secretary stating that "Absent domestic protection the senator will have to invoke the jurisdiction of the European Court of Human Rights".[8] In addition Strasbourg case law was employed in the arguments presented to the court. It might therefore have been anticipated that reference would be made to the Convention, particularly given that the Convention jurisprudence has much to say with regard to allegations of bias and the need for an impartial tribunal.

THE ARGUMENTS REGARDING THE POSSIBILITY OF BIAS

The basis of Senator Pinochet's appeal was the relationship between Lord Hoffmann and Amnesty International ("AI").[9] AI had been an intervener in *Pinochet 1* and in *Pinochet 2* it was stated that, "By seeking to intervene in this appeal and being allowed so to intervene, in practice AI became a party to the appeal".[10] Lord Browne-Wilkinson summarised Pinochet's petition as follows:

> The sole ground relied upon was that Lord Hoffmann's links with AI were such as to give the appearance of possible bias. It is important to stress that Senator Pinochet makes no allegation of *actual bias* against Lord Hoffmann; his claim is based on the requirement that justice should be seen to be done as well as actually being done. There is no allegation that any other member of the Committee has fallen short in the performance of his judicial duties.[11]

In order to determine the petition, the House of Lords examined the links between AI and Lord Hoffmann. In the various opinions their Lordships express their views as to the relationship differently. Lord Browne-Wilkinson analysed the links between AI, Amnesty International Limited ("AIL") and Amnesty's charity arm Amnesty International Charity Limited ("AICL")[12], of which Lord Hoffmann was a director and chairman, concluding that there was a "close interaction between the functions of AICL and AI". He referred to certain facts he had elicited from the report of the Directors of AICL for the year ended 31 December 1993, noting, firstly, that "AICL commissioned AIL to carry out charitable activities on its behalf" which included research publications and reports,

[7] The Home Secretary, Jack Straw, stated that the Government "plan to bring the remaining provisions of the Human Rights Act 1998 into force throughout the United Kingdom on 2 October 2000". (HC WA, 19 July 1999).

[8] *Pinochet 2*, n 1 supra, at 277; Annex, p 187.

[9] Senator Pinochet's legal representatives had initially made representations to the Home Secretary regarding Lord Hoffmann's wife's connections with AI. Senator Pinochet's legal team were subsequently informed of Lord Hoffmann's role in AICL.

[10] *Pinochet 2*, n 1 supra, at 282; Annex, p 188.

[11] Ibid, at 278; Annex, p 184.

[12] Ibid, quotations from 278–80; Annex, pp 185–6.

one of which was a 1993 publication relating to "not only the occurrence and nature of breaches of human rights within Chile, but also the progress of cases being brought against those alleged to have infringed human rights by torture and otherwise in the courts of Chile." Lord Browne-Wilkinson noted Amnesty's concern expressed in the report that "no one was convicted during the year for past human rights violations. The military courts continued to claim jurisdiction over human rights cases in civilian courts and to close cases covered by the 1978 Amnesty law." He also noted, particularly relevant to this case, that "Amnesty International continued to call for full investigation into human rights violations and for those responsible to be brought to justice." Lord Browne-Wilkinson concluded that: "Therefore AICL was involved in the reports of AI urging the punishment of those guilty in Chile for past breaches of human rights and also referring to such work as being part of the work that it supported."

As a director of AICL, Lord Hoffmann could be presumed to have been acquainted with AICL's research publications. It might therefore appear that he had the opportunity to have formed an opinion as to matters relating to the extradition of Senator Pinochet for human rights abuses in Chile prior to the extradition appeal being heard. As will be discussed later, this is a potentially important issue when applying the case law of the European Court of Human Rights. However, Lord Browne-Wilkinson did not consider the case in this context, although he, nevertheless, found that Lord Hoffmann had an interest in the proceedings sufficient to give rise to "an automatic disqualification".[13]

Lords Goff and Hope similarly looked at the association between AI and AICL, Lord Goff noting:

> The effect for present purposes is that Lord Hoffmann, as chairperson of one member of that organisation, AICL, is so closely associated with another member of that organisation, AI, that he can properly be said to have an interest in the outcome of proceedings to which AI has become party.[14]

For his part Lord Hope considered that:

> the connections which existed between Lord Hoffmann and Amnesty International were of such a character, in view of their duration and proximity, as to disqualify him on this ground. In view of his links with Amnesty International as the chairman and a director of Amnesty International Charity Limited he could not be seen to be impartial.[15]

It was therefore Lord Hoffmann's association with AI, a party to the proceedings against Senator Pinochet, which disqualified him. This approach based primarily on English case law and the identification of an interest on the part of Lord Hoffmann in the case can be contrasted with the approach likely to have

---

[13] Ibid, at 284; Annex, p 190. See also Evadne Grant (Chapter Three in this collection).
[14] Ibid, at 287; Annex, p 193.
[15] Ibid, at 291; Annex, p 196.

been taken if one were to apply the jurisprudence of the European Court of Human Rights.

Article 6(1) of the ECHR states:

> In the determination of his civil rights and obligations or of any criminal charge against him, everyone is entitled to a fair and public hearing within a reasonable time by an independent and impartial tribunal established by law. Judgment shall be pronounced publicly but the press and public may be excluded from all or part of the trial in the interests of morals, public order or national security in a democratic society, where the interests of juveniles or the protection of the private life of the parties so require, or to the extent strictly necessary in the opinion of the court in special circumstances where publicity would prejudice the interests of justice.

Under Article 6(1) Senator Pinochet's claim, regarding his treatment at the extradition appeal in the House of Lords, could be pursued both with respect to, firstly, the requirement of a fair hearing, based on the equality of arms principle, and, secondly, the right to be heard before an independent and impartial tribunal.

The right to a fair hearing; the principle of equality of arms

Two cases brought against the Belgian State are particularly pertinent to Senator Pinochet's position. *De Haes and Gijsels* v. *Belgium* considered the principle of equality of arms, which is fundamental to a fair hearing. This was given a broad interpretation such that:

> . . . the principle of equality of arms—a component of the broader concept of a fair trial—requires that each party must be afforded a reasonable opportunity to present his case under conditions that do not place him at a substantial disadvantage vis-à-vis his opponent.[16]

In the case of *Borgers* v. *Belgium* relating to the role of an officer from the procureur général's department, the court noted:

> No one questions the objectivity with which the *procureur général's* department at the Court of Cassation discharges its functions. . . . Nevertheless the opinion of the *procureur général's* department cannot be regarded as neutral from the point of view of the parties to the cassation proceedings. By recommending that an accused's appeal be allowed or dismissed, the official of the *procureur général's* department becomes,

---

[16] *De Haes and Gijsels* v. *Belgium* (1998) 25 EHRR 1 at para 53. This interpretation was originally stated in *Dombo Beheer B.V.* v. *The Netherlands* (1994) 18 EHRR 213.

objectively speaking, his ally or his opponent. In the latter event, Article 6 (1) requires that the rights of defence and the principle of equality of arms be respected.[17]

In the light of these cases it might be argued, that Lord Hoffmann's role in Pinochet's appeal against extradition could be said to place the senator at a "substantial disadvantage vis-à-vis his opponent" or, at least, vis-à-vis one of the interveners, AI. Lord Hoffmann could be seen to have a far more significant role in the determination of the case than the official of the procureur général's department.[18] He was able to, and did,[19] take part in the questioning of Pinochet's legal representatives and not only gave his own decisive opinion,[20] but may have influenced other members of the House of Lords hearing the appeal. Therefore, it is arguable that Lord Hoffmann, given his links with AI and his even greater opportunity to influence the proceedings and the final decision, would not be considered to be "neutral from the point of view of the parties" and that his presence as a judge in the case would render the trial unfair applying the equality of arms principle.

The right to be tried by an impartial tribunal

The case law of the European Court of Human Rights regarding what constitutes an impartial tribunal is extensive. In the *Piersack* judgment, the court considered a two part test of bias. The first test is subjective, "endeavouring to ascertain the personal conviction of a given judge in a given case"; the second is objective and is concerned with "determining whether he [the judge] offered guarantees sufficient to exclude any legitimate doubt in this respect".[21] With reference to the subjective test, the court has stated that the impartiality of a judge must be presumed unless there is evidence to the contrary.[22] The objective test requires consideration as to who should be satisfied by the guarantees offered by the judge against charges of partiality, in examining this the court has stated that "the standpoint of the accused is important but not decisive".[23]

---

[17] (1993) 15 EHRR 92 at para 26.

[18] The avocat général, representing the procureur général's department, had an advisory role in the court's deliberations. The Strasbourg court was particularly concerned that this gave him "an additional opportunity to promote, without fear of contradiction by the applicant, his submissions to the effect that the appeal should be dismissed." As a result the court concluded that *Borgers* had been denied a fair trial. Ibid, at para 28.

[19] Clare Montgomery QC, representing Senator Pinochet in the House of Lords, is quoted as having described Lord Hoffmann as " 'an active and hostile interrogator' who had frequently supported arguments by lawyers for the Spanish government and Amnesty International"—World Socialist Web Site http://www.wsws.org/news/1998/dec1998/pin-d18.shtml 17.07.99.

[20] The decision of the House of Lords on 25 November was split 3–2. Lords Nicholls, Steyn and Hoffmann holding that Senator Pinochet could be extradited to face charges in Spain. *Pinochet 1*, n 2 supra.

[21] (1983) 5 EHRR 169 at para 30.

[22] *Castillo-Algar v. Spain* (79/1997/863/1074) Hudoc REF00001049 at para 43 and *Hauschildt v. Denmark* (1990) 12 EHRR 266 at para 47.

[23] *Hauschildt v. Denmark* (1990) 12 EHRR 266 at para 48.

In *Pinochet 2* the "sole ground relied upon was that Lord Hoffmann's links with AI were such as to give the appearance of possible bias." Senator Pinochet's legal representatives were not alleging "actual bias".[24] Therefore it is the objective test of bias which is relevant here, the impartiality of a judge being presumed unless there is evidence to the contrary. The case law of the European Court of Human Rights suggests that, in applying the objective test, consideration must be given to whether there is a legitimate reason to fear a lack of impartiality. The Strasbourg court tests this by examining whether the guarantees offered by the court or the judge were sufficient to exclude any legitimate doubt of impartiality.

A number of Strasbourg cases have considered the involvement of officials and judges in the deliberations of a court or tribunal when they have previously been involved in pre-trial hearings relating to the case.[25] In assessing the legitimacy of an applicant's doubts regarding the impartiality of the tribunal, the European Court of Human Rights has looked at the extent to which the judge could have formed an opinion regarding the applicant's case prior to it being heard. The court has said:

> whether these misgivings should be treated as objectively justified depends on the circumstances of each particular case; the mere fact that a trial judge has also dealt with the case at the pre-trial stage cannot be held as in itself justifying fears as to his impartiality.[26]

In *De Cubber* v. *Belgium* the Strasbourg court considered the role of a judge, who had been involved in the case prior to the trial hearing, and concluded:

> the judge in question, unlike his colleagues, will already have acquired well before the hearing a particularly detailed knowledge of the—sometimes voluminous—file or files which he has assembled. Consequently, it is quite conceivable that he might, in the eyes of the accused, appear, firstly, to be in a position enabling him to play a crucial role in the trial court and, secondly, even to have a pre-formed opinion which is liable to weigh heavily in the balance at the moment of the decision.[27]

In these cases the Strasbourg court is declaring that the hearing of a case by a court, tribunal or judge, which gives the appearance that one or more of those

[24] *Pinochet 2*, n 1 supra, at 278; Annex 2, p 184.
[25] Cases in which the Strasbourg court have been called upon to consider the previous involvement of a judge in the case prior to trial include *Piersack* v. *Belgium* (1983) 5 EHRR 169, *De Cubber* v. *Belgium* (1985) 7 EHRR 236, *Hauschildt* v. *Denmark* (1990) 12 EHRR 266, *Ben Yaacoub* v. *Belgium* (1991) 13 EHRR 418, *Pfeifer and Plankl* v. *Austria* (1992) 14 EHRR 692, *Sainte-Marie* v. *France* (1993) 16 EHRR 116, *Fey* v. *Austria* (1993) 16 EHRR 387, *Padovani* v. *Italy* judgment of 26 February 1993, Series A no. 257–B, *Nortier* v. *the Netherlands* (1994) 17 EHRR 273, *Saraiva de Carvalho* v. *Portugal* (1994) 18 EHRR 534, *Oberschlick* v. *Austria* (1995) 19 EHRR 389, *Bulut* v. *Austria* (1997) 24 EHRR 84, *Castillo-Algar* v. *Spain* (79/1997/863/1074) Hudoc REF00001049.
[26] *Bulut* v. *Austria* (1997) 24 EHRR 84 at para 33. See also *Hauschildt* v. *Denmark* (1990) 12 EHRR 266 at paras 49–50, *Nortier* v. *The Netherlands* (1994) 17 EHRR 273 at para 33 and *Castillo-Algar* v. *Spain* (79/1997/863/1074) Hudoc REF00001049 at para 46.
[27] *De Cubber* v. *Belgium* (1985) 7 EHRR 236 at para 29.

sitting in judgment have already formed a view on the merits of the case, is contrary to the Convention. In *De Cubber* the court stated:

> appearances may be important; in the words of the English maxim . . . "justice must not only be done: it must also be seen to be done." . . . any judge in respect of whom there is a legitimate reason to fear a lack of impartiality must withdraw. What is at stake is the confidence which the courts in a democratic society must inspire in the public and above all, as far as criminal proceedings are concerned, in the accused.[28]

This approach has been gradually developed. In 1997 in the *Castillo-Algar* case the Strasbourg court stated that the objective test will be used to determine whether "irrespective of the judge's personal conduct, there are ascertainable facts which may raise doubts as to his impartiality". The court asserted that "[w]hat is decisive is whether this fear can be held to be objectively justified".[29]

The jurisprudence of the European Court of Human Rights in this area, as in others, is constantly developing. The court will look at its previous decisions and often bases decisions on statements of principle made in previous cases. However, unlike the English courts, the Strasbourg court does not operate within a system of binding precedent, and directions in which the law appears to be developing may be reversed.[30] This can lead to the Strasbourg court being criticised for uncertainty.[31] However, even with this proviso, it is apparent that certain areas of Strasbourg jurisprudence have become well-established. As Judge De Meyer, one of the critics of some of the approaches adopted by his fellow judges in this area,[32] points out:

> It is obviously not appropriate that someone who has already dealt with the case as a party or representative of a party, whether on the prosecution side or for the defence and even if only minimally or purely formally, should subsequently deal with it as a member of a trial court. That is wholly unhealthy.[33]

It is arguable that Lord Hoffmann's involvement with AI, through his directorship of AICL, could be equated with a judge who has been involved in the case prior to the trial hearing. Applying the reasoning in *De Cubber* to Lord Hoffmann's position, Amnesty's research would have given him the opportu-

---

[28] Ibid, para 26.

[29] *Castillo-Algar* v. *Spain* (79/1997/863/1074) Hudoc REF00001049 at para 45.

[30] For an evaluation of the use of precedent by the Strasbourg Court see JG Merrills, *The Development of International Law by the European Court of Human Rights* (2nd edn, Manchester University Press, 1995) at 12–16.

[31] Judge de Meyer in his separate opinion in *Bulut* v. *Austria* stated "it may be thought that our case-law on the concept of an 'impartial tribunal' has become very 'uncertain'." Looking at how much detailed knowledge of a case was required to constitute a breach of Article 6(1) he continued his criticism "These over-subtle distinctions, which give rise to uncertainty and confusion, are scarcely compatible with legal certainty." (1997) 24 EHRR 84 at paras B11 and B13.

[32] See, for example, his separate opinion in *Bulut* v. *Austria*, where he is critical of the reasoning adopted by his fellow judges, particularly he comments "[we must] not be obsessed with 'appearances', as we too often are in the reasoning of our judgments, but simply take into account the reality of the proceedings, in the light of what common sense tells us." Ibid, at para B13.

[33] Ibid, at para B14.

nity to acquire "particularly detailed knowledge" of human rights abuses in Chile. As a result "in the eyes of the accused" he might be viewed as having "a pre-formed opinion . . . liable to weigh heavily in the balance at the moment of the decision."

Article 6(1) of the Convention has also been found to have been contravened where a member of the tribunal or court, considering the applicant's case, has links with an organisation which has an interest in the matter being heard; where this might lead to the conclusion that the member's impartiality could be affected by loyalty to the organisation concerned. In such cases the European Court of Human Rights has been sensitive to appearances in considering claims that courts were biased. In *Baberà Messegué and Jabardo* v. *Spain*, a trial involving Catalan separatists, the wearing of Francoist insignia by the judge on his tie and cufflinks was a relevant factor in determining that there had been a breach of Article 6(1).[34] Arguably Lord Hoffmann's links with AI go beyond the wearing of insignia. In *Holm* v. *Sweden*, the Strasbourg court decided that the inclusion of five jury members with affiliations to a political party, criticised in the book which was the subject matter of a libel trial, contravened Article 6 (1).[35] Similarly in *Demicoli* v. *Malta* it held that there had been a breach of the requirement of impartiality when:

> The two Members of the House whose behaviour in Parliament was criticised in the impugned article and who raised the breach of privilege in the House participated throughout in the proceedings against the accused, including the finding of guilt and . . . the sentencing . . . the impartiality of the adjudicating body in these proceedings would appear to be open to doubt and the applicant's fears in this connection were justified.[36]

In both *Demicoli* and *Holm* political allegiances were relevant, which it might be argued differed from Lord Hoffmann's position as a director of a fund-raising institution. However, in many ways their positions are analogous. AICL, while a charitable body, was closely linked to AI, an organisation which though not party political was clearly political in its aims and those aims had been strongly asserted in relation to the bringing to justice of those responsible for human rights abuses in Chile. Lord Hoffmann's effectiveness as a fund raiser for AICL might be limited were he to indicate that he did not support Amnesty International in such a high profile case, the subject matter of which was so closely related to Amnesty's core aims and objectives. The Strasbourg case law requires that to be impartial a judge must be free from outside pressures.[37] Is it possible to argue that the links between Lord Hoffmann and AI would not have

---

[34] (1989) 11 EHHR 360 at para 59.

[35] (1994) 18 EHRR 79.

[36] (1992) 14 EHRR 47 at para 41.

[37] This is usually considered in the context of the independence of the tribunal. Often these cases have turned on whether the court was free from pressure from government, see *Lauko* v. *Slovakia* (4/1998/907/1119) Hudoc REF000010004, or from army links *Findlay* v. *United Kingdom* (1997) 24 EHRR 221, *Çiraklar* v. *Turkey* (70/1997/854/1061) Hudoc REF00001043.

created just this sort of pressure? Could Lord Hoffmann have retained his cred-
ibility as a director and chairman of AICL if he had ruled against the extradition
of Senator Pinochet?

Furthermore, as was noted earlier, given Lord Hoffmann's connections with
AI and AICL and their research into human rights abuses in Chile, an appearance of bias could have arisen because of fears that he had formed an opinion of
the appellant before the trial. A decisive factor in determining whether such
fears are justified is whether the tribunal or court provided sufficient guarantees
against such a charge of bias. Lord Hoffmann failed to disclose his links with AI
and his judicial oath of impartiality would seem an insufficient guarantee as
similar oaths have been considered inadequate by the Strasbourg court.[38] It
would appear that no persuasive argument could be raised to show that the trial
satisfied the requirements of Article 6(1) regarding the test of objective impartiality.

Thus, it seems likely that applying the case law of the European Court of
Human Rights to the facts of *Pinochet 2* the court could have found breaches of
two of the rights protected by Article 6(1). That is the right to a fair trial,
because of the breach of the equality of arms principle, and the right to an
impartial hearing. Whether it would have sought proof of both is a moot point,
proof of either would be sufficient to establish a breach of Article 6(1). The reasoning would have differed substantially from that employed by the House of
Lords, but the result would most likely have been the same irrespective of which
of the two relevant parts of Article 6(1) are applied. *Pinochet 2* would therefore
seem to have provided an opportunity for the House of Lords to use the
jurisprudence of the European Court of Human Rights to inform the common
law. It failed to do so.

THE HUMAN RIGHTS ACT 1998

Section 2 (1) of the Human Rights Act 1998 requires that:

> A court or tribunal determining a question which has arisen in connection with a
> Convention right must take into account any—(a) judgment, decision, declaration or
> advisory opinion of the European Court of Human Rights . . . whenever made or
> given, so far as, in the opinion of the court or tribunal, it is relevant to the proceedings
> in which that question has arisen.

Though the Act had received royal assent prior to the House of Lords' hearing,
section 2 has not yet been brought into force in English law. Therefore in
Pinochet 2 the House of Lords was not bound to take the Convention and its
case law into account. However, it is interesting to speculate why the House of
Lords did not even consider in their opinions the Strasbourg court's approach,

---

[38] In *Findlay* v. *United Kingdom* the taking of an oath was not sufficient to guarantee the impartiality of a court martial (1997) 24 EHRR. 221 at para 78.

particularly given the extremely high profile nature of the case, the comments of Senator Pinochet's lawyers concerning resorting to the European Court of Human Rights, and the fact that Strasbourg case law was cited in argument by counsel. This failure is highlighted by their Lordships' consideration of the law applying in other jurisdictions. While the main provisions of the 1998 Human Rights Act have not yet come into effect, the Act's existence makes the Strasbourg case law very relevant to the future determination of such issues.

The impact of the Convention on English law was explored by the Court of Appeal in *ex parte Kebilene*.[39] Laws LJ said that the "ECHR . . . has plainly informed the common law",[40] and Lord Bingham CJ outlined the traditional position of the courts since ratification of the Convention as being:

> Unless and until those central provisions are brought into force, and so become part of our domestic law they have no more binding effect than they ever had. Thus reference may be made to the Convention to resolve ambiguity or to inform the exercise of administrative discretion.[41]

This echoes the approach adopted by Gibson LJ in *Derbyshire County Council v. Times Newspapers Ltd.*, that where a matter "is not clear [by reference to] established principles of our law . . . this court must . . . have regard to the principles stated in the Convention".[42] However, some judges have been more assertive in their application of the Convention. Lord Scarman, in *Attorney-General v. BBC* stated that:

> If the issue should ultimately be . . . a question of legal policy, we must have regard to the country's international obligation to observe the Convention as interpreted by the Court of Human Rights.[43]

Pinochet 2 required the application of the common law to a situation which Lord Browne-Wilkinson described as "novel",[44] and which had major international implications.[45] In Lord Browne-Wilkinson's opinion the previous cases had "all dealt with automatic disqualification on the grounds of pecuniary inter-

---

[39] [1999] 3 WLR 175.

[40] Ibid, at 200.

[41] In doing so he was paraphrasing the submission made on behalf of the Director of Public Prosecutions by David Pannick QC. Ibid, at 186.

[42] [1992] 3 WLR 26 at 50.

[43] [1980] 3 WLR 109 at 130.

[44] *Pinochet 2*, n 1 supra, at 282; Annex, p 188.

[45] As Lord Browne-Wilkinson himself noted: "This wide public interest was reflected in the very large number attending the hearings before the Appellate Committee including representatives of the world press. The Palace of Westminster was picketed throughout. The announcement of the final result gave rise to worldwide reactions. In the eyes of very many people the issue was not a mere legal issue but whether or not Senator Pinochet was to stand trial and therefore, so it was thought, the cause of human rights triumph. Although the members of the Appellate Committee were in no doubt as to their function, the issue for many people was one of moral, not legal, right or wrong." *Pinochet 2*, n 1 supra, at 276; Annex, p 183. See Judith Hendrick (Chapter Five in this collection) for discussion on law and morality in relation to the Pinochet case.

[46] *Pinochet 2*, n 1 supra, at 283; Annex 2, p 189.

est",[46] whereas Lord Hoffmann's interest was non-pecuniary. It is a moot point whether this puts the case into Gibson LJ's category of matters which were not clear by reference to "established principles of law" or Lord Scarman's test as to whether it was "a question of legal policy".[47] Either way, the House of Lords could have used the Convention to inform the common law, if nothing else.

In *ex parte Kebilene*, the Lord Chief Justice stated that "The Convention, despite its recent advance towards incorporation, has not crossed the Rubicon which separates prospective law from binding law. Prospective law cannot override binding law".[48] While this statement seems traditional in its tone, the solution proposed by the Court of Appeal in *Kebilene* was radical. The Court of Appeal recognised the Convention was a relevant consideration for a prosecuting authority because the main provisions of the Human Rights Act 1998 might be in force by the time any appeal against conviction was heard.[49] Accepting that there are major differences in the issues under consideration in *Pinochet 2* and *Kebilene*,[50] the point is that the Court of Appeal obviously considered Convention case law relevant to the interpretation of English law in the period before the Human Rights Act takes full effect.[51]

In *Kebilene* the impending change in English law was acknowledged, in *Pinochet 2* it was not. While one explanation for this difference might have been that in *Kebilene* Convention rights formed the basis of the appellants' submissions, whereas in *Pinochet 2* they did not, in fact this is not the case. Seven decisions of the Strasbourg court were cited in argument in *Pinochet 2*,[52] although none were referred to in their Lordships' opinions. Clearly a different approach to European Court of Human Rights case law was adopted in the House of Lords from that adopted by the Court of Appeal in *Kebilene*. As the House of Lords made no reference to the submissions of the parties regarding Strasbourg case law, it is only possible to speculate as to their reasons. A

---

[47] Lord Browne-Wilkinson saw no problem in extending the established principles of law in this area. He stated "there is no good reason in principle for so limiting automatic disqualification. The rationale of the whole rule is that a man cannot be a judge in his own cause." Ibid.

[48] N 39 supra, at 186.

[49] This was a relevant consideration because the applicants would succeed on appeal if at the time of that appeal the Human Rights Act was in force and the relevant provisions of the Prevention of Terrorism (Temporary Provisions) Act 1989 were held to be contrary to the Convention. Assuming this hypothesis was correct, even if the relevant provisions of the Human Rights Act were not in force: "the applicants would in due course succeed in showing a violation of the Convention by the United Kingdom and so would obtain a decision in their favour in the European Court and, perhaps, recover compensation and achieve their release". Ibid, at 187.

[50] *Ex parte Kebilene* concerned the interpretation of statute law, its compatibility with the Convention and the use of the discretion to prosecute.

[51] The House of Lords' views as to the Court of Appeal's reasoning will become clearer when it considers the Director of Public Prosecutions' appeal in *Kebilene*. This may shed some light on how the House of Lords considers Convention law should be viewed before the main provisions of the Human Rights Act become law in England.

[52] *Campbell and Fell* v. *United Kingdom* (1984) 7 EHRR 165, *De Cubber* v. *Belgium* (1984) 7 EHRR 266, *Gregory* v. *United Kingdom* (1997) 25 EHRR 577, *Hauschildt* v. *Denmark* (1989) 12 EHRR 266, *Holm* v. *Sweden* (1993) 18 EHRR 79, *Langborger* v. *Sweden* (1989) 12 EHRR 416, *Pfeifer and Plankl* v. *Austria* (1992) 14 EHRR 692.

possible explanation could be based on the attitudes which some of the law lords have exhibited towards the Convention.

Lord Hoffmann, for instance, has stated his antipathy to the idea of applying European Court of Human Rights' decisions to English law. He concludes his article in *Modern Law Review*, with the following comment:

> I realise that in the present political climate, it would be very difficult for the government to withdraw from the Strasbourg court. When we joined, indeed, took the lead in the negotiation of the European Convention, it was not because we thought it would affect our own law, but because we thought it right to set an example for others and to help to ensure that all the member states respected those basic human rights which were not culturally determined but reflected our common humanity. There is still a great need throughout the world for the enforcement of such minimal human rights. But the jurisprudence of the Strasbourg court does create a dilemma because it seems to me to have passed far beyond its original modest ambitions and is seeking to impose a Voltairean uniformity of values upon all the member states. This I hope we shall resist. The White Paper which introduced the Human Rights Bill was called *Rights Brought Home*. Now that they have been brought home, I hope that we shall be able to keep them here.[53]

To the extent that Lord Hoffmann's views reflect those of his fellow law lords, this may go a long way to explaining the House of Lords' reluctance to embrace the jurisprudence of the Strasbourg court.

Other members of the House of Lords and of the Strasbourg court have also discussed why the courts of member states may be slow in applying European Court of Human Rights' case law. Sibrand Martens, President of the Supreme Court of the Netherlands and a former judge of the European Court of Human Rights, commenting on the role of the judiciary in incorporating the European Convention on Human Rights into United Kingdom law, spoke of the experience of the Dutch courts. He stated:

> Our experience has been that it takes a certain time before the bar has learnt to use the ECHR [the Convention] as an effective tool, as a means of scrutinizing long-accepted notions of domestic law, of holding them up to the new light of to-day's ideas on the fundamental freedoms of the individual as exemplified in the case law of the Strasbourg Court. Experience has taught us, furthermore, that it is only when the bar has learned to do so expertly that courts will become aware of their responsibilities under the ECHR and will feel called upon to respond in a similar vein.[54]

He estimated that this process took more than a quarter of a century in Holland. If the Dutch experience proves to be true in England, this could explain the failure to consider the Strasbourg jurisprudence in this case.

Lord Steyn, a current law lord, reinforces Martens' view about the unpreparedness of the judiciary to take on board the decisions of the European Court

---

[53] "Human Rights and the House of Lords" (1999) 62 *MLR* 159 at 166.
[54] "Opinion: Incorporating the European Convention: The Role of the Judiciary" [1998] 1 *EHRLR* 10.

of Human Rights. In an article, based on an address given in December 1997, he is far more welcoming towards the Strasbourg jurisprudence than Lord Hoffmann, but acknowledges the problems facing the English courts. He comments, with reference to incorporation:

> Clearly, these are great challenges for the courts. It will be necessary to teach judges new techniques of interpretation and adjudication. Academic lawyers and practitioners will have to educate the judges. The educational task will be incomplete unless it embraces the constitutional underpinning and theoretical foundations of their new tasks. In the House of Lords we are certainly in need of continuing education. After all, it is only a few weeks since we at last acquired a set of reports of the ECHR [European Court of Human Rights]. You are entitled to wonder how some of those great cases would have been decided if the purchase had been made earlier.[55]

Given that the United Kingdom was involved in the drafting of the European Convention on Human Rights and Fundamental Freedoms, was the first nation to ratify the Convention in 1951 and has, since December 1965, accepted the right of individual petition to the European Court of Human Rights, it is surprising that it was not until 1997 that the House of Lords obtained its own copy of the case law.

In *Pinochet 2* the House of Lords was hearing a politically sensitive and embarrassing case. Indeed, as the Guardian stated:

> The Hoffmann fiasco has focused public attention for the first time on the lottery element of justice in our highest court. Had Hoffmann disqualified himself, which a fresh panel said he should have done, and another judge taken his place, the result could well have gone the other way. The court sets precedents which determine the direction of the law for generations, yet outcomes are strongly influenced by which five of the 12 law lords (plus retired law lords, current and retired Lord Chancellors, and peers who have held high judicial office, who can also sit) happen to hear the case.[56]

At least by deciding the case primarily on the basis of previous English case law, the House of Lords was able to convey the impression that, while this was a novel situation, the existing rules were sufficient to deal with it. Had the House of Lords based their decision on the Convention, the impact of the decision would have seemed more revolutionary and would quite possibly have resulted in tabloid headlines to the effect that the highest court in the land was now ruled by Europe. As it was, by finding for Senator Pinochet there was no risk of the case being appealed to Strasbourg, and European judges would not be called upon to sit in judgment on the impartiality, or otherwise, of a case heard by the House of Lords.

On a more practical note they postponed other difficult questions which will have to be decided when Article 6(1) falls to be considered by the English courts. Not the least of which is the role of the Lord Chancellor and how this may affect

---

[55] "Current Topic: Incorporation and Devolution—A Few Reflections on the Changing Scene" [1998] 2 *EHRLR* 156.

[56] *The Guardian*, 2 February 1999; and see David Robertson, Chapter Two in this collection.

the impartiality and independence of the House of Lords when he is sitting in judgment. The recent Commission decision in *McGonnell* v. *the United Kingdom*[57] has considered the role of the Bailiff in Guernsey. The Bailiff was found to be:

> not only a senior member of the judiciary of the Island, but was also a senior member of the legislature[58] . . . and, in addition, a senior member of the executive.[59] . . . taking into account the Bailiff's roles in the administration of Guernsey, . . . the fact that he has executive and legislative functions means that his independence and impartiality are capable of appearing open to doubt.

Like the Bailiff, the Lord Chancellor is a senior member of the judiciary, legislature and administration. The impartiality and independence of the House of Lords when he is sitting in judgment may therefore be open to question in the light of this Commission decision.

However, it is not only the Lord Chancellor's position that may be suspect should the European Court of Human Rights follow the Commission's decision. The law lords may also be vulnerable, given that they act as legislators as well as judges. Their position might be distinguished from that of the Bailiff of Guernsey, in that, while they sit in Parliament as members of the House of Lords, they might not be viewed as having a sufficient legislative role to warrant their exclusion from the judiciary. The extent of their legislative involvement may be crucial in determining whether their independence and impartiality as judges will be thought capable of appearing open to doubt under Article 6(1).[60]

The House of Lords' decision in *Pinochet 2* is immensely significant. It opens the way to many more challenges by parties alleging that judges have an interest in the case. Lord Browne-Wilkinson anticipated this when he commented that "there may well be other exceptional cases in which the judge would be well advised to disclose a possible interest".[61] This has already occurred, Judge Hootton disqualifying himself from hearing an appeal against conviction for aggravated trespass on land being used for a pheasant shoot. The judge cited his support for shooting and the fact that he was a member of the Countryside Alliance as grounds for withdrawing from the case.[62] Before long the courts will

[57] Report of the Commission adopted on 20 October 1998 (Application No 28488/9).

[58] As President of the States of Deliberation.

[59] As titular head of the administration presiding over a number of important committees.

[60] The Royal Commission on the Reform of the House of Lords is already considering the judicial functions of the House of Lords and its consultation paper discusses the matter as follows: "The Appellate Committee of the House of Lords is the highest court of appeal in all criminal cases and for all civil cases in England, Wales and Northern Ireland. The Lord Chancellor still presides in the House of Lords, is head of the judiciary and may join in hearing appeals. Are these arrangements still appropriate, particularly in the light of the Human Rights Act which will give the courts a greater responsibility for determining cases which challenge the actions of the Executive and Acts of Parliament? Could this undermine, or appear to undermine, the independence and impartiality of this court of appeal? Should a separate 'Supreme Court' be created?".

[61] *Pinochet 2*, n 1 supra, at 284; Annex, p 191.

[62] *The Times*, 6 August 1999.

have to take into account the Convention and its case law when deciding cases where the impartiality of the court is challenged. In failing to provide courts with guidance as to how to interpret Article 6(1) in such cases, the House of Lords has missed a great opportunity to provide leadership in assisting courts in the proper application of the Convention.

Part 2

Pinochet, Justice, and International Law

5

Pinochet and Issues of Morality and Justice

JUDITH HENDRICK

INTRODUCTION

The rulings of the House of Lords in *Pinochet 1* and *Pinochet 3*,[1] which denied Pinochet sovereign immunity, and the Home Secretary's decision that the extradition process should be continued, had obvious implications for the development of both national and international law. The contribution of the various legal decisions to the jurisprudence concerning crimes against humanity is also self evident. But Pinochet's arrest, the lengthy judicial processes and the fact that he will almost certainly be tried in Spain for crimes of torture and conspiracy to torture have a larger resonance. They reflect "the growing internationalisation of bringing gross criminals to justice and the obligation of every state to put the perpetrators of crimes against humanity on trial in its own courts".[2]

This is not to suggest, of course, that the outcome to date of the various court proceedings have been universally welcomed. For, as the widespread public debate has revealed, while many, probably the majority, are indifferent to the Senator's fate, the attitudes of others are polarised. Thus for those, as Lord Browne-Wilkinson observed in *Pinochet 3* "of left-wing political convictions [he] is seen as an arch-devil; [but] to those of right-wing persuasions he is seen as the saviour of Chile".[3] But whatever the final outcome of the extradition process and whether or not Pinochet is tried in Spain, the saga to date arguably marks one of the most important developments of law and morality this century.

What then are the moral issues which underpin the Pinochet affair? The concept of justice is certainly the most pervasive. For example, Jack Straw's decision that Pinochet could be extradited was described as a "force for justice" and the only one he could have taken which "combines justice and moral vision".[4]

---

[1] R v. *Bow Street Metropolitan Stipendiary Magistrate and Others, ex parte Pinochet Ugarte* [1998] 3 WLR 1456; R v. *Bow Street Metropolitan Stipendiary Magistrate and Others, ex parte Pinochet Ugarte (No 3)* [1999] 2 WLR 827.
[2] *The Guardian*, 6 April 1999.
[3] N 1 supra.
[4] *The Guardian*, 26 November 1998.

Many, cautiously anticipating the "right" decisions by the law lords, also demanded that he should "face or be brought to justice", or that "justice should be exacted from him". In addition, it was argued that there would never be justice in Chile while an amnesty law, decreed by Pinochet to pardon himself, existed. Similarly, claims were made that those "fighting for justice" did not want compensation but had instead a "right to justice". These various observations about justice are clearly imprecise and ill-defined, but they, nevertheless, captured, what can be called, the ordinary understanding of the notion of justice; namely, a belief that Pinochet should be punished for his alleged involvement in the murder, torture and disappearances of thousands of innocent victims in Chile and elsewhere. Establishing his precise role, in other words his responsibility, both individually and in his capacity as a public official, is, however, another matter. This then is the second major issue raised by the saga.[5]

JUSTICE AND PUNISHMENT

Although justice is a moral value which most consider desirable, in the sense that the "right" course of action is, or should be, determined by what is just, the way in which it is defined and interpreted is subject to considerable variation. Yet, however it is defined, its link with punishment is undeniable. Lucas, for example, asserts that "punishment illuminates justice",[6] while Solomon argues that punishment is the:

> original meaning of justice and no doubt one of its most enduring aspects as in all societies (irrespective of whether they are free market or socialist, democracies or ruthless dictatorships) there are always those who break the law and violate whatever there is of a public trust, and they must be punished.[7]

Punishment is, in short, deeply entrenched in our moral thinking, being rooted in our beliefs about what is right and wrong. The problem is that, while everyone has some idea of what it is and thinks that there are occasions when someone should be punished, as a concept, it, like justice, is elusive and not easy to elucidate. Nonetheless, in a very general sense, "punishment" can be described as:

> something unwelcome, deliberately imposed on somebody by someone claiming to act disinterestedly on behalf of some society or community, on account of some wrong he has allegedly done, and understood as such.[8]

---

[5] The literature on punishment and responsibility is vast. What follows is therefore inevitably a selective, introductory account of those aspects the author considers most relevant.

[6] J R Lucas, *On Justice* (Clarendon Press, 1980) p 124.

[7] R Solomon and M C Murphy (eds), *What is Justice? Classic and Contemporary Readings* (OUP, 1990) p 241.

[8] J R Lucas, *Responsibility* (Clarendon Press, 1995) p 90.

This simple definition incorporates all the criteria, which are now widely accepted as essential to any formulation of punishment. However, some have argued that punishment can only be "legal" if it has an expressive function. In other words, the essential feature of legal punishment is to express and convey certain attitudes, such as, resentment, reprobation and condemnation. Legal punishment therefore has a symbolic significance sending complex messages of disapproval not just to the person who is to be punished, but to his or her victim and society as a whole.[9] Yet because any act of punishment (legal or otherwise) almost inevitably involves suffering, something which itself is generally considered immoral, it requires moral justification.

How then can punishment be justified? The debate about the morality of punishment, its nature and function, has a history which can be traced back to ancient Athens. However, a useful starting point is the Bible, if only because it contains one of the most well known and frequently quoted passages in this context. Thus the Old Testament states:

> And if a man cause a blemish in his neighbour; as he hath done, so shall it be done to him: breach for breach, eye for eye, tooth for tooth; as he hath caused a blemish in a man, so it shall be rendered unto him.[10]

In contrast to this apparent basic urge for retribution (i.e. "measure for measure") the New Testament pleads for mercy and the virtue of "turning the other cheek". Accordingly, we are told:

> Ye have heard that it was said, An eye for an eye, and a tooth for a tooth: but I say unto you, Resist not him that is evil: but whosoever smiteth thee on thy right cheek, turn to him the other also. And if any man would go to law with thee, and take away thy coat, let him have that cloak also.[11]

These two passages enshrine what later developed into the two dominant theories of punishment. The first, the so-called forward-looking theories, justify punishment on the basis of the alleged beneficial consequences, that is, those, which it is anticipated, will happen in the future. Such theories are consequentialist because they do not regard punishment as good in itself but justifiable only on utilitarian grounds, namely that it prevents even greater suffering or brings about greater good. So, if punishment reduces crimes by deterring people from repeating their criminal acts, or deters potential offenders from carrying out similar crimes (deterrence), a good consequence is achieved, which far outweighs any harm to the "punished" offender. A similar good outcome is achieved if criminals return to society as responsible and productive citizens (rehabilitation). The second group of theories, which are described as backward-looking or desert based, look back in time, to the past wrongful

---

[9] J Feinberg, "What is legal punishment?" in J Feinberg and H Gross (eds), *Philosophy of Law* (5th edn, Wadsworth, 1995).

[10] Leviticus 24:17–22.

[11] Matthew 5:38–42. See also St Paul's exhortation that we "should overcome evil with good", Romans 12:17–21.

action, and derive from the retributivist principle that wrongdoers deserve to be punished.)

Retributivist and consequentialist approaches therefore have very different theoretical frameworks. Nevertheless both theories can lead to the same practical conclusions. They would, for example, normally agree who should be punished and there is frequently consensus on the severity of the sentence. It is partly because of these similarities and partly because pure[12] retributivist and consequentialist, or utilitarian, theories are thought by many to be too extreme to be credible, that some writers have adopted a mixed theory, namely one which combines elements of retributivist and consequentialist principles.[13] In the context of *Pinochet*, however, it is the retributivist justification of punishment which seems most pertinent, for while some who call for "justice to be done" may be simply hoping that a trial (with or without a conviction) will deter other leaders from committing crimes against humanity, the majority who make this plea want the senator to be punished for his previous wrongdoing. In other words, implicit in their appeal for justice is a strongly held belief that he deserves to be "paid back" for his alleged involvement in the atrocities committed during his regime. Exacting justice from Pinochet thus means exacting the debt he owes to society for his previous wrongdoing.

RETRIBUTIVISM

As noted above, retributivism is a backward-looking theory which looks to past wrongdoing and guilt. There are several versions of the theory[14] but, in its strongest form, it asserts that the state has both a moral right and a duty to punish.[15] The most famous and influential proponent of retributivism was the German eighteenth-century philosopher Immanuel Kant. In his classical formulation of the theory he stated that:

> Judicial punishment can never be used merely as a means to promote some other good for the criminal himself or for civilised society, but instead it must in all cases be imposed on him only on the ground that he has committed a crime. . . . He must first be found to be deserving of punishment before any consideration is given to the utility of punishment for himself or for his fellow citizens. . . . The law concerning punishment is a categorical imperative, and woe to him who rummages around in the winding paths of a theory of happiness looking for some advantage

---

[12] The word "pure" indicates that the theory is not "contaminated" by any element borrowed from any other competing theory.

[13] One of the most influential proponents being John Rawls (see J Rawls, "Two Concepts of Rules", *The Philosophical Review* 64 (1955) 3–13; see also Table 6.1, "The Which Guide to Punishment" in Lucas, *On Justice*, n 6 supra, p 92 for a brief comparison between the various theories. A more detailed comparison is contained in Appendix 2, p 280).

[14] Broadly categorised as minimal, normal and "hard-line" see, Lucas, n 8 supra, p 281.

[15] See T Honderich, *Punishment:The Supposed Justifications* (Polity Press, 1989) pp 21–6.

to be gained by releasing the criminal from punishment or by reducing the amount of it.[16]

The desert principle which underpins Kant's retributivism provides that a person should be punished, if, and only if, he or she deserves to be punished, irrespective of whether or not the punishment produces any good consequences to the offender, the victim(s), or society at large. It therefore holds that it is morally wrong to punish the innocent and also wrong not to punish anyone who deserves punishment. But the desert principle in itself fails to provide any guidance on what is the "right" amount of punishment. For Kant, the answer to this question turned on the principle of equality. Under this principle:

> any undeserved evil that you inflict on someone else . . . is the one you do to yourself. If you vilify him, you vilify yourself; if you kill him you kill yourself. Only the law of retribution (*jus talionis*) can determine exactly the type of punishment. . . . All other standards . . . cannot be compatible with the principle of pure and strict legal justice.[17]

The principle of proportionality, namely that the punishment should not only fit but also be equal to the crime, is Kant's second principle. In other words, the more serious the crime—in terms of the gravity of the harm caused and degree of responsibility—the more severe the punishment. It would seem, therefore, that moral culpability and blameworthiness play an important role in fixing the appropriate measure of punishment.

Since Kant, many different versions of retributivism have been formulated but, according to Feinberg, the core elements of pure moralistic retributivism (the most popular variant) can be reduced to the following basic propositions:

- moral guilt is a necessary condition for justified punishment.
- moral guilt is a sufficient condition (irrespective of consequences) for justified punishment.
- the proper amount of punishment to be inflicted upon the morally guilty offender is that amount which matches, or is proportionate to, the moral gravity of the offence.[18]

It is perhaps because retributivism fits so well with most people's commonsense intuitions, that it has survived so long as a theory of punishment and has in recent years enjoyed a revival.[19] Yet few retributivists can explain clearly why previous wrongdoing justifies punishment. Many, for example, will simply assert that it just does, without providing any further explanation. In short, they regard the moral basis of the desert principle as self-evident. Others, on the other hand, may acknowledge that the principle is a puzzling one but their

[16] Immanuel Kant, *The Metaphysical Elements of Justice* (J Ladd, trans, Indianapolis: Bobbs-Merill, 1965) pp 100–1.
[17] Ibid.
[18] J Feinberg, "What, If Anything Justifies Legal Punishment? The Classic Debate" *Philosophy of Law*, p 614, n 9 supra.
[19] In the form of the "justice model", see M Cavadino and J Digman, *The Penal System: An Introduction* (2nd edn, Sage, 1997) chapter 2.

explanations are so unconvincing that, as Lacey points out, it seems: "that the claim that X ought to be punished because she deserves to be punished merely amounts to the claim that X ought to be punished because she ought to be punished".[20] Or to put it another way it is right to punish criminals because doing so is right!

Given these responses, it is unlikely that those who consider that Pinochet deserves to be punished could satisfactorily explain why his past behaviour justifies a trial in Spain, not least because neither his conviction nor any sentence could remove the harm that has been done to those who were tortured, murdered or who disappeared. Furthermore it could be argued that the effect of punishing Pinochet would simply be to add his suffering to that of the victims and their families thereby making things "worse" overall by increasing the amount of misery in the world.

How then can the popularity of retributivism, described recently as arguably the most influential philosophical justification for punishment in present day America,[21] be explained? Is it simply that punishment for past wrongdoing accords with our moral gut reactions and so satisfies some unconscious yet deeply rooted vengeful impulse? The idea that vengeance is our natural sense of retribution, rather than a philosophical abstraction, is one which few philosophers like to acknowledge. Perhaps this is because vengeance fits so uneasily in a world which is more comfortable with virtues like mercy and the notion of "forgiving and forgetting", however unrealistic they may be, than with the public and private reality of revenge, and its "unsettling echoes of the primitive and inescapable reminder of the fragility of the human order".[22] Yet it has been claimed that vengeance is the original meaning of justice, for example, in the Old Testament and in Homer, "justice" virtually always refers to revenge. In addition, as Solomon points out, throughout history the concept of justice has been far more concerned with the punishment of crimes and the balancing of wrongs than it has been with the fair distribution of goods and services. This is why the phrase, "getting even", has always been "one of the most basic metaphors of our moral vocabulary" and why "the frightening emotion of righteous wrathful anger is an essential part of the emotional basis for our sense of justice".[23] Today, however, revenge is often referred to in contemptuous terms and dismissed as an irrational, unenlightened, and vindictive emotion, one which is "blind", likely to "know no end" or to "get out of hand". It is, moreover, one which, by its very nature, is violent and disruptive and, as a consequence, therefore is seen as having no place in modern jurisprudence or in our modern thinking about justice.

[20] N Lacey, *State Punishment: Political Implications and Community Values* (Routledge, 1988) p 17.
[21] D Dolinko, "Retributivism, Consequentialism, And The Intrinsic Goodness of Punishment" (1997) 16 *Law and Philosophy* 507.
[22] S Jacoby, "Wild Justice" in R Soloman and M C Murphy (eds), *What is Justice? Classic and Contemporary Readings* (OUP, 1990) p 287.
[23] Ibid, p 292.

It is therefore not surprising that many writers are keen to deny the accusation that retribution is legalised revenge, carried out under the auspices of the state legal system. Accordingly, they almost always attempt to separate retribution from vengeance. Nozick, for example, distinguishes between the two by contrasting the emotionality of revenge with the impersonality and coolness of retribution. He insists that, while revenge has no limits, retribution is always done in response to a wrong and not merely because of personal harm or offence and that it sets strict limits to punishment.[24] Others, for example, Nuttal, assert that revenge is associated with personal satisfaction, with getting one's own back, whereas retribution is concerned with what someone deserves, irrespective of whether it gives satisfaction or benefits others.[25]

More recently, Rachels, in a robust defence of retributivism, which, he claims, is fairer and more just than other theories, dismisses objections to the desire for revenge as misguided. He argues that the idea that wrongdoers should be "paid back" for their wickedness is not merely a demand for primitive vengeance but is:

> part of a moral view with a subtle and complicated structure, that can be supported by a surprisingly strong array of arguments. The key idea is that people deserve to be treated in the same way that they voluntarily choose to treat others.[26]

However, even if we accept that revenge, although not an objective response, has a place in our modern conception of punishment, we still have to establish criteria to determine how much and what type of punishment should be imposed. Supposing, for example, Pinochet is convicted. What punishment should he receive? As noted above, the retributivist answer lies in the principle of proportionality, i.e. that the punishment should "fit" the crime. Thus the more serious the crime and the greater the moral culpability of the offender, the more severe the punishment and so forth. One of the simplest and oldest ways of ensuring that the punishment is proportionate, albeit not one universally accepted by retributivists, is the biblical principle *lex talionis*: an eye for an eye, a life for a life, and so on. As traditionally understood, the general principle of *lex talionis* is equivalence between harm done and punishment imposed. As Davis (who describes the principle as a slogan rather than theory) points out, the punishment is not for an act as such, that is, not for what was intended or risked, but for what was done. So, for example, to kill someone, even "by accident" would justify the same penalty as would killing deliberately.[27] But despite its appeal—the principle appears simple and straightforward, even if it does seem

---

[24] R Nozick, "Retribution and Revenge" in *Philosophical Explanations* (Harvard University Press, 1981), cited in Solomon and Murphy, n 22 supra, p 281.

[25] J Nutall, *Moral Questions: An Introduction to Ethics* (Polity Press, 1993) p 52.

[26] J Rachels, "Punishment and Desert" in Hugh LaFolette (ed.), *Ethics In Practice: An Anthology* (Blackwell, 1997) chapter 44. For another strong defence of retributivism see also S Dimock "Retributivism and Trust" (1997) 16 *Law and Philosophy*, pp 37–62.

[27] M Davis, "How Much Punishment Does a Bad Samaritan Deserve?" (1996) 15 *Law and Philosophy* 97.

to require the severest penalty a legal system can allow—it is seriously flawed as a reliable *tariff* system. As Lord Blackstone asked in the eighteenth century: what is the equivalent harm when a two-eyed man knocks out the eye of a one-eyed man? Or in the modern context, how can the *lex talionis* be applied to *Pinochet*? What punishment, for example, would "equal" the torture he is alleged to have condoned, if not ordered?

A more serious criticism of the *lex talionis* principle is that it seems to ignore mental states, that is, whether the offence was committed intentionally, accidentally, negligently, or, perhaps, for the very best of motives. In other words, the *lex talionis* fails to capture what has been described as one of retributivism's greatest strengths, namely "its accommodation of a strong principle of responsibility generating limitations on who may properly be punished".[28] Indeed, the concept of responsibility underpins the desert principle, in that someone can only be said to deserve punishment in the retributivist sense, if he, or she, has exercised a free choice and acted truly voluntarily. Or to put it another way, the idea that people should be punished for what they have done is based on the assumption that we all sometimes make free choices for which we can be held responsible. An understanding of the concept of responsibility is therefore crucial in so far as it arguably shapes how we instinctively judge people's actions.

RESPONSIBILITY

The nature of responsibility continues to be subject to considerable discussion. It is a multi-layered term and, when unravelled, it is soon apparent that it is also ambiguous, not least because it is often used interchangeably with a wide range of different, yet related, ideas, such as, "responsible", "responsible for" and "accountability". Indeed, ritual demands for accountability and "taking responsibility" are now so commonplace that the terms have been extended to embrace not just individuals, notably war criminals who have committed crimes against humanity, but also corporations which have profited from past unethical practices. One such example is the Deutsche Bank, Germany's largest financial institution, which has been forced to admit that it financed Aushwitz and even lent money to the company which produced Zyklon B, the gas which was used to kill millions.

Against this background, it is not surprising that claims have been made that Pinochet was responsible, and/or that he must take individual responsibility, for the atrocities committed during his regime. But how do we ascribe responsibility to him? This requires, first, an assumption that people have free will and so can, and do, make choices about how to run their lives. Such an assumption is denied by those who believe that all our actions are causally determined. Indeed, according to some theories of strict determinism, all actions are the inevitable

---

[28] Lacey, n 20 supra p 17.

causal consequence of things that happened in the past, which now cannot be altered, certainly not by the individual concerned. As Lucas wryly observes:

> they are not really my actions and I [therefore] cannot be held responsible for what my hormones, my genes, my childhood traumas, or the state of the universe at the Big Bang have made me do.[29]

The debate over free will and determinism is one of the oldest in philosophy.[30] However, in the context of *Pinochet*, the conception of responsibility, which informs discussion, is almost certainly based on the belief that he had control of his actions, that is, that he acted voluntarily, of his own accord, and therefore need not have done what he did.

In assessing Pinochet's "responsibility", several different approaches can be taken. According to Hart, for example, the "welter of distinguishable senses of the word 'responsibility' can be reduced to four different categories, notably role-responsibility, causal-responsibility, liability-responsibility and capacity-responsibility."[31] Since Pinochet was leader of the military junta which evicted President Allende, the focus here will be on role-responsibility. As Hart explains:

> whenever a person occupies a distinctive place or office in a social organisation, to which specific duties are attached to provide for the welfare of others or to advance in some specific way the aims or purposes of the organisation, he is properly said to be responsible for the performance of those duties, or for doing what is necessary to fulfil them.[32]

Hart's assertion that responsibility and duty are correlative is echoed by Lucas who also claims that, if someone is to have responsibility for something, then he, or she, has to have the authority and power to act to discharge that responsibility. For Lucas, therefore, responsibility implies, or is almost equivalent to, "power" or "authority" in modern usage.[33] As head of state, Pinochet's authority and power, likewise his "distinctive place", is difficult to deny. It was a role which gave him absolute control, effectively from 11 September 1973 until he handed over the Presidential sash to Patricio Aylwin in 1990, not just because he was directly in charge of the armed forces, including the police, but also the security agencies, notably the National Intelligence Directorate (DINA) and the National Intelligence Bureau (CNI, which replaced DINA).

The role responsibility of Pinochet as head of state is therefore self-evident. It is a special type of responsibility, also sometimes called command responsibility, which has long been acknowledged. Shakespeare, for example, made the

---

[29] Lucas, n 8 supra, p 13.
[30] For a useful and brief introduction to determinism see R Young, "The Implications of Determinism" in P Singer (ed.), *A Companion to Ethics* (Blackwell, 1991) chapter 47.
[31] H L A Hart, *Punishment and Responsibility: Essays in the Philosophy of Law* (Clarendon Press, 1968) chapter 9.
[32] Ibid, p 212.
[33] Lucas, n 8 supra, p 182.

responsibility of leaders for crimes a central theme in his plays and, by so doing, shed light on the antecedents of our notions of personal responsibility and the "intellectual genealogy of modern humanitarian law".[34] His notion of responsibility is thus very pertinent to modern times. The special responsibility of leaders for certain crimes has been recognised more recently in international law. At Nuremberg, for example, only high-level German officials were tried, the implication being that holding high office was indicative of greater guilt, rather than a mitigating factor. So significant was this implication that it was enshrined in Article 7 of the Charter[35] which states that:

> official positions of defendants, whether as Heads of State or responsible officials in Government Departments, shall not be considered as freeing them from responsibility or mitigating punishment.

This Article (and the Charter's definition of war crimes) were innovatory in suggesting that responsibility for criminal activities ultimately rested with those who governed or commanded. No longer could those at the top shelter behind their official positions. The formulation of Article 7 was not surprising, given the influence of the US Prosecutor, Robert H Jackson, Associate Justice of the Supreme Court. Jackson, who played a major role in the preliminary negotiations which led to the approval of the Charter and in the trial itself, was insistent that those in command should bear the brunt of responsibility for the acts of their underlings. He therefore consistently refused to accept the "paradox that responsibility should be least where the power is the greatest".[36]

As head of state, Pinochet could also arguably be implicated under the so-called *Yamashita* doctrine (or at least the principles it enshrines). This doctrine has been described as the first authoritative statement of the modern rule of command responsibility, under which the commander must enforce the law and make those subject to his command accountable for compliance with the norms.[37] It was explicitly recognised in 1977[38] but derives from the prosecution of General Yamashita by the American army in 1946. Yamashita was the commander of the Japanese forces in the Philippines in 1944–5. He was charged with having failed to discharge his duty to control the actions of those under his command, who had violated the laws of war by murdering and raping both civilians and prisoners of war. Yamashita, like Pinochet, protested that he had not personally either committed, or directed, the commission of those atrocities. He was nonetheless convicted on the basis that commanders must be responsible for the acts of their subordinates. According to one judge in the case, Justice Stone, the doctrine imposed an affirmative duty to take such measures to protect prisoners and civilians as were within the commander's power and

---

[34] T Meron, *War Crimes Law Comes of Age* (Clarendon Press, 1998) chapter 3, p 67.

[35] The Charter is an international agreement, which led to the establishment of an "International Military Tribunal for the just and prompt trial and punishment of the major war criminals of the European Axis". Article 7 is referred to throughout *Pinochet 1* and *3*.

[36] A Tusa and J Tusa, *The Nuremberg Trial* (Papermac, 1983) p 73.

[37] Meron, n 34 supra, p 87.

appropriate in the circumstances. In the absence of such a duty, commanders who failed to take reasonable measures to that end, would escape unpunished, and the purpose of the law of war, to protect people from brutality, would largely be defeated.

CONCLUSION

It would seem plausible to suggest, therefore, that Pinochet's role as head of state imposed a special responsibility on him, not least because of the authority he held and the power he had to prevent violations of human rights carried out by his subordinates. Yet many may be uncomfortable with the idea that Pinochet should be held personally responsible for the offences of torture and conspiracy to torture, when, as it has been conceded, he did not personally murder or torture any victims by his own hands. Furthermore he has repeatedly claimed that he had "no time to control what others were doing" and "never accepted torture".[39] Notwithstanding these denials, it may, nevertheless, still be possible to implicate Pinochet, although this depends on the truth of the allegations which have been made against him. As reported in *Pinochet 3*, it has, for example, been alleged that he "was the prime example of an official torturer who for state purposes resort[ed] to torture".[40] Several references to his alleged involvement were also made by other law lords. Hence Lord Steyn referred to the allegations that agents of DINA committed the acts of torture but that DINA was directly answerable to General Pinochet rather than to the military junta, and that DINA undertook and arranged the killings, disappearances and torturing of victims on the orders of General Pinochet. In other words, "what is alleged against General Pinochet is not constructive criminal responsibility, the case is that he ordered and procured the criminal acts".[41] Similarly, Lord Browne-Wilkinson notes the allegation that the atrocities were done at Pinochet's "instigation and with his knowledge".[42] Even more compelling is the assertion that Pinochet "incurred direct criminal responsibility for his own acts in ordering and directing a campaign of terror involving the use of torture".[43] Moreover, Lord Hope's interpretation of the conspiracy to torture charge was broad enough to include the ancillary offences of counselling, procuring, commanding, aiding and abetting, or being an accessory before or after the fact to these acts of torture.[44]

---

[38] In Article 86(2) of Protocol 1 Additional to the Geneva Conventions of 12 August 1949, and Relating to the Protection of Victims of International Armed Conflicts.

[39] *The Guardian*, 19 July 1999.

[40] *Pinochet 3*, n 1 supra, at 903, per Lord Saville; Annex, p 268.

[41] *Pinochet 1*, n 1 supra, at 1504; Annex, p 176.

[42] *Pinochet 3*, n 1 supra, at 834; Annex, p 203.

[43] Ibid, at 914, per Lord Millet; Annex, p 278.

[44] Ibid, at 875; Annex, p 232.

Evidence of Pinochet's precise role has yet to be assessed but the declassification of Pentagon papers, which include one stating that General Contreras, the head of DINA with whom Pinochet breakfasted every morning, "reports exclusively to and receives orders from President Pinochet",[45] is likely to make his assertion of innocence untenable. Until such time as the evidence comes under further legal scrutiny it is, of course, only possible to speculate on Pinochet's personal responsibility. But, even if he is found not guilty, his "connection" with the harm suffered by those who were tortured is, for many, strong enough to justify continued moral condemnation. It seems unlikely too that in the meantime they will be assuaged by Pinochet's objection that he was "kidnapped" in England and treated as a "common bandit",[46] nor will the formal apology, given to the victims and their families on behalf of the state by President Aylwin in 1991, do much to lessen Pinochet's alleged moral responsibility, especially since the Chilean army, under his command, refused to co-operate with the Rettig Truth Commission, which implicated the military and secret police at the highest levels.[47] Moreover, while Pinochet may now be a frail old man, that cannot diminish the moral blame many believe he should carry for the death or disappearance of more than 3000 people and the torture, forced exile and grave human rights violations of tens of thousands of others.

[45] *The Guardian*, 23 July 1999.
[46] Ibid.
[47] Y Beigbeder, *Judging War Criminals: The Politics of International Justice* (Macmillan Press, 1999) p 108. The Rettig Commission was set up in 1990 and investigated 2920 cases involving death (by 1994 the total number of people who had been officially acknowledged to be more than 3000).

6

Sovereign Immunity Under International Law: The Case of Pinochet

JONATHAN BLACK-BRANCH

INTRODUCTION

Traditionally, sovereign immunity has been a well-accepted legal principle both within international and municipal fora. Heads of state and former heads of state enjoyed immunity to conduct the affairs of state, largely free from legal repercussions. The House of Lords' ruling on Senator Pinochet is set to change this long-standing doctrine. It marks an end to state immunity, ultimately setting the stage for a wider international jurisdiction as it pertains to crimes of torture, in particular, and broader human rights abuses generally.

Although this ruling may at first appear to be the right answer on humanitarian grounds, it may well be wrong according to customary international law and thus ultimately destructive to global political stability and security, not to mention the protection of human rights. The House of Lords' ruling to allow Senator Pinochet to face extradition has many implications for heads of state in every jurisdiction, not only those perceived as unfavourable dictators.

The Government of Spain requested the extradition of Senator Agusto Pinochet Ugarte to stand trial for alleged crimes committed during his period of office first as General[1] and then as Head of State of Chile. Initially accused of three categories of crimes, namely, torture, genocide and taking hostages between 1973 (later dated as 1 January 1972) and 1990, the charges changed during the process. After a protracted series of appeals, the House of Lords ruled that Senator Pinochet should stand trial for extradition for offences of torture and conspiracy to torture occurring after 8 December 1988. The main question was whether the English court could assert any criminal jurisdiction over acts committed by Senator Pinochet while head of state. The answer turned on whether he was immune from these proceedings.

---

[1] The Spanish Government submitted that Senator Pinochet's conduct extended back to when he was merely a General, before he actually became head of state; a time period for which he should not be granted immunity.

In *Pinochet 3*, the extradition charges were considered in light of the double criminality rule, governing whether the conduct in question actually amounts to an extradition crime. Examining this issue in depth to determine which charges, if any, would apply to Senator Pinochet, the House of Lords greatly reduced the number of charges to be examined in an extradition hearing. Those remaining charges failed to meet the immunity test as interpreted by the majority of the House of Lords. The primary purpose of this essay is to argue that the immunity principle was wrongly interpreted. English courts should not have asserted criminal jurisdiction over acts committed by Senator Pinochet in his capacity as head of state. Senator Pinochet should have been granted immunity under international law and, as a consequence, should not be subjected to extradition.

JUS GENTIUM: THE LAW OF NATIONS

A fitting place to begin any discussion on international law is the concept itself. International law may best be summed up in its Latin term, *jus gentium*, the law of nations. It is a system of law regulating the interrelationship of sovereign states, including their rights and duties,[2] and their responsibilities and obligations to one another. The principal sources of international law, as followed by the International Court of Justice,[3] are international treaties and conventions; international custom;[4] general principles of law recognised by civilised nations; judicial decisions; and, as a subsidiary means of determining rules of law, the writings of jurists.[5] Of these principal sources, treaties and customs are paramount. In the event of a conflict between treaties and customs, treaty provisions will override customary practices provided they are clear and unambiguously written.[6]

The principal treaties relating to immunity are the *Vienna Convention on Diplomatic Relations 1961* and the *European Convention on State Immunity (and Additional Protocol)* which was adopted in Basel in 1972. The *Vienna Convention* provides for immunity from civil and criminal process for diplomats both while posted, and indeed thereafter, in respect of conduct which they committed in the performance of their official functions while in post. The European Treaty, although a regional treaty, has since served as the basis for domestic legislation in various State Signatories. A distinguishing feature of this convention is that it gives effect to the principle of "relative" immunity, as opposed to "absolute" immunity. This convention has since formed the basis of

---

[2] *Oxford Dictionary of Law* (3rd edn, OUP, 1997) p 207.

[3] Article 38(1) Statute of the International Court of Justice.

[4] In so far as such custom is generally practiced and followed, and evidence of such actions is accepted as legally binding.

[5] See I A Shearer, *Starke's International Law* (11th edn, Butterworths, 1994) p 29; D H Harris, *Cases and Materials on International Law* (5th edn, Sweet & Maxwell, 1998).

[6] *The United Nations Charter* is the main source of international law taking precedence over all other treaties, and indeed customs.

the 1978 State Immunity Act of the United Kingdom, discussed in detail later in this essay. Although this convention is important, the principal source of international law on state immunity lies in custom.

Custom is best defined as, "a clear and continuous habit of doing certain actions which has grown up under the conviction that these actions are, according to international law, obligatory or right".[7] De Visscher highlights the merits of custom as a primary source of international law, stating:

> What gives international custom its special value and its superiority over conventional institutions, in spite of the inherent imprecision of its expression, is the fact that, developing by spontaneous practice, it reflects a deeply felt community of law. Hence the density and stability of its rules.[8]

The concept of state/sovereign immunity has come to be well-entrenched in international customary law. There is no doubt that formerly Senator Pinochet would not have been the subject of an extradition hearing. This would have been ruled to be out of the domain of the British State under customary international law.

STATE IMMUNITY

Immunity for a head of state is a creature of customary international law, similar to the principle of sovereign immunity. Although the terms "state immunity" and "sovereign immunity" are often used interchangeably, it would seem they are separate concepts rooted in the same principle, sovereign independence.[9] Formerly, to sue a head of state effectively meant suing the state itself, extraterritorially. Customary practice was not to sue another nation. Sovereign nations were sovereign in their own right. Throughout the 1800s this principle of immunity came to be well-accepted both in international political practices and in legal circles.

In 1812 in *The Schooner Exchange* v. *McFaddon*,[10] Marshall CJ of the US Supreme Court justified the doctrine of state immunity on the basis of the equality, independence and dignity of individual sovereign states. Here, American parties to a legal action sought possession of a French naval vessel which docked in Philadelphia for repairs following a storm. They argued the French vessel was their ship, the Schooner Exchange, which had been seized on the high seas in 1810. The US Attorney-General submitted that the French were immune from prosecution and the court should decline jurisdiction. Marshall CJ accepted this argument stating:

---

[7] Sir Robert Jennings QC and Sir Arthur Watts QC (eds), *Oppenheim's International Law* (9th edn, 1992) p 27.

[8] *De Visscher*, pp 161–2, as cited in Harris, *Cases and Materials on International Law*, p 45.

[9] *The Suchariktul Report to the International Law Commission* (1980) Vol II Doc A (LN 4–331 and Add J).

[10] *The Schooner Exchange* v. *McFaddon* (1812) 7 Cranch 116.

> The jurisdiction of the nation within its own territory is necessarily exclusive and absolute. It is susceptible of no limitation not imposed by itself.

Moreover:

> This full and absolute territorial jurisdiction being alike the attribute of every sovereign, and being incapable of conferring extra-territorial power, would not seem to contemplate foreign sovereigns nor their sovereign rights as its objects.

He continued:

> One sovereign being in no respect amenable to another, and being bound by obligations of the highest character not to degrade the dignity of his nation, by placing him or its sovereign rights within the jurisdiction of another, can be supposed to enter a foreign territory only under an express license, or in the confidence that the immunities belonging to his independent sovereign station, though not expressly stipulated, are reserved by implication, and will be extended to him.

This case reiterated the custom of the day, *par in parem non habet imperium* (an equal [state] has no domain over an equal); a custom which stands today.

In 1848 the Lord Chancellor issued a similar ruling regarding extra-territorial legal disputes in *The Duke of Brunswick* v. *The King of Hanover*,[11] stating that a "foreign Sovereign . . . cannot be made responsible here for an act done in his Sovereign character in his own country".[12] This ruling illustrates the widely accepted customary practice of the day, and was upheld in 1982 in *Buttes Gas and Oil Co.* v. *Hammer*.[13] Indeed, through custom and practice, state immunity came to be recognised in two separate areas, immunity as to the process of the court and immunity with respect to property belonging to the foreign state or sovereign.[14] Shearer concludes that: "the English authorities laid it down that the courts would not by their process 'implead' a foreign state or foreign sovereign; in other words, they would not, against its will, make it a party to legal proceedings".[15] In the case of Pinochet, the English authorities should have followed this practice and not "impleaded" a foreign state or foreign sovereign. They should not have made him a party to legal proceedings.

GENERAL PRINCIPLES OF LAW

General principles of law recognised by civilised nations are also included in the list of sources of law under Article 38(1) of the Statute of the International Court of Justice. Jurists such as Verdross[16] saw this as a means of incorporating principles of natural law into the international area, while others, such as

---

[11] *Duke of Brunswick* v. *The King of Hanover* (1848) 2 HL Cas 1.
[12] Ibid, p 17.
[13] *Buttes Gas and Oil Co* v. *Hammer* [1982] AC 888.
[14] Shearer, *Starke's International Law*, n 5 supra, p 192.
[15] Ibid.
[16] As cited in Harris, *Cases and Materials on International Law*, n 5 supra, p 47.

Guggenheim,[17] argued it meant nothing more than reiterating those principles previously covered in treaties and customs. Asked to elaborate on this notion Lord Phillimore of the United Kingdom, who co-authored the provision with his US counterpart Mr Root, stated that, "the general principles referred to . . . were those which were accepted by all nations *in foro domestico*, such as principles of procedure, the principle of good faith, and the principle of *res judicata*, etc".[18] He subsequently stated that what he meant by "general principles" was "maxims of law". In this regard, it could be argued on Pinochet's behalf that a well-accepted maxim of international law is "*par in parem imperium non habet*", an equal has no domain over an equal. Indeed, such has been upheld in *The Schooner Exchange*, as noted above.[19]

JUDICIAL DECISIONS

Judicial decisions are also valuable in shaping international opinion in relation to legal matters. Previously decided cases can provide persuasive arguments pertaining to current issues. In relation to the *Pinochet* case, Lord Phillips stated that there was no case law which actually supported his claim to immunity, *per se*. He said the closest Chile could find to illustrate its point was the *obiter* opinion of the Swiss Federal Tribunal in *Marcos and Marcos*,[20] which stated:

> The privilege of the immunity from criminal jurisdiction of heads of state . . . has not been fully codified in the Vienna Convention [on Diplomatic Relations]. . . . But it cannot be concluded that the texts of conventions drafted under the aegis of the United Nations grant a lesser protection to heads of foreign states than to the diplomatic representatives of the state which those heads of state lead or universally represent. . . . Articles 32 and 39 of the Vienna Convention must therefore apply by analogy to heads of state.[21]

Lord Phillips saw this apparent lack of firm case precedents as a negative point against Senator Pinochet. Alternatively, it could be argued that the lack of case law supporting immunity for Pinochet's case is due to the fact that, under customary law, cases of this nature were not heard and therefore no firm body of case law has developed to support his cause. Indeed the cases discussed earlier support the concept of "absolute" immunity. More recent cases tend to focus on immunity as it relates to commercial actions, which are somewhat different from the acts of a head of state. Although there was no firm case law directly in his support, conversely, there was no strong judicial precedent against him either.

---

[17] "Traite de droit international public", I, p 152, as cited in Harris, ibid, p 47.
[18] As cited in Harris, ibid, p 49.
[19] N 10 supra.
[20] *Marcos and Marcos* v. *Federal Department of Police* (1989) 102 ILR 198.
[21] Ibid, at 202–3.

Indeed, in the *King of Hanover*,[22] noted above, the Lord Chancellor made it perfectly clear that it was improper for a foreign court to interfere in the King's home affairs stating:

> A foreign Sovereign, coming into this country cannot be made responsible here for an act done in his Sovereign character in his own country; whether it be an act right or wrong, whether according to the constitution of that country or not, the Courts of this country cannot sit in judgment upon an act of a Sovereign, effected by virtue of his Sovereign authority abroad, an act not done as a British subject, but supposed to be done in the exercise of his authority vested in him as Sovereign.[23]

In relation to the *Pinochet* case, the *Hanover* ruling establishes three important points under international case law to which we will return below. First, heads of state are immune. Secondly, it does not matter whether or not the "act is according to the constitution of that country". Thus, even if there are statutory provisions in the country, which are being violated, this is quite irrelevant. Thirdly, it is irrelevant whether the act spoken of is right or wrong. There is therefore no place for judicial intervention in these affairs, even if they may be "wrong". This is a point the Lord Chancellor reiterated later in the judgment

> If it be a matter of sovereign authority we cannot try that fact, whether it be right or wrong. The allegation that it is contrary to the laws of Hanover, taken in conjunction with the allegation of the authority under which the defendant had acted, must be conceded to be an allegation, not that it was contrary to the existing laws as regulating the right of individuals, but that it was contrary to the laws and duties and rights and powers of a Sovereign exercising Sovereign authority. If that be so, it does not require another observation to shew, because it has not been doubted, that no Court in this country can entertain questions to bring Sovereigns to account for their acts done in their sovereign capacities abroad.[24]

Moreover, this case precedent was upheld in the United Kingdom in 1982 by Lord Wilberforce, who referred to *Hanover* as "a case in this House which is still authoritative and which has influenced the law both here and overseas",[25] and accepted by Lord Slynn in *Pinochet 1* as relevant law, being cited both in judicial decisions and in the writing of eminent jurists.[26]

Another important decision in relation to *Pinochet* is *Hatch v. Baez* (1876),[27] where the plaintiff claimed that he had suffered injuries in the Dominican Republic as a result of acts done by the defendant in his official capacity of President of that Republic. Because the defendant was in New York State, the court accepted territorial jurisdiction to hear the case. However, it noted:

---

[22] N 11 supra.
[23] Ibid, at 17.
[24] Ibid, at 22.
[25] N 13 supra, at 932.
[26] *R v. Bow Street Metropolitan Stipendiary Magistrate and Others, en parte Pinochet Ugarte* [1998] 3 WLR 1465; Annex, p 144.
[27] *Hatch v. Baez* (1876) 7 Hun 596.

But the immunity of individuals from suits brought in foreign tribunals for acts done within their own States, in the exercise of the sovereignty thereof, is essential to preserve the peace and harmony of nations, and has the sanction of the most approved writers on international law. It is also recognized in all the judicial decisions on the subject that have come to my knowledge. . . . The fact that the defendant has ceased to be president of St. Domingo does not destroy his immunity. That springs from the capacity in which the acts were done, and protects the individual who did them, because they emanated from a foreign and friendly government.[28]

These cases would seem to demonstrate that, in the final analysis, there are indeed judicial decisions which support Pinochet's case.

WRITINGS OF AUTHORS

Wolfke states that the role of authors in international law today is to analyse facts and opinions; to draw conclusions relating to binding customary rules. He says that, "Such conclusions, like all generalizations of this kind, involve unrestricted supplementation by introducing elements lacking and hence, a creative factor".[29] Moreover, through appraisal, the writers indirectly influence the evolution of international law, thus assisting in the development of its customs. In relation to *Pinochet* there have been numerous writings by learned authors and renowned jurists in support of the immunity claim asserted on behalf of Senator Pinochet.

The position of a former head of state as accepted in the *King of Hanover* continues to be cited as authoritative amongst jurists. Similarly, the principle in *Hatch* is still broadly applied. In that regard, in *Oppenheim's International Law* editors, Sir Robert Jennings QC and Sir Arthur Watts QC, maintain that:

> All privileges mentioned must be granted to a head of state only so long as he holds that position. Therefore . . . he may be sued, at least in respect of obligations of a private character entered into while head of state. For his official acts as head of state he will, like any other agent of a state, enjoy continuing immunity.[30]

The same point is affirmed in Satow's *Guide to Diplomatic Practice*.[31] In relation to the position of a visiting head of state, after considering the relevant conventions (Vienna Convention on Diplomatic Relations 1961, New York Convention on Special Missions 1969 and European Convention on State Immunity 1972), the editors conclude that:

> The personal status of a head of a foreign state therefore continues to be regulated by long-established rules of international law which can be stated in simple terms. He is entitled to immunity—probably without exception—from criminal and civil jurisdiction.[32]

[28] Ibid, at 600.
[29] As cited in Harris, n 5 supra, p 57.
[30] *Oppenheim's International Law*, n 7 supra, pp 1043–4, para 456.
[31] *Satow's Guide to Diplomatic Practice* (4th edn, 1957).
[32] Ibid, pp 9–10.

Note that this ninth edition of the volume was published in 1992, some four years after the Torture Convention took effect in domestic law and after Pinochet ceased to hold power. No commentator appears to have speculated on a change of immunity for him, or indeed other leaders in a similar position.

Furthermore, Satow's *Guide to Diplomatic Practice* highlights that:

> A head of state who has been deposed or replaced or has abdicated or resigned is of course no longer entitled to privileges or immunities as a head of state. He will be entitled to continuing immunity in regard to acts which he performed while head of state, provided that the acts were performed in his official capacity; in this his position is no different from that of any agent of the state.[33]

Sir Arthur Watts in his noted work[34] discusses the loss of immunity of a head of state who is deposed on a foreign visit:

> A head of state's official acts, performed in his public capacity as head of state, are however subject to different considerations. Such acts are acts of the state rather than the head of state's personal acts, and he cannot be sued for them even after he has ceased to be head of state. The position is similar to that of acts performed by an ambassador in the exercise of his functions, for which immunity continues to subsist even after the ambassador's appointment has come to an end.[35]

In *Pinochet 3* Lord Phillips dismissed these observations, stating: "I do not find these writings . . . a compelling foundation for the immunity in respect of criminal proceedings that is asserted". It must be argued, however, that these submissions are *most* compelling. They represent the five primary sources of international law, as established under Article 38(1) of the Statute of the International Court of Justice. Specifically, they interpret statutory international law as it relates to treaties and conventions. They provide measured commentary on accepted and long-established customs in international law. They highlight general principles recognised by civilised nations. They base their works on judicial decisions which have been issued in the area of law. They are the works of renowned jurists and respected practitioners working in the area of international law. Theirs is a most compelling stand on the issue of immunity. Indeed, these writings are authoritative and relevant to the matter at hand. They affirm in no uncertain terms that Senator Pinochet is immune as former head of state according to the principles of international law.

JUS COGENS

An overriding principle of international law is the doctrine of *jus cogens*. Effectively, this principle establishes that a rule or principle in international law

---

[33] *Satow's Guide to Diplomatic Practice* (4th edn, 1957).

[34] Sir Arthur Watts, "The Legal Position in International Law of Heads of State, Heads of Government and Foreign Ministers" (1994) 247 *Recueil des cours* III.

[35] Ibid, pp 88–9.

is so fundamental that it binds all states and does not allow any exceptions. These rules are often referred to as "peremptory norms". In recent years many authorities have agreed that laws prohibiting acts such as genocide are *jus cogens* laws. Others suggest that human rights abuses and international crimes generally should also be *jus cogens* laws. It would seem that the principle of immunity is *jus cogens* law on its own. Learned writers and jurists cited throughout this paper affirm that immunity for heads of state is a well-recognised principle of international law, a "peremptory norm" widely accepted throughout the global community, in relation to "official acts as head of state . . . like any other agent of a state, . . . [and] continuing immunity"[36] thereafter for those acts. Indeed, a head of state "is entitled to immunity—probably without exception—from criminal and civil jurisdiction",[37] and "the position is similar to that of acts performed by an ambassador in the exercise of his functions, for which immunity continues to subsist even after the ambassador's appointment has come to an end".[38]

So, on the one hand, it could be argued that crimes of torture are *jus cogens* law, but it would seem that state immunity also holds such weight. Indeed, customary practice, as evidenced by the writings of eminent jurists, indicates it is a long-standing and well-established set of principles within the international community. In addition, "A treaty which conflicts with an existing *jus cogens* rule is void".[39] In this regard, state immunity has had longer support in more countries throughout the world and therefore takes priority in the hierarchy of principles. Thus, it could be argued that the applicable parts of the Torture Convention are void to the extent they conflict with the *jus cogens* laws of state immunity. Surely the framers of the legislation would not have intended this conflict. Moreover, given the special position of heads of state as it relates to immunity, had the framers intended former heads of state to be liable for alleged acts, they would have made express reference to such leaders. In that regard it is highly unlikely that Pinochet would have signed a document which would eventually render himself liable. It is ironic that the very convention which Pinochet, as head of state, signed has led to his possible extradition to Spain for alleged acts of torture.

COMITY OF NATIONS

While it could be argued that holding those responsible, or allegedly responsible, in the *Pinochet* case, for crimes of torture should be an overriding principle of international law, which is above that of state immunity, it could, alternatively, be contended that the smooth working of international relations, as it

[36] *Oppenheim's International Law*, n 7 supra, pp 1043–4, para 456.
[37] *Satow's Guide to Diplomatic Practice*, n 31 supra, pp 9–10.
[38] Sir Arthur Watts, n 34 supra, pp 88–9.
[39] *Oxford Dictionary of Law*, n 2 supra, pp 218–19.

relates to heads of state and former heads of state, is a more pressing international concern. Indeed, this itself formulates a long-standing principle of international law known as comity. Comity of nations operates on the basis that nations are willing to grant privileges, not as a right as such, but as a matter of good will, for the smooth functioning of international affairs. Comity of nations is thus defined as:

> the recognition one nation allows within its territory to legislative, executive, or judicial acts of another nation, having due regard both to international duty and convenience and to the rights of its own citizens or of other persons who are under the protection of its laws.[40]

Under this principle, the United Kingdom should respect the wishes of Chile as a sovereign nation and allow Senator Pinochet to return home.

Moreover, this is a principle supported by the courts. In *Buck* v. *Attorney General* (1965)[41] Diplock LJ stated:

> As a member of the family of nations, the Government of the United Kingdom (of which this court forms part of the judicial branch) observes the rules of comity, videlicet, the accepted rules of mutual conduct as between state and state which each state adopts in relation to other states to adopt in relation to itself. One of those rules is that it does not purport to exercise jurisdiction over the internal affairs of any other independent state, or to apply measures of coercion to it or to its property, except in accordance with the rules of public international law. One of the commonest applications of this rule by the judicial branch of the United Kingdom Government is the well-known doctrine of sovereign immunity. A foreign state cannot be impleaded in the English courts without its consent.... That would be a breach of the rules of comity.[42]

The principles of comity, as it pertains to heads of state, are even more fundamental to international law and politics than many others and thus must be respected. That is not to say that human rights issues are not important. It is only to say that fostering good relations between, and among, states may be more productive in the long run. It is not a principle extended to everyone, only heads and former heads of state. Non-heads or former heads who commit acts of torture can, and indeed should, be tried. Additionally, this will not give world leaders a carte blanche to commit torture and other atrocities. It highlights that these are issues which are not adequately provided for under international law and those desiring a world-wide jurisdiction for crimes of this nature, including for heads of state, should press for clarity on this point under international law. Several examples of this sort currently exist, for example, the international tribunals for the former Yugoslavia (1993) and for Rwanda (1994) make express provisions to try heads and former heads of state. In addition, the Rome Statute of the International Criminal Court makes similar references.

---

[40] *Black's Law Dictionary* (5th edn, West Publishing Co, 1979) p 242.
[41] *Buck* v. *Att. Gen* [1965] Ch 475, 770.
[42] Ibid.

EROSION OF ABSOLUTE IMMUNITY IN BRITAIN

Prior to the 1950s, Britain mainly supported state immunity in an absolute form. But in 1952 under the infamous "Tate Letter" the government began to curtail this doctrine indicating a more "restrictive" notion of immunity. In May of that year Mr Jack Tate, Acting Legal Adviser to the United States Department of State, sent a letter to the Acting US Attorney-General declaring the discontinuance of the doctrine of sovereign immunity as absolute. The Government would take a more restrictive approach while considering such requests from foreign governments. This development was soon mirrored by the judiciary. In 1957, Lord Denning[43] voiced his opposition to the granting of immunity to foreign governments in relation to commercial matters. Some twenty years later the Judicial Committee of the Privy Council[44] held that a foreign state did not have absolute immunity from jurisdiction in relation to an action in *rem* during commercial activities, while the Court of Appeal held the Central Bank of Nigeria was not a department or extension of government but a legal "entity" in its own right and thus had no entitlement to jurisdictional immunity in relation to proceedings in *personam*.[45] In this decision, Lord Denning, Master of the Rolls, stated in no uncertain terms that the court should not be "bound by any idea of *stare decisis* in international law".[46] Although highly significant, in, and of, itself, in serving to transform the doctrine of "absolute" immunity to a more "restrictive" form, this restrictiveness seemed largely to affect commercial transactions and not the acts of heads of state performing public functions, as such. So it would appear that these rulings have little, if any, bearing on the *Pinochet* case. Indeed, they implicitly act in his favour. While restrictions were placed on immunity in one sense, no mention was made of heads of state performing official public functions.

Aside from these decisions, there have also been statutory developments, which actually serve to affirm immunity for heads of state acting in their country's interest. In 1972 the European Convention on State Immunity and Additional Protocol were adopted in Basle, giving effect to what may be called "relative" immunity. This Convention later formed the basis of the 1978 State Immunity Act of the United Kingdom, which is directly applicable to *Pinochet*. The long title of the Act states that it is, first, "to make new provision in respect of proceedings in the United Kingdom by or against other States" and, secondly, "to make new provision with respect to the immunities and privileges of Heads of State". Part I of the Act, entitled, "General Immunity from Jurisdiction", provides that: "A State is immune from the jurisdiction of the Courts of the United

---

[43] *Rahimtoola* v. *Nizam of Hyderabad* [1957] 3 All ER 441, at 463.
[44] *The Philippine Admiral (Owners)* v. *Wallem Shipping (Hong Kong) Ltd* [1977] AC 373; [1976] All ER 78.
[45] *Trendtex Trading Corpn* v. *Central Bank of Nigeria* [1977] QB 529; [1977] 1 All ER 881.
[46] Ibid.

Kingdom, except as provided in the following provisions of this Part of this Act".[47] The noted exceptions presented in sections relate largely to matters of a commercial nature, contracts of employment and injuries to persons and property. The Act does not expressly indicate whether these matters apply to civil or criminal matters, or both. However, in *Pinochet 1* Lord Slynn indicated that "some of these exceptions . . . are capable of being construed to include both civil and criminal proceedings".[48]

Section 1 of the Act provides little guidance as to what the concept of "state" entails, that is, who it involves and in which capacity. It simply refers to "the State". Section 14, however, elaborates upon the concept of state and its various organs, specifying that, "references to a State include references to (a) the sovereign or other head of that State in his public capacity; (b) the government of that State; and (c) any department of that government, but not to any entity . . . which is distinct from the executive organs of the government of the State and capable of suing or of being sued".[49] Moreover, section 16(4), specifies that, "this Part of this Act does not apply to criminal proceedings". It would seem that Senator Pinochet could not rely on such immunities under this Part of the State Immunity Act.

However, he could rely on Part III, which states that, "the Diplomatic Privileges Act 1964 shall apply to (a) A sovereign or other head of State; (b) members of his family forming part of his household; and (c) his private servants, as it applies to the head of a diplomatic mission, to members of his family forming part of his household and to his private servants".[50] Further, 20(5) specifies that, "This section applies to the sovereign or other head of any State on which immunities and privileges are conferred by Part I of this Act and is without prejudice to the application of that Part to any such sovereign or head of State in his public capacity". These provisions affirm that state immunity for heads of state should continue, thus indicating that Pinochet is immune under United Kingdom domestic law as well as according to international treaties, custom and practice.[51]

---

[47] The State Immunity Act 1978, section 1.
[48] Supra n 26; Annex, p 140.
[49] The State Immunity Act 1978, section 14(1).
[50] Ibid, section 20(1).
[51] Lord Slynn, in his dissenting judgment in *Pinochet 1* (at 1465–8) contended that a direct reference to the Diplomatic Privileges Act 1964 in Part III clarified the issue. He noted section 1 provides the Act will "have effect in substitution for any previous enactment or rule of law". By section 2, articles of the Vienna Convention on Diplomatic Relations (1961) set out in the Schedule, "shall have the force of law in the United Kingdom". He referred to the Preamble to the Convention, together with its provisions, and concluded that their main intent is "to recognize a head of state as a 'diplomatic agent' " and to provide that "a head of state shall be inviolable, not liable to any form of arrest or detention (article 29), and shall enjoy immunity from criminal jurisdiction (article 31(1)". Moreover, he argued "there is nothing to indicate that this immunity is limited to acts done within the State of which the person concerned is Head". This indicates that Pinochet is immune under UK domestic law as well as according to international treaties, custom and practice.

THE PRINCIPLE OF INVIOLABILITY

It is a generally accepted principle of international law that a head of state is inviolable. As discussed above, British domestic law serves to support this principle. In the words of Lord Phillips:

> A head of state on a visit to another country is inviolable. He cannot be arrested or detained, let alone removed against his will to another country, and he is not subject to the judicial processes, whether civil or criminal, of the courts of the state that he is visiting.[52]

Lord Phillips stated that Senator Pinochet would be granted such immunity if he were still head of state. "[H]e and Chile would be in a position to complain that the entire extradition process was a violation of the duties owed under international law to a person of his status".[53] However, according to Lord Phillips, because he is a former head of state, Pinochet loses his status and is thus violable under English jurisdiction.

Surely this proposition cannot be so. Individuals should not lose their rights simply because of a change of circumstances, especially a change which is virtually inevitable. That is, every head of state will eventually become a former head of state, unless, of course, they die in office. They cannot be told that they are inviolable at one stage, that is, during their leadership, and later that they are violable due to their change of circumstance (no longer being in office). That is not to say that as former head of state the leader in question should be allowed to continue acting in this capacity and remain immune. It is simply to say that those acts alleged to have been committed while head of state should remain inviolable. Acts committed as former head of state are thus inviolable. It seems that both Pinochet and the state of Chile itself are in a position to complain that the entire extradition process has violated various obligations under international law. Under the inviolability principle, alone, Senator Pinochet is immune.

IMMUNITY *RATIONE PERSONAE* AND IMMUNITY *RATIONE MATERIAE*

The immunity of a head of state operates under the Latin term "*ratione personae*" which means by reason of the person concerned.[54] Lord Phillips pointed out that, "While a head of state is serving, his status ensures him immunity".[55] So by virtue of being head of state, the person in question is inviolable. Once he ceases to be head of state, however, the principle of *ratione personae* no longer

---

[52] *R v Bow Street Metropolitan Stipendary Magistrate and Others, ex parte Pinochet Ugarte* [1999] 2 WLR 827 at 915; Annex, p 280.
[53] Ibid.
[54] *Black's Law Dictionary*, n 40 supra, p 1136.
[55] Supra n 52.

applies to that individual. Immunity is claimed, *ratione materiae*, by reason of the subject matter involved.[56] Lord Phillips stated that:

> This is an immunity of the state which applies to preclude the courts of another state from asserting jurisdiction in relation to a suit brought against an official or other agent of the state, present or past, in relation to the conduct of the business of the state while in office.[57]
>
> Once he is out of office, he is in the same position as any other state official and any immunity will be based upon the nature of the subject matter of the litigation.[58]

In the case of *United States of America* v. *Noriega* (1990)[59] immunity granted for a head of state was to ensure that "leaders are free to perform their Governmental duties without being subject to detention, arrest or embarrassment in a foreign country's legal system". Lord Slynn concludes that this reasoning, in, and of, itself, is sufficient for continuing to apply the immunity *ratione materiae* in respect of a former head of state. There have been a number of civil proceedings where questions were raised, regarding whether a former head of state acted in a public or private capacity.[60] These cases, however, are not particularly helpful for the present case, other than to point out that there is a distinction between private matters and public acts of state.

In this instance the subject matter of the extradition process is that of alleged actions conducted by Senator Pinochet, while head of state. As a result:

> There is no distinction to be made between a head of state, a former head of state, a state official or a former state official in respect of official acts performed under colour of their office. Immunity will attach to all official acts which are imputable or attributable to the state. It is therefore the nature of the conduct and the capacity of the Respondent at the time of the conduct alleged, not the capacity of the Respondent at the time of any suit, that is relevant.

It would seem that the acts in question were clearly in connection with official functions when he was head of Chile. Whether or not one agrees with such actions is another matter, they were not administered in a personal and private capacity, they were in exercise of his public role based on what the government of the day felt was in the best interest of the state. As amply demonstrated through the various sources of international law, it is contrary to international law to prosecute someone who was once head of state, or a state official, in respect of acts committed in his official capacity. Senator Pinochet should not be held personally responsible unless either Chile itself moves to try him, or the United Nations does under the aegis of a broader international tribunal such as the Nuremberg Trials and those in the former Yugoslavia and Rwanda.

---

[56] *Black's Law Dictionary*, n 40 supra, p 1136.
[57] Supra n 52.
[58] Ibid, at 921; Annex, p 285.
[59] *United States of America* v. *Noriega* (1990) 746 F. Supp 1506.
[60] *Ex King Farouk of Egypt* v. *Christian Dior*, SARL (1957) 24 ILR 228; *Soc. Jean Desses* v. *Prince Farouk* (1963) 65 ILR 37; *Jiminez* v. *Aristeguieta* 311 F 2d 547; *U.S.* v. *Noriega* (1997) 117 F 3rd 1206.

ACT OF STATE DOCTRINE

In situations where the state itself is not impleaded, by the former head, as in *Pinochet*, the English and American courts have exercised much judicial restraint. This was noted by Lord Phillips, who, applying, what has become known as, the "act of state" doctrine, indicated in *Pinochet 3* that the courts were not competent to hear cases, which turn on the validity of the public acts of a foreign state. This doctrine essentially "precludes the courts of this country from inquiring into the validity of governmental acts of a recognized foreign sovereign committed within its territory".[61] As Lord Slynn noted, the American courts, in particular, have upheld this principle largely on the basis of comity between nations (described above), beginning with *The Schooner Exchange* v. *McFaddon*.

There are a number of cases which demonstrate the attitude of the American courts. Notably, in *Underhill* v. *Hernandez* (1897),[62] Fuller CJ stated that:

> Every sovereign state is bound to respect the independence of every other sovereign state, and the courts of one country will not sit in judgment on the acts of the government of another done within its own territory. Redress of grievances by reason of such acts must be obtained through the means open to be availed of by sovereign powers as between themselves . . . The immunity of individuals from suits brought in foreign tribunals for acts done within their own states, in the exercise of governmental authority, whether as civil officers or as military commanders, must necessarily extend to the agents of governments ruling by paramount force as matter of fact.[63]

In *Banco National de Cuba* v. *Sabbatino* (1961)[64] it was said that:

> the Act of State Doctrine briefly stated holds that American Courts will not pass on the validity of the acts of foreign governments performed in their capacities as sovereigns within their own territories . . . This doctrine is one of the conflict of laws rules applied by American Courts; it is not itself a rule of international law . . . it stems from the concept of the immunity of the sovereign because "the sovereign can do no wrong".[65]

More recently, in *International Association of Machinists* v. *Opec* [1981][66] the Ninth Circuit Court of Appeals went even further in its discussion, stating:

> The doctrine of sovereign immunity is similar to the Act of State Doctrine in that it also represents the need to respect the sovereignty of foreign states. The law of sovereign immunity goes to the jurisdiction of the Court. The Act of State Doctrine is not jurisdictional . . . Rather it is a procedural doctrine designed to avoid action in sensitive areas. Sovereign immunity is a principle of international law, recognized in the

---

[61] *Black's Law Dictionary*, n 40 supra, p 32.
[62] *Underhill* v. *Hernandez* (1897) 168 US 456.
[63] Ibid, at 457.
[64] *Banco National de Cuba* v. *Sabbatino* 307F 2d 845 (1961).
[65] Ibid, at 855.
[66] *International Association of Machinists* v. *Opec* (649F 2d 134) [1981].

United States by statutes. It is the states themselves, as defendants, who may claim sovereign immunity.

It must be said, however, that although the two doctrines, sovereign immunity and act of state, are separate, they often run parallel. As noted by Lord Slynn, the law of sovereign immunity is now contained in the US Foreign Sovereign Immunities Act,[67] in respect of civil matters, and many of the decisions on sovereign immunity in the United States turn on whether the exemption to a general state immunity from suit falls within one of the specific exemptions. The Act itself does not deal with the immunity of a head of state from criminal acts, but in the United States the courts would normally follow a decision of the executive as to the grant or denial of immunity and it is only when the executive does not take a position that "Courts should make an independent determination regarding immunity".[68] Moreover, in the case of *Kirkpatrick* v. *Environmental Tectonics* (1990)[69] the court said that, having begun with comity of nations as the basis for the act of state doctrine, more recently it regarded comity as springing from the sense that if the judiciary adjudicated on the validity of foreign acts of state, this might serve to hinder the conduct of foreign affairs. The Supreme Court ruled that "Act of State issues only arise when a Court must decide—that is when the outcome of the case turns upon—the effect of official action by a foreign Sovereign".[70]

The position in English law is, according to Lord Slynn, much the same as it was in the earlier US cases. Thus the act of state doctrine:

> is to the effect that the Courts of one State do not, as a rule, question the validity or legality of the official acts of another Sovereign State or the official or officially avowed acts of its agents, at any rate in so far as those acts involve the exercise of the State's public authority, purport to take effect within the sphere of the latter's own jurisdiction. . . .[71]

In *Buttes Gas* Lord Wilberforce spoke of the normal meaning of acts of state as being "action taken by a Sovereign State within its own territory". He later asked whether, apart from cases concerning acts of British officials outside this country and cases concerned with the examination of the applicability of foreign municipal legislation within the territory of a foreign state, there was not "a more general principle that the Courts will not adjudicate upon the transactions of foreign Sovereign States"—a principle to be considered if it existed "not as a variety of 'acts of State', but one of judicial restraint or abstention". This was the approach adopted by Lord Slynn and it would seem persuasive. The United Kingdom courts should not therefore have adjudicated on the facts of the

---

[67] 28 USSC–1602.
[68] Stated by Kravitch SCJ in *US* v. *Noriega*.
[69] *Kirkpatrick* v. *Environmental Tectonics* 493 U.S. 403 110 S Ct 701 (1990).
[70] Ibid, at 705.
[71] *Oppenheim's International Law*, n 7 supra, p 365.

Pinochet case but should have exercised judicial restraint or, more appropriately, abstention.

ACTS OF HEAD OF STATE

Questions are raised as to what actually constitutes official acts in the exercise of the functions as head of state. The multitude of duties and functions performed by a head of state are voluminous and the list would vary from one country to the next, based on their respective constitutions, their location in the world, and their unique arrangements with other states. Nevertheless, it has been asserted that certain functions are not to be equated with heads of state, for instance, acts of genocide, torture, and crimes against humanity, in general. While there is little doubt that the world would be a better place if such atrocities were eradicated, it is difficult to determine whether certain acts of state, which amount to these types of actions, are legitimate within the political context within a given state, at a given time. If today there is a concerted world movement to eradicate these types of abuses, then the United Nations (UN) should deal with them decisively and agree to institute clear legislation with enforcement mechanisms.

Sir Arthur Watts, QC in his Hague Lectures has stated:

> A Head of State clearly can commit a crime in his personal capacity; but it seems equally clear that he can, in the course of his public functions as Head of State, engage in conduct which may be tainted by criminality or other forms of wrongdoing. The critical test would seem to be whether the conduct was engaged in under colour of or in ostensible exercise of the Head of State's public authority. If it was, it must be treated as official conduct, and so not a matter subject to the jurisdiction of other States whether or not it was wrongful or illegal under the law of his own State.[72]

In relation to the *Pinochet* case, Lord Slynn drew attention to the fact that it was accepted in the international warrant of arrest that in relation to the repression alleged, "the plans and instructions established beforehand from the Government enabled these actions to be carried out . . . In this sense [the] Commander in Chief of the Armed Forces and Head of the Chilean Government at the time committed punishable acts". Although one may disagree with the actions taken by Pinochet, this provides evidence that the acts in question were undertaken as part of Pinochet's functions when he was head of state, and as a consequence, take immunity.

LIKE WITH LIKE

Commentators have drawn comparisons to Hitler's Germany and to modern-day Milosevic's Serbia. But such comparisons fail to compare like with like. The

[72] Sir Arthur Watts, n 34 supra, pp 56–7.

situations in Germany and Serbia were somewhat different from that in Chile. To begin with there was an overwhelming consensus in the Western world that Hitler "must be stopped". Indeed, the allied countries eventually waged war against Germany to put an end to his rule. Similarly, Serbia NATO offences aimed to put an end to Milosevic's aggressive practices which were perceived to jeopardise world peace and security, such, at the time, was the collective voice of the major Western countries led by NATO. The actions of General Pinochet were somewhat different. It must be said that a number of UN bodies and the International American Commission on Human Rights have documented systematic kidnapping, torture and murder. And indeed, if tried, Pinochet might well be found guilty of some or all of these alleged crimes. But there was never the same degree of collective Western resolve to oust Pinochet from office as with Hitler or Milosevic. In fact, he was recognised and received as head of state in the United Kingdom and other countries. Leaders may not have agreed with the practices with which he is charged, but, by receiving him and granting diplomatic privileges as head of state during his rule, they indicated a tacit approval of such alleged wrong-doings.

If the family of nations feel that redress is necessary then it is up to the world body to instigate such proceedings. It is not for two individual states in Europe (Spain and Britain) to settle the issue. This should be a responsibility of the UN. In the past the community of nations has taken the lead in setting up international tribunals to adjudicate on specific sets of atrocities. The Nuremberg Charter in 1945, for example, gave jurisdiction to try crimes against peace, war crimes and crimes against humanity.[73] Article 7 specifically addressed the issue of immunity for heads of state and their agents stating "the official position of defendants, whether as a Heads of State or responsible officials in Government Departments shall not be considered as freeing them from responsibility or mitigating punishment". Similar provisions were found in the Tokyo Convention 1946.

More recently, in 1993 an international tribunal was established to deal with atrocities in the former Yugoslavia. This tribunal was granted power to prosecute persons "responsible for serious violations of international humanitarian law".[74] In relation to individual criminal responsibility it is provided that "the official position of any accused person whether as Head of State or Government or as a responsible Government Official shall not relieve such person of criminal responsibility".[75] A year later a similar tribunal was set up in Africa under the Statute of the International Tribunal for Rwanda (1994). This statute granted the tribunal the power to prosecute persons committing genocide and specified crimes against humanity "when committed as part of a widespread or systematic attack against any civilian population on national political ethnic or

[73] The Nuremberg Charter 1945, Article 6.
[74] See Ben Chigara (Chapter Seven in this collection) for further discussion on this and other tribunals.
[75] Article 7, The International Criminal Tribunal for the former Yugoslavia (ICTY).

other specified grounds". In relation to heads of state, a similar clause to that of the Yugoslavia tribunal was listed in the statute establishing the Rwanda tribunal, i.e. the official position of any accused person whether as head of state or government or as a responsible government official shall not relieve such person of criminal responsibility. The most recent development of this sort of collective UN action relates to the Rome Statute of the International Criminal Court which provides for jurisdiction in respect of genocide and crimes against humanity, as respectively defined, with regard to crimes committed after the entry into force of this statute. Notably, official capacity as a head of state or government shall in no case exempt the person from criminal responsibility under this statute. These examples give weight to the argument that UN action can be taken on a collective front to address the violations of human rights, even by heads of state and their officials. More importantly, it would seem that collective world action of this sort would be both more appropriate in the *Pinochet* case, and indeed the most effective means of dealing with the issue.

Alternatively, it may sometimes be appropriate for individual countries to come to grips with their own past so as to create a sense of moral redress while maintaining political stability. Examples surface, including Chile itself. Following Pinochet's time in power, the newly-elected democratic government appointed a Commission for Truth and Reconciliation, consisting of eight civilians of varying political persuasions under the chairmanship of Don Raul Rettig. Their remit was to investigate all violations of human rights between 1973 and 1990, and to make recommendations in relation thereto. The Commission reported its findings in February 1991. The notion of such commissions has since gained popularity, the most celebrated of which was the Commission for Truth and Reconciliation set up in South Africa. In the past many of these commissions have had the blessing of the UN, as a means of helping to restore peace and stability in the country in question. Another approach has been to declare an amnesty in relation to human rights abuses. For example, an amnesty was declared at the end of the Franco-Algerian War in 1962. Similarly, in 1971 India and Bangladesh agreed not to pursue charges of genocide against Pakistan troops accused of killing some one million East Pakistanis. Other general amnesties have been declared in other countries throughout the world, especially in South America.

CONCLUSION

The House of Lords' decision will invariably be noted by heads of state and former heads of state. To some extent the ruling may he heralded by human rights activists as a step towards bringing unsavoury leaders to trial. But the actions and practices of all leaders, even those promoting humanitarian causes, will come under scrutiny. A recent example relates to the NATO air campaign against the Federal Republic of Yugoslavia. It could be argued that NATO's campaign had no basis in international law and therefore its air attacks were, strictly speaking, "illegal". Some would circumvent this argument by stating that the attacks were justified on humanitarian grounds. But a quick purview of international law reveals no apparent "right" to humanitarian intervention. Indeed, NATO officials were cautious not to claim such a "right" themselves. Instead they pointed to the political need to prevent maverick states from exercising their will against the general consensus of the Western alliance. Whether they were morally right (a judgment) or not, NATO could be construed by Serbia to have committed barbarous acts against its citizenry. As a result, Serbia may well decide to hold the heads of state of the various NATO countries at the time of the air campaign, liable for crimes against humanity. Whether or not such an action would succeed in the end is secondary at this point. The main point is that eventually all of these NATO allies will become former heads of state. Based on the House of Lords' ruling, in such a scenario the United Kingdom would be impelled to hear the case in the first instance and, in addition, a persuasive precedent has now been set which means immunity as former head of state is doubtful under international law.

Other comparable instances are sure to arise as well. For instance, in relation to the Gulf War, a request might be made for former US President Bush to be extradited to Iraq for his role in the attacks. Similarly, the extradition of former Prime Minister Margaret (Baroness) Thatcher might be requested by Argentina, on the grounds of her role in the Falklands War. That is not to say that heads of state and former heads of state should have a *carte blanche* to do whatever they wish and not be held responsible for their actions in any way at all. It is to say that hitherto under international law they have enjoyed immunity and have been led to believe that they could be immune from extradition orders of this nature. This may no longer be the case.

If universal consensus today is that such leaders should be held accountable for alleged human rights abuses and crimes, including torture, then it is incumbent on the international community to take the lead and initiate the necessary steps to achieve this aim. They should agree and implement laws to this effect. It should not be left to individual states to become the human rights police of the world. It should be a collective and collaborative effort at the international level. One could argue that the Convention on Torture seeks to achieve this end. It is the collective will of the world, an international treaty to deter torture. As a result, people, such as Senator Pinochet, should be tried pursuant to it for his alleged crimes. On the other hand, it must be stated that had world opinion wanted former heads of state, such as Senator Pinochet, to stand trial, then it should have specified these aims in clear and unambiguous language within the provisions of the Convention.

Perhaps the notion of sovereign/state immunity is an old-fashioned, outdated, antiquated concept. Perhaps it is time to redefine it within a modern-day, international legal context. But, that is exactly the point. If nothing else, the *Pinochet* case calls for increased clarity in the law both in municipal and international fora. Whilst the *Pinochet* case may be forgotten, many questions relating to state immunity remain. This essay has argued that it is now up to the UN to clarify the intent of the law and to take the necessary action to provide clear and unambiguous guidance in this area of law and practice. Conventions which apply to former heads of state should state so expressly and unambiguously. Moreover, individual member states must mirror this clarity in their respective domestic legislation. They must specify the intent of the law and the penalties for violations thereof. In addition, if it is truly the will of the international community that those accused of torture should stand trial, as in the case of *Pinochet*, then, giving effect to this will, should be delegated to an international tribunal. The UN should ask Chile to extradite the senator in order to stand trial for his alleged crimes. It is not for one state to take unilateral action, as Spain sought to do.

7

Pinochet and the Administration of International Criminal Justice

BEN CHIGARA

INTRODUCTION

The purpose of international law from the very beginning has been the regulation of the rights and duties of states. States are the fundamental or primary subjects of the international legal system. Cassese[1] writes that they are the backbone of the international community, so that if they should disappear, present international society would either fall apart or change radically. Because statehood rides upon notions of sovereign independence and self-determination, it is neither intended nor desirable that there should be a legal superior in the international legal process. Though they may not be equal socially, states are legal equals,[2] and, the international legal system ought to reflect this.[3] For this reason, fundamental principles of international law, which include the principles of sovereign equality of states, prohibition of the threat or use of force, non-intervention in the internal or external affairs of other states, the peaceful settlement of disputes, international co-operation, good-faith and respect for human rights, support and maintain the power of the state. Yet in Pinochet 3[4] it was the apparent pursuit of the principle of respect for human rights, despite a tension with other substantive principles listed above, that triggered debate on the coherence of international law.

In the United Kingdom at least, the Pinochet case[5] has foregrounded several issues regarding this principle. One of them is the role of independent sovereign states in the administration of international criminal justice. Because Pinochet is charged with crimes allegedly committed while head of state, this case raises the

---

[1] International Law in a Divided World (Clarendon Press Oxford,1994) p 74; see also D Parry, "The Function of Law in the International Community" in M Sorensen (ed), Manual of Public International Law (Macmillan, 1968) p 1.

[2] For a lucid consideration of this phenomenon, see M Byers, Custom, Power and the Power of Rules (Cambridge University Press, 1999).

[3] See M Dixon, International Law (Blackstone, 1998) p 2; L Henkin, "How Nations Behave" (1965) 114 Recueil Des Cours, p 175.

[4] R v. Bow Street Metropolitan Stipendiary Magistrate and Others, ex parte Pinochet Ugarte (No 3) [1999] 2 WLR 827.

[5] Ibid.

question of whether the strategy of one state (Chile), for dealing with its past by granting amnesty for crimes against humanity,[6] could be challenged legally by another state (Spain) in order to punish those crimes. It also rehearses, on a practical level, the immense difficulties which arise where the state (Spain), zealous to try crimes against humanity, can only reach the person accused (Chile's Pinochet) by invoking against a third state (United Kingdom) the international law duty to either punish or extradite the accused person to their own jurisdiction. While upholding the common view that there exists universal jurisdiction for crimes against humanity,[7] by which states can try in their national courts persons alleged to have committed crimes against humanity, this writer argues that the *Pinochet* case indicates, first, that a state which, for whatever reason, grants amnesty to persons, who would otherwise be charged with crimes against humanity, should register such an amnesty with the United Nations, to ensure the acceptance or acquiescence by other states of that decision; and secondly, that international crimes should at all times be tried by international tribunals. The essay assesses the place in international law of national amnesties as a mechanism by which a state may choose to deal with an uncomfortable immediate past with the hope of securing a future that is entirely different and which marks a new stage in the nation's history.

THE LEGAL BASIS OF PROCEEDINGS AGAINST SENATOR PINOCHET UGARTE

The arrest in London on 16 October 1998 of Senator Pinochet under a provisional warrant issued by a metropolitan stipendiary magistrate pursuant to section 8(1) of the Extradition Act 1989[8] was triggered by the issue on the same day in Madrid of an international warrant of arrest. On 22 October 1998, a second section 8(1) warrant was issued upon receipt of a second international warrant of arrest issued by the Spanish Court alleging that during his rule of Chile, between 1973 and 1990, Senator Pinochet Ugarte had ordered his officials to commit acts of torture and of hostage taking.[9] Thus, Senator Pinochet was alleged to have breached norms of international law founded on customary international law, conventions and treaties. At least one of these norms, namely the prohibition of torture "has evolved into a peremptory norm of *jus cogens*, that is, a norm that enjoys a higher rank in the international hierarchy than treaty law and even 'ordinary customary' rules".[10] The seriousness of norms of

---

[6] Not an uncommon way of dealing with atrocities committed in the transition from oppressive rule to democratic rule. Chile, South Africa, Guatemala, El Salvador and Haiti are recent examples. In support of this approach in third-world countries, see A Cassese, "Reflections on International Criminal Justice" (1998) 61 *Modern Law Review* 1, p 1 at 3.

[7] J Birkett, "International Legal Theories Evolved at Nuremberg" (1947) 23 *International Affairs*, pp 317–25; B F Smith, *Reaching Judgment at Nuremberg* (Basic Books Inc, New York, 1977).

[8] This Act gives effect to the European Convention on Extradition (ETS No 24, Paris, 13 December 1957).

[9] *Pinochet 3*, n 4 supra, at 834; Annex, p 203.

[10] Per Lord Browne-Wilkinson, ibid at 841; Annex, p 209.

jus cogens has been underlined in various places. The Vienna Convention on the Law of Treaties (1969),[11] itself a definitive guide on the codification of norms of international law, is perhaps the best place to look for guidance on the quality of such norms. It provides in Article 53 that:

> A treaty is void, if, at the time of its conclusion, it conflicts with a peremptory norm of general international law. For the purposes of the present Convention, a peremptory norm of general international law is a norm accepted and recognised by the international community of States as a whole as a norm from which no derogation is permitted and which can be modified only by a subsequent norm of general international law having the same character.

Article 64 adds: "If a new peremptory norm of general international law emerges, any existing treaty which is in conflict with that norm becomes void and terminates".

This special character of norms of *jus cogens* justifies the views of Lord Millett and Lord Phillips that, "[t]he systematic use of torture was an international crime for which there could be no immunity even before the Convention came into effect and consequently there is no immunity under customary international law for the offences relating to torture alleged against the applicant".[12] Their Lordships' view is shared also by the judges of the Spanish National Court Criminal Division who held in a Plenary Session of 5 November 1998 that "Spain is competent to judge the events by virtue of the principle of universal prosecution for certain crimes—a category of international law—established by our internal legislation".[13]

The two treaties most applicable to this case, the Convention against Torture and Other Cruel, Inhuman or Degrading Treatment or Punishment (1984), which came into force on 26 June 1987,[14] and the International Convention Against the Taking of Hostages (1979), which came into force in 1983,[15] both authorise states to adopt measures for their enforcement. By Article 2 of the Convention Against Torture, each state-party is obligated to take effective legislative, administrative, judicial or other measures to prevent acts of torture in any territory under its jurisdiction. This same provision rules out, as a justification of torture, any exceptional circumstances whatsoever, whether a state of war or a threat of war, internal political instability or any other public emergency. Moreover, an order from a superior officer or a public authority may not be invoked as a justification of torture. More importantly, perhaps, for the purposes of this discussion, by Article 5(1) each state party shall take such measures as may be necessary to establish its jurisdiction over the offences referred to in

---

[11] The Vienna Convention on The Law Of Treaties (23 May 1969, UN Doc A/Conf 39/27; UKTS 58 (1980) Cmnd 7964.

[12] *Pinochet 3*, n 4 supra, at 829; Annex, p 277.

[13] R v. *Bow Street Metropolitan Stipendiary Magistrate and Others, ex parte Pinochet Ugarte*, [1998] 3 WLR 1456 at 1463; Annex, p 138.

[14] GA Res 39/46, annex, 39 UN GAOR Supp (No 51) at 197, UN Doc A/39/51 (1984).

[15] UKTS 81 (1983) Cmnd; ILM (1979) 18, p 1456.

Article 4 in cases: (a) when the offences are committed in any territory under its jurisdiction or on board a ship or aircraft registered that state; (b) when the alleged offender is a national of that state; and (c) when the victim is a national of that state if that state considers it appropriate.

It is not uncommon for international conventions and treaties to delegate enforcement of their norms to national legal systems. Section 134 of the Criminal Justice Act 1988 brings this Convention into English law.[16] This is consistent with the intention and purpose of the said convention. As noted by Lord Browne-Wilkinson,[17] the *jus cogens* nature of the international crime of torture justifies states in taking universal jurisdiction over torture wherever committed. Offences *jus cogens* may be punished by any state because the offenders are common enemies of all mankind and all nations have an equal interest in their apprehension and prosecution. One of the purposes of the Convention Against Torture was to introduce the principle *aut dedere aut punire*, that is, either you extradite or you punish perpetrators of torture.[18] Therefore international crimes of this type, which Senator Pinochet is alleged to have committed, can legitimately be considered in national jurisdictions, including Spain and the United Kingdom.

The Taking of Hostages Convention (1979)[19] grants to states similar authority,[20] providing that each state-party shall take such measures as may be necessary to establish its jurisdiction over any of the offences listed[21] and over an alleged offender, present in its territory, whom it does not extradite to any of the other party-states.[22] The Convention[23] also enjoins states to co-operate in the prevention of the offences by: (a) taking all practicable measures to prevent preparations in their respective territories for the commission of those offences within or outside their territories, including measures to prohibit in their territories illegal activities of persons, groups and organisations that encourage, instigate, organise or engage in the perpetration of acts of taking of hostages; and (b) exchanging information and co-ordinating the taking of administrative and other measures as appropriate to prevent the commission of those offences. The Convention is given effect in the United Kingdom by the Taking of Hostages Act 1982.[24] The co-operation of states is recognised in the Convention itself as the primary *modus operandi* for its enforcement. Thus Spain's engage-

---

[16] For commentary see D J Harris, *Cases and Materials on International Law* (5th edn, Sweet and Maxwell, 1998) pp 715–9; D McGoldrick, *The Human Rights Committee: Its Role in the Development of the International Covenant on Civil and Political Rights* (Clarendon Press Oxford, 1991) pp 362–82.

[17] *Pinochet 3*, n 4 supra, at 841; Annex, p 210.

[18] Ibid, at 843; Annex, p 211.

[19] UN Doc A/C6/34/L23, 4 December 1979.

[20] See Harris, n 16 supra, p300.

[21] Article 5(1); offences are set out in Article 1, as are the states who are a party to the Convention.

[22] Ibid, Article 5 (2) and see also Article 5(2) of the Convention Against Torture (1984).

[23] Ibid, Article 4.

[24] See Harris, n 16 supra, p 300.

ment of the United Kingdom, in an effort that partly seeks to enforce the said Convention, appears legitimate. This legitimacy is reinforced by the extradition arrangements between the two countries.[25]

Thus, Senator Pinochet faces charges which include not only violation of rules of *jus cogens* but also of Conventional rules, to which both the United Kingdom and Spain are party, and which the United Kingdom has brought into domestic law. Not only does international law allow states to exercise a universal jurisdiction over offences *jus cogens*, but the specific treaty obligations of the United Kingdom require it to establish such a jurisdiction to be exercised as an alternative to extradition for the offence of torture.

INDIVIDUAL RESPONSIBILITY UNDER THE INTERNATIONAL LEGAL SYSTEM

It is clear from the intention and purpose of the conventions upon which the charges against Senator Pinochet are based that international law now also regulates the rights and duties of individuals. As stated by Lord Browne-Wilkinson:

The jurisdiction being established by the Torture Convention and the Hostages Convention is one where existing domestic Courts of all the countries are being authorised and required to take jurisdiction internationally.[26]

Although being developed with new vigour, the liability of individuals in international law is well established. The first such trial recorded is the fifteenth century trial at Bresach of a war criminal accused of trampling underfoot the laws of God and humanity[27]—the equivalent of the modern day charge of crimes against humanity, for which there is universal jurisdiction to try suspects.[28] The Nuremberg proceedings,[29] for all their weaknesses, especially the common charge of victors' justice,[30] affirmed that same principle that individuals who breach international criminal law shall be made to answer in a court of law for those breaches. In recent times tribunals have been established to try persons alleged to have committed grave breaches of international law. These include the tribunals for war crimes committed in the former Yugoslavia,[31] resident in The Hague, and for war crimes committed in and around Rwanda, resident in Arusha, Tanzania.[32] The purpose of these tribunals is to hear cases against individuals accused of violating international criminal law.

[25] The European Convention on Extradition binds the two countries to co-operate on this subject.

[26] *Pinochet 3*, n 4 supra, at 847; Annex, p 215.

[27] See Birkett, n 7 supra, p 317.

[28] Per Lord Browne-Wilkinson, *Pinochet 3*, n 4 supra, at 843; Annex, p 211.

[29] Judgment of the Nuremberg International Military Tribunal (1947) 41 *American Journal of International Law*, p 172.

[30] See generally Smith, *Reaching Judgment at Nuremberg* (Basic Books Inc., New York, 1977).

[31] Annexe to Security Council Resolution 827 (1993) 32 *International Legal Materials*, p 1203.

[32] Security Council resolution 955 (1994) 33 *International Legal Materials*, p 1600.

On 7 May 1997 the International Tribunal for the Prosecution of Persons Responsible for Serious Violations of International Humanitarian Law Committed in the Territory of the former Yugoslavia since 1991 (ICTY), found Dusko Tadic, a citizen of the former Yugoslavia, who was of Serb ethnic descent and a resident of the Republic of Bosnia and Herzegovina at the time of the alleged crimes, guilty of crimes against humanity under Article 5 of the Statute of the International Tribunal. These included "persecution", "inhumane acts" and violations of the laws or customs of war under Article 3 of the Statute, including the "cruel treatment" of civilians contrary to Article 3 common to the Geneva Conventions of 12 August 1949.[33] Subsequently, on appeal to the Tribunal's Appeals Chamber, on 15 July 1999 Dusko Tadic was found guilty on nine additional counts of grave breaches of international criminal law,[34] namely, wilful killing, torture or inhuman treatment, wilfully causing great suffering or serious injury to body or health, and murder.

The pursuit by international law of individuals who participate in international crimes is further demonstrated by the Statute of the International Criminal Tribunal for Rwanda, (ICTR),[35] Article 6(1) of which provides:

> A person who planned, instigated, ordered, committed or otherwise aided and abetted in the planning, preparation or execution of a crime referred to in articles 2 to 4 of the present Statute, shall be individually responsible for the crime.

In the Tribunal's jurisprudence, this means that in addition to responsibility as principal perpetrator, a person accused of such breaches of international criminal law can be held responsible for the criminal acts of others where he plans with them, instigates them, orders them or aids and abets them to commit those acts.[36] The parallel with Senator Pinochet is clear.[37] Thus, Article 6(1) covers various stages of the commission of a crime, ranging from its initial planning through its organisation to its execution. This is consistent with the view of the International Law Commission which, in the Draft Code of Crimes Against the Peace and Security of Mankind,[38] reaffirmed the principle of individual respon-

---

[33] *Prosecutor v. Tadic* (1997) 4 *International Human Rights Reports* 645; *International Legal Materials* 36 (1997) 908.

[34] A press release (Communiqué de presse) of 15 July 1999 TH/ PIS/ 419–e.

[35] The Tribunal was established by the United Nations Security Council by its resolution 955 of 8 November 1994. Resolution 955 charges all states with a duty to co-operate fully with the Tribunal and its organs in accordance with the Statute of the Tribunal, and to take any measures necessary under their domestic law to implement the provisions of the Statute, including compliance with requests for assistance or orders issued by the Tribunal . Subsequently, by its resolution 978 of 27 February 1995, the Security Council "urge[d] the States to arrest and detain, in accordance with their national law and relevant standards of international law, pending prosecution by the International Tribunal for Rwanda or by the appropriate national authorities, persons found within their territory against whom there is sufficient evidence that they were responsible for acts within the jurisdiction of the International Tribunal for Rwanda".

[36] See Tribunal's judgment *in Prosecutor v. Jean-Paul Akayesu*,Case No ICTR–96–4–T Decision of 2 September 1998.

[37] *Pinochet 3*, n 4 supra, at 834; Annex, p 203.

[38] Article 2(3).

sibility for the five forms of participation deemed criminal by Article 6(1) of the Statute of the ICTR,[39] as outlined above, and, with the exception of aiding and abetting, which is akin to complicity and therefore implies a principal offence, consistently included the phrase "which in fact occurs". In this respect, the International Criminal Tribunal for the former Yugoslavia (ICTY) found in the Tadic case[40] that:

> A person may only be criminally responsible for conduct where it is determined that he knowingly participated in the commission of an offence . . . [and] . . . his partici- pation directly and substantially affected the commission of that offence through sup- porting the actual commission before, during, or after the incident.

According to the ICTR, this intent can be inferred from a certain number of facts, as concerns genocide, crimes against humanity and war crimes, including for instance, their massive and/or systematic nature or their atrocity.[41] Jean- Paul Akayesu was on 2 September 1998 found guilty on nine counts of genocide and crimes against humanity and sentenced to life imprisonment by Trial Chamber I of the ICTR.[42] Other people convicted of similar crimes by the ICTR include the former Prime Minister, Jean Kambanda.[43] Taking the work of these two tribunals together, it is clear that:

> For international conduct which is so serious as to be tainted with criminality to be regarded as attributable only to the personal State and not to individuals who ordered or perpetrated it is both unrealistic and offensive to common notions of justice. The idea that individuals who commit international crimes are internationally accountable for them has now become an accepted part of international law.[44]

The adoption on 17 July 1999 in Rome by 120 states of the Statute of the International Criminal Court[45] is clear evidence that the international commu- nity wants persons who breach norms of international criminal law to respond to the charges preferred against them in a court of law. In addition, by adopting

---

[39] Article 6 provides that: (1) A person who planned, instigated, ordered, committed or otherwise aided and abetted in the planning, preparation or execution of a crime referred to in Articles 2 to 4 of the present Statute, shall be individually responsible for the crime. (2) The official position of any accused person, whether as Head of State or Government or as a responsible Government official, shall not relieve such person of criminal responsibility nor mitigate punishment. (3) The fact that any of the acts referred to in articles 2 to 4 of the present Statute was committed by a subordinate does not relieve his or her superior of criminal responsibility if he or she knew or had reason to know that the subordinate was about to commit such acts or had done so and the superior failed to take the necessary and reasonable measures to prevent such acts or to punish the perpetrators thereof. (4) The fact that an accused person acted pursuant to an order of a Government or of a superior shall not relieve him or her of criminal responsibility, but may be considered in mitigation of punishment if the International Tribunal for Rwanda determines that justice so requires.

[40] (1997) 36 *International Legal Materials* 908.

[41] *Prosecutor v. Jean-Paul Akayesu*, n 36 supra.

[42] http://www.ictr.org.

[43] *Prosecutor v. Jean Kambanda*, Case No ICTR–97–23–I.

[44] Per Lord Browne-Wilkinson, (citing Sir Arthur Watts) *Pinochet 3*, n 4 supra, at 846; Annex, p 214.

[45] For commentary see D Sarooshi, "The Statute of the International Criminal Court" (1999) 48 *International and Comparative Law Quarterly* 2 at 387.

the Convention setting up the International Criminal Court, the international community demonstrated that it preferred allegations of breaches of international criminal law to have a legal rather than a political resolution. The existence of a permanent court for these purposes has several advantages. One is that because of its singular and particular procedure,[46] litigants will not endure prolonged periods of procedural or substantive uncertainty, often witnessed when two, or several, national legal systems combine to deal with a case. Another is that of predictability. A steady jurisprudence will shorten the time taken to resolve cases because both the prosecution and defence attorneys will have previous cases of the same court to guide them.

The problems accompanying any effort to bring together the national laws of two states, for the purpose of enforcing international standards, has exercised the judiciary in both Spain and Britain in *Pinochet*. The first extradition application by Spain proved deficient because it failed to meet the requirement that the crimes for which Spain wanted Senator Pinochet Ugarte extradited had to be crimes under English law at the material time.[47] This illegality would have provided useful evidence to those commentators who view this case as a political trial that violates the international law rule that no sovereign state can adjudicate on the conduct of a foreign state.[48] A second application had to be made within days of the said discovery.[49] However this episode is interpreted, it makes clear that the interaction of any pair of legal systems for the purpose of enforcing international criminal law, can set off substantive hurdles whose crossing might jeopardise public perception of the purpose of the whole process. This is important in jurisdictions such as ours, which honour the principle that justice must not only be done, but it must also be seen to be done.

Thus, Senator Pinochet faces charges which the international community has shown an increasing willingness to resolve through international juridical bodies. There are advantages to resolution at this level, rather than at the domestic level discussed in the preceding section. Kelsen thought that the punishment of international crimes by an international tribunal, "and particularly the punishment of crimes which have the character of acts of State", would certainly meet with much less resistance than national punishment because it would not hurt national feelings as much.[50] Linked to this emotional welfare of state consideration, is the ability of international judges to investigate crimes with ramifications in many States more easily than national judges.[51]

---

[46] On jurisdiction, admissibility and applicable law, see Articles 5–21. On composition and administration of the Court, see Articles 34–52. On investigation and prosecution, see Articles 53–61. On trial and penalties, see Articles 62–80.

[47] *Pinochet 3*, n 4 supra, at 836–8; Annex, pp 205–8.

[48] Ibid, at 844; Annex, p 212.

[49] Ibid, at 834; Annex, p 203.

[50] Quoted in Cassese, "Reflections on International Criminal Justice", n 6 supra, p 7.

[51] Ibid, p 8.

STATE PRACTICE ON THE RESOLUTION OF OFFENCES *JUS COGENS*

Against this activity of domestic and international bodies to try these charges, and the individual liability of those accused of such offences, there must be regard for the specific context of the civil life of Chile. The removal of Senator Pinochet and the army from the civil administration of Chile, and the restoration of civilian rule, was part of a process that also sought to envelop and cater for potential legal repercussions against the outgoing military government or its members—a political settlement.[52] That settlement contained a precarious balancing act. On the one hand, it granted to the head of the military, General Pinochet, a constitutionally recognised life senatorship of Chile,[53] something that Gareton[54] regards as "an act of great symbolic violence against an as yet incomplete democratisation process". Perhaps Gareton does not properly consider that such were the first steps towards the process of restoring democracy to Chile, and the sequence of events that he would have preferred was not favoured by the practical reality of Chile at that time. On the other hand, a commission was set up to establish how many Chileans had disappeared, following the military coup against President Salvador Allende's Government in September 1973. Again the motive behind this development is not certain, especially because the settlement had previously conferred on the military immunity from prosecution for acts done during its reign.[55] The paradox that this settlement created has been helpfully summarised in the following manner:

> according to surveys, through the last eight years of democratic rule about 70% of Chileans have considered that violations of human rights under the dictatorship should be clarified or punished, and feel frustration because it has not happened. They are of course not willing to risk a regression concerning what they have conquered so far, but they do not see any risk of that in Pinochet's detention and, though they preferred that justice be meted out in Chile, regarded its application in a foreign country with approval, recognising the impossibility of pursuing it at home.[56]

Such frustration is almost always bound to result where political settlements extend immunity from prosecution to people alleged to have committed grave breaches of international criminal law. The question which, between justice, revenge, amnesia and amnesty the international community should pursue in such situations does not find an easy answer. Justice denied or delayed may create in the victims' psyche an almost insatiable desire for revenge. The massacre on 24 July of fourteen Serb farmers in Kosovo, the worst incident since NATO

[52] G Hawthorn, "Pinochet: the Politics" (1999) 75 *International Affairs* 2, p 253.
[53] Ibid.
[54] M A Gareton, "Chile 1997–1998: The Revenge of Incomplete Democratisation" (1999) 75 *International Affairs* 2, p 261.
[55] Though some of the decisions of the courts allow investigations to be made into human rights violations which occurred under the military regime, even by-passing the amnesty law itself. See Gareton, ibid p 262.
[56] Ibid, p 263.

peacekeepers were deployed in the troubled region,[57] probably reflects this. Justice and revenge have been helpfully differentiated in the following manner:

> Revenge is undoubtedly a primitive form of justice—a private system of law enforcement. It has, however, an altogether different foundation from justice—an implacable logic of hatred and retaliation. . . . As the history of the Armenian genocide illustrates, when there is no justice in response to the extermination of a people, the result is that victims are led to take the law into their own hands, both to exact retribution and to draw attention to the denied historical fact.[58]

But amnesties, including the Senator Pinochet political settlement type, are common-place. At Zimbabwe's independence in 1980, President Mugabe's public policy of reconciliation served to anaesthetise and confine under the carpet of amnesia grave breaches of international criminal law by both warring factions, during the sixteen-year civil war between Ian Smith's Government and the liberation movements led by Joshua Nkomo and Robert Mugabe. The hope was that forgetting about the past would catalyse the transition to a more peaceful and prosperous future for all the peoples of Zimbabwe. Optimists would say that in the event, the amnesia effect worked to great effect, and perhaps they are right. But to the dismay of others, the fate of many, including Edison Sithole, a brilliant and much liked black lawyer who disappeared mysteriously, remains unknown.[59] The case for privileging juridical resolutions of violations of international criminal law over political amnesties was in the event made more apparent by the subsequent murder of a white farmer and the trial for that murder of Edgar Tekere, a member of President Mugabe's cabinet. In his defence, Tekere, himself a former detainee, argued, among other things, that the victim of the murder had personally been responsible for torturing black detainees during the civil war.

AMNESTIES AND INTERNATIONAL LAW

Are amnesties for breaches of international criminal law consistent with international law? Orentlicher is a fervent proponent of the view that amnesties are contrary to international law.[60] Cassese[61] distinguishes between situations where amnesties will be exceptional in international law, and situations where they will contradict it. Exceptional cases include situations like 1980 Zimbabwe, 1993 South Africa and 1990 Chile, where the nation is engaged in the process of

---

[57] J Strauss, "Jackson Orders Manhunt after Massacre of Serb Families" (1999) *The Sunday Telegraph* 25 July 1999, p 1.

[58] Cassese, n 6 supra, p 1; and see Hendrick (Chapter Five in this collection) for discussion on justice.

[59] D Martin and P Johnson, *The Struggle for Zimbabwe* (Zimbabwe Publishing House, Harare, 1981) p 206.

[60] "Settling Accounts: the Duty to Prosecute Human Rights Violations of a Prior Regime" (1991) 100 *Yale Law Journal* 2537.

[61] Cassese, n 6 supra, pp 3–5.

freeing itself from a regime of terror and undergoing a transition to democracy. He writes that amnesty and truth commissions are favourable when the society in question is too fragile to survive the destabilising effects of politically charged trials, noting, "There is need to empty wounds of all the old infection before healing can start. But in some countries, like Angola and Mozambique, I'm not sure you'd have anything left if you cleaned out all the infection".[62] Cases of amnesties, which are outrightly contrary to international law, include situations like the former Yugoslavia, where the society is:

> still riven by, and built on, ethnic divisions and where the perpetrators of atrocities still preach the gospel of ethnic separation, or for a society such as that of Rwanda where ethnic hatred still persists and the victims of genocide, or their relatives, demand that the culprits be duly punished.[63]

More recently, the work of South Africa's Truth and Reconciliation Commission bears the same trademark of granting amnesty to people who would otherwise be liable for grave breaches of international criminal law. El Salvador, Guatemala and Argentina have all utilised this approach in dealing with their immediate past.

The hope in all these cases is that these amnesties will capture and harness the national mood and psyche to positively imagine and recast a better future for the good of the country. But do amnesties have this talisman effect? Often they depict serious, genuine and desperate efforts by affected states to establish normality. The perceived opportunity for peace and tranquillity is sometimes used as a justification for privileging the amnesia effect over the juridical process. A zealous pursuit for justice becomes extravagance. The long nightmare cannot transform into a new dawn unless some sacrifice has been made. But to forget the executed, deported, tortured, orphaned and those who disappeared boarders on a kind of recklessness that only serves to embolden would-be tyrants of the future. For this reason, it has been argued that in situations where the trial of individuals, alleged to have committed grave breaches of international criminal law, is likely to disrupt the emerging national fabric, the answer lies not in opting for political amnesties, but the creation of an international tribunal which "could conduct the work at a distance—both physical and political—from destabilising national forces".[64] This has the added advantage of answering those who often argue that international criminal law is applied selectively when opportunity permits, and using only small and poor states as targets.[65] International law has a long history of subjecting to criminal arbitration those alleged to have breached international criminal law.[66] There is nothing to recommend that this standard should suddenly be compromised. Providing

---

[62] Ibid, p 4, quoting a US State Department official.
[63] Ibid.
[64] Ibid, p 3.
[65] Talking of the new international politics based on opportunism, arbitrariness and the seizing of the political moment, see among others, Hawthorn, n 52 supra, pp 254–7.
[66] Ibid.

Senator Pinochet with a chance to answer in a court of law the grave breaches of international law alleged against him, has the benefit of stopping victims of his alleged crimes from resorting to revenge, and of recording finally the crimes of which he is accused. Moreover, whatever the outcome of such a trial, the (international community would also have demonstrated that it will not give way to individuals who violate norms of international criminal law.)

But if Senator Pinochet were extradited and tried for the crimes alleged against him by the Spanish courts, the political settlement, as a legal contract, which saw Chile's return to civilian rule, would have been breached, even fraudulently. This fact is acknowledged in the effort by the Chilean Government to impede the extradition proceedings in London, first, by pleading immunity on behalf of Senator Pinochet—a diplomatic effort, and, second, by applying to be enjoined as a party to the proceedings in London—a juridical effort.[67] In reliance upon the constitutionally recognised promise of immunity from prosecution for events that took place in Chile while he was head of government, General, now Senator, Pinochet preferred a civilian administration to his military one. Could it be said that contractually, the doctrine of estoppel—which requires that where A has by his words or conduct justified B in believing that a certain state of facts exists, and B has acted upon such belief to his prejudice, A is not permitted to affirm against B that a different state of facts existed at the same time[68]—could now be invoked correctly as a shield and not sword, to require Chile to prevent extradition to Spain of Senator Pinochet ?

The political settlement of 1990 was very much a contract recorded in the constitution itself. That international criminal law is now set to supersede this internal agreement between the civilian government of Chile (as representative of the people of Chile) and the military would suggest that national amnesties are always subject to acceptance by the international community. But if they are, does it mean also that unilaterally, international law can alter the *grundnorm*[69] of any member-state of the United Nations? Kelsen[70] foresaw the possibility of a change of the basic norm through constitutional means, i.e. as stipulated in the constitution itself. He also accepted that political uprisings, including a *coup d'état*, might result in a new basic norm. It is questionable that national constitutions can be altered/changed by unilateral intervention of international law. It has to be said that as a monist, Kelsen thought that international law occupied a higher level in the hierarchy of norms. But that is not to say that he privileged international law over domestic law.

---

[67] See Lord Browne-Wilkinson's judgment, *Pinochet 3*, n 4 supra, at 836; Annex, p 204.
[68] Per Lord Birkenhead in *Maclaine* v. *Gatty* [1921] 1 AC 376, at 386.
[69] German for constitution. Also referred to as the basic norm.
[70] See H Kelsen, *The General Theory of Law and State* (3rd edn, Harvard University Press Massachusetts, 1949).

CONCLUSION

This essay considered international law's response to the way states respond to violations of criminal international law by previous governments, their agents or individual citizens. State practice has been shown to vary. Sometimes states go for political settlements involving the granting of amnesty to previous governments, its agents or individuals who would otherwise be charged with breaches of criminal international law. Sometimes states opt for a juridical resolution which results in the trial by a court of those accused of breaches of criminal international law. There are no clear indicators for when a political settlement applies though cases where they have occurred abound. These cases are so dissimilar that it is not easy to draw from them an indicative list of such determinants. Parallel to these are juridical settlement cases. It is not clear what sets these two cases apart. What is unquestionable though is the international community's commitment to punish those cases that it regards as imperative juridical settlement type. International law's universal jurisdiction for crimes against humanity makes it possible for all countries to claim jurisdiction over charges of breach of criminal international law. Indeed states have a duty to punish perpetrators of crimes against humanity or to extradite them.

Where a nation takes the latter approach, the risk is that instead of extinguishing the smouldering cycle of violence and hatred, the trial of members of a former government, or its agents, or individuals who sympathised with it, may rekindle unrest. National judges involved in such trials may not easily be perceived to be impartial, both in their investigations and in their verdicts, because of their closeness to the social and political milieu that they now seek to preside over. Thus, it might be said that the political settlement that brought to an end Senator Pinochet's rule of Chile attempted to forestall such a dilemma by granting to him amnesty for acts done while the military government was in power. However, such political settlements do not address the effects of violations of criminal international law beyond the boundaries of the afflicted nation. Yet breaches of criminal international law affect both the national and international psyches, which is why international law recognises universal jurisdiction for crimes *jus cogens*, and orders states to either punish offenders or extradite them to those willing to punish them.

This writer shares the view that international crimes are best dealt with by international tribunals rather than national courts. A compelling reason, vindicated also in the current *Pinochet* proceedings in the United Kingdom, is that of national pride. To try in the national courts of Spain or Britain, a Chilean citizen for breaches of criminal international law in his own country may offend Chile's national pride and stir emotional resentment of Chileans. The relative success and international approval of the work of the ICTY and the ICTR, suggests that complaints about national pride being offended do not arise when nationals are tried for breaches of criminal international law by an international tribunal. Therefore, the establishment of the International Criminal Court is a welcome development.

Nonetheless, the *Pinochet* case confirms that far from being hollow and inadequate, international law in general, and criminal international law in particular, affects international life so as to punish offences *jus cogens.* It affirms the international will to deny offenders the opportunity to hide behind state immunity and state sovereignty for individual acts inconsistent with appropriate state behaviour. Explicitly, it makes clear that the doctrine of state immunity applies to exonerate from prosecution heads of states or former heads of states only for those of their acts that properly fall into the category of "official duties". Their official duties properly construed exclude the commission of crimes which international law prescribes against by way of customary international law, convention or *jus cogens*.[71]

Because there appears no other valid defence against the extradition of Senator Pinochet to Spain, than that the political settlement of 1990 promised him immunity from any such charges, indirectly this case points to a gap in the development of international law at this stage. This gap lies between what states can legitimately do in their own right by means of granting amnesties, which deliver political settlements, and what they cannot do, because international law can intervene to annul such settlements, and to put on trial those who had helped achieve such settlements. This gap could be addressed by establishing a requirement that all political settlements which seek to erase charges of crimes against humanity against certain individuals must be registered with the UN. Registration of any such amnesty could be initiated in the form of an application by the state granting it. The UN would either ratify the amnesty or reject it, before persons who are subject to them are shocked by being served with warrants of arrest, while on holiday anywhere in the world, or while receiving medical treatment in London.

---

[71] Per Lord Browne-Wilkinson, *Pinochet 3*, n 4 supra, at 846; Annex, p 214.

Bibliography

Aronson, M and Dyer, B, *Judicial Review of Administrative Action* (LBC Information Services, 1996)

Beigbeder, Y, *Judging War Criminals* (Macmillan Press, 1999)

Bell, J, *Policy Arguments in Judicial Decisions* (Clarendon Press, 1983)

Birkett, J, "International Legal Theories Evolved At Nuremberg" (1947) 23 *International Affairs* 317

Black, H C, *Law Dictionary; definitions of the terms and phrases of American and English jurisdictions, ancient and modern* (5th edn, St Paul's, Minnesotta, West Publishing Co, 1979)

Brazier, R, *Constitutional Reform* (2nd edn, OUP, 1998)

Byers, M, *Custom, Power and the Power of Rules* (Cambridge University Press, 1999)

Cassese, A, *International Law in a Divided World* (Clarendon Press, 1994)

—— "Reflections on International Criminal Justice" (1998) 61 *Modern Law Review* 1

Cavdino, M and Dignan, J, *The Penal System: An Introduction* (2nd edn, Sage, 1997)

Craig, P P, *Administrative Law* (3rd edn, Sweet and Maxwell, 1994)

Davis, M, "How Much Punishment Does a Bad Samaritan Deserve?" (1996) 15 *Law and Philosophy* 97

—— *International Law* (Blackstone Press, 1998)

De Smith, Woolf and Jowell, *Judicial Review of Administrative Action* (5th edn, Sweet and Maxwell, 1995)

Dicey, A V, *Introduction to the Study of the Law of the Constitution* (Macmillan, 1967)

Dickson, B and Carmichael, P (eds), *The House of Lords: its Parliamentary and Judicial Roles* (Hart Publishing, 1999)

Dimock, S, "Retributivism and Trust" (1997) 16 *Law and Philosophy* 37

Dixon, M, *International Law* (Blackstone, 1998)

Dolinko, D, "Retributivism, Consequentialism and the Intrinsic Goodness of Punishment" (1997) 16 *Law and Philosophy* 507

Feinberg, J, "What is Legal Punishment?" in Feinberg, J and Gross, H, *Philosophy of Law* (5th edn, Wadsworth, 1995)

—— "What, if Anything, Justifies Legal Punishment? The Classic Debate" in Feinberg, J and Gross, H, *Philosophy of Law* (5th edn, Wadsworth, 1995)

—— and Gross, H, *Philosophy of Law* (5th edn, Wadsworth, 1995)

Feldman, D, "Remedies for Violations of Convention Rights under the Human Rights Act" [1998] *European Human Rights Law Review* 691

—— "The Human Rights Act 1998 and constitutional principles" (1999) 19 *Legal Studies* 165

Fitzpatrick, B, "A Dualist House of Lords in a Sea of Monist Community Law" in Dickson, B and Carmichael, P (eds), *The House of Lords: its Parliamentary and Judicial Roles* (Hart Publishing, 1999)

Gareton, M A, "Chile 1997–1998: The Revenge of Incomplete Democratisation" (1999) 75 *International Affairs* 2 at 259

Hacker, P M S and Raz, J (eds), *Law, Morality and Society: Essays in Honour of H L A Hart* (Clarendon Press, 1997)

Harris, D J, *Cases and Materials on International Law* (5th edn, Sweet and Maxwell, 1998)

Hart, H L A, *Punishment and Responsibility: Essays in the Philosophy of Law* (Clarendon Press, 1968)

Hawthorn, G, "Pinochet: the Politics" (1999) 75 *International Affairs* 2 at 253

Hazell, R, *Constitutional Futures* (OUP, 1999)

Henkin, L, "How Nations Behave" (1965) 114 *Recueil Des Cours* 1 at 175

Hoffmann, Lord, "Human Rights and the House of Lords" (1998) 62 *Modern Law Review* 2 at 166

Honderich, T, *Punishment: The Supposed Justifications* (Polity Press, 1989)

Jacoby, S, "Wild Justice" in Solomon, R and Murphy, M C (eds), *What is Justice? Classic and Contemporary Readings* (OUP, 1990)

Jennings, Sir Robert and Watts, Sir Arthur, *Oppenheim's International Law* (9th edn, 1992)

Kant, I, *The Metaphysical Elements of Justice* (translated by Ladd, J, Indianapolis, Bobbs-Merill, 1965)

Kelsen, H, *The General Theory of Law and State* (3rd edn, Harvard University Press, 1945)

Lacey, N, *State Punishment: Political Principles and Community Values* (Routledge, 1988)

LaFollette, H (ed), *Ethics in Practice: An Anthology* (Blackwell, 1997)

Lucas, R J, *On Justice* (Clarendon Press, 1980)

—— *Responsibility* (Clarendon Press, 1995)

Marens, S, "Opinion: Incorporating the European Convention: The Role of the Judiciary" [1998] 1 *European Human Rights Law Review* 10

Marshall, H H, *Natural Justice* (Sweet and Maxwell, 1959)

Martin, D and Johnson, P, *The Struggle for Zimbabwe* (Zimbabwe Publishing House, Harare, 1981)

Martin, E A (ed), *Oxford Dictionary of Law* (3rd edn, OUP, 1996)

Maxwell, P, "The House of Lords as a Constitutional Court: The Implications of *Ex p EOC*" in Dickson, B and Carmichael, P (eds), *The House of Lords: its Parliamentary and Judicial Roles* (Hart Publishing, 1999)

McGoldrick, D, *The Human Rights Committee: Its Role in the Development of the International Covenant on Civil and Political Rights* (Clarendon Press, 1990)

Meron, T, *War Crimes Law Comes of Age* (Clarendon Press, 1998)

Merrills, J G, *The Development of International Law by the European Court of Human Rights* (2nd edn, Manchester University Press, 1995)

Morowitz, T, *The Philosophy of Law: An Introduction* (Macmillan, 1980)

Morrison, W, *Jurisprudence: From the Greeks to post-modernism* (Cavendish, 1997)

Norrie, A, *Law Ideology and Punishment* (Kluwer, 1991)

Nozick, R, "Retribution and Revenge", *Philosophical Explanations* (Harvard University Press, 1981)

Nuttal, J, *Moral questions: An Introduction to Ethics* (Polity Press, 1993)

Olowofoyeku, A, "State Liability for the Exercise of Judicial Power" [1999] *Public Law* 4

Orentlicher, "Settling Accounts: the Duty to Prosecute Human Rights Violations of a Prior Regime" (1991) 100 *Yale Law Journal* 2537

Pannick, D, *Judges* (OUP, 1988)

Parry, D, "The Function of Law in the International Community", in Sorensen, M (ed), *Manual of Public International Law* (Macmillan, 1968)

Posner, R A, *Overcoming Law* (Massachusetts, Harvard University Press, 1995)

Rachels, J, "Punishment and Desert" in LaFollete, H (ed), *Ethics in Practice: An Anthology* (Blackwell, 1997)

Rawls, J, "Two Concepts of Rules" (1955) 64 *The Philosophical Review* 3

Robertson, D, *Judicial Discretion in the House of Lords* (Clarendon Press, 1998)

Rozenberg, J, "Analysis" [1999] *Public Law* 181

Sarooshi, D, "The Statute of the International Criminal Court" (1999) 48 *International and Comparative Law Quarterly* 2 at 387

Satow, *Guide to Diplomatic Practice* (4th edn, 1957)

Shearer, I A, *Starke's International law* (11th edn, Butterworths, 1994)

Shetreet, S, *Judges on Trial* (North Holland Publishing Company, 1976)

Singer, P (ed), *A Companion Guide to Ethics* (Blackwell, 1991)

Smith, B F, *Reaching Judgment at Nuremberg* (Basic Books Inc., New York, 1977)

Smith, S H and Gunn, M J, *Smith and Bailey on the Modern English Legal System* (3rd edn, Sweet and Maxwell, 1996)

Solomon, R, and Murphy, M (eds), *What Is Justice? Classic and Contemporary Readings* (OUP, 1990)

Stevens, R, *Law and Politics: The House of Lords as a Judicial Body 1800–1976* (Weidenfeldt and Nicholson, 1979)

—— *The Independence of the Judiciary* (OUP, 1993)

Steyn, Lord, "Current Topic: Incorporation and Devolution—A few Reflections on the Changing Scene" [1998] 2 *European Human Rights Law Review* 156

Sykes, E I, Lanham, D J, Tracey, R R S, Esser, K W, *General Principles of Administrative Law* (4th edn, Butterworths, 1997)

Tilmouth, S and Williams, G, "The High Court and the Disqualification of one of its own" (1999) 73 *Australian Law Journal* 72

Tusa, A and Tusa, J, *The Nuremberg Trial* (Papermac, 1983)

Wade, H W R and Forsyth, C F, *Administrative Law* (7th edn, OUP, 1994)

Walker, N, *Why Punish?* (OUP, 1991)

Young, R, "The Implications of Determinism" in Singer, P (ed), *A Companion Guide to Ethics* (Blackwell, 1991)

Annex

Pinochet 1
Pinochet 2
Pinochet 3

HOUSE OF LORDS

Lord Slynn of Hadley   Lord Lloyd of Berwick   Lord Nicholls of Birkenhead
Lord Steyn   Lord Hoffmann

OPINIONS OF THE LORDS OF APPEAL FOR JUDGMENT IN THE CAUSE

Regina v. *Bartle and the Commissioner of Police for the Metropolis and Others*
(appellants)

Ex parte Pinochet (respondent) (on appeal from a Divisional Court of the Queen's
Bench division)

Regina v. *Evans and Another and the Commissioner of Police
for the Metropolis and Others* (appellants)

Ex parte Pinochet (respondent) (on appeal from a Divisional Court of the Queen's
Bench Division)

on 25 November 1998

UNAMENDED

LORD SLYNN OF HADLEY:

My Lords,
   The respondent to this appeal is alleged to have committed or to have been responsible for the commission of the most serious of crimes—genocide, murder on a large scale, torture, the taking of hostages. In the course of 1998, eleven criminal suits have been brought against him in Chile in respect of such crimes. Proceedings have also now been brought in a Spanish court. The Spanish Court has, however, held that it has jurisdiction to try him. In the latter proceedings, none of these specific crimes is said to have been committed by the respondent himself.
   If the question for your Lordships on the appeal were whether these allegations should be investigated by a Criminal Court in Chile or by an international tribunal, the answer, subject to the terms of any amnesty, would surely be yes. But that is not the question and it is necessary to remind oneself throughout that it is not the question. Your Lordships are not being asked to decide whether proceedings should be brought against the respondent, even whether he should in the end be extradited to another country (that is a question for the Secretary of State) let alone whether he in particular is guilty of the commission or responsible for the commission of these crimes. The sole question is whether he is entitled to immunity as a former Head of State from arrest and extradition proceedings in the United Kingdom in respect of acts alleged to have been committed whilst he was Head of State.

The proceedings

The proceedings have arisen in this way. On 16 October 1998 Mr. Nicholas Evans, a Metropolitan Magistrate, issued a provisional warrant for the arrest of the respondent pursuant to section 8(1)(b) of the Extradition Act 1989 on the basis that there was evidence that he was accused that:

> "between 11 September 1973 and 31 December 1983 within the jurisdiction of the Fifth Central Magistrate of the National Court of Madrid did murder Spanish citizens in Chile within the jurisdiction of the Government of Spain."

A second warrant was issued by Mr. Ronald Bartle, a Metropolitan Magistrate, on 22 October 1998 on the application of the Spanish Government, but without the respondent being heard, despite a written request that he should be heard to oppose the application. That warrant was issued on the basis that there was evidence that he was accused:

> "between 1 January 1988 and December 1992 being a public official intentionally inflicted severe pain or suffering on another in the performance or purported performance of his official duties within the jurisdiction of the Government of Spain."

Particulars of other alleged offences were set out, namely:

(i) between 1 January 1988 and 31 December 1992, being a public official, conspired with persons unknown to intentionally inflict severe pain or suffering on another in the performance or purported performance of his official duties;

(ii) Between 1 January 1982 and 31 January 1992: (a) he detained; (b) he conspired with persons unknown to detain other persons ("the hostages") and in order to compel such persons to do or to abstain from doing any act, threatened to kill, injure or continue to detain the hostages;

(iii) Between January 1976 and December 1992, conspired together with persons unknown to commit murder in a Convention country.

It seems, however, that there are alleged at present to have been only one or two cases of torture between 1 January 1988 and 11 March 1990.

The respondent was arrested on that warrant on 23 October.

On the same day as the second warrant was issued, and following an application to the Home Secretary to cancel the warrant pursuant to section 8(4) of the Extradition Act 1989, solicitors for the respondent issued a summons applying for an order of Habeas Corpus. Mr. Michael Caplan, a partner in the firm of solicitors, deposed that the plaintiff was in hospital under medication following major surgery and that he claimed privilege and immunity from arrest on two grounds. The first was that, as stated by the Ambassador of Chile to the Court of St. James's, the respondent was "President of the Government Junta of Chile" according to Decree No. 1, dated 11 September 1973 from 11 September 1973 until 26 June 1974 and "Head of State of the Republic of Chile" from 26 June 1974 until 11 March 1990 pursuant to Decree Law No. 527, dated 26 June 1974, confirmed by Decree Law No. 806, dated 17 December 1974, and subsequently by the 14th Transitory Provision of the Political Constitution of the Republic of Chile 1980. The second ground was that the respondent was not and had not been a subject of Spain and accordingly no extradition crime had been identified.

An application was also made on 22 October for leave to apply for judicial review to quash the first warrant of 16 October and to direct the Home Secretary to cancel the warrant. On 26 October a further application was made for Habeas Corpus and judicial review of the second warrant. The grounds put forward were (in addition to the claim for immunity up to 1990) that all the charges specified offences contrary to English statutory provisions which were not in force when the acts were done. As to the fifth charge of murder in a Convention country, it was objected that this charged murder in Chile (not a Convention country) by someone not a Spanish national or a national of a Convention country. Objection was also taken to the issue of a second provisional warrant when the first was treated as being valid.

These applications were heard by the Divisional Court on 26 and 27 October. On 28 October leave was given to the respondent to move for certiorari and the decision to issue the provisional warrant of 16 October was quashed. The Magistrate's decision of 22 October to issue a provisional warrant was also quashed, but the quashing of the second warrant was stayed pending an appeal to your Lordships' House for which leave was given on an undertaking that the Commissioner of Police and the Government of Spain would lodge a petition to the House on 2 November 1998. It was ordered that the applicant was not to be released from custody other than on bail, which was granted subsequently. No order was made on the application for Habeas Corpus, save to grant leave to appeal and as to costs.

The Divisional Court certified:

> "that a point of law of general public importance is involved in the Court's decision, namely the proper interpretation and scope of the immunity enjoyed by a former Head of State from arrest and extradition proceedings in the United Kingdom in respect of acts committed when he was Head of State".

The matter first came before your Lordships on Wednesday 5 November. Application for leave to intervene was made first by Amnesty International and others representing victims of the alleged activities. Conditional leave was given to these intervenors, subject to the parties showing cause why they should not be heard. It was ordered that submissions should so far as possible be in writing, but that, in view of the very short time available before the hearing, exceptionally leave was given to supplement those by oral submissions, subject to time limits to be fixed. At the hearing no objection was raised to Professor Brownlie, Q.C. on behalf of these intervenors being heard. Leave was also given to other intervenors to apply to put in written submissions, although an application to make oral submissions was refused. Written submissions were received on behalf of these parties. Because of the urgency and the important and difficult questions of international law which appeared to be raised, the Attorney General, at your Lordships request, instructed Mr. David Lloyd Jones as amicus curiae and their Lordships are greatly indebted to him for the assistance he provided in writing and orally at such very short notice. Many cases have been cited by counsel, but I only refer to a small number of them.

At the date of the provisional warrants and of the judgment of the Divisional Court no extradition request had been made by Spain, a party to the European Convention on Extradition, nor accordingly any authority to proceed from the Secretary of State under the Extradition Act 1989.

The Divisional Court held that the first warrant was defective. The offence specified of murder in Chile was clearly not said to be committed in Spain so that section 2(1)(a) of the 1989 Act was not satisfied. Nor was section 2(1)(b) of the Act satisfied since the United Kingdom Courts could only try a defendant for murder outside the United Kingdom if the defendant was a British citizen (section 9 of the Offences Against the Person Act 1861 as amended). Moreover, section 2(3)(a) was not satisfied, since the accused is not a citizen of Spain and it is not sufficient that the victim was a citizen of Spain. The Home Secretary, however, was held not to have been in breach of his duty by not cancelling the warrants. As for the second provisional warrant, the Divisional Court rejected the respondent's argument that it was unlawful to proceed on the second warrant and that the Magistrate erred in not holding an inter partes hearing. The Court did not rule at that stage on the respondent's argument that the acts alleged did not constitute crimes in the United Kingdom at the time they were done, but added that it was not necessary that the conduct alleged did constitute a crime here at the time the alleged crime was committed abroad.

As to the sovereign immunity claim, the Court found that from the earliest date in the second warrant (January 1976), the respondent was Head of State of Chile and, although he ceased to be Head of State in March 1990, nothing was relied on as having taken place after March 1990 and indeed the second international warrant issued by the Spanish Judge covered the period from September 1973 to 1979. Section 20 in Part III of the State Immunity Act 1978 was held to apply to matters which occurred before the coming into force of the Act. The Court read the international warrant as accusing the respondent not of personally torturing or murdering victims or causing their disappearance, but of using the powers of the State of which he was Head to do that. They rejected the argument that section 20(1) of the 1970 Act and Article 39 of the Vienna Convention only applied to acts done in the United Kingdom, and held that the applicant was entitled to immunity as a former Head of State from the criminal and civil process of the English Courts.

A request for the extradition of the respondent, signed in Madrid on 3 November 1998 by the same judge who signed the international warrant, set out a large number of alleged murders, disappearances and cases of torture which, it is said, were in breach of Spanish law relating to genocide, to torture and to terrorism. They occurred mainly in Chile, but there are others outside Chile—e.g. an attempt to murder in Madrid, which was abandoned because of the danger to the agent concerned. The respondent personally is said to have met an agent of the intelligence services of Chile (D.I.N.A.) following an attack in Rome on the Vice-President of Chile in October 1975 and to have set up and directed "Operation Condor" to eliminate political adversaries, particularly in South America.

> "These offences have presumably been committed, by Augusto Pinochet Ugarte, along with others in accordance with the plan previously established and designed for the systematic elimination of the political opponents, specific segments of sections of the Chilean national groups, ethnic and religious groups, in order to remove any ideological dispute and purify the Chilean way of life through the disappearance and death of the most prominent leaders and other elements which defended Socialist, Communist (Marxist) positions, or who simply disagreed."

By order of 5 November 1998, the Judges of the National Court Criminal Division in Plenary Session held that Spain had jurisdiction to try crimes of terrorism, and genocide even committed abroad, including crimes of torture which are an aspect of genocide and not merely in respect of Spanish victims.

> "Spain is competent to judge the events by virtue of the principle of universal prosecution for certain crimes—a category of international law—established by our internal legislation. It also has a legitimate interest in the exercise of such jurisdiction because more than 50 nationals were killed or disappeared in Chile, victims of the repression reported in the proceedings."

The validity of the arrest

Although before the Divisional Court the case was argued on the basis that the respondent was at the relevant times Head of State, it was suggested that he was not entitled to such recognition, at any rate for the whole of the period during which the crimes were alleged to have been committed and for which immunity is claimed. An affidavit sworn on 2 November 1974 was produced from Professor Faundez to support this. His view was that by Decree Law No. 1 of 11 September 1973, the respondent was only made President of the Military Junta; that Decree Law was in any event unconstitutional. By Decree Law No. 527 of 26 June 1974, the respondent was designated "Supreme Chief of the Nation" and by Decree Law No. 806 of 17 December 1974, he was given the title President of the Republic of Chile. This, too, it is said was unconstitutional, as was the Decree Law No. 788 of 4 December 1974 purporting to reconcile the Decree Laws with the Constitution. He was not, in any event, appointed in a way recognised by the Constitution. It seems clear, however, that the respondent acted as Head of State. In affidavits from the Ambassador of Chile to the Court of St. James's, sworn on 21 October 1998, and by affidavits of two former Ambassadors, his position has been said to be that of President of the Junta from 11 September 1973 until 26 June 1974 and then Head of State from 26 June 1974 until 11 March 1990. Moreover, it was the respondent who signed the letters of credential presented to The Queen by the Chilean Ambassador to the United Kingdom on 26 October 1973. Further, in the request for extradition dated 3 November 1998, the Spanish Government speak of him as being Head of State. He is said not to have immunity "in regard to the allegedly criminal acts committed when [the respondent] was Head of State in Chile" and in considering whether an immunity should be accorded, it was relevant to take into account that "Mr. Pinochet became Head of State after overthrowing a democratically elected Government by force". I accordingly accept for the purposes of this appeal that, although no certificate has been issued by the Secretary of State pursuant to Section 21(a) of the State Immunity Act 1978, on the evidence at all maternal times until March 1990 the respondent was Head of State of Chile.

The protection claimed by the respondent is put essentially on two different bases, one a procedural bar to the proceedings for extradition and the other an objection that the issues raised are not justiciable before the English Courts. They are distinct matters, though there are common features. See for example Argentina v. Amerada Hess 488 U.S. 428, Filartiga v. Pena-Irala (1984) 577 F.Supp. 860, Siderman de Blake v. Republic of Argentina(1992) 965 F 2d 699, and Al Adsani v. Kuwait 107 I.L.R. 536.

The claim of immunity

Chronologically, it is the procedural bar which falls to be considered first. Can the respondent say either that because the State is immune from proceedings he cannot be brought before the Court, or can he say that as a former Head of State he has an immunity of his own which, as I see it, is a derivative of the principle of State immunity. The starting point for both these claims is now the State Immunity Act 1978. The long title of that Act states that this is to (a) make new provision in respect of proceedings in the United Kingdom by or against other States and (b) to make new provision with respect to the immunities and privileges of Heads of State.

Part I deals with (a); Part III with (b).

Part I

By section 1 headed "General Immunity from Jurisdiction", it is provided: "(1) A State is immune from the jurisdiction of the Courts of the United Kingdom except as provided in the following provisions of this Part of this Act".

The first part of the sentence is general and the exceptions which follow in sections 2 to 11 relate to specific matters—commercial transactions, certain contracts of employment and injuries to persons and property caused by acts or omissions in the United Kingdom—and do not indicate whether the general rule applies to civil or criminal matters, or both. Some of these exceptions—patents, trademarks and business names, death or personal injury—are capable of being construed to include both civil and criminal proceedings.

Section 1 refers only to States and there is nothing in its language to indicate that it covers emanations or officials of the State. I read it as meaning States as such. Section 14, however, goes much further, since references to a State:

> "include references to (a) the sovereign or other head of that State in his public capacity; (b) the government of that State; and (c) any department of that government, but not to any entity (hereinafter referred to as a separate entity) which is distinct from the executive organs of the government of the State and capable of suing or of being sued".

A "separate entity" is immune from jurisdiction "if, and only if—(a) the proceedings relate to anything done by it in the exercise of sovereign authority and (b) the circumstances are such that a State . . . would have been so immune." This section does not deal expressly with the position of a former Head of State.

Section 16(4), however, under the heading "Excluded Matters", provides that "this Part of this Act does not apply to criminal proceedings". Mr. Nicholls, Q.C. contends that this must be read subject to the terms of the provision of Section 1(1) which confers absolute immunity from jurisdiction on States. Section 16(4) therefore excludes criminal proceedings from the exceptions provided in sections 2 to 11, but it does not apply to section 1(1), so that a State is immune from criminal proceedings and accordingly Heads of State enjoy immunity from criminal proceedings under section 14. I am not able to accept this. Section 16(4) is in quite general terms and must be read as including section 1 as well as sections 2 to 11 of the Act. It is hardly surprising that crimes are excluded from section 1, since the number of crimes which may be committed by the State as opposed to by individuals seems likely to be limited. It is also consistent with the Foreign Sovereign Immunity Act of the United States which, as I understand it, does not apply to criminal proceedings. Since extradition proceedings in respect of criminal charges are themselves regarded as criminal proceedings, the respondent cannot rely on Part I of the 1978 Act.

Part III

Part III of the Act contains the provisions of this Act on which it seems that this claim turns, curiously enough under the heading, "Miscellaneous and Supplementary". By section 20(1), "Heads of State", it is provided that:

> "subject to the provisions of this section and to any necessary modifications, the Diplomatic Privileges Act 1964 shall apply to (a) A sovereign or other head of State; (b) members of his family forming part of his household; and (c) his private servants, as it applies to the head of a diplomatic mission, to members of his family forming part of his household and to his private servants.
> . . .
> (5) This section applies to the sovereign or other head of any State on which immunities and privileges are conferred by Part I of this Act and is without prejudice to the application of that Part to any such sovereign or head of State in his public capacity".

Again there is no mention of a former Head of State.

The Diplomatic Privileges Act 1964, unlike the 1978 Act, provides in section 1 that the provisions of the Act, "with respect to the matters dealt with shall "have effect in substitution for any previous enactment or rule of law". By section 2, Articles of the Vienna Convention on Diplomatic Relations (1961) set out in the Schedule, "shall have the force of law in the United Kingdom."

The Preamble to the Vienna Convention (which though not part of the Schedule may in my view be looked at in the interpretation of the articles so scheduled) refers to the fact that an International Convention on Diplomatic Privileges and Immunities would contribute to the development of friendly relations among nations "irrespective of the differing constitutional and social systems" and records that the purpose of such privileges and immunities is "not to benefit individuals, but to ensure the efficient performance of the functions of diplomatic missions as representing States." It confirmed, however, "that the rules of customary international law should continue to govern questions not expressly regulated by the provisions of the present Convention."

It is clear that the provisions of the Convention were drafted with the Head and the members of a diplomatic staff of the mission of a sending State (whilst in the territory of the receiving State and carrying out diplomatic functions there) in mind and the specific functions of a diplomatic mission are set out in article 3 of the Convention. Some of the provisions of the Vienna Convention thus have little or no direct relevance to the Head of State: those which are relevant must be read "with the necessary modifications".

The relevant provisions for present purposes are:

(i) Article 29:

"The person of a diplomatic agent shall be inviolable. He shall not be liable to any form of arrest or detention. The receiving State shall treat him with due respect and shall take all appropriate steps to prevent any attack on his person, freedom or dignity."

(ii) By Article 31(1), a diplomatic agent shall enjoy immunity from the criminal jurisdiction of the receiving State

(iii) By Article 39:

"1. Every person entitled to privileges and immunities shall enjoy them from the moment he enters the territory of the receiving State on proceeding to take up his post or, if already in its territory, from the moment when his appointment is notified to the Ministry for Foreign Affairs or such other ministry as may be agreed. 2. When the functions of a person enjoying privileges and immunities have come to an end, such privileges and immunities shall normally cease at the moment when he leaves the country, or on expiry of a reasonable period in which to do so, but shall subsist until that time, even in case of armed conflict. However, with respect to acts performed by such a person in the exercise of his functions as a member of the mission, immunity shall continue to subsist."

It is also to be noted that in article 38, for diplomatic agents who are nationals of or resident in the receiving State, immunity is limited. Such immunity is only in respect of "official" acts performed in the exercise of his functions.

Reading the provisions "with the necessary modifications" to fit the position of a Head of State, it seems to me that when references are made to a "diplomatic agent" one can in the first place substitute only the words "Head of State". The provisions made cover, prima facie, a Head of State whilst in office. The next question is how to relate the time limitation in article 39(1) to a Head of State. He does not, in order to take up his post as Head of State, "enter the territory of a receiving State", i.e. a country other than his own, in order to take up his functions or leave it when he finishes his term of office. He may, of course, as Head of State visit another State on an official visit and it is suggested that his immunity and privileges are limited to those visits. Such an interpretation would fit into a strictly literal reading of article 39. It seems to me, however, to be unreal and cannot have been intended. The principle functions of a Head of State are performed in his own country and it is in respect of the exercise of those functions that if he is to have immunity that immunity is most needed. I do not accept therefore that section 20 of the 1978 Act read with article 39(2) of the Vienna Convention is limited to visits abroad.

Nor do I consider that the general context of this Convention indicates that it only grants immunity to acts done in a foreign state or in connection only with international diplomatic activities as normally understood. The necessary modification to "the moment he enters the territory of the receiving State on proceeding to take up his post" and to "the moment when he leaves the country" is to the time when he "becomes Head of State" to the time "when he ceases to be Head of State". It therefore covers acts done by him whilst in his own State and in post. Conversely there is nothing to indicate that this immunity is limited to acts done within the State of which the person concerned is Head.

If these limitations on his immunity do not apply to a Head of State they should not apply to the position of a former Head of State, whom it is sought to sue for acts done during his period as Head of State. Another limitation has, however, been suggested. In respect of acts performed by a person in the exercise of his functions as head of a mission, it is said that it is only "immunity" which continues to subsist, whereas "privileges and immunities normally cease at the moment when he leaves the country [sc. when he finishes his term of office]." It is suggested that all the provisions of article 29 are privileges not immunities. Mr. Nicholls, Q.C. replies that even if being treated with respect and being protected from an attack on his person, freedom or dignity are privileges, the provision that a diplomatic agent [sc. Head of State] "shall not be liable to any form of arrest or detention" is an immunity. As a matter of ordinary language and as a matter of principle it seems to me that Mr. Nicholls is plainly right. In any event, by article 31 the diplomatic agent/Head of State has immunity from the criminal jurisdiction of the receiving State: that immunity would cover immunity from arrest as a first step in criminal proceedings. Immunity in article 39(2) in relation to former Heads of State in my view covers immunity from arrest, but so also does article 29.

Where a diplomatic agent [Head of State] is in post, he enjoys these immunities and privileges as such—i.e. ratione personae just as in respect of civil proceedings he enjoys immunity from the jurisdiction of the Courts of the United Kingdom under section 14 of the 1978 Act because of his office.

For one who ceases to occupy a post "with respect to acts performed by such a person in the exercise of his functions as a member of the mission [Head of State] immunity shall continue to subsist." This wording is in one respect different from the wording in article 38 in respect of a diplomat who is a national of the receiving State. In that case, he has immunity in respect of "official" acts performed in the exercise of his function, but as Mrs. Denza suggests, the two should be read in the same way [see Diplomatic Law, 2nd Edition, p. 363].

The question then arises as to what can constitute acts (i.e. official acts) in the exercise of his functions as Head of State.

It is said (in addition to the argument that functions mean only international functions which I reject):

(i) that the functions of the Head of State must be defined by international law, they cannot be defined simply as a matter of national law or practice; and

(ii) genocide, torture and the taking of hostages cannot be regarded as the functions of a Head of State within the meaning of international law when international law regards them as crimes against international law.

As to (i), I do not consider that international law prescribes a list of those functions which are, and those which are not, functions for the purposes of article 32. The role of a Head of State varies very much from country to country, even as between Presidents in various States in Europe and the United States. International law recognises those functions which are attributed to him as Head of State by the law, or in fact, in the country of which he is Head as being functions for this purpose, subject to any general principle of customary international law or national law, which may prevent what is done from being regarded as a function.

As to (ii), clearly international law does not recognise that it is one of the specific functions of a Head of State to commit torture or genocide. But the fact that in carrying out other functions, a Head of State commits an illegal act does not mean that he is no longer to be regarded as carrying out one of his functions. If it did, the immunity in respect of criminal acts would be deprived of much of its content. I do not think it right to draw a distinction for this purpose between acts whose criminality and moral obliquity is more or less great. I accept the approach of Sir Arthur Watts, Q.C. in his Hague Lectures at pp. 56–57:

> "A Head of State clearly can commit a crime in his personal capacity; but it seems equally clear that he can, in the course of his public functions as Head of State, engage in conduct which may be tainted by criminality or other forms of wrongdoing. The critical test would seem to be whether the conduct was engaged in under colour of or in ostensible exercise of the Head of State's public authority90. If it was, it must be treated as official conduct, and so not a matter subject to the jurisdiction of other States whether or not it was wrongful or illegal under the law of his own State.91"

In the present case it is accepted in the international warrant of arrest that in relation to the repression alleged "the plans and instructions established beforehand from the Government enabled these actions to be carried out". "In this sense [the] Commander in Chief of the Armed Forces and Head of the Chilean Government at the time committed punishable acts . . ."

I therefore conclude that in the present case the acts relied on were done as part of the carrying out of his functions when he was Head of State.

The next question is, therefore, whether this immunity in respect of functions is cut down as a matter of the interpretation of the Vienna Convention and the Act. The provisions of the Act "fall to be considered against the background of those principles of public international law as are generally recognised by the family of nations" (Alcom Ltd. v. Republic of Colombia [1984] A.C. 580, 597 per Lord Diplock). So also as I see it must the Convention be interpreted.

The original concept of the immunity of a Head of State in customary international law in part arose from the fact that he or she was a Monarch who by reason of personal dignity and respect ought not to be impleaded in a foreign State: it was linked no less to the idea that the Head of State was, or represented, the State and that to sue him was tantamount to suing an independent State extra-territorially, something which the comity of nations did not allow. Moreover, although the concepts of State immunity and Sovereign immunity have different origins, it seems to me that the latter is an attribute of the former and that both are essentially based on the principles of Sovereign independence and dignity, see for example, Suchariktul in his report to the International Law Commission (1980) Vol. II Doc. A (LN 4—331 and Add.J.) Marshall C.J. in the Schooner Exchange v. M'Faddon (1812) 11 US (7 Cranch) 116.

In the Duke of Brunswick v. The King of Hanover (1848) 2 H.L. Cas. 1 the Duke claimed that the King of Hanover had been involved in the removal of the Duke from his position as reigning Duke and in the maladministration of his estates. The Lord Chancellor said:

> "A foreign Sovereign, coming into this country cannot be made responsible here for an act done in his Sovereign character in his own country; whether it be an act right or wrong, whether according to the constitution of that country or not, the Courts of this country cannot sit in judgment upon an act of a Sovereign, effected by virtue of his Sovereign authority abroad, an act not done as a British subject, but supposed to be done in the exercise of his authority vested in him as Sovereign."

He further said:

> "If it be a matter of sovereign authority, we cannot try that fact, whether it be right or wrong. The allegation that it is contrary to the laws of Hanover, taken in conjunction with the allegation of the authority under which the defendant had acted, must be conceded to be an allegation, not that it was contrary to the existing laws as regulating the right of individuals, but that it was contrary to the laws and duties and rights and powers of a Sovereign exercising Sovereign authority. If that be so, it does not require another observation to shew, because it has not been doubted, that no Court in this country can entertain questions to bring Sovereigns to account for their acts done in their sovereign capacities abroad."

This case has been cited since both in judicial decisions and in the writing of jurists and in Buttes Gas and Oil Co. v. Hammer [1982] A.C. 888 was said by Lord Wilberforce to be "a case in this House which is still authoritative and which has influenced the law both here and overseas" (p. 932). In Hatch v. Baez (1876) 7 Hun. 596, the plaintiff claimed that he had suffered injuries in the Dominican Republic as a result of acts done by the defendant in his official capacity of President of that Republic. The Court accepted that because the defendant was in New York, he was within the territorial jurisdiction of the State. The Court said, however:

> "But the immunity of individuals from suits brought in foreign tribunals for acts done within their own States, in the exercise of the sovereignty thereof, it is essential to preserve the peace and harmony of nations, and has the sanction of the most approved writers on international law. It is also recognised in all the judicial decisions on the subject that have come to my knowledge . . .
>
> "The fact that the defendant has ceased to be president of St. Domingo does not destroy his immunity. That springs from the capacity in which the acts were done, and protects the individual who did them, because they emanated from a foreign and friendly government."

Jurists since have regarded this principle as still applying to the position of a former Head of State. Thus in the 9th edition of Oppenheim's International Law (1992 Sir Robert Jennings, Q.C. and Sir Arthur Watts, Q.C.) it is said that a Head of State enjoys all the privileges set out as long as he holds that position (i.e. ratione personae) but that thereafter he may be sued in respect of obligations of a private character.

> "For his official acts as Head of State, he will like any other agent of the State enjoy continuing immunity."

Satow in Guide to Diplomatic Practice, Fifth Edition, is to the same effect. Having considered the Vienna Convention on Diplomatic Relations of 1961, the New York Convention on Special Missions of 1969 and the European Convention on State Immunity, the editors conclude at page 9:

> "2. The personal status of a head of a foreign state therefore continues to be regulated by long established rules of customary international law which can be stated in simple terms. He is entitled to immunity—probably without exception—from criminal and civil jurisdiction."
>
> "2.4. A head of state who has been deposed or replaced or has abdicated or resigned is of course no longer entitled to privileges or immunities as a head of state. He will be entitled to continuing immunity in regard to acts which he performed while head of state, provided that the acts were performed in his official capacity; in this his position is no different from that of any agent of the state. He cannot claim to be entitled to privileges as of right, although he may continue to enjoy certain privileges in other states on a basis of courtesy."

In his Hague Lectures on "The Legal Position in International Law on Heads of States et al", Sir Arthur Watts, Q.C. wrote that a former Head of State had no immunity in respect of his private activities taking place whilst he was Head of State. "A Head of State's official acts, performed in his public capacity as Head of State, are however subject to different considerations. Such acts are acts of the State rather than the Head of State's personal acts and he cannot be sued for them even after he has ceased to be Head of State" ().

One critical difference between a Head of State and the State of course resides in the fact that a Head of State may resign or be removed. As these writers show, customary international law whilst continuing to hold immune the Head of State for acts performed in such capacity during his tenure of the office, did not hold him immune from personal acts of his own. The distinction may not always be easy to draw, but examples can be found. On the one side in the United States was Hatch v. Baez to which I have referred, and Nobili v. Charles I of Austria (1921) (Annual Digest of Public International Law Cases, Volume I 1932, Case No. 90, page 136). On the other side, in France is the case of Mellerio v. Isabel de Bourbon ex Queen of Spain, Journal of International Law (1974) (page 32); more recently the former King Farouk was held not immune from suits for goods supplied to his former wife whilst he was Head of State (Review Critique 1964, page 689).

The reasons for this immunity as a general rule both for the actual and a former Head of State still have force and, despite the changes in the role and the person of the Head of State in many countries, the immunity still exists as a matter of customary international law. For an actual Head of State as was said in United States of America v. Noriega (1990) 746 F. Supp. 1506 the reason was to ensure that "leaders are free to perform their Governmental duties without being subject to detention, arrest or embarrassment in a foreign country's legal system." There are in my view analogous if more limited reasons for continuing to apply the immunity ratione materiae in respect of a former Head of State.

Rules of customary international law change, however, and as Lord Denning, M.R. said in Trendtex Trading Corporation v. Central Bank of Nigeria [1977] 1 Q.B. 529, "we should give effect to those changes and not be bound by any idea of stare decisis in international law". Thus, for example, the concept of absolute immunity for a Sovereign has changed to adopt a theory of restrictive immunity in so far as it concerns the activities of a State engaging in trade (I Congresso del Partido [1983] A.C. 244). One must therefore ask is there "sufficient evidence to show that the rule of international law has changed?" (p. 556).

This principle of immunity has, therefore, to be considered now in the light of developments in international law relating to what are called international crimes. Sometimes these developments are through Conventions. Thus, for example, the International Convention against the Taking of Hostages 1979 provides that:

"Any person who seizes or detains and threatens to kill, to injure . . . another person . . . in order to compel a third party, namely a State, an international inter-governmental organisation, a natural or juridical person, or a group of persons, to do or to abstain from doing any act as an explicit or implicit condition for the release of the hostage commits the offence of taking hostages."

States undertake to prosecute if they do not extradite an offender (any offender "without exception whatsoever") through proceedings in accordance with the law of that State, but subject to "enjoyment of all the rights and guarantees provided by the law of the State in the territory of which he is present." This Convention entered into force on 3 June 1983 and was enacted in the United Kingdom in the Taking of Hostages Act 1982 which came into force on 26 November 1982.

By the Genocide Convention of 1948,

"the Contracting Parties confirmed that genocide (being any of the acts specified in article II of the Convention), whether committed in time of peace or in time of war, is a crime under international law which they undertake to prevent and punish".

By article IV,

"Persons committing genocide or any of the other acts enumerated in article III shall be punished, whether they are constitutionally responsible rulers, public officials or private individuals."

The Genocide Act 1969 made the acts specified in article II of the Convention the criminal offence of genocide, but it is to be noted that article IV of the Convention which on the face of it would cover a Head of State was not enacted as part of domestic law. It is, moreover, provided in article VI that persons charged with genocide "shall be tried by a competent tribunal of the State in the territory in which the act was committed, or by such international penal tribunal as may have jurisdiction." It seems to me to follow that if an immunity otherwise exists, it would only be taken away in respect of the State where the crime was committed or before an international tribunal.

There have in addition been a number of Charters or Statutes setting up international tribunals, there is the Nuremberg Charter in 1945 which gave jurisdiction to try crimes against peace, war crimes and crimes against humanity (Article 6). By Article 7 "the official position of defendants, whether as a Heads of State or responsible officials in Government Departments shall not be considered as freeing them from responsibility or mitigating punishment." A similar provision was found in the Tokyo Convention. In 1993 the international tribunal for the former Yugoslavia was given power to prosecute persons "responsible for serious violations of international humanitarian law" including grave breaches of the Geneva Conventions of 1949, torture and taking civilians as hostages, genocide, crimes against humanity "when committed in armed conflict whether international or internal in character, and directed against any civilian population" including murder, torture, persecution on political racial or religious grounds. In dealing with individual criminal responsibility it is provided in Article 7 that "the official position of any accused person whether as Head of State or Government or as a responsible Government Official shall not relieve such person of criminal responsibility."

The Statute of the International tribunal for Rwanda (1994) also empowered the tribunal to prosecute persons committing genocide and specified crimes against humanity "when committed as part of a widespread or systematic attack against any civilian population on national political ethnic or other specified grounds." The same clause as to Head of State as in the Yugoslav tribunal is in this Statute.

The Rome Statute of the International Criminal Court provides for jurisdiction in respect of genocide as defined, crimes against humanity as defined but in each case only with respect to crimes committed after the entry into force of this statute. Official capacity as a Head of State or Government shall in no case exempt the person from criminal responsibility under this statute. Although it is concerned with jurisdiction, it does indicate the limits which States were prepared to impose in this area on the tribunal.

There is thus no doubt that States have been moving towards the recognition of some crimes as those which should not be covered by claims of State or Head of State or other official or diplomatic immunity when charges are brought before international tribunals.

Movement towards the recognition of crimes against international law is to be seen also in the decisions of National Courts, in the resolution of the General Assembly of the United Nations 1946, in the reports of the International Law Commission and in the writings of distinguished international jurists.

It has to be said, however, at this stage of the development of international law that some of those statements read as aspirations, as embryonic. It does not seem to me that it has been shown that there is any State practice or general consensus let alone a widely supported convention that all crimes against international law should be justiciable in National Courts on the basis of the universality of jurisdiction. Nor is there any jus cogens in respect of such breaches of international law which require that a claim of State or Head of State immunity, itself a well established principle of international law, should be overridden. I am not satisfied that even now there would be universal acceptance of a definition of crimes against humanity. They had their origin as a concept after the 1914 War and were recognised in the Nuremberg Tribunal as existing at the time of international armed conflicts. Even later it was necessary to spell out that humanitarian crimes could be linked to armed conflict internally and that it was not necessary to show that they occurred in international conflict. This is no doubt a developing area but states have proceeded cautiously.

That international law crimes should be tried before international tribunals or in the perpetrator's own state is one thing; that they should be impleaded without regard to a long-established customary international law rule in the Courts of other states is another. It is significant that in respect of serious breaches of "intransgressible principles of international customary law" when tribunals have been set up it is with carefully defined powers and jurisdiction as accorded by the states involved; that the Genocide Convention provides only for jurisdiction before an international tribunal or the Courts of the state where the crime is committed, that the Rome Statute of the International Criminal Court lays down jurisdiction for crimes in very specific terms but limits its jurisdiction to future acts.

So, starting with the basic rule to be found both in Article 39(2) and in customary international law that a former Head of State is entitled to immunity from arrest or prosecution in respect of official acts done by him in the exercise of his functions as Head of State, the question is what effect, if any, the recognition of acts as international crimes has in itself on that immunity. There are two extreme positions. The first is that such recognition has no effect. Head of State immunity is still necessary for a former Head of State in respect of his official acts; it is long established, well recognised and based on sound reasons. States must be treated as recognising it between themselves so that it over-rides any criminal act, whether national or international. This is a clear cut rule, which for that reason has considerable attraction. It, however, ignores the fact that international law is not static and that the principle may be modified by changes introduced in State practice, by Conventions and by the informed opinions of international jurists. Just as it is now accepted that, contrary to an earlier principle of absolute immunity, States may limit State immunity to acts of sovereign authority (acta jure imperii) and exclude commercial acts (acta jure gestionis) as the United Kingdom has done and just as the immunity of a former Head of State is now seen to be limited to acts which he did in his official capacity and to exclude private acts, so it is argued, the immunity should be treated as excluding certain acts of a criminal nature.

The opposite extreme position is that all crimes recognised as, or accepted to be, international crimes are outside the protection of the immunity in respect of former Heads of State. I do not accept this. The fact even that an act is recognised as a crime under international law does not mean that the Courts of all States have jurisdiction to try it, nor in my view does it mean that the immunity recognised by States as part of their international relations is automatically taken away by international law. There is no universality of jurisdiction for crimes against international law: there is no universal rule that all crimes are outside immunity ratione materiae.

There is, however, another question to be asked. Does international law now recognise that some crimes are outwith the protection of the former Head of State immunity so that immunity in Article 39 (2) is equally limited as part of domestic law; if so, how is that established? This is the core question and it is a difficult question.

It is difficult partly because changes in international law take place slowly as states modify existing principles. It is difficult because in many aspects of this problem the appropriate principles of international law have not crystallised. There is still much debate and it seems to me still much uncertainty so that a national judge should proceed carefully. He may have to say that the position as to State practice has not reached the stage when he can identify a positive rule at the particular time when he has to consider the position. This is clearly shown by the developments which have taken place in regard to crimes against humanity. The concept that such crimes might exist was as I have said recognised, for Nuremburg and the Tokyo Tribunals in 1946 in the context of international armed conflict when the tribunals were given jurisdiction to try crimes against humanity. The Affirmation of the Principles of International Law adopted by the United Nations General Assembly in December 1945, the International Law Commission reports and the European Convention on Human Rights and Fundamental Freedoms also recognised these crimes as international crimes. Since then there have been, as I have shown, conventions dealing with specific crimes and tribunals have been given jurisdiction over international crimes with a mandate not to treat as a defence to such crimes the holding of official office including that of Head of State. National Courts as in the Eichmann Case held that they had jurisdiction to deal with international crimes (see also Re Honecker (1984) 80 I.L.R. 36, and Demanjanjuk 776 F 2d 511).

But except in regard to crimes in particular situations before international tribunals these measures did not in general deal with the question as to whether otherwise existing immunities were taken away. Nor did they always specifically recognise the jurisdiction of, or confer jurisdiction on, National Courts to try such crimes.

I do not find it surprising that this has been a slow process or that the International Law Commission eventually left on one side its efforts to produce a convention dealing with Head of State immunity. Indeed, until Prosecutor v. Tadic (105 I.L.R. 419) after years of discussion and perhaps even later there was a feeling that crimes against humanity were committed only in connection with armed conflict even if that did not have to be international armed conflict.

If the States went slowly so must a national judge go cautiously in finding that this immunity in respect of former Heads of State has been cut down. Immunity, it must be remembered, reflects the particular relationship between states by which they recognise the status and role of each others Head and former Head of State.

So it is necessary to consider what is needed, in the absence of a general international convention defining or cutting down Head of State immunity, to define or limit the former Head of State immunity in particular cases. In my opinion it is necessary to find provision in an international convention to which the State asserting, and the State being asked to refuse, the immunity of a former Head of State for an official act is a party; the convention must clearly define a crime against international law and require or empower a state to prevent or prosecute the crime, whether or not committed in its jurisdiction and whether or not committed by one of its nationals; it must make it clear that a National Court has jurisdiction to try a crime alleged against a former Head of State, or that having been a Head of State is no defence and that expressly or impliedly the immunity is not to apply so as to bar proceedings against him. The convention must be given the force of law in the National Courts of the State; in a dualist country like the United Kingdom that means by legislation, so that with the necessary procedures and machinery the crime may be prosecuted there in accordance with the conditions to be found in the convention.

In that connection it is necessary to consider when the pre-existing immunity is lost. In my view it is from the date when the national legislation comes into force, although I recognise that there is an argument that it is when the convention comes into force, but in my view nothing earlier will do. Acts done thereafter are not protected by the immunity; acts done before, so long as otherwise qualifying, are protected by the immunity. It seems to me wrong in principle to say that once the immunity is cut down in respect of particular crimes it has gone even for acts done when the immunity existed and was believed to exist. Equally, it is artificial to say that an evil act can be treated as a function of a Head of State until an international convention says that the act is a crime when it ceases ex post facto to have been a function. If that is the right test, then it gives a clear date from which the immunity was lost. This may seem a strict test and a cautious approach, but in laying down when States are to be taken to be taken as abrogating a long established immunity it is necessary to be satisfied that they have done so.

The crimes alleged

What is the position in regard to the three groups of crimes alleged here: torture, genocide and taking hostages?

The Torture Convention of 10 December 1984 defines torture as severe pain or suffering intentionally inflicted for specific purposes, "by or at the instigation of or with the consent or acquiescence of a public official or other person acting in an official capacity."

Each State Party is to ensure that all acts of torture are offences under its criminal law and to establish jurisdiction over offences committed in its territory, or by a national of that State or, if the State considers it appropriate, when the victim is a national of that

State (Article 5). It must also establish jurisdiction where, "the alleged offender is present under its jurisdiction and it does not extradite pursuant to Article 8." Thus, where a person is found in the territory of a State in the cases contemplated in Article 5, then the State must, by Article 7: "if it does not extradite him, submit the case to its competent authorities for the purpose of prosecution." States are to give each other the greatest measure of assistance in connection with criminal proceedings.

The important features of this Convention are: (1) that it involves action "by a public official or other person acting in an official capacity"; (2) that by Articles 5 and 7, if not extradited, the alleged offender must be dealt with as laid down; and (3) Chile was a State Party to this Convention and it therefore accepted that, in respect of the offence of torture, the United Kingdom should either extradite or take proceedings against offending officials found in its jurisdiction.

That Convention was incorporated into English law by section 134 of the Criminal Justice Act 1988. Section 134(1) and (2) provides:

"(1) A public official or person acting in an official capacity, whatever his nationality, commits the offence of torture if in the United Kingdom or elsewhere he intentionally inflicts severe pain or suffering on another in the performance or purported performance of his official duties."
"(2) A person not falling within subsection (1) above commits the offence of torture, whatever his nationality, if: (a) in the United Kingdom or elsewhere he intentionally inflicts severe pain or suffering on another at the instigation or with the consent or acquiescence:
(i) of a public official; or (ii) of a person acting in an official capacity; and (b) the official or other person is performing or purporting to perform his official duties when he instigates the commission of the offence or consents to or acquiesces in it."

If committed other than in the United Kingdom lawful authority, justification or excuse under the law of the place where the torture was inflicted is a defence, but in Chile the constitution forbids torture.

It is thus plain that torture was recognised by the State Parties as a crime which might be committed by the persons, and be punishable in the States, referred to. In particular, the Convention requires that the alleged offender, if found in the territory of a State Party, shall be, if not extradited, submitted to the prosecution authorities.

This, however, is not the end of the enquiry. The question remains—have the State Parties agreed, and in particular have the United Kingdom and Chile, which asserts the immunity, agreed that the immunity enjoyed by a former Head of State for acts ratione materiae, shall not apply to alleged crimes of torture? That depends on whether a Head of State, and therefore a former Head of State, is covered by the words "a public official or a person acting in that capacity". As a matter of ordinary usage, it can obviously be argued that he is. But your Lordships are concerned with the use of the words in their context in an international Convention. I find it impossible to ignore the fact that in the very Conventions and Charters relied on by the appellants as indicating that jurisdiction in respect of certain crimes was extended from 1945 onwards, there are specific provisions in respect of Heads of State as well as provisions covering officials. These provisions may relate to jurisdiction, or to the removal of a defence, and immunity of course is different from each, both as a concept and in that it is only pleadable in bar to proceedings in National Courts. These provisions do, however, serve as a guide to indicate whether States have generally accepted that former Heads of State are to be regarded as "public officials" and accordingly that the immunity has been taken away from former Heads of State in the Torture Convention.

Thus, in the Nuremberg Charter 1945 (Article 7), the official position of defendants "whether as Heads of State or responsible officials" does not free them from responsibility. In the Genocide Convention (1948) persons committing the act shall be punished "whether they are constitutionally responsible rulers, public officials or private individuals". In the Yugoslav and Rwanda Tribunals,

> "The official position of any accused person, whether as Head of State or Government or as a responsible Government official"

is not a defence (Article 7). Even as late as the Rome Statute on the International Criminal Court by Article 27 "official capacity as a Head of State or Government . . . or Government official" is not exempted from criminal responsibility.

In these cases, States have not taken the position that the words public or government official are wide enough to cover Heads of State or former Heads of State, but that a specific exclusion of a defence or of an objection to jurisdiction on that basis is needed. It is nothing to the point that the reference is only to Head of State. A Head of State on ceasing to be a Head of State is not converted into a public official in respect of the period when he was a Head of State if he was not so otherwise. This is borne out by the experience of the International Law Commission in seeking to produce a draft in respect of State immunity. The reports of its meeting show the difficulties which arose in seeking to deal with the position of a Head of State.

I conclude that the reference to public officials in the Torture Convention does not include Heads of State or former Heads of State, either because States did not wish to provide for the prosecution of Heads of State or former Heads of State or because they were not able to agree that a plea in bar to the proceedings based on immunity should be removed. I appreciate that there may be considerable political and diplomatic difficulties in reaching agreement, but if States wish to exclude the long established immunity of former Heads of State in respect of allegations of specific crimes, or generally, then they must do so in clear terms. They should not leave it to National Courts to do so because of the appalling nature of the crimes alleged.

The second provisional warrant does not mention genocide, though the international warrant and the request for extradition do. The Genocide Convention in Article 6 limits jurisdiction to a tribunal in the territory in which the act was committed and is not limited to acts by public officials. The provisions in Article 4 making "constitutionally responsible rulers" liable to punishment is not incorporated into the English Genocide Act of 1948. Whether or not your Lordships are concerned with the second international warrant and the request for extradition (and Mr. Nicholls, Q.C. submits that you are not), the Genocide Convention does not therefore satisfy the test which I consider should be applied.

The Taking of Hostages Convention which came into force in 1983 and the Taking of Hostages Act 1982 clearly make it a crime for "any person, whatever his nationality" who "in the United Kingdom or elsewhere to take hostages for one of the purposes specified." This again indicates the scope both of the substantive crime and of jurisdiction, but neither the Convention nor the Act contain any provisions which can be said to take away the customary international law immunity as Head of State or former Head of State.

It has been submitted that a number of other factors indicate that the immunity should not be refused by the United Kingdom—the United Kingdom's relations with Chile, the fact that an amnesty was granted, that great efforts have been made in Chile to restore democracy and that to extradite the respondent would risk unsettling what has been achieved, the length of time since the events took place, that prosecutions have already been launched against the respondent in Chile, that the respondent has, it is said, with the United Kingdom Government's approval or acquiescence, been admitted into this country and been received in official quarters. These are factors, like his age, which may be relevant on the question whether he should be extradited, but it seems to me that they are for the Secretary of State (the executive branch) and not for your Lordships on this occasion.

The alternative basis—Acts of State—and non-justiciability

United States Courts have been much concerned with the defence of act of state as well as of sovereign immunity. They were put largely on the basis of comity between nations beginning with the Schooner Exchange v. M'Faddon (supra). See also Underhill v. Hernandez 168 US 250. In Banco National de Cuba v. Sabbatino 307F 2d 845 (1961) it was said that "the Act of State Doctrine briefly stated that American Courts will not pass on the validity of the acts of foreign governments performed in their capacities as sovereigns within their own territories . . . This doctrine is one of the conflict of laws rules applied by American Courts; it is not itself a rule of international law . . . it stems from the concept of the immunity of the sovereign because "the sovereign can do no wrong" (page 855). See also the 3rd Restatement of the Law paragraph 443/444. In International Association of Machinists v. Opec (649F 2d 134) [1981] the 9th Circuit Court of Appeals took the matter further

> "The doctrine of sovereign immunity is similar to the Act of State Doctrine in that it also represents the need to respect the sovereignty of foreign states. The law of sovereign immunity goes to the jurisdiction of the Court. The Act of State Doctrine is not jurisdictional . . . Rather it is a procedural doctrine designed to avoid action in sensitive areas. Sovereign immunity is a principle of international law, recognised in the United States by statutes. It is the states themselves, as defendants, who may claim sovereign immunity."

The two doctrines are separate, but they are often run together. The law of Sovereign immunity is now contained in the Foreign Sovereign Immunities Act (28 USSC–1602) ("F.S.I.A.") in respect of civil matters and many of the decisions on sovereign immunity in the United States turn on the question whether the exemption to a general State immunity from suit falls within one of the specific exemptions. The F.S.I.A. does not deal with criminal Head of State immunity. In the United States the Courts would normally follow a decision of the executive as to the grant or denial of immunity and it is only when the executive does not take a position that "Courts should make an independent determination regarding immunity" (Kravitch S.C.J. in US v. Noriega (7 July 1997)).

In Kirkpatrick v. Environmental Tectonics (493 U.S. 403 110 S. Ct. 701 (1990)) the Court said that, having begun with comity as the basis for the act of State doctrine, the Court more recently regarded it as springing from the sense that if the judiciary adjudicated on the validity of foreign acts of State, it might hinder the conduct of foreign affairs. The Supreme Court said that "Act of State issues only arise when a Court must decide—that is when the outcome of the case turns upon—the effect of official action by a foreign Sovereign" (p. 705).

In English law the position is much the same as it was in the earlier statements of the United States Courts. The act of State doctrine "is to the effect that the Courts of one

State do not, as a rule, question the validity or legality of the official acts of another Sovereign State or the official or officially avowed acts of its agents, at any rate in so far as those acts involve the exercise of the State's public authority, purport to take effect within the sphere of the latter's own jurisdiction and are not in themselves contrary to international law" (Oppenheim 9th edition, page 365). In Buttes Gas (supra), Lord Wilberforce spoke of the normal meaning of acts of State as being "action taken by a Sovereign State within its own territory." In his speech, only a year before International Association of Machinists v. Opec., Lord Wilberforce asked whether, apart from cases concerning acts of British officials outside this country and cases concerned with the examination of the applicability of foreign municipal legislation within the territory of a foreign State, there was not "a more general principle that the Courts will not adjudicate upon the transactions of foreign Sovereign States"—a principle to be considered if it existed "not as a variety of 'acts of State', but one of judicial restraint or abstention".

Despite the divergent views expressed as to what is covered by the Act of State doctrine, in my opinion once it is established that the former Head of State is entitled to immunity from arrest and extradition on the lines I have indicated, United Kingdom Courts will not adjudicate on the facts relied on to ground the arrest, but in Lord Wilberforce's words, they will exercise "judicial restraint or abstention."

Accordingly, in my opinion, the respondent was entitled to claim immunity as a former Head of State from arrest and extradition proceedings in the United Kingdom in respect of official acts committed by him whilst he was Head of State relating to the charges in the provisional warrant of 22 October 1998. I would accordingly dismiss the appeal.

LORD LLOYD OF BERWICK

My Lords,

Background

On 11 September 1973 General Augusto Pinochet Ugarte assumed power in Chile after a military coup. He was appointed president of the Governing Junta the same day. On 22 September the new regime was recognised by Her Majesty's Government. By a decree dated 11 December 1974 General Pinochet assumed the title of President of the Republic. In 1980 a new constitution came into force in Chile, approved by a national referendum. It provided for executive power in Chile to be exercised by the President of the Republic as head of state. Democratic elections were held in December 1989. As a result, General Pinochet handed over power to President Aylwin on 11 March 1990.

In opening the appeal before your Lordships Mr. Alun Jones Q.C. took as the first of the three main issues for decision whether General Pinochet was head of state throughout the whole period of the allegations against him. It is clear beyond doubt that he was. So I say no more about that.

I return to the narrative. On 19 April 1978, while General Pinochet was still head of state, the senate passed a decree granting an amnesty to all persons involved in criminal acts (with certain exceptions) between 11 September 1973 and 10 March 1978. The purpose of the amnesty was stated to be for the "general tranquillity, peace and order" of the nation. After General Pinochet fell from power, the new democratic government appointed a Commission for Truth and Reconciliation, thus foreshadowing the appointment of a similar commission in South Africa. The Commission consisted of eight civilians of varying political viewpoints under the chairmanship of Don Raul Rettig. Their terms of reference were to investigate all violations of human rights between 1973 and 1990, and to make recommendations. The Commission reported on 9 February 1991.

In 1994 Senator Pinochet came to the United Kingdom on a special diplomatic mission: (he had previously been appointed senator for life). He came again in 1995 and 1997. According to the evidence of Professor Walters, a former foreign minister and ambassador to the United Kingdom, Senator Pinochet was accorded normal diplomatic courtesies. The Foreign Office was informed in advance of his visit to London in September 1998, where at the age of 82 he has undergone an operation at the London Clinic.

At 11.25 p.m. on 16 October he was arrested while still at the London Clinic pursuant to a provisional warrant ("the first provisional warrant") issued under section 8(1)(b) of the Extradition Act 1989. The warrant had been issued by Mr. Evans, a metropolitan stipendiary magistrate, at his home at about 9 p.m. the same evening. The reason for the urgency was said to be that Senator Pinochet was returning to Chile the next day. We do not know the terms of the Spanish international warrant of arrest, also issued on 16 October. All we know is that in the first provisional warrant Senator Pinochet was accused of the murder of Spanish citizens in Chile between 11 September 1973 and 31 December 1983.

For reasons explained by the Divisional Court the first provisional warrant was bad on its face. The murder of Spanish citizens in Chile is not an extradition crime under section 2(1)(b) of the Extradition Act for which Senator Pinochet could be extradited, for the simple reason that the murder of a British citizen in Chile would not be an offence against our law. The underlying principle of all extradition agreements between states, including the European Extradition Convention of 1957, is reciprocity. We do not extradite for offences for which we would not expect and could not request extradition by others.

On 17 October the Chilean Government protested. The protest was renewed on 23 October. The purpose of the protest was to claim immunity from suit on behalf of Senator Pinochet both as a visiting diplomat and as a former head of state, and to request his immediate release.

Meanwhile the flaw in the first provisional warrant must have become apparent to the Crown Prosecution Service, acting on behalf of the State of Spain. At all events, Judge Garzon in Madrid issued a second international warrant of arrest dated 18 October, alleging crimes of genocide and terrorism. This in turn led to a second provisional warrant of arrest in England issued on this occasion by Mr. Ronald Bartle. Senator Pinochet was re-arrested in pursuance of the second warrant on 23 October.

The second warrant alleges five offences, the first being that Senator Pinochet "being a public official conspired with persons unknown to intentionally inflict severe pain or suffering on another in the . . . purported performance of his official duties . . . within the jurisdiction of the government of Spain." In other words, that he was guilty of torture. The reason for the unusual language is that the second provisional warrant was carefully drawn to follow the wording of section 134 of the Criminal Justice Act 1988 which itself reflects article 1 of the Convention Against Torture and Other Cruel, Inhuman or Degrading Treatment or Punishment (1984). Section 134(1) provides:

> "A public official or person acting in an official capacity, whatever his nationality, commits the
> offence of torture if in the United Kingdom or elsewhere he intentionally inflicts severe pain or
> suffering on another in the performance or purported performance of his official duties."

It will be noticed that unlike murder, torture is an offence under English law wherever the act of torture is committed. So unlike the first provisional warrant, the second provisional warrant is not bad on its face. The alleged acts of torture are extradition crimes under section 2 of the Extradition Act, as article 8 of the Convention required, and as Mr. Nichols conceded. The same is true of the third alleged offence, namely, the taking of hostages. Section 1 of the Taking of Hostages Act 1982 creates an offence under English law wherever the act of hostage-taking takes place. So hostage taking, like torture, is an extradition crime. The remaining offences do not call for separate mention.

It was argued that torture and hostage-taking only became extradition crimes after 1988 (torture) and 1982 (hostage-taking) since neither section 134 of the Criminal Justice Act 1988, nor section 1 of the Taking of Hostages Act 1982 are retrospective. But I agree with the Divisional Court that this argument is bad. It involves a misunderstanding of section 2 of the Extradition Act. Section 2(1)(a) refers to conduct which would constitute an offence in the United Kingdom now. It does not refer to conduct which would have constituted an offence then.

The torture allegations in the second provisional warrant are confined to the period from 1 January 1988 to 31 December 1992. Mr. Alun Jones does not rely on conduct subsequent to 11 March 1990. So we are left with the period from 1 January 1988 to 11 March 1990. Only one of the alleged acts of torture took place during that period. The hostage-taking allegations relate to the period from 1 January 1982 to 31 January 1992. There are no alleged acts of hostage-taking during that period. So the second provisional warrant hangs on a very narrow thread. But it was argued that the second provisional warrant is no longer the critical document, and that we ought now to be looking at the complete list of crimes alleged in the formal request of the Spanish Government. I am content to assume, without deciding, that this is so.

Returning again to the narrative, Senator Pinochet made an application for certiorari to quash the first provisional warrant on 22 October and a second application to quash the second provisional warrant on 26 October. It was these applications which succeeded before the Divisional Court on 28 October 1998, with a stay pending an appeal to your Lordships' House. The question certified by the Divisional Court was as to "the proper interpretation and scope of the immunity enjoyed by a former head of state from arrest and extradition proceedings in the United Kingdom in respect of acts committed while he was head of state."

On 3 November 1998 the Chilean Senate adopted a formal protest against the manner in which the Spanish courts had violated the sovereignty of Chile by asserting extra-territorial jurisdiction. They resolved also to protest that the British Government had disregarded Senator Pinochet's immunity from jurisdiction as a former head of state. This latter protest may be based on a misunderstanding. The British Government has done nothing. This is not a case where the Secretary of State has already issued an authority to proceed under section 7 of the Extradition Act, since the provisional warrants were issued without his authority (the case being urgent) under section 8(1)(b) of the Act. It is true that the Secretary of State might have cancelled the warrants under section 8(4). But as the Divisional Court pointed out, it is not the duty of the Secretary of State to review the validity of provisional warrants. It was submitted that it should have been obvious to the Secretary of State that Senator Pinochet was entitled to immunity as a former head of state. But the Divisional Court rejected that submission. In the event leave to move against the Secretary of State was refused.

There are two further points made by Professor Walters in his evidence relating to the present state of affairs in Chile. In the first place he gives a list of 11 criminal suits which have been filed against Senator Pinochet in Chile and five further suits where the Supreme Court has ruled that the 1978 amnesty does not apply. Secondly, he has drawn attention to public concern over the continued detention of Senator Pinochet.

> "I should add that there are grave concerns in Chile that the continued detention and attempted prosecution of Senator Pinochet in a foreign court will upset the delicate political balance and transition to democracy that has been achieved since the institution of democratic rule in Chile. It is felt that the current stable position has been achieved by a number of internal measures including the establishment and reporting of the Rettig Commission on Truth and Reconciliation. The intervention of a foreign court in matters more proper to internal domestic resolution may seriously undermine the balance achieved by the present democratic government."

Summary of issues

The argument has ranged over a very wide field in the course of a hearing lasting six days. The main issues which emerged can be grouped as follows:

(1) Is Senator Pinochet entitled to immunity as a former head of state at common law? This depends on the requirements of customary international law, which are observed and enforced by our courts as part of the common law.
(2) Is Senator Pinochet entitled to immunity as a former head of state under Part 1 of the State Immunity Act 1978? If not, does Part 1 of the State Immunity Act cut down or affect any immunity to which he would otherwise be entitled at common law?
(3) Is Senator Pinochet entitled to immunity as a former head of state under Part 3 of the State Immunity Act, and the articles of the Vienna Convention as set out in the schedule to the Diplomatic Privileges Act 1964? It should be noticed that despite an assertion by the Chilean Government that Senator Pinochet is present in England on a diplomatic passport at the request of the Royal Ordnance, Miss Clare Montgomery Q.C. does not seek to argue that he is entitled to diplomatic immunity on that narrow ground, for which, she says, she cannot produce the appropriate evidence.
(4) Is this a case where the court ought to decline jurisdiction on the ground that the issues raised are non-justiciable?

The last of these four heads is sometimes referred to as "the Act of State" doctrine, especially in the United States. But Act of State is a confusing term. It is used in different senses in many different contexts. So it is better to refer to non-justiciability. The principles of sovereign immunity and non-justiciability overlap in practice. But in legal theory they are separate. State immunity, including head of state immunity, is a principle of public international law. It creates a procedural bar to the jurisdiction of the court. Logically therefore it comes first. Non-justiciability is a principle of private international law. It goes to the substance of the issues to be decided. It requires the court to withdraw from adjudication on the grounds that the issues are such as the court is not competent to decide. State immunity, being a procedural bar to the jurisdiction of the court, can be waived by the state. Non-justiciability, being a substantive bar to adjudication, cannot.

Issue one: head of state immunity at common law

As already mentioned, the common law incorporates the rules of customary international law. The matter is put thus in Oppenheim's International Law 9th ed. 1992, p. 57:

"The application of international law as part of the law of the land means that, subject to the overriding effect of statute law, rights and duties flowing from the rules of customary international law will be recognised and given effect by English courts without the need for any specific Act adopting those rules into English law."

So what is the relevant rule of customary international law? I cannot put it better than it is put by the appellants themselves in para. 26 of their written case:

"No international agreement specifically provides for the immunities of a former head of state. However, under customary international law, it is accepted that a state is entitled to expect that its former head of state will not be subjected to the jurisdiction of the courts of another state for certain categories of acts performed while he was head of state unless immunity is waived by the current government of the state of which he was once the head. The immunity is accorded for the benefit not of the former head of state himself but for the state of which he was once the head and any international law obligations are owed to that state and not to the individual."

The important point to notice in this formulation of the immunity principle is that the rationale is the same for former heads of state as it is for current heads of state. In each case the obligation in international law is owed to the state, and not the individual, though in the case of a current head of state he will have a concurrent immunity ratione personae. This rationale explains why it is the state, and the state alone, which can waive the immunity. Where, therefore, a state is seeking the extradition of its own former head of state, as has happened in a number of cases, the immunity is waived ex hypothesi. It cannot be asserted by the former head of state. But here the situation is the reverse. Chile is not waiving its immunity in respect of the acts of Senator Pinochet as former head of state. It is asserting that immunity in the strongest possible terms, both in respect of the Spanish international warrant, and also in respect of the extradition proceedings in the United Kingdom.

Another point to notice is that it is only in respect of "certain categories of acts" that the former head of state is immune from the jurisdiction of municipal courts. The distinction drawn by customary international law in this connection is between private acts on the one hand, and public, official or governmental acts on the other. Again I cannot put it better than it is put by the appellants in para. 27 of their written case. Like para. 26 it has the authority of Professor Greenwood; and like para. 26 it is not in dispute.

"It is generally agreed that private acts performed by the former head of state attract no such immunity. Official acts, on the other hand, will normally attract immunity. . . . Immunity in respect of such acts, which has sometimes been applied to officials below the rank of head of state, is an aspect of the principle that the courts of one state will not normally exercise jurisdiction in respect of the sovereign acts of another state."

The rule that a former head of state cannot be prosecuted in the municipal courts of a foreign state for his official acts as head of state has the universal support of writers on international law. They all speak with one voice. Thus Sir Arthur Watts K.C.M.G. Q.C. in his monograph on the Legal Position in International Law of Heads of States, Heads of Governments and Foreign Ministers (1994) Recueil des Cours vol. 247 at p. 89 says:

"A head of state's official acts, performed in his public capacity as head of state, are however subject to different considerations. Such acts are acts of the state rather than the head of state's personal acts, and he cannot be sued for them even after he has ceased to be head of state."

In Satow's Guide to Diplomatic Practice 5th ed. we find:

> "2.2 The personal status of a head of a foreign state therefore continues to be regulated by long-established rules of customary international law which can be stated in simple terms. He is entitled to immunity—probably without exception—from criminal and civil jurisdiction . . . 2.4 A head of state who has been deposed or replaced or has abdicated or resigned is of course no longer entitled to privileges or immunities as a head of state. He will be entitled to continuing immunity in regard to acts which he performed while head of state, provided that the acts were performed in his official capacity; in this his position is no different from that of any agent of the state."

In Oppenheim's International Law 9th ed. para. 456, we find:

> "All privileges mentioned must be granted to a head of state only so long as he holds that position. Therefore, after he has been deposed or has abdicated, he may be sued, at least in respect of obligations of a private character entered into while head of state. For his official acts as head of state he will, like any other agent of a state, enjoy continuing immunity."

It was suggested by Professor Brownlie that the American Restatement of the Foreign Relations Law of the United States was to the contrary effect. But I doubt if this is so. In vol. 1, para. 464 we find:

> "Former heads of state or government have sometimes sought immunity from suit in respect of claims arising out of their official acts while in office. Ordinarily, such acts are not within the jurisdiction to prescribe of other states. However a former head of state appears to have no immunity from jurisdiction to adjudicate."

The last sentence means only that it is competent for the court of the foreign state to inquire whether the acts complained of were official acts of the head of state, or private acts. Unless the court is persuaded that they were private acts the immunity is absolute.

Decided cases support the same approach. In Duke of Brunswick v. King of Hanover (1848) 2 H.L. Cas. p. 1, a case discussed by Professor F. A. Mann in his illuminating article published in 59 L.Q.R. (1943) p. 42, the reigning King of Hanover (who happened to be in England) was sued by the former reigning Duke of Brunswick. It was held by this House that the action must fail, not on the ground that the King of Hanover was entitled to personal immunity so long as he was in England (ratione personae) but on the wider ground (ratione materiae) that a foreign sovereign

> "cannot be made responsible here for an act done in his sovereign character in his own country; whether it be an act right or wrong, whether according to the constitution of that country or not, the courts of this country cannot sit in judgment upon an act of a sovereign, effected by virtue of his sovereign authority abroad."

In Hatch v. Baez (1876) 7 Hun. 596 the plaintiff complained of an injury which he sustained at the hands of the defendant when president of the Dominican Republic. After the defendant had ceased to be president, he was arrested in New York at the suit of the plaintiff. There was a full argument before what would now, I think, be called the Second Circuit Court of Appeals, with extensive citation of authority including Duke of Brunswick v. King of Hanover. The plaintiff contended (just as the appellants have contended in the present appeal) that the acts of the defendant must be regarded as having been committed in his private capacity. I quote from the argument at p. 596–597:

> "No unjust or oppressive act committed by his direction upon any one of his subjects, or upon others entitled to protection, is in any true sense the act of the executive in his public and representative capacity, but of the man simply, rated as other men are rated in private stations; for in the perpetration of unauthorised offences of this nature, he divests himself of his "regal preroga-

tives" and descends to the level of those untitled offenders, against whose crimes it is the highest purpose of government to afford protection."

But the court rejected the plaintiff's argument. At p. 599 Gilbert J. said:

"The wrongs and injuries of which the plaintiff complains were inflicted upon him by the Government of St. Domingo, while he was residing in that country, and was in all respects subject to its laws. They consist of acts done by the defendant in his official capacity of president of that republic. The sole question is, whether he is amenable to the jurisdiction of the courts of this state for those acts."

A little later we find, at p. 600:

"The general rule, no doubt, is that all persons and property within the territorial jurisdiction of a state are amenable to the jurisdiction of its courts. But the immunity of individuals from suits brought in foreign tribunals for acts done within their own states, in the exercise of the sovereignty thereof, is essential to preserve the peace and harmony of nations, and has the sanction of the most approved writers on international law. It is also recognised in all the judicial decisions on the subject that have come to my knowledge."

The court concluded:

"The fact that the defendant has ceased to be president of St. Domingo does not destroy his immunity. That springs from the capacity in which the acts were done, and protects the individual who did them, because they emanated from a foreign and friendly government."

In Underhill v. Hernandez (1897) 168 U.S. 250 the plaintiff was an American citizen resident in Venezuela. The defendant was a general in command of revolutionary forces, which afterwards prevailed. The plaintiffs brought proceedings against the defendant in New York, alleging wrongful imprisonment during the revolution. In a celebrated passage Chief Justice Fuller said, at 252:

"Every sovereign state is bound to respect the independence of every other sovereign state, and the courts of one country will not sit in judgment on the acts of the government of another done within its own territory. Redress of grievances by reason of such acts must be obtained through the means open to be availed of by sovereign powers as between themselves."

The Supreme Court approved, at p. 254 a statement by the Circuit Court of Appeals "that the acts of the defendant were the acts of the government of Venezuela, and as such are not properly the subject of adjudication in the courts of another government."

On the other side of the line is Jimenez v. Aristeguieta (1962) 311 F. 2d547. In that case the State of Venezuela sought the extradition of a former chief executive alleging four charges of murder, and various financial crimes. There was insufficient evidence to connect the defendant with the murder charges. But the judge found that the alleged financial crimes were committed for his private financial benefit, and that they constituted "common crimes committed by the Chief of State done in violation of his position and not in pursuance of it." The defendant argued that as a former chief executive he was entitled to sovereign immunity, and he relied on Underhill v. Hernandez. Not surprisingly the Fifth Circuit Court of Appeals rejected this argument. At p. 557, they said:

"It is only when officials having sovereign authority act in an official capacity that the act of state doctrine applies."

To the same effect is United States of America v. Noriega (1990) 746 F.Supp. 1506. The defendant was charged with various drug offences. He claimed immunity as de facto head of the Panamanian government. The court considered the claim under three heads, sovereign immunity, the act of state doctrine and diplomatic immunity. Having referred to Hatch v. Baez and Underhill v. Hernandez the court continued, at pp. 1521–1522:

> "In order for the act of state doctrine to apply, the defendant must establish that his activities are 'acts of state', i.e. that they were taken on behalf of the state and not, as private acts, on behalf of the actor himself. . . . That the acts must be public acts of the sovereign has been repeatedly affirmed. . . . Though the distinction between the public and private acts of government officials may prove elusive, this difficulty has not prevented courts from scrutinising the character of the conduct in question."

The court concluded that Noriega's alleged drug trafficking could not conceivably constitute public acts on behalf of the Panamanian state.

These cases (and there are many others to which we were referred) underline the critical distinction between personal or private acts on the one hand, and public or official acts done in the execution or under colour of sovereign authority on the other. Despite the plethora of authorities, especially in the United States, the appellants were unable to point to a single case in which official acts committed by a head of state have been made the subject of suit or prosecution after he has left office. The nearest they got was Hilao v. Marcos (1994) 25 F. 3d 1467, in which a claim for immunity by the estate of former President Marcos failed. But the facts were special. Although there was no formal waiver of immunity in the case, the government of the Philippines made plain their view that the claim should proceed. Indeed they filed a brief in which they asserted that foreign relations with the United States would not be adversely affected if claims against ex-President Marcos and his estate were litigated in U.S. courts. There is an obvious contrast with the facts of the present case.

So the question comes to this: on which side of the line does the present case come? In committing the crimes which are alleged against him, was Senator Pinochet acting in his private capacity or was he acting in a sovereign capacity as head of state? In my opinion there can be only one answer. He was acting in a sovereign capacity. It has not been suggested that he was personally guilty of any of the crimes of torture or hostage-taking in the sense that he carried them out with his own hands. What is alleged against him is that he organised the commission of such crimes, including the elimination of his political opponents, as head of the Chilean government, and that he did so in co-operation with other governments under Plan Condor, and in particular with the government of Argentina. I do not see how in these circumstances he can be treated as having acted in a private capacity.

In order to make the above point good it is necessary to quote some passages from the second international warrant.

> "It can be inferred from the inquiries made that, since September 1973 in Chile and since 1976 in the Republic of Argentina a series of events and punishable actions were committed under the fiercest ideological repression against the citizens and residents in these countries. The plans and instructions established beforehand from the government enabled these actions to be carried out.
> . . .
>   It has been ascertained that there were coordination actions at international level that were called 'Operativo Condor' in which different countries, Chile and Argentina among them, were involved and whose purpose was to coordinate the oppressive actions among them.
>   In this sense Augusto Pinochet Ugarte, Commander-in-Chief of the Armed Forces and head of the Chilean government at the time, committed punishable acts in coordination with the military authorities in Argentina between 1976 and 1983 . . . as he gave orders to eliminate, torture and

kidnap persons and to cause others to disappear, both Chileans and individuals from different nationalities, in Chile and in other countries, through the actions of the secret service (D.I.N.A.) and within the framework of the above-mentioned 'Plan Condor'."

Where a person is accused of organising the commission of crimes as the head of the government, in cooperation with other governments, and carrying out those crimes through the agency of the police and the secret service, the inevitable conclusion must be that he was acting in a sovereign capacity and not in a personal or private capacity.

But the appellants have two further arguments. First they say that the crimes alleged against Senator Pinochet are so horrific that an exception must be made to the ordinary rule of customary international law. Secondly they say that the crimes in question are crimes against international law, and that international law cannot both condemn conduct as a breach of international law and at the same time grant immunity from prosecution. It cannot give with one hand and take away with the other.

As to the first submission, the difficulty, as the Divisional Court pointed out, is to know where to draw the line. Torture is, indeed, a horrific crime, but so is murder. It is a regrettable fact that almost all leaders of revolutionary movements are guilty of killing their political opponents in the course of coming to power, and many are guilty of murdering their political opponents thereafter in order to secure their power. Yet it is not suggested (I think) that the crime of murder puts the successful revolutionary beyond the pale of immunity in customary international law. Of course it is strange to think of murder or torture as "official" acts or as part of the head of state's "public functions." But if for "official" one substitutes "governmental" then the true nature of the distinction between private acts and official acts becomes apparent. For reasons already mentioned I have no doubt that the crimes of which Senator Pinochet is accused, including the crime of torture, were governmental in nature. I agree with Collins J. in the Divisional Court that it would be unjustifiable in theory, and unworkable in practice, to impose any restriction on head of state immunity by reference to the number or gravity of the alleged crimes. Otherwise one would get to this position: that the crimes of a head of state in the execution of his governmental authority are to be attributed to the state so long as they are not too serious. But beyond a certain (undefined) degree of seriousness the crimes cease to be attributable to the state, and are instead to be treated as his private crimes. That would not make sense.

As to the second submission, the question is whether there should be an exception from the general rule of immunity in the case of crimes which have been made the subject of international conventions, such as the International Convention against the Taking of Hostages (1980) and the Convention against Torture (1984). The purpose of these conventions, in very broad terms, was to ensure that acts of torture and hostage-taking should be made (or remain) offences under the criminal law of each of the state parties, and that each state party should take measures to establish extra-territorial jurisdiction in specified cases. Thus in the case of torture a state party is obliged to establish extra-territorial jurisdiction when the alleged offender is a national of that state, but not where the victim is a national. In the latter case the state has a discretion: see article 5.1(b) and (c). In addition there is an obligation on a state to extradite or prosecute where a person accused of torture is found within its territory—aut dedere aut judicare: see article 7. But there is nothing in the Torture Convention which touches on state immunity. The contrast with the Convention on the Prevention and Punishment of the Crime of Genocide (1948) could not be more marked. Article 4 of the Genocide Convention provides:

"Persons committing genocide or any of the other acts enumerated in article 3 shall be punished whether they are constitutionally responsible rulers or public officials or private individuals."

There is no equivalent provision in either the Torture Convention or the Taking of Hostages Convention.

Moreover when the Genocide Convention was incorporated into English law by the Genocide Act 1969, article 4 was omitted. So Parliament must clearly have intended, or at least contemplated, that a head of state accused of genocide would be able to plead sovereign immunity. If the Torture Convention and the Taking of Hostages Convention had contained a provision equivalent to article 4 of the Genocide Convention (which they did not) it is reasonable to suppose that, as with genocide, the equivalent provisions would have been omitted when Parliament incorporated those conventions into English law. I cannot for my part see any inconsistency between the purposes underlying these Conventions and the rule of international law which allows a head of state procedural immunity in respect of crimes covered by the Conventions.

Nor is any distinction drawn between torture and other crimes in state practice. In Al-Adsani v. Government of Kuwait (1996) 107 I.L.R. 536 the plaintiff brought civil proceedings against the government of Kuwait alleging that he had been tortured in Kuwait by government agents. He was given leave by the Court of Appeal to serve out of the jurisdiction on the ground that state immunity does not extend to acts of torture. When the case came back to the Court of Appeal on an application to set aside service, it was argued that a state is not entitled to immunity in respect of acts that are contrary to international law, and that since torture is a violation of jus cogens, a state accused of torture forfeits its immunity. The argument was rejected. Stuart Smith L.J. observed that the draftsman of the State Immunity Act must have been well aware of the numerous international conventions covering torture (although he could not, of course, have been aware of the convention against torture in 1984). If civil claims based on acts of torture were intended to be excluded from the immunity afforded by section 1(1) of the Act of 1978, because of the horrifying nature of such acts, or because they are condemned by international law, it is inconceivable that section 1(1) would not have said so.

The same conclusion has been reached in the United States. In Siderman de Blake v. Republic of Argentina (1992) 965F 2d 699 the plaintiff brought civil proceedings for alleged acts of torture against the Government of Argentina. It was held by the 9th Circuit Court of Appeals that although prohibition against torture has attained the status of jus cogens in international law (citing Filartiga v. Pena-Irala (1980) 630F 2d 876) it did not deprive the defendant state of immunity under the Foreign Sovereign Immunities Act.

Admittedly these cases were civil cases, and they turned on the terms of the Sovereign Immunity Act in England and the Foreign Sovereign Immunity Act in the United States. But they lend no support to the view that an allegation of torture "trumps" a plea of immunity. I return later to the suggestion that an allegation of torture excludes the principle of non-justiciability.

Further light is shed on state practice by the widespread adoption of amnesties for those who have committed crimes against humanity including torture. Chile was not the first in the field. There was an amnesty at the end of the Franco-Algerian War in 1962. In 1971 India and Bangladesh agreed not to pursue charges of genocide against Pakistan troops accused of killing about 1 million East Pakistanis. General amnesties have also become common in recent years, especially in South America, covering members of former regimes accused of torture and other atrocities. Some of these have had the blessing of the United Nations, as a means of restoring peace and democratic government.

In some cases the validity of these amnesties has been questioned. For example, the Committee against Torture (the body established to implement the Torture Convention under article 17) reported on the Argentine amnesty in 1990. In 1996 the Inter-American Commission investigated and reported on the Chilean amnesty. It has not been argued that these amnesties are as such contrary to international law by reason of the failure to prosecute the individual perpetrators. Notwithstanding the wide terms of the Torture Convention and the Taking of Hostages Convention, state practice does not at present support an obligation to extradite or prosecute in all cases. Mr. David Lloyd Jones (to whom we are all much indebted for his help as amicus) put the matter as follows:

> "It is submitted that while there is some support for the view that generally applicable rules of state immunity should be displaced in cases concerning infringements of jus cogens, e.g. cases of torture, this does not yet constitute a rule of public international law. In particular it must be particularly doubtful whether there exists a rule of public international law requiring states not to accord immunity in such circumstances. Such a rule would be inconsistent with the practice of many states."

Professor Greenwood took us back to the charter of the International Military Tribunal for the trial of war criminals at Nuremburg, and drew attention to article 7, which provides:

> "The official position of defendants, whether as heads of state or responsible officials in government departments, shall not be considered as freeing them from responsibility or mitigating punishment."

One finds the same provision in almost identical language in article 7(2) of the Statute of the International Tribunal for the Former Yugoslavia (1993), article 6(2) of the Statue of the International Tribunal for Rwanda (1994) and most recently in article 27 of the Statute of the International Criminal Court (1998). Like the Divisional Court, I regard this as an argument more against the appellants than in their favour. The setting up of these special international tribunals for the trial of those accused of genocide and other crimes against humanity, including torture, shows that such crimes, when committed by heads of state or other responsible government officials cannot be tried in the ordinary courts of other states. If they could, there would be little need for the international tribunal.

Professor Greenwood's reference to these tribunals also provides the answer to those who say, with reason, that there must be a means of bringing such men as Senator Pinochet to justice. There is. He may be tried (1) in his own country, or (2) in any other country that can assert jurisdiction, provided his own country waives state immunity, or (3) before the International Criminal Court when it is established, or (4) before a specially constituted international court, such as those to which Professor Greenwood referred. But in the absence of waiver he cannot be tried in the municipal courts of other states.

On the first issue I would hold that Senator Pinochet is entitled to immunity as former head of state in respect of the crimes alleged against him on well established principles of customary international law, which principles form part of the common law of England.

Issue two: immunity under Part I of the State Immunity Act 1978

The long title of the State Immunity Act 1978 states as its first purpose the making of new provision with respect to proceedings in the United Kingdom by or against other states.

Other purposes include the making of new provision with respect to immunities and privileges of heads of state. It is common ground that the Act of 1978 must be read against the background of customary international law current in 1978; for it is highly unlikely, as Lord Diplock said in Alcom Ltd. v. Republic of Colombia [1984] 4 A.C. 580 at p. 600 that Parliament intended to require United Kingdom courts to act contrary to international law unless the clear language of the statute compels such a conclusion. It is for this reason that it made sense to start with customary international law before coming to the statute.

The relevant sections are as follows:

"1. General immunity from jurisdiction
(1) A state is immune from the jurisdiction of the courts of the United Kingdom except as provided in the following provisions of this Part of this Act.
(2) A court shall give effect to the immunity conferred by this section even though the state does not appear in the proceedings in question.
"14. States entitled to immunities and privileges
"(1) The immunities and privileges conferred by this Part of this Act apply to any foreign or commonwealth state other than the United Kingdom; and references to a state include references to:
(a) the sovereign or other head of that state in his public capacity;
(b) the government of that state; and
(c) any department of that government,
but not to any entity (hereafter referred to as a 'separate entity') which is distinct from the executive organs of the government of the state and capable of suing or being sued.
(2) A separate entity is immune from the jurisdiction of the courts of the United Kingdom if, and only if:
(a) the proceedings relate to anything done by it in the exercise of sovereign authority; . . .
"16. Excluded matters
(1) This Part of this Act does not affect any immunity or privilege conferred by the Diplomatic Privileges Act 1964 . . .
(4) This Part of this Act does not apply to criminal proceedings."

Mr. Nichols drew attention to the width of section 1(1) of the Act. He submitted that it confirms the rule of absolute immunity at common law, subject to the exceptions contained in sections 2–11, and that the immunity covers criminal as well as civil proceedings. Faced with the objection that Part I of the Act is stated not to apply to criminal proceedings by virtue of the exclusion in section 16(4), he argues that the exclusion applies only to sections 2–11. In other words section 16(4) is an exception on an exception. It does not touch section 1. This was a bold argument, and I cannot accept it. It seems clear that the exclusions in section 16(2)(3) and (5) all apply to Part I as a whole, including section 1(1). I can see no reason why section 16(4) should not also apply to section 1(1). Mr. Nichols referred us to an observation of the Lord Chancellor in moving the Second Reading of the Bill in the House of Lords: Hansard 17 January 1978 col. 52. In relation to Part I of the Bill he said "immunity from criminal jurisdiction is not affected, and that will remain." I do not see how this helps Mr. Nicholls. It confirms that the purpose of Part I was to enact the restrictive theory of sovereign immunity in relation to commercial transactions and other matters of a civil nature. It was not intended to affect immunity in criminal proceedings.

The remaining question under this head is whether the express exclusion of criminal proceedings from Part I of the Act, including section 1(1), means that the immunity in respect of criminal proceedings which exists at common law has been abolished. In Al Adsani v. Government of Kuwait 107 I.L.R. 536 at 542 Stuart Smith L.J. referred to the

State Immunity Act as providing a "comprehensive code." So indeed it does. But obviously it does not provide a code in respect of matters which it does not purport to cover. In my opinion the immunity of a former head of state in respect of criminal acts committed by him in exercise of sovereign power is untouched by Part I of the Act.

Issue three: *immunity under Part III of the State Immunity Act*

The relevant provision is section 20 which reads:

"(1) Subject to the provisions of this section and to any necessary modifications, the Diplomatic Privileges Act 1964 shall apply to:
(a) a sovereign or other head of State;
(b) members of his family forming part of his household; and
(c) his private servants,
as it applies to the head of a diplomatic mission, to members of his family forming part of his household and to his private servants. . . .
"(5) This section applies to the sovereign or other head of any state on which immunities and privileges are conferred by Part I of this Act and is without prejudice to the application of that Part to any such sovereign or head of state in his public capacity."

The Diplomatic Privileges Act 1964 was enacted to give force to the Vienna Convention on diplomatic privileges. Section 1 provides that the Act is to have effect in substitution for any previous enactment or rule of law.

So again the question arises whether the common law immunities have been abolished by statute. So far as the immunities and privileges of diplomats are concerned, this may well be the case. Whether the same applies to heads of state is more debatable. But it does not matter. For in my view the immunities to which Senator Pinochet is entitled under section 20 of the State Immunity Act are identical to the immunities which he enjoys at common law.

The Vienna Convention provides as follows:

"Article 29: The person of a diplomatic agent shall be inviolable. He shall not be liable to any form of arrest or detention. . . .
"Article 31: A diplomatic agent shall enjoy immunity from the criminal jurisdiction of the receiving state. . . .
"Article 39(1): Every person entitled to privileges and immunities shall enjoy them from the moment he enters the territory of the receiving state on proceedings to take up his post or, if already in its territory, from the moment when his appointment is notified to the Ministry for Foreign Affairs or such other ministry as may be agreed.
(2) When the functions of a person enjoying privileges and immunities have come to an end, such privileges and immunities shall normally cease at the moment when he leaves the country, or on expiry of a reasonable period in which to do so, but shall subsist until that time, even in case of armed conflict. However, with respect to acts performed by such a person in the exercise of his functions as a member of the mission, immunity shall continue to subsist.

The critical provision is the second sentence of article 39(2). How is this sentence to be applied (as it must) to a head of state? What are the "necessary modifications" which are required under section 20 of the State Immunity Act? It is a matter of regret that in such an important sphere of international law as the immunity of heads of state from the jurisdiction of our courts Parliament should have legislated in such a round-about way. But we must do our best.

The most extreme view, advanced only, I think, by Professor Brownlie for the Interveners and soon abandoned, is that the immunity extends only to acts performed by a visiting head of state while within the United Kingdom. I would reject this submission. Article 39(2) is not expressly confined to acts performed in the United Kingdom, and it is difficult to see what functions a visiting heads of state would be able to exercise in the United Kingdom as head of state other than purely ceremonial functions.

A less extensive view was advanced by Mr. Alun Jones as his first submission in reply. This was that the immunity only applies to the acts of heads of state in the exercise of their external functions, that is to say, in the conduct of international relations and foreign affairs generally. But in making the "necessary modifications" to article 39 to fit a head of state, I see no reason to read "functions" as meaning "external functions." It is true that diplomats operate in foreign countries as members of a mission. But heads of state do not. The normal sphere of a head of state's operations is his own country. So I would reject Mr. Alun Jones's first submission.

Mr. Alun Jones's alternative submission in reply was as follows:

"However, if this interpretation is wrong, and Parliament's intention in section 20(1)(a) of the State Immunity Act was to confer immunity in respect of the exercise of the internal, as well as the external, functions of the head of state, then the second sentence of article 39(2) must be read as if it said: 'with respect to official acts performed by a head of state in the exercise of his functions as head of state, immunity shall continue to subsist.' "

Here Mr. Alun Jones hits the mark. His formulation was accepted as correct by Mr. Nicholls and Miss Clare Montgomery on behalf of the respondents, and by Mr. David Lloyd Jones as amicus curiae.

So the question on his alternative submission is whether the acts of which Senator Pinochet is accused were "official acts performed by him in the exercise of his functions as head of state." For the reasons given in answer to issue 1, the answer must be that they were.

So the answer is the same whether at common law or under the statute. And the rationale is the same. The former head of state enjoys continuing immunity in respect of governmental acts which he performed as head of state because in both cases the acts are attributed to the state itself.

Issue four: non-justiciability

If I am right that Senator Pinochet is entitled to immunity at common law, and under the statute, then the question of Non-justiciability does not arise. But I regard it as a question of overriding importance in the present context, so I intend to say something about it.

The principle of non-justiciability may be traced back to the same source as head of state immunity, namely, the Duke of Brunswick v. The King of Hanover. Since then the principles have developed separately; but they frequently overlap, and are sometimes confused. The authoritative expression of modern doctrine of non-justiciability is to be found in the speech of Lord Wilberforce in Buttes Gas and Oil Co. v. Hammer [1982] A.C. 888. One of the questions in that case was whether there exists in English law a general principle that the courts will not adjudicate upon the transactions of foreign sovereign states. Lord Wilberforce answered the question in the affirmative. At 932 he said:

"In my opinion there is, and for long has been, such a general principle, starting in English law, adopted and generalised in the law of the United States of America which is effective and compelling in English courts. This principle is not one of discretion, but is inherent in the very nature of the judicial process."

Lord Wilberforce traces the principle from Duke of Brunswick v. King of Hanover through numerous decisions of the Supreme Court of the United States including Underhill v. Hernandez, Oetjen v. Central Leather Co. (1918) 246 U.S. 297 and Banco Nacional de Cuba v. Sabbatino (1964) 376 U.S. 398. In the latter case Lord Wilberforce detected a more flexible use of the principle on a case-by-case basis. This is borne out by the most recent decision of the Supreme Court in W.S. Kirkpatrick & Co. Inc. v. Environmental Tectonics Corporation International (1990) 493 U.S. 400. These and other cases are analysed in depth by Mance J. in his judgment in Kuwait Airways Corporation v. Iraqi Airways Co. (unreported) 29 July 1998, from which I have derived much assistance. In the event Mance J. held that judicial restraint was not required on the facts of that case. The question is whether it is required (or would be required if head of state immunity were not a sufficient answer) on the facts of the present case. In my opinion there are compelling reasons for regarding the present case as falling within the non-justiciability principle.

In the Buttes Gas case the court was being asked "to review transactions in which four sovereign states were involved, which they had brought to a precarious settlement, after diplomacy and the use of force, and to say that at least part of these were 'unlawful' under international law." Lord Wilberforce concluded that the case raised issues upon which a municipal court could not pass. In the present case the State of Spain is claiming the right to try Senator Pinochet, a former head of state, for crimes committed in Chile, some of which are said to be in breach of international law. They have requested his extradition. Other states have also requested extradition. Meanwhile Chile is demanding the return of Senator Pinochet on the ground that the crimes alleged against him are crimes for which Chile is entitled to claim state immunity under international law. These crimes were the subject of a general amnesty in 1978, and subsequent scrutiny by the Commission of Truth and Reconciliation in 1990. The Supreme Court in Chile has ruled that in respect of at least some of these crimes the 1978 amnesty does not apply. It is obvious, therefore, that issues of great sensitivity have arisen between Spain and Chile. The United Kingdom is caught in the crossfire. In addition there are allegations that Chile was collaborating with other states in South America, and in particular with Argentina, in execution of Plan Condor.

If we quash the second provisional warrant, Senator Pinochet will return to Chile, and Spain will complain that we have failed to comply with our international obligations under the European Convention on Extradition. If we do not quash the second provisional warrant, Chile will complain that Senator Pinochet has been arrested in defiance of Chile's claim for immunity, and in breach of our obligations under customary international law. In these circumstances, quite apart from any embarrassment in our foreign relations, or potential breach of comity, and quite apart from any fear that, by assuming jurisdiction, we would only serve to "imperil the amicable relations between governments and vex the peace of nations" (see Oetjen v. Central Leather Co. (1918) 246 U.S. 297 at 304) we would be entering a field in which we are simply not competent to adjudicate. We apply customary international law as part of the common law, and we give effect to our international obligations so far as they are incorporated in our statute law; but we are not an international court. For an English court to investigate and pronounce on the validity of the amnesty in Chile would be to assert jurisdiction over the internal affairs of that state at the very time when the Supreme Court in Chile is itself performing the same task. In my view this is a case in which, even if there were no valid claim to sovereign immunity, as I think there is, we should exercise judicial restraint by declining jurisdiction.

There are three arguments the other way. The first is that it is always open to the Secretary of State to refuse to make an order for the return of Senator Pinochet to Spain in the exercise of his discretion under section 12 of the Extradition Act. But so far as Chile is concerned, the damage will by then have been done. The English courts will have condoned the arrest. The Secretary of State's discretion will come too late. The fact that these proceedings were initiated by a provisional warrant under section 8(1)(b) without the Secretary of State's authority to proceed, means that the courts cannot escape responsibility for deciding now whether or not to accept jurisdiction.

Secondly it is said that by allowing the extradition request to proceed, we will not be adjudicating ourselves. That will be the task of the courts in Spain. In an obvious sense this is true. But we will be taking an essential step towards allowing the trial to take place, by upholding the validity of the arrest. It is to the taking of that step that Chile has raised objections, as much as to the trial itself.

Thirdly it is said that in the case of torture Parliament has removed any concern that the court might otherwise have by enacting section 134 of the Criminal Justice Act 1988 in which the offence of torture is defined as the intentional infliction of severe pain by "a public official or . . . person acting in an official capacity." I can see nothing in this definition to override the obligation of the court to decline jurisdiction (as Lord Wilberforce pointed out it is an obligation, and not a discretion) if the circumstances of the case so require. In some cases there will be no difficulty. Where a public official or person acting in an official capacity is accused of torture, the court will usually be competent to try the case if there is no plea of sovereign imunity, or if sovereign immunity is waived. But here the circumstances are very different. The whole thrust of Lord Wilberforce's speech was that non-justiciability is a flexible principle, depending on the circumstances of the particular case. If I had not been of the view that Senator Pinochet is entitled to immunity as a former head of state, I should have held that the principle of non-justiciability applies.

For these reasons, and the reasons given in the judgment of the Divisional Court with which I agree, I would dismiss the appeal.

Lord Nicholls

My Lords,

This appeal concerns the scope of the immunity of a former head of state from the criminal processes of this country. It is an appeal against a judgment of the Divisional Court of the Queen's Bench Division which quashed a provisional warrant issued at the request of the Spanish Government pursuant to section 8(b)(i) of the Extradition Act 1989 for the arrest of the respondent Senator Augusto Pinochet. The warrant charged five offences, but for present purposes I need refer to only two of them. The first offence charged was committing acts of torture contrary to section 134(1) of the Criminal Justice Act 1988. The Act defines the offence as follows:

"A public official or person acting in an official capacity, whatever his nationality, commits the offence of torture if in the United Kingdom or elsewhere he intentionally inflicts severe pain or suffering on another in the performance or purported performance of his official duties."

The third offence charged was hostage-taking contrary to section 1 of the Taking of Hostages Act 1982. Section 1 defines the offence in these terms:

"A person, whatever his nationality, who, in the United Kingdom or elsewhere:
(a) detains any other person ('the hostage'), and

(b) in order to compel a State, international governmental organisation or person to do or abstain from doing any act, threatens to kill, injure, or continue to detain the hostage, commits an offence."

Both these offences are punishable with imprisonment for life. It is conceded that both offences are extradition crimes within the meaning of the Extradition Act.

The Divisional Court quashed the warrant on the ground that Senator Pinochet was head of the Chilean state at the time of the alleged offences and therefore, as a former sovereign, he is entitled to immunity from the criminal processes of the English courts. The court certified, as a point of law of general public importance, "the proper interpretation and scope of the immunity enjoyed by a former head of state from arrest and extradition proceedings in the United Kingdom in respect of acts committed while he was head of state", and granted leave to appeal to your Lordships' House. On this appeal I would admit the further evidence which has been produced, setting out the up-to-date position reached in the extradition proceedings.

There is some dispute over whether Senator Pinochet was technically head of state for the whole of the period in respect of which charges are laid. There is no certificate from the Foreign and Commonwealth Office, but the evidence shows he was the ruler of Chile from 11 September 1973, when a military junta of which he was the leader overthrew the previous government of President Allende, until 11 March 1990 when he retired from the office of president. I am prepared to assume he was head of state throughout the period.

Sovereign immunity may have been a single doctrine at the time when the laws of nations did not distinguish between the personal sovereign and the state, but in modern English law it is necessary to distinguish three different principles, two of which have been codified in statutes and the third of which remains a doctrine of the common law. The first is state immunity, formerly known as sovereign immunity, now largely codified in Part I of the State Immunity Act 1978. The second is the Anglo-American common law doctrine of act of state. The third is the personal immunity of the head of state, his family and servants, which is now codified in section 20 of the State Immunity Act 1978. Miss Montgomery Q.C., in her argument for Senator Pinochet, submitted that in addition to these three principles there is a residual state immunity which protects former state officials from prosecution for crimes committed in their official capacities.

State immunity

Section 1 of the State Immunity Act 1978 provides that "a State is immune from the jurisdiction of the courts of the United Kingdom", subject to exceptions set out in the following sections, of which the most important is section 3 (proceedings relating to a commercial transaction). By section 14(1) references to a state include references to the sovereign or other head of that state in his public capacity, its government and any department of its government. Thus the immunity of the state may not be circumvented by suing the head of state, or indeed, any other government official, in his official capacity.

It should be noted that the words "in his public capacity" in section 14(1), read with section 1, refer to the capacity in which the head of state is sued, rather than the capacity in which he performed the act alleged to give rise to liability. Section 1 of the Act deals with proceedings which, at the time they are started, are in form or in substance proceedings against the state, so that directly or indirectly the state will be affected by the judgment. In the traditional language of international law, it is immunity ratione personae and not ratione materiae. It protects the state as an entity. It is not concerned with the nature of the transaction alleged to give rise to liability, although this becomes important when applying the exceptions in later sections. Nor is it concerned with whether, in an action against an official or former official which is not in substance an action against the state, he can claim immunity on the ground that in doing the acts alleged he was acting in a public capacity. Immunity on that ground depends upon the other principles to which I shall come. Similarly, Part I of the Act does not apply to criminal proceedings (section 16(4)). On this section 16(4) is unambiguous. Contrary to the contentions of Mr. Nicholls Q.C., section 16(4) cannot be read as applying only to the exceptions to section 1.

In cases which fall within section 1 but not within any of the exceptions, the immunity has been held by the Court of Appeal to be absolute and not subject to further exception on the ground that the conduct in question is contrary to international law: see Al-Adsani v. Government of Kuwait (1996) 107 I.L.R. 536, where the court upheld the government's plea of state immunity in proceedings where the plaintiff alleged torture by government officials. A similar conclusion was reached by the United States Supreme Court on the interpretation of the Foreign Sovereign Immunities Act 1976 in Argentine Republic v. Amerada Hess Shipping Corporation (1989) 109 S.Ct. 683. This decision was followed by the Court of Appeals for the Ninth Circuit, perhaps with a shade of reluctance, in Siderman de Blake v. Republic of Argentina 965 F.2d 699 (9th Cir. 1992), also a case based upon allegations of torture by government officials. These decisions are not relevant in the present case, which does not concern civil proceedings against the state. So I shall say no more about them.

Act of state: non-justiciability

The act of state doctrine is a common law principle of uncertain application which prevents the English court from examining the legality of certain acts performed in the exercise of sovereign authority within a foreign country or, occasionally, outside it. Nineteenth century dicta (for example, in Duke of Brunswick v. King of Hanover (1848) 2 H.L.Cas. 1 and Underhill v. Hernandez (1897) 169 U.S. 456) suggested that it reflected a rule of international law. The modern view is that the principle is one of domestic law which reflects a recognition by the courts that certain questions of foreign affairs are not justiciable (Buttes Gas and Oil Co. v. Hammer [1982] A.C. 888) and, particularly in the United States, that judicial intervention in foreign relations may trespass upon the province of the other two branches of government (Banco Nacional de Cuba v. Sabbatino 376 U.S. 398).

The doctrine has sometimes been stated in sweepingly wide terms; for instance, in a celebrated passage by Chief Justice Fuller in Underhill v. Hernandez (1897) 169 U.S. 456:

> "Every sovereign state is bound to respect the independence of every other sovereign state, and the courts of one country will not sit in judgment on the acts of the government of another done within its own territory."

More recently the courts in the United States have confined the scope of the doctrine to instances where the outcome of the case requires the court to decide the legality of the sovereign acts of foreign states: W. S. Kirkpatrick & Co. Inc. v. Environmental Tectonics Corporation, International (1990) 110 S.Ct. 701.

However, it is not necessary to discuss the doctrine in any depth, because there can be no doubt that it yields to a contrary intention shown by Parliament. Where Parliament has shown that a particular issue is to be justiciable in the English courts, there can be no place for the courts to apply this self-denying principle. The definition of torture in section 134(1) of the Criminal Justice Act 1988 makes clear that prosecution will require an investigation into the conduct of officials acting in an official capacity in foreign countries. It must follow that Parliament did not intend the act of state doctrine to apply in such cases. Similarly with the taking of hostages. Although section 1(1) of the Taking of Hostages Act 1982 does not define the offence as one which can be committed only by a public official, it is really inconceivable that Parliament should be taken to have intended that such officials should be outside the reach of this offence. The Taking of Hostages Act was enacted to implement the International Convention against the Taking of Hostages, and that convention described taking hostages as a manifestation of international terrorism. The convention was opened for signature in New York in December 1979, and its immediate historical background was a number of hostage-taking incidents in which states were involved or were suspected to have been involved. These include the hostage crisis at the United States embassy in Teheran earlier in that year, several hostage-takings following the hijacking of aircraft in the 1970s, and the holding hostage of the passengers of an El-Al aircraft at Entebbe airport in June 1976.

Personal immunity

Section 20 of the State Immunity Act 1978 confers personal immunity upon a head of state, his family and servants by reference ("with necessary modifications") to the privileges and immunities enjoyed by the head of a diplomatic mission under the Vienna Convention on Diplomatic Relations 1961, which was enacted as a schedule to the Diplomatic Privileges Act 1964. These immunities include, under article 31, "immunity from the criminal jurisdiction of the receiving state." Accordingly there can be no doubt that if Senator Pinochet had still been head of the Chilean state, he would have been entitled to immunity.

Whether he continued to enjoy immunity after ceasing to be head of state turns upon the proper interpretation of article 39.2 of the convention:

"When the functions of a person enjoying privileges and immunities have come to an end, such privileges and immunities shall normally cease at the moment when he leaves the country, or on expiry of a reasonable period in which to do so, but shall subsist until that time, even in case of armed conflict. However, with respect to acts performed by such a person in the exercise of his functions as a member of the mission, immunity shall continue to subsist."

The "necessary modification" required by section 20 of the 1978 Act is to read "as a head of state" in place of "as a member of the mission" in the last sentence. Writ large, the effect of these provisions can be expressed thus:

"A former head of state shall continue to enjoy immunity from the criminal jurisdiction of the United Kingdom with respect to acts performed by him in the exercise of his functions as a head of state."

Transferring to a former head of state in this way the continuing protection afforded to a former head of a diplomatic mission is not an altogether neat exercise, as their functions are dissimilar. Their positions are not in all respects analogous. A head of mission operates on the international plane in a foreign state where he has been received; a head of state operates principally within his own country, at both national and international levels. This raises the question whether, in the case of a former head of state, the continuing immunity embraces acts performed in exercise of any of his "functions as a head of state" or is confined to such of those acts as have an international character. I prefer the former, wider interpretation. There is no reason for cutting down the ambit of the protection, so that it will embrace only some of the functions of a head of state. (I set out below the test for determining what are the functions of a head of state.)

The question which next arises is the crucial question in the present case. It is whether the acts of torture and hostage-taking charged against Senator Pinochet were done in the exercise of his functions as head of state. The Divisional Court decided they were because, according to the allegations in the Spanish warrant which founded the issue of the provisional warrant in this country, they were committed under colour of the authority of the government of Chile. Senator Pinochet was charged, not with personally torturing victims or causing their disappearance, but with using the power of the state of which he was the head to that end. Thus the Divisional Court held that, for the purposes of article 39.2, the functions of head of state included any acts done under purported public authority in Chile. The Lord Chief Justice said the underlying rationale of the immunity accorded by article 39.2 was "a rule of international comity restraining one sovereign state from sitting in judgment on the sovereign behaviour of another." It therefore applied to all sovereign conduct within Chile.

Your Lordships have had the advantage of much fuller argument and the citation of a wider range of authorities than the Divisional Court. I respectfully suggest that, in coming to this conclusion, the Lord Chief Justice elided the domestic law doctrine of act of state, which has often been stated in the broad terms he used, with the international law obligations of this country towards foreign heads of state, which section 20 of the 1978 Act was intended to codify. In my view, article 39.2 of the Vienna Convention, as modified and applied to former heads of state by section 20 of the 1978 Act, is apt to confer immunity in respect of acts performed in the exercise of functions which international law recognises as functions of a head of state, irrespective of the terms of his domestic constitution. This formulation, and this test for determining what are the functions of a head of state for this purpose, are sound in principle and were not the subject of controversy before your Lordships. International law does not require the grant of any wider immunity. And it hardly needs saying that torture of his own subjects, or of aliens, would not be regarded by international law as a function of a head of state. All states disavow the use of torture as abhorrent, although from time to time some still resort to it. Similarly, the taking of hostages, as much as torture, has been outlawed by the international community as an offence. International law recognises, of course, that the functions of a head of state may include activities which are wrongful, even illegal, by the law of his own state or by the laws of other states. But international law has made plain that certain types of conduct, including torture and hostage-taking, are not acceptable conduct on the part of anyone. This applies as much to heads of state, or even more so, as it does to everyone else; the contrary conclusion would make a mockery of international law.

This was made clear long before 1973 and the events which took place in Chile then and thereafter. A few references will suffice. Under the charter of the Nurnberg International Military Tribunal (8 August 1945) crimes against humanity, committed before as well as during the second world war, were declared to be within the jurisdiction of the tribunal, and the official position of defendants, "whether as heads of state or responsible officials in government", was not to free them from responsibility (articles 6 and 7). The judgment of the tribunal included the following passage:

"The principle of international law which, under certain circumstance, protects the representatives of a state cannot be applied to acts condemned as criminal by international law. The authors of these acts cannot shelter themselves behind their official position to be freed from punishment."

With specific reference to the laws of war, but in the context the observation was equally applicable to crimes against humanity, the tribunal stated:

"He who violates the laws of war cannot obtain immunity while acting in pursuance of the authority of the state if the state in authorising action moves outside its competence under international law."

By a resolution passed unanimously on 11 December 1946, the United Nations general assembly affirmed the principles of international law recognised by the charter of the Nurnberg tribunal and the judgment of the tribunal. From this time on, no head of state could have been in any doubt about his potential personal liability if he participated in acts regarded by international law as crimes against humanity. In 1973 the United Nations put some of the necessary nuts and bolts into place, for bringing persons suspected of having committed such offences to trial in the courts of individual states. States were to assist each other in bringing such persons to trial, asylum was not to be granted to such persons, and states were not to take any legislative or other measures which might be prejudicial to the international obligations assumed by them in regard to the arrest, extradition and punishment of such persons. This was in resolution 3074 adopted on 3 December 1973.

Residual immunity

Finally I turn to the residual immunity claimed for Senator Pinochet under customary international law. I have no doubt that a current head of state is immune from criminal process under customary international law. This is reflected in section 20 of the State Immunity Act 1978. There is no authority on whether customary international law grants such immunity to a former head of state or other state official on the ground that he was acting under colour of domestic authority. Given the largely territorial nature of criminal jurisdiction, it will be seldom that the point arises.

A broad principle of international law, according former public officials a degree of personal immunity against prosecution in other states, would be consistent with the rationale underlying section 20 of the 1978 Act. It would also be consistent with changes in the way countries are governed. In times past, before the development of the concept of the state as a separate entity, the sovereign was indistinguishable from the state: l'Etat, c'est moi. It would be expected therefore that in those times a former head of state would be accorded a special personal immunity in respect of acts done by him as head of state. Such acts were indistinguishable from acts of the state itself. Methods of state governance have changed since the days of Louis XIV. The conduct of affairs of state is often in the hands of government ministers, with the head of state having a largely ceremonial role. With this change in the identity of those who act for the state, it would be attractive for personal immunity to be available to all former public officials, including a former head of state, in respect of acts which are properly attributable to the state itself. One might expect international law to develop along these lines, although the personal immunity such a principle affords would be largely covered also by the act of state doctrine.

Even such a broad principle, however, would not assist Senator Pinochet. In the same way as acts of torture and hostage-taking stand outside the limited immunity afforded to a former head of state by section 20, because those acts cannot be regarded by international law as a function of a head of state, so for a similar reason Senator Pinochet cannot bring himself within any such broad principle applicable to state officials. Acts of torture and hostage-taking, outlawed as they are by international law, cannot be attributed to the state to the exclusion of personal liability. Torture is defined in the torture convention (the Convention against torture and other cruel, inhuman or degrading treatment or punishment (1984)) and in the United Kingdom legislation (section 134 of the Criminal Justice Act 1984) as a crime committed by public officials and persons acting in a public capacity. As already noted, the Convention against the taking of hostages (1979) described hostage-taking as a manifestation of international terrorism. It is not consistent with the existence of these crimes that former officials, however senior, should be immune from prosecution outside their own jurisdictions. The two international conventions made clear that these crimes were to be punishable by courts of individual states. The torture convention, in articles 5 and 7, expressly provided that states are permitted to establish jurisdiction where the victim is one of their nationals, and that states are obliged to prosecute or extradite alleged offenders. The hostage-taking convention is to the same effect, in articles 5 and 8.

I would allow this appeal. It cannot be stated too plainly that the acts of torture and hostage-taking with which Senator Pinochet is charged are offences under United Kingdom statute law. This country has taken extra-territorial jurisdiction for these crimes. The sole question before your Lordships is whether, by reason of his status as a former head of state, Senator Pinochet is immune from the criminal processes of this country, of which extradition forms a part. Arguments about the effect on this country's diplomatic relations with Chile if extradition were allowed to proceed, or with Spain if refused, are not matters for the court. These are, par excellence, political matters for consideration by the Secretary of State in the exercise of his discretion under section 12 of the Extradition Act.

LORD STEYN

My Lords,

The way in which this appeal comes before the House must be kept in mind. Spain took preliminary steps under the Extradition Act 1989 to obtain the extradition of General Pinochet, the former Head of State of Chile, in respect of crimes which he allegedly committed between 11 September 1973 and March 1990 when he ceased to be the President of Chile. General Pinochet applied to the Divisional Court for a ruling that he is entitled to immunity as a former Head of State from criminal and civil process in the English courts. He obtained a ruling to that effect. If that ruling is correct, the extradition proceedings are at an end. The issues came to the Divisional Court in advance of the receipt of a particularized request for extradition by Spain. Such a request has now been received. Counsel for General Pinochet has argued that the House ought to refuse to admit the request in evidence. In my view it would be wrong to ignore the material put forward in Spain's formal request for extradition. This case ought to be decided on the basis of all the relevant materials before the House. And that involves also taking into account the further evidence lodged on behalf of General Pinochet.

In an appeal in which no fewer than 16 barristers were involved over six days it is not surprising that issues proliferated. Some of the issues do not need to be decided. For example, there was as an issue as to the date upon which General Pinochet became the Head of State of Chile. He undoubtedly became the Head of State at least by 26 June 1974; and I will assume that from the date of the coup d'etat on 11 September 1973 he was the Head of State. Rather than attempt to track down every other hare that has been started, I will concentrate my observations on three central issues, namely (1) the nature of the charges brought by Spain against General Pinochet; (2) the question whether he is entitled to former Head of State immunity under the applicable statutory provisions; (3) if he is not entitled to such immunity, the different question whether under the common law act of state doctrine the House ought to declare that the matters involved are not justiciable in our courts. This is not the order in which counsel addressed the issues but the advantage of so considering the issues is considerable. One can only properly focus on the legal issues before the House when there is clarity about the nature of the charges in respect of which General Pinochet seeks to establish immunity or seeks to rely on the act of state doctrine. Logically, immunity must be examined before act of state. The act of state issue will only arise if the court decides that the defendant does not have immunity. And I shall attempt to show that the construction of the relevant statutory provisions relating to immunity has a bearing on the answer to the separate question of act of state.

The case against General Pinochet

In the Divisional Court the Lord Chief Justice summarized the position by saying that the thrust of the warrant "makes it plain that the applicant is charged not with personally torturing or murdering victims or ordering their disappearance, but with using the power of the State to that end". Relying on the information contained in the request for extradition, it is necessary to expand the cryptic account of the facts in the warrant. The request alleges a systematic campaign of repression against various groups in Chile after the military coup on 11 September 1973. The case is that of the order of 4,000 individuals were killed or simply disappeared. Such killings and disappearances mostly took place in Chile but some also took place in various countries abroad. Such acts were committed during the period from 11 September 1973 until 1990. The climax of the repression was reached in 1974 and 1975. The principal instrumentality of the oppression was the Direction de Inteligencia Nacional (DINA), the secret police. The subsequent renaming of this organization is immaterial. The case is that agents of DINA, who were specially trained in torture techniques, tortured victims on a vast scale in secret torture chambers in Santiago and elsewhere in Chile. The torturers were invariably dressed in civilian clothes. Hooded doctors were present during torture sessions. The case is not one of interrogators acting in excess of zeal. The case goes much further. The request explains:

> "The most usual method was 'the grill' consisting of a metal table on which the victim was laid naked and his extremities tied and electrical shocks were applied to the lips, genitals, wounds or metal prosthesis; also two persons, relatives or friends, were placed in two metal drawers one on top of the other so that when the one above was tortured the psychological impact was felt by the other; on other occasions the victim was suspended from a bar by the wrists and/or the knees, and over a prolonged period while held in this situation electric current was applied to him, cutting wounds were inflicted or he was beaten; or the 'dry submarine' method was applied, i.e. placing

a bag on the head until close to suffocation, also drugs were used and boiling water was thrown on various detainees to punish them as a foretaste for the death which they would later suffer."

As the Divisional Court observed it is not alleged that General Pinochet personally committed any of these acts by his own hand. The case is, however, that agents of DINA committed the acts of torture and that DINA was directly answerable to General Pinochet rather than to the military junta. And the case is that DINA undertook and arranged the killings, disappearances and torturing of victims on the orders of General Pinochet. In other words, what is alleged against General Pinochet is not constructive criminal responsibility. The case is that he ordered and procured the criminal acts which the warrant and request for extradition specify. The allegations have not been tested in a court of law. The House is not required to examine the correctness of the allegations. The House must assume the correctness of the allegations as the backcloth of the questions of law arising on this appeal.

The former Head of State immunity

It is now possible to turn to the point of general public importance involved in the Divisional Court's decision, namely "the proper interpretation and scope of the immunity enjoyed by a former Head of State from arrest and extradition proceedings in the United Kingdom in respect of acts committed while he was Head of State". It is common ground that a Head of State while in office has an absolute immunity against civil or criminal proceedings in the English courts. If General Pinochet had still been Head of State of Chile, he would be immune from the present extradition proceedings. But he has ceased to be a Head of State. He claims immunity as a former Head of State. Counsel for General Pinochet relied on provisions contained in Part I of the State Immunity Act 1978. Part I does not apply to criminal proceedings: see Section 16(4). It is irrelevant to the issues arising on this appeal. The only arguable basis for such an immunity originates in Section 20 of the Act of 1978. It provides as follows:

"Subject to the provisions of this section and to any necessary modifications, the Diplomatic Privileges Act 1964 shall apply to:

(a) a sovereign or other head of State;
(b) members of his family forming part of his household; and
(c) his private servants. as it applies to the head of a diplomatic mission, to members of his family forming part of his household and to his private servants."

It is therefore necessary to turn to the relevant provisions of the Diplomatic Privileges Act 1964. The relevant provisions are contained in Articles 31, 38 and 39 of the Vienna Convention on Diplomatic Relations which in part forms Schedule 1 to the Act of 1964. Article 31 provides that a diplomatic agent shall enjoy immunity from criminal jurisdiction in the receiving state. Article 38(1) reads as follows:

"Except in so far as additional privileges and immunities may be granted by the receiving State, a diplomatic agent who is a national of or permanently resident in that State shall enjoy only immunity from jurisdiction and inviolability in respect of *official acts performed in the exercise of his functions.*" (My emphasis)

Article 39 so far as it is relevant reads as follows:

"1. Every person entitled to privileges and immunities shall enjoy them from the moment he enters the territory of the receiving State. . . .

2. When the functions of a person enjoying privileges and immunities have come to an end, such privileges and immunities shall normally cease at the moment when he leaves the country or on expiry of a reasonable period in which to do so but shall subsist until that time even in case of armed conflict. However, with respect to acts performed by such a person in the exercise of his functions as a member of the mission, immunity shall continue to subsist." (My emphasis)

Given the different roles of a member of a diplomatic mission and a Head of State, as well as the fact that a diplomat principally acts in the receiving state whereas a Head of State principally acts in his own country, the legislative technique of applying Article 39(2) to former a Head of State is somewhat confusing. How the necessary modifications required by Section 20 of the Act of 1978 are to be achieved is not entirely straightforward. Putting to one side the immunity of a serving Head of State, my view is that Section 20 of the 1978 Act, read with the relevant provisions of the schedule to the 1964 Act, should be read as providing that a former Head of State shall enjoy immunity from the criminal jurisdiction of the United Kingdom with respect to his official acts performed in the exercise of his functions as Head of State. That was the synthesis of the convoluted provisions helpfully offered by Mr Lloyd Jones, who appeared as amicus curiae. Neither counsel for General Pinochet nor counsel for the Spanish Government questioned this formulation. For my part it is the only sensible reconstruction of the legislative intent. It is therefore plain that statutory immunity in favour of a former Head of State is not absolute. It requires the coincidence of two requirements: (1) that the defendant is a former Head of State (ratione personae in the vocabulary of international law) and (2) that he is charged with official acts performed in the exercise of his functions as a Head of State (ratione materiae). In regard to the second requirement it is not sufficient that official acts are involved: the acts must also have been performed by the defendant in the exercise of his functions as Head of State.

On the assumption that the allegations of fact contained in the warrant and the request are true, the central question is whether those facts must be regarded as official acts performed in the exercise of the functions of a Head of State. The Lord Chief Justice observed that a former Head of State is clearly entitled to immunity from process in respect of some crimes. I would accept this proposition. Rhetorically, The Lord Chief Justice then posed the question: "Where does one draw the line?" After a detailed review of the case law and literature, he concluded that even in respect of acts of torture the former Head of State immunity would prevail. That amounts to saying that there is no or virtually no line to be drawn. Collins J. went further. He said:

> "The submission was made that it could never be in the exercise of such functions to commit crimes as serious as those allegedly committed by the applicant. Unfortunately history shows that it has indeed on occasions been state policy to exterminate or to oppress particular groups. One does not have look very far back in history to see examples of the sort of thing having happened. There is in my judgment no justification for reading any limitation based on the nature of the crimes committed into the immunity which exists."

It is inherent in this stark conclusion that there is no or virtually no line to be drawn. It follows that when Hitler ordered the "final solution" his act must be regarded as an official act deriving from the exercise of his functions as Head of State. That is where the reasoning of the Divisional Court inexorably leads. Counsel for General Pinochet submitted that this conclusion is the inescapable result of the statutory wording.

My Lords, the concept of an individual acting in his capacity as Head of State involves a rule of law which must be applied to the facts of a particular case. It invites classification of the circumstances of a case as falling on a particular side of the line. It contemplates at the very least that some acts of a Head of State may fall beyond even the most enlarged meaning of official acts performed in the exercise of the functions of a Head of State. If a Head of State kills his gardener in a fit of rage that could by no stretch of the imagination be described as an act performed in the exercise of his functions as Head of State. If a Head of State orders victims to be tortured in his presence for the sole purpose of enjoying the spectacle of the pitiful twitchings of victims dying in agony (what Montaigne described as the farthest point that cruelty can reach) that could not be described as acts undertaken by him in the exercise of his functions as a Head of State. Counsel for General Pinochet expressly, and rightly, conceded that such crimes could not be classified as official acts undertaken in the exercise of the functions of a Head of State. These examples demonstrate that there is indeed a meaningful line to be drawn.

How and where the line is to be drawn requires further examination. Is this question to be considered from the vantage point of the municipal law of Chile, where most of the acts were committed, or in the light of the principles of customary international law? Municipal law cannot be decisive as to where the line is to be drawn. If it were the determining factor, the most abhorrent municipal laws might be said to enlarge the functions of a Head of State. But I need not dwell on the point because it is conceded on behalf of General Pinochet that the distinction between official acts performed in the exercise of functions as a Head of State and acts not satisfying these requirements must depend on the rules of international law. It was at one stage argued that international law spells out no relevant criteria and is of no assistance. In my view that is not right. Negatively, the development of international law since the Second World War justifies the conclusion that by the time of the 1973 coup d'etat, and certainly ever since, international law condemned genocide, torture, hostage taking and crimes against humanity (during an armed conflict or in peace time) as international crimes deserving of punishment. Given this state of international law, it seems to me difficult to maintain that the commission of such high crimes may amount to acts performed in the exercise of the functions of a Head of State.

The essential fragility of the claim to immunity is underlined by the insistence on behalf of General Pinochet that it is not alleged that he "personally" committed any of the crimes. That means that he did not commit the crimes by his own hand. It is apparently conceded that if he personally tortured victims the position would be different. This distinction flies in the face of an elementary principle of law, shared by all civilized legal systems, that there is no distinction to be drawn between the man who strikes, and a man who orders another to strike. It is inconceivable that in enacting the Act of 1978 Parliament would have wished to rest the statutory immunity of a former Head of State on a different basis.

On behalf of General Pinochet it was submitted that acts by police, intelligence officers and military personnel are paradigm official acts. In this absolute form I do not accept the proposition. For example, why should what was allegedly done in secret in the torture chambers of Santiago on the orders of General Pinochet be regarded as official acts? Similarly, why should the murders and disappearances allegedly perpetrated by DINA in secret on the orders of General Pinochet be regarded as official acts? But, in any event, in none of these cases is the further essential requirement satisfied, viz. that in an international law sense these acts were part of the functions of a Head of State. The normative principles of international law do not require that such high crimes should be classified as acts performed in the exercise of the functions of a Head of State. For my part I am satisfied that as a matter of construction of the relevant statutory provisions the charges brought by Spain against General Pinochet are properly to be classified as conduct falling beyond the scope of his functions as Head of State. Qualitatively, what he is alleged to have done is no more to be categorized as acts undertaken in the exercise of the functions of a Head of State than the examples already given of a Head of State murdering his gardener or arranging the torture of his opponents for the sheer spectacle of it. It follows that in my view General Pinochet has no statutory immunity.

Counsel for General Pinochet further argued that if he is not entitled to statutory immunity, he is nevertheless entitled to immunity under customary international law. International law recognizes no such wider immunity in favour of a former Head of State. In any event, if there had been such an immunity under international law Section 20, read with Article 39(2), would have overridden it. General Pinochet is not entitled to an immunity of any kind.

The act of state doctrine

Counsel for General Pinochet submitted that, even if he fails to establish the procedural bar of statutory immunity, the House ought to uphold his challenge to the validity of the warrant on the ground of the act of state doctrine. They argued that the validity of the warrant and propriety of the extradition proceedings necessarily involve an investigation by the House of governmental or official acts which largely took place in Chile. They relied on the explanation of the doctrine of act of state by Lord Wilberforce in Buttes Gas and Oil Co v. Hammer [1982] A.C. 888. Counsel for General Pinochet further put forward wide-ranging political arguments about the consequences of the extradition proceedings, such as adverse internal consequences in Chile and damage to the relations between the United Kingdom and Chile. Plainly it is not appropriate for the House to take into account such political considerations. And the same applies to the argument suggesting past "acquiescence" by the United Kingdom government.

Concentrating on the legal arguments, I am satisfied that there are several reasons why the act of state doctrine is inapplicable. First the House is not being asked to investigate, or pass judgment on, the facts alleged in the warrant or request for extradition. The task of the House is simply to take note of the allegations and to consider and decide the legal issues of immunity and act of state. Secondly, the issue of act of state must be approached on the basis that the intent of Parliament was not to give statutory immunity to a former Head of State in respect of the systematic torture and killing of his fellow citizens. The ground of this conclusion is that such high crimes are not official acts committed in the exercise of the functions of a Head of State. In those circumstances it cannot be right for the House to enunciate an enlarged act of state doctrine, stretching far beyond anything said in Buttes Gas, to protect a former Head of State from the consequences of his private crimes. Thirdly, any act of state doctrine is displaced by Section 134(1) of the Criminal Justice Act 1988 in relation to torture and Section (1)(1) of the Taking of Hostages Act 1982 . Both Acts provide for the taking of jurisdiction over foreign governmental acts. Fourthly, and more broadly, the Spanish authorities have relied on crimes of genocide, torture, hostage taking and crimes against humanity. It has in my view been clearly established that by 1973 such acts were already condemned as high crimes by customary international law. In these circumstances it would be wrong for the English courts now to extend the act of state doctrine in a way which runs counter to the state of customary international law as it existed in 1973. Since the act of state doctrine depends on public policy as perceived by the courts in the forum at the time of the suit the developments since 1973 are also relevant and serve to reinforce my view. I would endorse the observation in the Third Restatement of The Foreign Relations Law of the United States, published in 1986 by the American Law Institute, Volume 1, at 370, to the effect that: "A claim arising out of an alleged violation of fundamental human rights—for instance, a claim on behalf of a victim of torture or genocide—would (if otherwise sustainable) probably not be defeated by the act of state doctrine, since the accepted international law of human rights is well established and contemplates external scrutiny of such acts." But in adopting this formulation I would remove the word "probably" and substitute "generally." Finally, I must make clear that my conclusion does not involve the expression of any view on the interesting arguments on universality of jurisdiction in respect of certain international crimes and related jurisdictional questions. Those matters do not arise for decision.

I conclude that the act of state doctrine is inapplicable.

Conclusions

My Lords, since the hearing in the Divisional Court the case has in a number of ways been transformed. The nature of the case against General Pinochet is now far clearer. And the House has the benefit of valuable submissions from distinguished international lawyers. In the light of all the material now available I have been persuaded that the conclusion of the Divisional Court was wrong. For the reasons I have given I would allow the appeal.

LORD HOFFMANN

My Lords,

I have had the advantage of reading in draft the speech of my noble and learned friend Lord Nicholls of Birkenhead and for the reasons he gives I too would allow this appeal.

Prepared 25 November 1998

HOUSE OF LORDS

Lord Browne-Wilkinson   Lord Goff of Chieveley   Lord Nolan
Lord Hope of Craighead   Lord Hutton

Opinions of the Lords of Appeal for Judgment in the Cause in re Pinochet

Oral Judgment: 17 December 1998
Reasons: 15 January 1999

LORD BROWNE-WILKINSON

My Lords,

Introduction

This petition has been brought by Senator Pinochet to set aside an order made by your Lordships on 25 November 1998. It is said that the links between one of the members of the Appellate Committee who heard the appeal, Lord Hoffmann, and Amnesty International ("AI") were such as to give the appearance that he might have been biased against Senator Pinochet. On 17 December 1998 your Lordships set aside the order of 25 November 1998 for reasons to be given later. These are the reasons that led me to that conclusion.

Background facts

Senator Pinochet was the Head of State of Chile from 11 September 1973 until 11 March 1990. It is alleged that during that period there took place in Chile various crimes against humanity (torture, hostage taking and murder) for which he was knowingly responsible.

In October 1998 Senator Pinochet was in this country receiving medical treatment. In October and November 1998 the judicial authorities in Spain issued international warrants for his arrest to enable his extradition to Spain to face trial for those alleged offences. The Spanish Supreme Court has held that the courts of Spain have jurisdiction to try him. Pursuant to those international warrants, on 16 and 23 October 1998 Metropolitan Stipendiary Magistrates issued two provisional warrants for his arrest under section 8(1)(b) of the Extradition Act 1989. Senator Pinochet was arrested. He immediately applied to the Queen's Bench Divisional Court to quash the warrants. The warrant of 16 October was quashed and nothing further turns on that warrant. The second warrant of 23 October 1998 was quashed by an order of the Divisional Court of the Queen's Bench Division (Lord Bingham of Cornhill C.J., Collins and Richards JJ.) However, the quashing of the second warrant was stayed to enable an appeal to be taken to your Lordships' House on the question certified by the Divisional Court as to "the proper interpretation and scope of the immunity enjoyed by a former Head of State from arrest and extradition proceedings in the United Kingdom in respect of acts committed while he was Head of State."

As that question indicates, the principle point at issue in the main proceedings in both the Divisional Court and this House was as to the immunity, if any, enjoyed by Senator Pinochet as a past Head of State in respect of the crimes against humanity for which his extradition was sought. The Crown Prosecution Service (which is conducting the proceedings on behalf of the Spanish Government) while accepting that a foreign Head of State would, during his tenure of office, be immune from arrest or trial in respect of the matters alleged, contends that once he ceased to be Head of State his immunity for crimes against humanity also ceased and he can be arrested and prosecuted for such crimes committed during the period he was Head of State. On the other side, Senator Pinochet contends that his immunity in respect of acts done whilst he was Head of State persists even after he has ceased to be Head of State. The position therefore is that if the view of the CPS (on behalf of the Spanish Government) prevails, it was lawful to arrest Senator Pinochet in October and (subject to any other valid objections and the completion of the extradition process) it will be lawful for the Secretary of State in his discretion to extradite Senator Pinochet to Spain to stand trial for the alleged crimes. If, on the other hand, the contentions of Senator Pinochet are correct, he has at all times been and still is immune from arrest in this country for the alleged crimes. He could never be extradited for those crimes to Spain or any other country. He would have to be immediately released and allowed to return to Chile as he wishes to do.

The court proceedings

The Divisional Court having unanimously quashed the provisional warrant of 23 October on the ground that Senator Pinochet was entitled to immunity, he was thereupon free to return to Chile subject only to the stay to permit the appeal to your Lordships' House. The matter proceeded to your Lordships' House with great speed. It was heard on 4, 5 and 9–12 November 1998 by a committee consisting of Lord Slynn of Hadley, Lord Lloyd of Berwick, Lord Nicholls of Birkenhead, Lord Steyn and Lord Hoffmann. However, before the main hearing of the appeal, there was an interlocutory decision of the greatest importance for the purposes of the present application. Amnesty International ("AI"), two other human rights bodies and three individuals petitioned for leave to intervene in the appeal. Such leave was granted by a committee consisting of Lord Slynn, Lord Nicholls and Lord Steyn subject to any protest being made by other parties at the start of the main hearing. No such protest having been made AI accordingly became an intervener in the appeal. At the hearing of the appeal AI not only put in written submissions but was also represented by counsel, Professor Brownlie Q.C., Michael Fordham, Owen Davies and Frances Webber. Professor Brownlie addressed the committee on behalf of AI supporting the appeal.

The hearing of this case, both before the Divisional Court and in your Lordships' House, produced an unprecedent degree of public interest not only in this country but worldwide. The case raises fundamental issues of public international law and their interaction with the domestic law of this country. The conduct of Senator Pinochet and his regime have been highly contentious and emotive matters. There are many Chileans and supporters of human rights who have no doubt as to his guilt and are anxious to bring him to trial somewhere in the world. There are many others who are his supporters and believe that he was the saviour of Chile. Yet a third group believe that, whatever the truth of the matter, it is a matter for Chile to sort out internally and not for third parties to interfere in the delicate balance of contemporary Chilean politics by seeking to try him outside Chile.

This wide public interest was reflected in the very large number attending the hearings before the Appellate Committee including representatives of the world press. The Palace of Westminster was picketed throughout. The announcement of the final result gave rise to worldwide reactions. In the eyes of very many people the issue was not a mere legal issue but whether or not Senator Pinochet was to stand trial and therefore, so it was thought, the cause of human rights triumph. Although the members of the Appellate Committee were in no doubt as to their function, the issue for many people was one of moral, not legal, right or wrong.

The decision and afterwards

Judgment in your Lordships' House was given on 25 November 1998. The appeal was allowed by a majority of three to two and your Lordships' House restored the second warrant of 23 October 1998. Of the majority, Lord Nicholls and Lord Steyn each delivered speeches holding that Senator Pinochet was not entitled to immunity: Lord Hoffmann agreed with their speeches but did not give separate reasons for allowing the appeal. Lord Slynn and Lord Lloyd each gave separate speeches setting out the reasons for their dissent.

As a result of this decision, Senator Pinochet was required to remain in this country to await the decision of the Home Secretary whether to authorise the continuation of the proceedings for his extradition under section 7(1) of the Extradition Act 1989. The Home Secretary had until the 11 December 1998 to make that decision, but he required anyone wishing to make representations on the point to do so by the 30 November 1998.

The link between Lord Hoffmann and AI

It appears that neither Senator Pinochet nor (save to a very limited extent) his legal advisers were aware of any connection between Lord Hoffmann and AI until after the judgment was given on 25 November. Two members of the legal team recalled that they had heard rumours that Lord Hoffmann's wife was connected with AI in some way. During the Newsnight programme on television on 25 November, an allegation to that effect was made by a speaker in Chile. On that limited information the representations made on Senator Pinochet's behalf to the Home Secretary on 30 November drew attention to Lady Hoffmann's position and contained a detailed consideration of the relevant law of bias. It then read:

> "It is submitted therefore that the Secretary of State should not have any regard to the decision of Lord Hoffmann. The authorities make it plain that this is the appropriate approach to a decision that is affected by bias. Since the bias was in the House of Lords, the Secretary of State represents the senator's only domestic protection. Absent domestic protection the senator will have to invoke the jurisdiction of the European Court of Human Rights."

After the representations had been made to the Home Office, Senator Pinochet's legal advisers received a letter dated 1 December 1998 from the solicitors acting for AI written in response to a request for information as to Lord Hoffmann's links. The letter of 1 December, so far as relevant, reads as follows:

> "Further to our letter of 27 November, we are informed by our clients, Amnesty International, that Lady Hoffmann has been working at their International Secretariat since 1977. She has always been employed in administrative positions, primarily in their department dealing with

press and publications. She moved to her present position of Programme Assistant to the Director of the Media and Audio Visual Programme when this position was established in 1994.

"Lady Hoffmann provides administrative support to the Programme, including some receptionist duties. She has not been consulted or otherwise involved in any substantive discussions or decisions by Amnesty International, including in relation to the Pinochet case."

On 7 December a man anonymously telephoned Senator Pinochet's solicitors alleging that Lord Hoffmann was a Director of the Amnesty International Charitable Trust. That allegation was repeated in a newspaper report on 8 December. Senator Pinochet's solicitors informed the Home Secretary of these allegations. On 8 December they received a letter from the solicitors acting for AI dated 7 December which reads, so far as relevant, as follows:

"On further consideration, our client, Amnesty International have instructed us that after contacting Lord Hoffmann over the weekend both he and they believe that the following information about his connection with Amnesty International's charitable work should be provided to you.

"Lord Hoffmann is a Director and Chairperson of Amnesty International Charity Limited (AICL), a registered charity incorporated on 7 April 1986 to undertake those aspects of the work of Amnesty International Limited (AIL) which are charitable under UK law. AICL files reports with Companies' House and the Charity Commissioners as required by UK law. AICL funds a proportion of the charitable activities undertaken independently by AIL. AIL's board is composed of Amnesty International's Secretary General and two Deputy Secretaries General.

"Since 1990 Lord Hoffmann and Peter Duffy Q.C. have been the two Directors of AICL. They are neither employed nor remunerated by either AICL or AIL. They have not been consulted and have not had any other role in Amnesty International's interventions in the case of Pinochet. Lord Hoffmann is not a member of Amnesty International.

"In addition, in 1997 Lord Hoffmann helped in the organisation of a fund raising appeal for a new building for Amnesty International UK. He helped organise this appeal together with other senior legal figures, including the Lord Chief Justice, Lord Bingham. In February your firm contributed ú1,000 to this appeal. You should also note that in 1982 Lord Hoffmann, when practising at the Bar, appeared in the Chancery Division for Amnesty International UK."

Further information relating to AICL and its relationship with Lord Hoffmann and AI is given below. Mr. Alun Jones Q.C. for the CPS does not contend that either Senator Pinochet or his legal advisors had any knowledge of Lord Hoffmann's position as a Director of AICL until receipt of that letter.

Senator Pinochet's solicitors informed the Home Secretary of the contents of the letter dated 7 December. The Home Secretary signed the Authority to Proceed on 9 December 1998. He also gave reasons for his decision, attaching no weight to the allegations of bias or apparent bias made by Senator Pinochet.

On 10 December 1998, Senator Pinochet lodged the present petition asking that the order of 25 November 1998 should either be set aside completely or the opinion of Lord Hoffmann should be declared to be of no effect. The sole ground relied upon was that Lord Hoffmann's links with AI were such as to give the appearance of possible bias. It is important to stress that Senator Pinochet makes no allegation of actual bias against Lord Hoffmann; his claim is based on the requirement that justice should be seen to be done as well as actually being done. There is no allegation that any other member of the Committee has fallen short in the performance of his judicial duties.

Amnesty International and its constituent parts

Before considering the arguments advanced before your Lordships, it is necessary to give some detail of the organisation of AI and its subsidiary and constituent bodies. Most of the information which follows is derived from the Directors' Reports and Notes to the Accounts of AICL which have been put in evidence.

AI itself is an unincorporated, non profit making organisation founded in 1961 with the object of securing throughout the world the observance of the provisions of the Universal Declaration of Human Rights in regard to prisoners of conscience. It is regulated by a document known as the Statute of Amnesty International. AI consists of sections in different countries throughout the world and its International Headquarters in London. Delegates of the Sections meet periodically at the International Council Meetings to co-ordinate their activities and to elect an International Executive Committee to implement the Council's decisions. The International Headquarters in London is responsible to the International Executive Committee. It is funded principally by the Sections for the purpose of furthering the work of AI on a worldwide basis and to assist the work of Sections in specific countries as necessary. The work of the International Headquarters is undertaken through two United Kingdom registered companies Amnesty International Limited ("AIL") and Amnesty International Charity Limited ("AICL").

AIL is an English limited company incorporated to assist in furthering the objectives of AI and to carry out the aspects of the work of the International Headquarters which are not charitable.

AICL is a company limited by guarantee and also a registered charity. In McGovern v. Attorney-General [1982] Ch. 321, Slade J. held that a trust established by AI to promote certain of its objects was not charitable because it was established for political purposes; however the judge indicated that a trust for research into the observance of human rights and the dissemination of the results of such research could be charitable. It appears that AICL was incorporated on 7 April 1986 to carry out such of the purposes of AI as were charitable. Clause 3 of the Memorandum of Association of AICL provides:

"Having regard to the Statute for the time being of Amnesty International, the objects for which the Company is established are:
  (a) To promote research into the maintenance and observance of human rights and to publish the results of such research.
  (b) To provide relief to needy victims of breaches of human rights by appropriate charitable (and in particular medical, rehabilitational or financial) assistance.
  (c) To procure the abolition of torture, extra judicial execution and disappearance. . . ."

Under Article 3(a) of AICL the members of the Company are all the elected members for the time being of the International Executive Committee of Amnesty International and nobody else. The Directors are appointed by and removable by the members in general meetings. Since 8 December 1990 Lord Hoffmann and Mr. Duffy Q.C. have been the sole Directors, Lord Hoffmann at some stage becoming the Chairperson.

There are complicated arrangements between the International Headquarters of AI, AICL and AIL as to the discharge of their respective functions. From the reports of the Directors and the notes to the annual accounts, it appears that, although the system has changed slightly from time to time, the current system is as follows. The International

Headquarters of AI are in London and the premises are, at least in part, shared with AICL and AIL. The conduct of AI's International Headquarters is (subject to the direction of the International Executive Committee) in the hands of AIL. AICL commissions AIL to undertake charitable activities of the kind which fall within the objects of AI. The Directors of AICL then resolve to expend the sums that they have received from AI Sections or elsewhere in funding such charitable work as AIL performs. AIL then reports retrospectively to AICL as to the monies expended and AICL votes sums to AIL for such part of AIL's work as can properly be regarded as charitable. It was confirmed in the course of argument that certain work done by AIL would therefore be treated as in part done by AIL on its own behalf and in part on behalf of AICL.

I can give one example of the close interaction between the functions of AICL and AI. The report of the Directors of AICL for the year ended 31 December 1993 records that AICL commissioned AIL to carry out charitable activities on its behalf and records as being included in the work of AICL certain research publications. One such publication related to Chile and referred to a report issued as an AI report in 1993. Such 1993 reports covers not only the occurrence and nature of breaches of human rights within Chile, but also the progress of cases being brought against those alleged to have infringed human rights by torture and otherwise in the courts of Chile. It records that "no one was convicted during the year for past human rights violations. The military courts continued to claim jurisdiction over human rights cases in civilian courts and to close cases covered by the 1978 Amnesty law." It also records "Amnesty International continued to call for full investigation into human rights violations and for those responsible to be brought to justice. The organisation also continued to call for the abolition of the death penalty." Again, the report stated that "Amnesty International included references to its concerns about past human rights violations against indigenous peoples in Chile and the lack of accountability of those responsible." Therefore AICL was involved in the reports of AI urging the punishment of those guilty in Chile for past breaches of human rights and also referring to such work as being part of the work that it supported.

The Directors of AICL do not receive any remuneration. Nor do they take any part in the policy-making activities of AI. Lord Hoffmann is not a member of AI or of any other body connected with AI.

In addition to the AI related bodies that I have mentioned, there are other organisations which are not directly relevant to the present case. However, I should mention another charitable company connected with AI and mentioned in the papers, namely, "Amnesty International U.K. Section Charitable Trust" registered as a company under number 3139939 and as a charity under 1051681. That was a company incorporated in 1995 and, so far as I can see, has nothing directly to do with the present case.

The parties' submissions

Miss Montgomery Q.C. in her very persuasive submissions on behalf of Senator Pinochet contended:

1. That, although there was no exact precedent, your Lordships' House must have jurisdiction to set aside its own orders where they have been improperly made, since there is no other court which could correct such impropriety.
2. That (applying the test in Reg. v. Gough [1993] A.C. 646) the links between Lord Hoffmann and AI were such that there was a real danger that Lord Hoffmann was biased

in favour of AI or alternatively (applying the test in Webb v. The Queen (1994) 181 C.L.R. 41) that such links give rise to a reasonable apprehension or suspicion on the part of a fair minded and informed member of the public that Lord Hoffmann might have been so biased.

On the other side, Mr. Alun Jones Q.C. accepted that your Lordships had power to revoke an earlier order of this House but contended that there was no case for such revocation here. The applicable test of bias, he submitted, was that recently laid down by your Lordships in Reg. v. Gough and it was impossible to say that there was a real danger that Lord Hoffmann had been biased against Senator Pinochet. He further submitted that, by relying on the allegations of bias in making submissions to the Home Secretary, Senator Pinochet had elected to adopt the Home Secretary as the correct tribunal to adjudicate on the issue of apparent bias. He had thereby waived his right to complain before your Lordships of such bias. Expressed in other words, he was submitting that the petition was an abuse of process by Senator Pinochet. Mr. Duffy Q.C. for AI (but not for AICL) supported the case put forward by Mr. Alun Jones.

Conclusions

1. Jurisdiction
As I have said, the respondents to the petition do not dispute that your Lordships have jurisdiction in appropriate cases to rescind or vary an earlier order of this House. In my judgment, that concession was rightly made both in principle and on authority.

In principle it must be that your Lordships, as the ultimate court of appeal, have power to correct any injustice caused by an earlier order of this House. There is no relevant statutory limitation on the jurisdiction of the House in this regard and therefore its inherent jurisdiction remains unfettered. In Cassell & Co. Ltd. v. Broome (No. 2) [1972] A.C. 1136 your Lordships varied an order for costs already made by the House in circumstances where the parties had not had a fair opportunity to address argument on the point.

However, it should be made clear that the House will not reopen any appeal save in circumstances where, through no fault of a party, he or she has been subjected to an unfair procedure. Where an order has been made by the House in a particular case there can be no question of that decision being varied or rescinded by a later order made in the same case just because it is thought that the first order is wrong.

2. Apparent bias
As I have said, Senator Pinochet does not allege that Lord Hoffmann was in fact biased. The contention is that there was a real danger or reasonable apprehension or suspicion that Lord Hoffmann might have been biased, that is to say, it is alleged that there is an appearance of bias not actual bias.

The fundamental principle is that a man may not be a judge in his own cause. This principle, as developed by the courts, has two very similar but not identical implications. First it may be applied literally: if a judge is in fact a party to the litigation or has a financial or proprietary interest in its outcome then he is indeed sitting as a judge in his own cause. In that case, the mere fact that he is a party to the action or has a financial or proprietary interest in its outcome is sufficient to cause his automatic disqualification. The second application of the principle is where a judge is not a party to the suit and does not have a financial interest in its outcome, but in some other way his conduct or behaviour may give rise to a suspicion that he is not impartial, for example because of his friendship with a party. This second type of case is not strictly speaking an application of the principle that a man must not be judge in his own cause, since the judge will not normally be himself benefiting, but providing a benefit for another by failing to be impartial.

In my judgment, this case falls within the first category of case, viz where the judge is disqualified because he is a judge in his own cause. In such a case, once it is shown that the judge is himself a party to the cause, or has a relevant interest in its subject matter, he is disqualified without any investigation into whether there was a likelihood or suspicion of bias. The mere fact of his interest is sufficient to disqualify him unless he has made sufficient disclosure: see Shetreet, Judges on Trial, (1976), p. 303; De Smith, Woolf & Jowel, Judicial Review of Administrative Action, 5th ed. (1995), p. 525. I will call this "automatic disqualification."

In Dimes v. Proprietors of Grand Junction Canal (1852) 3 H.L. Cas. 759, the then Lord Chancellor, Lord Cottenham, owned a substantial shareholding in the defendant canal which was an incorporated body. In the action the Lord Chancellor sat on appeal from the Vice-Chancellor, whose judgment in favour of the company he affirmed. There was an appeal to your Lordships' House on the grounds that the Lord Chancellor was disqualified. Their Lordships consulted the judges who advised that Lord Cottenham was disqualified from sitting as a judge in the cause because he had an interest in the suit: at p. 786. This advice was unanimously accepted by their Lordships. There was no inquiry by the court as to whether a reasonable man would consider Lord Cottenham to be biased and no inquiry as to the circumstances which led to Lord Cottenham sitting. Lord Campbell said, at p. 793:

> "No one can suppose that Lord Cottenham could be, in the remotest degree, influenced by the interest he had in this concern; but, my Lords, it is of the last importance that the maxim that no man is to be a judge in his own cause should be held sacred. And that is not to be confined to a cause in which he is a party, but applies to a cause in which he has an interest." (Emphasis added)

On occasion, this proposition is elided so as to omit all references to the disqualification of a judge who is a party to the suit: see, for example, Reg. v. Rand (1866) L.R. 1 Q.B. 230; Reg. v. Gough at p. 661. This does not mean that a judge who is a party to a suit is not disqualified just because the suit does not involve a financial interest. The authorities cited in the Dimes case show how the principle developed. The starting-point was the case in which a judge was indeed purporting to decide a case in which he was a party. This was held to be absolutely prohibited. That absolute prohibition was then extended to cases where, although not nominally a party, the judge had an interest in the outcome.

The importance of this point in the present case is this. Neither AI, nor AICL, have any financial interest in the outcome of this litigation. We are here confronted, as was Lord Hoffmann, with a novel situation where the outcome of the litigation did not lead to financial benefit to anyone. The interest of AI in the litigation was not financial; it was its interest in achieving the trial and possible conviction of Senator Pinochet for crimes against humanity.

By seeking to intervene in this appeal and being allowed so to intervene, in practice AI became a party to the appeal. Therefore if, in the circumstances, it is right to treat Lord Hoffmann as being the alter ego of AI and therefore a judge in his own cause, then he must have been automatically disqualified on the grounds that he was a party to the appeal. Alternatively, even if it be not right to say that Lord Hoffmann was a party to the appeal as such, the question then arises whether, in non financial litigation, anything other than a financial or proprietary interest in the outcome is sufficient automatically to disqualify a man from sitting as judge in the cause.

Are the facts such as to require Lord Hoffmann to be treated as being himself a party to this appeal? The facts are striking and unusual. One of the parties to the appeal is an unincorporated association, AI. One of the constituent parts of that unincorporated association is AICL. AICL was established, for tax purposes, to carry out part of the functions of AI—those parts which were charitable—which had previously been carried on either by AI itself or by AIL. Lord Hoffmann is a Director and chairman of AICL which is wholly controlled by AI, since its members, (who ultimately control it) are all the members of the International Executive Committee of AI. A large part of the work of AI is, as a matter of strict law, carried on by AICL which instructs AIL to do the work on its behalf. In reality, AI, AICL and AIL are a close-knit group carrying on the work of AI.

However, close as these links are, I do not think it would be right to identify Lord Hoffmann personally as being a party to the appeal. He is closely linked to AI but he is not in fact AI. Although this is an area in which legal technicality is particularly to be avoided, it cannot be ignored that Lord Hoffmann took no part in running AI. Lord Hoffmann, AICL and the Executive Committee of AI are in law separate people.

Then is this a case in which it can be said that Lord Hoffmann had an "interest" which must lead to his automatic disqualification? Hitherto only pecuniary and proprietary interests have led to automatic disqualification. But, as I have indicated, this litigation is most unusual. It is not civil litigation but criminal litigation. Most unusually, by allowing AI to intervene, there is a party to a criminal cause or matter who is neither prosecutor nor accused. That party, AI, shares with the Government of Spain and the CPS, not a financial interest but an interest to establish that there is no immunity for ex-Heads of State in relation to crimes against humanity. The interest of these parties is to procure Senator Pinochet's extradition and trial—a non-pecuniary interest. So far as AICL is concerned, clause 3(c) of its Memorandum provides that one of its objects is "to procure the abolition of torture, extra-judicial execution and disappearance". AI has, amongst other objects, the same objects. Although AICL, as a charity, cannot campaign to change the law, it is concerned by other means to procure the abolition of these crimes against humanity. In my opinion, therefore, AICL plainly had a non-pecuniary interest, to establish that Senator Pinochet was not immune.

That being the case, the question is whether in the very unusual circumstances of this case a non-pecuniary interest to achieve a particular result is sufficient to give rise to automatic disqualification and, if so, whether the fact that AICL had such an interest necessarily leads to the conclusion that Lord Hoffmann, as a Director of AICL, was automatically disqualified from sitting on the appeal? My Lords, in my judgment, although the cases have all dealt with automatic disqualification on the grounds of pecuniary interest, there is no good reason in principle for so limiting automatic disqualification. The rationale of the whole rule is that a man cannot be a judge in his own cause. In civil litigation the matters in issue will normally have an economic impact; therefore a judge is automatically disqualified if he stands to make a financial gain as a consequence of his own decision of the case. But if, as in the present case, the matter at issue does not relate to money or economic advantage but is concerned with the promotion of the cause, the rationale disqualifying a judge applies just as much if the judge's decision will lead to the promotion of a cause in which the judge is involved together with one of the parties. Thus in my opinion if Lord Hoffmann had been a member of AI he would have been automatically disqualified because of his non-pecuniary interest in establishing that Senator Pinochet was not entitled to immunity. Indeed, so much I understood to have been conceded by Mr. Duffy.

Can it make any difference that, instead of being a direct member of AI, Lord Hoffmann is a Director of AICL, that is of a company which is wholly controlled by AI and is carrying on much of its work? Surely not. The substance of the matter is that AI, AIL and AICL are all various parts of an entity or movement working in different fields towards the same goals. If the absolute impartiality of the judiciary is to be maintained, there must be a rule which automatically disqualifies a judge who is involved, whether personally or as a Director of a company, in promoting the same causes in the same organisation as is a party to the suit. There is no room for fine distinctions if Lord Hewart's famous dictum is to be observed: it is "of fundamental importance that justice should not only be done, but should manifestly and undoubtedly be seen to be done." (see Rex v. Sussex Justices, Ex parte McCarthy [1924] K.B. 256, 259)

Since, in my judgment, the relationship between AI, AICL and Lord Hoffmann leads to the automatic disqualification of Lord Hoffmann to sit on the hearing of the appeal, it is unnecessary to consider the other factors which were relied on by Miss Montgomery, viz. the position of Lady Hoffmann as an employee of AI and the fact that Lord Hoffmann was involved in the recent appeal for funds for Amnesty. Those factors might have been relevant if Senator Pinochet had been required to show a real danger or reasonable suspicion of bias. But since the disqualification is automatic and does not depend in any way on an implication of bias, it is unnecessary to consider these factors. I do, however, wish to make it clear (if I have not already done so) that my decision is not that Lord Hoffmann has been guilty of bias of any kind: he was disqualified as a matter of law automatically by reason of his Directorship of AICL, a company controlled by a party, AI.

For the same reason, it is unnecessary to determine whether the test of apparent bias laid down in Reg. v. Gough ("is there in the view of the Court a real danger that the judge was biased?") needs to be reviewed in the light of subsequent decisions. Decisions in Canada, Australia and New Zealand have either refused to apply the test in Reg. v. Gough, or modified it so as to make the relevant test the question whether the events in question give rise to a reasonable apprehension or suspicion on the part of a fair-minded and informed member of the public that the judge was not impartial: see, for example, the High Court of Australia in Webb v. The Queen. It has also been suggested that the test in Reg. v. Gough in some way impinges on the requirement of Lord Hewart's dictum that justice should appear to be done: see Reg. v. Inner West London Coroner, Ex Parte Dallaglio [1994] 4 All E.R. 139 at page 152 A to B. Since such a review is unnecessary for the determination of the present case, I prefer to express no view on it.

It is important not to overstate what is being decided. It was suggested in argument that a decision setting aside the order of 25 November 1998 would lead to a position where judges would be unable to sit on cases involving charities in whose work they are involved. It is suggested that, because of such involvement, a judge would be disqualified. That is not correct. The facts of this present case are exceptional. The critical elements are (1) that AI was a party to the appeal; (2) that AI was joined in order to argue for a particular result; (3) the judge was a Director of a charity closely allied to AI and sharing, in this respect, AI's objects. Only in cases where a judge is taking an active role as trustee or Director of a charity which is closely allied to and acting with a party to the litigation should a judge normally be concerned either to recuse himself or disclose the position to the parties. However, there may well be other exceptional cases in which the judge would be well advised to disclose a possible interest.

Finally on this aspect of the case, we were asked to state in giving judgment what had been said and done within the Appellate Committee in relation to Amnesty International during the hearing leading to the Order of 25 November. As is apparent from what I have said, such matters are irrelevant to what we have to decide: in the absence of any disclosure to the parties of Lord Hoffmann's involvement with AI, such involvement either did or did not in law disqualify him regardless of what happened within the Appellate Committee. We therefore did not investigate those matters and make no findings as to them.

Election, waiver, abuse of process

Mr. Alun Jones submitted that by raising with the Home Secretary the possible bias of Lord Hoffmann as a ground for not authorising the extradition to proceed, Senator Pinochet had elected to choose the Home Secretary rather than your Lordships' House as the arbiter as to whether such bias did or did not exist. Consequently, he submitted, Senator Pinochet had waived his right to petition your Lordships and, by doing so immediately after the Home Secretary had rejected the submission, was committing an abuse of the process of the House.

This submission is bound to fail on a number of different grounds, of which I need mention only two. First, Senator Pinochet would only be put to his election as between two alternative courses to adopt. I cannot see that there are two such courses in the present case, since the Home Secretary had no power in the matter. He could not set aside the order of 25 November and as long as such order stood, the Home Secretary was bound to accept it as stating the law. Secondly, all three concepts—election, waiver and abuse of process—require that the person said to have elected etc. has acted freely and in full knowledge of the facts. Not until 8 December 1998 did Senator Pinochet's solicitors know anything of Lord Hoffmann's position as a Director and Chairman of AICL. Even then they did not know anything about AICL and its constitution. To say that by hurriedly notifying the Home Secretary of the contents of the letter from AI's solicitors, Senator Pinochet had elected to pursue the point solely before the Home Secretary is unrealistic. Senator Pinochet had not yet had time to find out anything about the circumstances beyond the bare facts disclosed in the letter.

Result

It was for these reasons and the reasons given by my noble and learned friend Lord Goff of Chieveley that I reluctantly felt bound to set aside the order of 25 November 1998. It was appropriate to direct a re-hearing of the appeal before a differently constituted Committee, so that on the re-hearing the parties were not faced with a Committee four of whom had already expressed their conclusion on the points at issue.

Lord Goff of Chieveley

My Lords,

I have had the opportunity of reading in draft the opinion prepared by my noble and learned friend, Lord Browne-Wilkinson. It was for the like reasons to those given by him that I agreed that the order of your Lordships' House in this matter dated 25 November

1998 should be set aside and that a rehearing of the appeal should take place before a differently constituted Committee. Even so, having regard to the unusual nature of this case, I propose to set out briefly in my own words the reasons why I reached that conclusion.

Like my noble and learned friend, I am of the opinion that the principle which governs this matter is that a man shall not be a judge in his own cause—nemo judex in sua causa: see Dimes v. Grand Junction Canal (1852) 3 H.L.C. 759, 793, per Lord Campbell. As stated by Lord Campbell in that case at p. 793, the principle is not confined to a cause to which the judge is a party, but applies also to a cause in which he has an interest. Thus, for example, a judge who holds shares in a company which is a party to the litigation is caught by the principle, not because he himself is a party to the litigation (which he is not), but because he has by virtue of his shareholding an interest in the cause. That was indeed the ratio decidendi of the famous case of Dimes itself. In that case the then Lord Chancellor, Lord Cottenham, affirmed an order granted by the Vice-Chancellor granting relief to a company in which, unknown to the defendant and forgotten by himself, he held a substantial shareholding. It was decided, following the opinion of the judges, that Lord Cottenham was disqualified, by reason of his interest in the cause, from adjudicating in the matter, and that his order was for that reason voidable and must be set aside. Such a conclusion must follow, subject only to waiver by the party or parties to the proceedings thereby affected.

In the present case your Lordships are not concerned with a judge who is a party to the cause, nor with one who has a financial interest in a party to the cause or in the outcome of the cause. Your Lordships are concerned with a case in which a judge is closely connected with a party to the proceedings. This situation has arisen because, as my noble and learned friend has described, Amnesty International ("AI") was given leave to intervene in the proceedings; and, whether or not AI thereby became technically a party to the proceedings, it so participated in the proceedings, actively supporting the cause of one party (the Government of Spain, represented by the Crown Prosecution Service) against another (Senator Pinochet), that it must be treated as a party. Furthermore, Lord Hoffmann is a Director and Chairperson of Amnesty International Charity Limited ("AICL"). AICL and Amnesty International Limited ("AIL") are United Kingdom companies through which the work of the International Headquarters of AI in London is undertaken, AICL having been incorporated to carry out those purposes of AI which are charitable under UK law. Neither Senator Pinochet nor the lawyers acting for him were aware of the connection between Lord Hoffmann and AI until after judgment was given on 25 November 1998.

My noble and learned friend has described in lucid detail the working relationship between AICL, AIL and AI, both generally and in relation to Chile. It is unnecessary for me to do more than state that not only was AICL deeply involved in the work of AI, commissioning activities falling within the objects of AI which were charitable, but that it did so specifically in relation to research publications including one relating to Chile reporting on breaches of human rights (by torture and otherwise) in Chile and calling for those responsible to be brought to justice. It is in these circumstances that we have to consider the position of Lord Hoffmann, not as a person who is himself a party to the proceedings or who has a financial interest in such a party or in the outcome of the proceedings, but as a person who is, as a director and chairperson of AICL, closely connected with AI which is, or must be treated as, a party to the proceedings. The question which arises is whether his connection with that party will (subject to waiver) itself disqualify him from sitting as a judge in the proceedings, in the same way as a significant shareholding in a party will do, and so require that the order made upon the outcome of the proceedings must be set aside.

Such a question could in theory arise, for example, in relation to a senior executive of a body which is a party to the proceedings, who holds no shares in that body; but it is, I believe, only conceivable that it will do so where the body in question is a charitable organisation. He will by reason of his position be committed to the well-being of the charity, and to the fulfilment by the charity of its charitable objects. He may for that reason properly be said to have an interest in the outcome of the litigation, though he has no financial interest, and so to be disqualified from sitting as a judge in the proceedings. The cause is "a cause in which he has an interest", in the words of Lord Campbell in Dimes at p. 793. It follows that in this context the relevant interest need not be a financial interest. This is the view expressed by Professor Shetreet in his book Judges on Trial at p. 310, where he states that "A judge may have to disqualify himself by reason of his association with a body that institutes or defends the suit", giving as an example the chairman or member of the board of a charitable organisation.

Let me next take the position of Lord Hoffmann in the present case. He was not a member of the governing body of AI, which is or is to be treated as a party to the present proceedings: he was chairperson of an associated body, AICL, which is not a party. However, on the evidence, it is plain that there is a close relationship between AI, AIL and AICL. AICL was formed following the decision in McGovern v. Attorney-General [1982] Ch. 321, to carry out the purposes of AI which were charitable, no doubt with the sensible object of achieving a tax saving. So the division of function between AIL and AICL was that the latter was to carry out those aspects of the work of the International Headquarters of AI which were charitable, leaving it to AIL to carry out the remainder, that division being made for fiscal reasons. It follows that AI, AIL and AICL can together be described as being, in practical terms, one organisation, of which AICL forms part. The effect for present purposes is that Lord Hoffmann, as chairperson of one member of that organisation, AICL, is so closely associated with another member of that organisation, AI, that he can properly be said to have an interest in the outcome of proceedings to which AI has become party. This conclusion is reinforced, so far as the present case is concerned, by the evidence of AICL commissioning a report by AI relating to breaches of human rights in Chile, and calling for those responsible to be brought to justice. It follows that Lord Hoffmann had an interest in the outcome of the present proceedings and so was disqualified from sitting as a judge in those proceedings.

It is important to observe that this conclusion is, in my opinion, in no way dependent on Lord Hoffmann personally holding any view, or having any objective, regarding the question whether Senator Pinochet should be extradited, nor is it dependent on any bias or apparent bias on his part. Any suggestion of bias on his part was, of course, disclaimed by those representing Senator Pinochet. It arises simply from Lord Hoffmann's involvement in AICL; the close relationship between AI, AIL and AICL, which here means that for present purposes they can be regarded as being, in practical terms, one organisation; and the participation of AI in the present proceedings in which as a result it either is, or must be treated as, a party.

LORD NOLAN

My Lords,
    I agree with the views expressed by noble and learned friends Lord Browne-Wilkinson

and Lord Goff of Chieveley. In my judgment the decision of 25 November had to be set aside for the reasons which they give.

I would only add that in any case where the impartiality of a judge is in question the appearance of the matter is just as important as the reality.

LORD HOPE OF CRAIGHEAD

My Lords,

I have had the advantage of reading in draft the speeches which have been prepared by my noble and learned friends, Lord Browne-Wilkinson and Lord Goff of Chieveley. For the reasons which they have given I also was satisfied that the earlier decision of this House cannot stand and must be set aside. But in view of the importance of the case and its wider implications, I should like to add these observations.

One of the cornerstones of our legal system is the impartiality of the tribunals by which justice is administered. In civil litigation the guiding principle is that no one may be a judge in his own cause: nemo debet esse judex in propria causa. It is a principle which is applied much more widely than a literal interpretation of the words might suggest. It is not confined to cases where the judge is a party to the proceedings. It is applied also to cases where he has a personal or pecuniary interest in the outcome, however small. In London and North-Western Railway Co. v. Lindsay (1858) 3 Macq. 99 the same question as that which arose in Dimes v. Proprietors of Grand Junction Canal (1852) 3 H.L.Cas. 759 was considered in an appeal from the Court of Session to this House. Lord Wensleydale stated that, as he was a shareholder in the appellant company, he proposed to retire and take no part in the judgment. The Lord Chancellor said that he regretted that this step seemed to be necessary. Although counsel stated that he had no objection, it was thought better that any difficulty that might arise should be avoided and Lord Wensleydale retired.

In Sellar v. Highland Railway Co. 1919 S.C. (H.L.) 19, the same rule was applied where a person who had been appointed to act as one of the arbiters in a dispute between the proprietors of certain fishings and the railway company was the holder of a small number of ordinary shares in the railway company. Lord Buckmaster, after referring to Dimes and Lindsay, gave this explanation of the rule at pp. 20–21:

> "The law remains unaltered and unvarying today, and, although it is obvious that the extended growth of personal property and the wide distribution of interests in vast commercial concerns may render the application of the rule increasingly irksome, it is none the less a rule which I for my part should greatly regret to see even in the slightest degree relaxed. The importance of preserving the administration of justice from anything which can even by remote imagination infer a bias or interest in the Judge upon whom falls the solemn duty of interpreting the law is so grave that any small inconvenience experienced in its preservation may be cheerfully endured. In practice also the difficulty is one easily overcome, because, directly the fact is stated, it is common practice that counsel on each side agree that the existence of the disqualification shall afford no objection to the prosecution of the suit, and the matter proceeds in the ordinary way, but, if the disclosure is not made, either through neglect or inadvertence, the judgment becomes voidable and may be set aside."

As my noble and learned friend Lord Goff of Chieveley said in Reg. v. Gough [1993] A.C. 646, 661, the nature of the interest is such that public confidence in the administration of justice requires that the judge must withdraw from the case or, if he fails to disclose his interest and sits in judgment upon it, the decision cannot stand. It is no answer for the judge to say that he is in fact impartial and that he will abide by his judicial oath. The purpose of the disqualification is to preserve the administration of justice from any suspicion of impartiality. The disqualification does not follow automatically in the strict sense of that word, because the parties to the suit may waive the objection. But no further investigation is necessary and, if the interest is not disclosed, the consequence is inevitable. In practice the application of this rule is so well understood and so consistently observed that no case has arisen in the course of this century where a decision of any of the courts exercising a civil jurisdiction in any part of the United Kingdom has had to be set aside on the ground that there was a breach of it.

In the present case we are concerned not with civil litigation but with a decision taken in proceedings for extradition on criminal charges. It is only in the most unusual circumstances that a judge who was sitting in criminal proceedings would find himself open to the objection that he was acting as a judge in his own cause. In principle, if it could be shown that he had a personal or pecuniary interest in the outcome, the maxim would apply. But no case was cited to us, and I am not aware of any, in which it has been applied hitherto in a criminal case. In practice judges are well aware that they should not sit in a case where they have even the slightest personal interest in it either as defendant or as prosecutor.

The ground of objection which has invariably been taken until now in criminal cases is based on that other principle which has its origin in the requirement of impartiality. This is that justice must not only be done; it must also be seen to be done. It covers a wider range of situations than that which is covered by the maxim that no-one may be a judge in his own cause. But it would be surprising if the application of that principle were to result in a test which was less exacting than that resulting from the application of the nemo judex in sua causa principle. Public confidence in the integrity of the administration of justice is just as important, perhaps even more so, in criminal cases. Article 6(1) of the European Convention on Fundamental Rights and Freedoms makes no distinction between civil and criminal cases in its expression of the right of everyone to a fair and public hearing within a reasonable time by an independent and impartial tribunal established by law.

Your Lordships were referred by Miss Montgomery Q.C. in the course of her argument to Bradford v. McLeod 1986 S.L.T. 244. This is one of only two reported cases, both of them from Scotland, in which a decision in a criminal case has been set aside because a full-time salaried judge was in breach of this principle. The other is Doherty v. McGlennan 1997 S.L.T. 444. In neither of these cases could it have been said that the sheriff had an interest in the case which disqualified him. They were cases where the sheriff either said or did something which gave rise to a reasonable suspicion about his impartiality.

The test which must be applied by the appellate courts of criminal jurisdiction in England and Wales to cases in which it is alleged that there has been a breach of this principle by a member of an inferior tribunal is different from that which is used in Scotland. The test which was approved by your Lordships' House in Reg. v. Gough [1993] A.C. 646 is whether there was a real danger of bias on the part of the relevant member of the tribunal. I think that the explanation for this choice of language lies in the fact that it was necessary in that case to formulate a test for the guidance of the lower appellate courts. The aim, as Lord Woolf explained at p. 673, was to avoid the quashing of convictions upon quite insubstantial grounds and the flimsiest pretexts of bias. In Scotland the High Court of Justiciary applies the test which was described in Gough as the reasonable suspicion test. In Bradford v. McLeod 1986 S.L.T. 244, 247 it adopted as representing the law of Scotland the rule which was expressed by Eve J. in Law v. Chartered Institute of Patent Agents [1919] 2 Ch. 276, 279 where he said:

> "Each member of the council in adjudicating on a complaint thereunder is performing a judicial duty, and he must bring to the discharge of that duty an unbiased and impartial mind. If he has a bias which renders him otherwise than an impartial judge he is disqualified from performing that duty. Nay, more (so jealous is the policy of our law of the purity of the administration of justice), if there are circumstances so affecting a person acting in a judicial capacity as to be calculated to create in the mind of a reasonable man a suspicion of that person's impartiality, those circumstances are themselves sufficient to disqualify although in fact no bias exists."

The Scottish system for dealing with criminal appeals is for all appeals from the courts of summary jurisdiction to go direct to the High Court of Justiciary in its appellate capacity. It is a simple, one-stop system, which absolves the High Court of Justiciary from the responsibility of giving guidance to inferior appellate courts as to how to deal with cases where questions have been raised about a tribunal's impartiality. Just as Eve J. may be thought to have been seeking to explain to members of the council of the Chartered Institute in simple language the test which they should apply to themselves in performing their judicial duty, so also the concern of the High Court of Justiciary has been to give guidance to sheriffs and lay justices as to the standards which they should apply to themselves in the conduct of criminal cases. The familiar expression that justice must not only be done but must also be seen to be done serves a valuable function in that context.

Although the tests are described differently, their application by the appellate courts in each country is likely in practice to lead to results which are so similar as to be indistinguishable. Indeed it may be said of all the various tests which I have mentioned, including the maxim that no-one may be a judge in his own cause, that they are all founded upon the same broad principle. Where a judge is performing a judicial duty, he must not only bring to the discharge of that duty an unbiased and impartial mind. He must be seen to be impartial.

As for the facts of the present case, it seems to me that the conclusion is inescapable that Amnesty International has associated itself in these proceedings with the position of the prosecutor. The prosecution is not being brought in its name, but its interest in the case is to achieve the same result because it also seeks to bring Senator Pinochet to justice. This distinguishes its position fundamentally from that of other bodies which seek to uphold human rights without extending their objects to issues concerning personal responsibility. It has for many years conducted an international campaign against those individuals whom it has identified as having been responsible for torture, extra-judicial executions and disappearances. Its aim is that they should be made to suffer criminal penalties for such gross violations of human rights. It has chosen, by its intervention in these proceedings, to bring itself face to face with one of those individuals against whom it has for so long campaigned.

But everyone whom the prosecutor seeks to bring to justice is entitled to the protection of the law, however grave the offence or offences with which he is being prosecuted. Senator Pinochet is entitled to the judgment of an impartial and independent tribunal on the question which has been raised here as to his immunity. I think that the connections which existed between Lord Hoffmann and Amnesty International were of such a character, in view of their duration and proximity, as to disqualify him on this ground. In view of his links with Amnesty International as the chairman and a director of Amnesty International

Charity Limited he could not be seen to be impartial. There has been no suggestion that he was actually biased. He had no financial or pecuniary interest in the outcome. But his relationship with Amnesty International was such that he was, in effect, acting as a judge in his own cause. I consider that his failure to disclose these connections leads inevitably to the conclusion that the decision to which he was a party must be set aside.

LORD HUTTON

My Lords,

I have had the advantage of reading in draft the speech of my noble and learned friend Lord Browne-Wilkinson. I gratefully adopt his account of the matters (including the links between Amnesty International and Lord Hoffmann) leading to the bringing of this petition by Senator Pinochet to set aside the order made by this House on 25 November 1998. I am in agreement with his reasoning and conclusions on the issue of the jurisdiction of this House to set aside that order and on the issues of election, waiver and abuse of process. In relation to the allegation made by Senator Pinochet, not that Lord Hoffmann was biased in fact, but that there was a real danger of bias or a reasonable apprehension or suspicion of bias because of Lord Hoffmann's links with Amnesty International, I am also in agreement with the reasoning and conclusion of Lord Browne-Wilkinson, and I wish to add some observations on this issue.

In the middle of the last century the Lord Chancellor, Lord Cottenham, had an interest as a shareholder in a canal company to the amount of several thousand pounds. The company filed a bill in equity seeking an injunction against the defendant who was unaware of Lord Cottenham's shareholding in the company. The injunction and the ancillary order sought were granted by the Vice-Chancellor and were subsequently affirmed by Lord Cottenham. The defendant subsequently discovered the interest of Lord Cottenham in the company and brought a motion to discharge the order made by him, and the matter ultimately came on for hearing before this House in Dimes v. Proprietors of Grand Junction Canal (1852) 3 H.L. Cas. 759. The House ruled that the decree of the Lord Chancellor should be set aside, not because in coming to his decision Lord Cottenham was influenced by his interest in the company, but because of the importance of avoiding the appearance of the judge labouring under the influence of an interest. Lord Campbell said at p. 793:

> "No one can suppose that Lord Cottenham could be, in the remotest degree, influenced by the interest that he had in this concern; but, my Lords, it is of the last importance that the maxim that no man is to be a judge in his own cause should be held sacred. And that is not to be confined to a cause in which he is a party, but applies to a cause in which he has an interest. Since I have had the honour to be Chief Justice of the Court of Queen's Bench, we have again and again set aside proceedings in inferior tribunals because an individual, who had an interest in a cause, took a part in the decision. And it will have a most salutary influence on these tribunals when it is known that this high Court of last resort, in a case in which the Lord Chancellor of England had an interest, considered that his decree was on that account a decree not according to law, and was set aside. This will be a lesson to all inferior tribunals to take care not only that in their decrees they are not influenced by their personal interest, but to avoid the appearance of labouring under such an influence."

In his judgment in Reg. v. Gough [1993] A.C. 646, 659G my noble and learned friend Lord Goff of Chieveley made reference to the great importance of confidence in the integrity of the administration of justice, and he said:

"In any event, there is an overriding public interest that there should be confidence in the integrity of the administration of justice, which is always associated with the statement of Lord Hewart C.J. in Rex v. Sussex Justices, Ex parte McCarthy [1924] 1 K.B. 256, 259, that it is 'of fundamental importance that justice should not only be done, but should manifestly and undoubtedly be seen to be done.' "

Then at p. 661B, referring to the case of Dimes, he said:

". . . I wish to draw attention to the fact that there are certain cases in which it has been considered that the circumstances are such that they must inevitably shake public confidence in the integrity of the administration of justice if the decision is to be allowed to stand. Such cases attract the full force of Lord Hewart C.J.'s requirement that justice must not only be done but must manifestly be seen to be done. These cases arise where a person sitting in a judicial capacity has a pecuniary interest in the outcome of the proceedings. In such a case, as Blackburn J. said in Reg. v. Rand (1866) L.R. 1 Q.B. 230, 232: 'any direct pecuniary interest, however small, in the subject of inquiry, does disqualify a person from acting as a judge in the matter.' The principle is expressed in the maxim that nobody may be judge in his own cause (nemo judex in sua causa). Perhaps the most famous case in which the principle was applied is Dimes v. Proprietors of Grand Junction Canal (1852) 3 H.L.Cas. 759, in which decrees affirmed by Lord Cottenham L.C. in favour of a canal company in which he was a substantial shareholder were set aside by this House, which then proceeded to consider the matter on its merits, and in fact itself affirmed the decrees. Lord Campbell said, at p. 793:

'No one can suppose that Lord Cottenham could be, in the remotest degree, influenced by the interest that he had in this concern; but, my Lords, it is of the last importance that the maxim that no man is to be a judge in his own cause should be held sacred.'

In such a case, therefore, not only is it irrelevant that there was in fact no bias on the part of the tribunal, but there is no question of investigating, from an objective point of view, whether there was any real likelihood of bias, or any reasonable suspicion of bias, on the facts of the particular case. The nature of the interest is such that public confidence in the administration of justice requires that the decision should not stand."

Later in his judgment Lord Goff said at p. 664F, agreeing with the view of Lord Woolf at p. 673F, that the only special category of case where there should be disqualification of a judge without the necessity to inquire whether there was any real likelihood of bias was where the judge has a direct pecuniary interest in the outcome of the proceedings. However I am of opinion that there could be cases where the interest of the judge in the subject matter of the proceedings arising from his strong commitment to some cause or belief or his association with a person or body involved in the proceedings could shake public confidence in the administration of justice as much as a shareholding (which might be small) in a public company involved in the litigation. I find persuasive the observations of Lord Widgery C.J. in Regina v. Altrincham Justices, Ex parte Pennington [1975] 1 Q.B. 549, 552F:

"There is no better known rule of natural justice than the one that a man shall not be a judge in his own cause. In its simplest form this means that a man shall not judge an issue in which he has a direct pecuniary interest, but the rule has been extended far beyond such crude examples and now covers cases in which the judge has such an interest in the parties or the matters in dispute as to make it difficult for him to approach the trial with the impartiality and detachment which the judicial function requires.

"Accordingly, application may be made to set aside a judgment on the so called ground of bias without showing any direct pecuniary or proprietary interest in the judicial officer concerned."

A similar view was expressed by Deane J. in Webb v. The Queen (1994) 181 C.L.R. 41, 74:

"The area covered by the doctrine of disqualification by reason of the appearance of bias encompasses at least four distinct, though sometimes overlapping, main categories of case. The first is disqualification by interest, that is to say, cases where some direct or indirect interest in the proceedings, whether pecuniary or otherwise, gives rise to a reasonable apprehension of prejudice, partiality or prejudgment. . . . The third category is disqualification by association. It will often overlap the first and consists of cases where the apprehension of prejudgment or other bias results from some direct or indirect relationship, experience or contact with a person or persons interested in, or otherwise involved in, the proceedings." (My emphasis)

An illustration of the approach stated by Lord Widgery and Deane J. in respect of a non-pecuniary interest is found in the earlier judgment of Lord Carson in Frome United Breweries Co. Ltd. v. Bath Justices [1926] A.C. 586, 618 when he cited with approval the judgments of the Divisional Court in Reg. v. Fraser (1893) 9 T.L.R. 613. Lord Carson described Fraser's case as one:

". . . where a magistrate who was a member of a particular council of a religious body one of the objects of which was to oppose the renewal of licences, was present at a meeting at which it was decided that the council should oppose the transfer or renewal of the licences, and that a solicitor should be instructed to act for the council at the meeting of the magistrates when the case came on. A solicitor was so instructed, and opposed the particular licence, and the magistrate sat on the bench and took part in the decision. The Court in that case came to the conclusion that the magistrate was disqualified on account of bias, and that the decision to refuse the licence was bad. No one imputed mala fides to the magistrate, but Cave J., in giving judgment, said: 'the question was, What would be likely to endanger the respect or diminish the confidence which it was desirable should exist in the administration of justice?' Wright J. stated that although the magistrate had acted from excellent motives and feelings, he still had done so contrary to a well settled principle of law, which affected the character of the administration of justice."

I have already stated that there was no allegation made against Lord Hoffmann that he was actually guilty of bias in coming to his decision, and I wish to make it clear that I am making no finding of actual bias against him. But I consider that the links, described in the judgment of Lord Browne-Wilkinson, between Lord Hoffmann and Amnesty International, which had campaigned strongly against General Pinochet and which intervened in the earlier hearing to support the case that he should be extradited to face trial for his alleged crimes, were so strong that public confidence in the integrity of the administration of justice would be shaken if his decision were allowed to stand. It was this reason and the other reasons given by Lord Browne-Wilkinson which led me to agree reluctantly in the decision of the Appeal Committee on 17 December 1998 that the order of 25 November 1998 should be set aside.

HOUSE OF LORDS

Lord Browne-Wilkinson   Lord Goff of Chieveley   Lord Hope of Craighead
Lord Hutton   Lord Saville of Newdigate   Lord Millett
Lord Phillips of Worth Matravers

OPINIONS OF THE LORDS OF APPEAL FOR JUDGMENT IN THE CAUSE

Regina v. *Bartle and the Commissioner of Police for the Metropolis and Others*
(appellants) ex parte *Pinochet* (respondent)

Regina v. *Evans and Another and the Commissioner of Police for the Metropolis and Others* (appellants)

Ex parte Pinochet (respondent) (on appeal from a Divisional Court of the Queen's Bench Division)

on 24 March 1999

LORD BROWNE-WILKINSON

My Lords,

As is well known, this case concerns an attempt by the Government of Spain to extradite Senator Pinochet from this country to stand trial in Spain for crimes committed (primarily in Chile) during the period when Senator Pinochet was head of state in Chile. The interaction between the various legal issues which arise is complex. I will therefore seek, first, to give a short account of the legal principles which are in play in order that my exposition of the facts will be more intelligible.

Outline of the law

In general, a state only exercises criminal jurisdiction over offences which occur within its geographical boundaries. If a person who is alleged to have committed a crime in Spain is found in the United Kingdom, Spain can apply to the United Kingdom to extradite him to Spain. The power to extradite from the United Kingdom for an "extradition crime" is now contained in the Extradition Act 1989. That Act defines what constitutes an "extradition crime". For the purposes of the present case, the most important requirement is that the conduct complained of must constitute a crime under the law both of Spain and of the United Kingdom. This is known as the double criminality rule.

Since the Nazi atrocities and the Nuremberg trials, international law has recognised a number of offences as being international crimes. Individual states have taken jurisdiction to try some international crimes even in cases where such crimes were not committed within the geographical boundaries of such states. The most important of such international crimes for present purposes is torture which is regulated by the International Convention Against Torture and other Cruel, Inhuman or Degrading Treatment or Punishment, 1984. The obligations placed on the United Kingdom by that Convention (and on the other 110 or more signatory states who have adopted the Convention) were incorporated into the law of the United Kingdom by section 134 of the

Criminal Justice Act 1988. That Act came into force on 29 September 1988. Section 134 created a new crime under United Kingdom law, the crime of torture. As required by the Torture Convention "all" torture wherever committed world-wide was made criminal under United Kingdom law and triable in the United Kingdom. No one has suggested that before section 134 came into effect torture committed outside the United Kingdom was a crime under United Kingdom law. Nor is it suggested that section 134 was retrospective so as to make torture committed outside the United Kingdom before 29 September 1988 a United Kingdom crime. Since torture outside the United Kingdom was not a crime under U.K. law until 29 September 1988, the principle of double criminality which requires an Act to be a crime under both the law of Spain and of the United Kingdom cannot be satisfied in relation to conduct before that date if the principle of double criminality requires the conduct to be criminal under United Kingdom law at the date it was committed. If, on the other hand, the double criminality rule only requires the conduct to be criminal under U.K. law at the date of extradition the rule was satisfied in relation to all torture alleged against Senator Pinochet whether it took place before or after 1988. The Spanish courts have held that they have jurisdiction over all the crimes alleged.

In these circumstances, the first question that has to be answered is whether or not the definition of an "extradition crime" in the Act of 1989 requires the conduct to be criminal under U.K. law at the date of commission or only at the date of extradition.

This question, although raised, was not decided in the Divisional Court. At the first hearing in this House it was apparently conceded that all the matters charged against Senator Pinochet were extradition crimes. It was only during the hearing before your Lordships that the importance of the point became fully apparent. As will appear, in my view only a limited number of the charges relied upon to extradite Senator Pinochet constitute extradition crimes since most of the conduct relied upon occurred long before 1988. In particular, I do not consider that torture committed outside the United Kingdom before 29 September 1988 was a crime under U.K. law. It follows that the main question discussed at the earlier stages of this case—is a former head of state entitled to sovereign immunity from arrest or prosecution in the U.K. for acts of torture—applies to far fewer charges. But the question of state immunity remains a point of crucial importance since, in my view, there is certain conduct of Senator Pinochet (albeit a small amount) which does constitute an extradition crime and would enable the Home Secretary (if he thought fit) to extradite Senator Pinochet to Spain unless he is entitled to state immunity. Accordingly, having identified which of the crimes alleged is an extradition crime, I will then go on to consider whether Senator Pinochet is entitled to immunity in respect of those crimes. But first I must state shortly the relevant facts.

The facts

On 11 September 1973 a right-wing coup evicted the left-wing regime of President Allende. The coup was led by a military junta, of whom Senator (then General) Pinochet was the leader. At some stage he became head of state. The Pinochet regime remained in power until 11 March 1990 when Senator Pinochet resigned.

There is no real dispute that during the period of the Senator Pinochet regime appalling acts of barbarism were committed in Chile and elsewhere in the world: torture, murder and the unexplained disappearance of individuals, all on a large scale. Although it is not alleged that Senator Pinochet himself committed any of those acts, it is alleged that they were done in pursuance of a conspiracy to which he was a party, at his instigation and with his knowledge. He denies these allegations. None of the conduct alleged was committed by or against citizens of the United Kingdom or in the United Kingdom.

In 1998 Senator Pinochet came to the United Kingdom for medical treatment. The judicial authorities in Spain sought to extradite him in order to stand trial in Spain on a large number of charges. Some of those charges had links with Spain. But most of the charges had no connection with Spain. The background to the case is that to those of left-wing political convictions Senator Pinochet is seen as an arch-devil: to those of right-wing persuasions he is seen as the saviour of Chile. It may well be thought that the trial of Senator Pinochet in Spain for offences all of which related to the state of Chile and most of which occurred in Chile is not calculated to achieve the best justice. But I cannot emphasise too strongly that that is no concern of your Lordships. Although others perceive our task as being to choose between the two sides on the grounds of personal preference or political inclination, that is an entire misconception. Our job is to decide two questions of law: are there any extradition crimes and, if so, is Senator Pinochet immune from trial for committing those crimes. If, as a matter of law, there are no extradition crimes or he is entitled to immunity in relation to whichever crimes there are, then there is no legal right to extradite Senator Pinochet to Spain or, indeed, to stand in the way of his return to Chile. If, on the other hand, there are extradition crimes in relation to which Senator Pinochet is not entitled to state immunity then it will be open to the Home Secretary to extradite him. The task of this House is only to decide those points of law.

On 16 October 1998 an international warrant for the arrest of Senator Pinochet was issued in Spain. On the same day, a magistrate in London issued a provisional warrant ("the first warrant") under section 8 of the Extradition Act 1989. He was arrested in a London hospital on 17 October 1998. On 18 October the Spanish authorities issued a second international warrant. A further provisional warrant ("the second warrant") was issued by the magistrate at Bow Street Magistrates Court on 22 October 1998 accusing Senator Pinochet of:

> "(1) Between 1 January 1988 and December 1992 being a public official intentionally inflicted severe pain or suffering on another in the performance or purported performance of his official duties;
>
> (2) Between the first day of January 1988 and 31 December 1992 being a public official, conspired with persons unknown to intentionally inflict severe pain or suffering on another in the performance or purported performance of his official duties;
>
> (3) Between the first day of January 1982 and 31 January 1992 he detained other persons (the hostages) and in order to compel such persons to do or to abstain from doing any act threatened to kill, injure or continue to detain the hostages;
>
> (4) Between the first day of January 1982 and 31 January 1992 conspired with persons unknown to detain other persons (the hostages) and in order to compel such persons to do or to abstain from doing any act, threatened to kill, injure or continue to detain the hostages.
>
> (5) Between January 1976 and December 1992 conspired together with persons unknown to commit murder in a Convention country."

Senator Pinochet started proceedings for habeas corpus and for leave to move for judicial review of both the first and the second provisional warrants. Those proceedings came before the Divisional Court (Lord Bingham of Cornhill C.J., Collins and Richards JJ.) which on 28 October 1998 quashed both warrants. Nothing turns on the first warrant which was quashed since no appeal was brought to this House. The grounds on which the Divisional Court quashed the second warrant were that Senator Pinochet (as former head of state) was entitled to state immunity in respect of the acts with which he was charged. However, it had also been argued before the Divisional Court that certain of the crimes alleged in the second warrant were not "extradition crimes" within the meaning of the Act of 1989 because they were not crimes under U.K. law at the date they were committed. Whilst not determining this point directly, the Lord Chief Justice held that, in order to be an extradition crime, it was not necessary that the conduct should be criminal at the date of the conduct relied upon but only at the date of request for extradition.

The Crown Prosecution Service (acting on behalf of the Government of Spain) appealed to this House with the leave of the Divisional Court. The Divisional Court certified the point of law of general importance as being "the proper interpretation and scope of the immunity enjoyed by a former head of state from arrest and extradition proceedings in the United Kingdom in respect of acts committed while he was head of state." Before the appeal came on for hearing in this House for the first time, on 4 November 1998 the Government of Spain submitted a formal Request for Extradition which greatly expanded the list of crimes alleged in the second provisional warrant so as to allege a widespread conspiracy to take over the Government of Chile by a coup and thereafter to reduce the country to submission by committing genocide, murder, torture and the taking of hostages, such conduct taking place primarily in Chile but also elsewhere.

The appeal first came on for hearing before this House between 4 and 12 November 1998. The Committee heard submissions by counsel for the Crown Prosecution Service as appellants (on behalf of the Government of Spain), Senator Pinochet, Amnesty International as interveners and an independent amicus curiae. Written submissions were also entertained from Human Rights Watch. That Committee entertained argument based on the extended scope of the case as put forward in the Request for Extradition. It is not entirely clear to what extent the Committee heard submissions as to whether all or some of those charges constituted "extradition crimes". There is some suggestion in the judgments that the point was conceded. Certainly, if the matter was argued at all it played a very minor role in that first hearing. Judgment was given on 25 November 1998 (see [1998] 3 W.L.R. 1456). The appeal was allowed by a majority (Lord Nicholls of Birkenhead, Lord Steyn and Lord Hoffmann, Lord Slynn of Hadley and Lord Lloyd of Berwick dissenting) on the grounds that Senator Pinochet was not entitled to immunity in relation to crimes under international law. On 15 January 1998 that judgment of the House was set aside on the grounds that the Committee was not properly constituted: see [1999] 2 W.L.R. 272. The appeal came on again for rehearing on 18 January 1999 before your Lordships. In the meantime the position had changed yet again. First, the Home Secretary had issued to the magistrate authority to proceed under section 7 of the Act of 1989. In deciding to permit the extradition to Spain to go ahead he relied in part on the decision of this House at the first hearing that Senator Pinochet was not entitled to immunity. He did not authorise the extradition proceedings to go ahead on the charge of genocide: accordingly no further arguments were addressed to us on the charge of genocide which has dropped out of the case.

Secondly, the Republic of Chile applied to intervene as a party. Up to this point Chile had been urging that immunity should be afforded to Senator Pinochet, but it now wished to be joined as a party. Any immunity precluding criminal charges against Senator Pinochet is the immunity not of Senator Pinochet but of the Republic of Chile. Leave to intervene was therefore given to the Republic of Chile. The same amicus, Mr. Lloyd Jones, was heard as at the first hearing as were counsel for Amnesty International. Written representations were again put in on behalf of Human Rights Watch.

Thirdly, the ambit of the charges against Senator Pinochet had widened yet again. Chile had put in further particulars of the charges which they wished to advance. In order to try to bring some order to the proceedings, Mr. Alun Jones Q.C., for the Crown Prosecution Service, prepared a schedule of the 32 U.K. criminal charges which correspond to the allegations made against Senator Pinochet under Spanish law, save that the genocide charges are omitted. The charges in that schedule are fully analysed and considered in the speech of my noble and learned friend, Lord Hope of Craighead who summarises the charges as follows:

Charges 1, 2 and 5: conspiracy to torture between 1 January 1972 and 20 September 1973 and between 1 August 1973 and 1 January 1990;
Charge 3: conspiracy to take hostages between 1 August 1973 and 1 January 1990;
Charge 4: conspiracy to torture in furtherance of which murder was committed in various countries including Italy, France, Spain and Portugal, between 1 January 1972 and 1 January 1990.
Charges 6 and 8: torture between 1 August 1973 and 8 August 1973 and on 11 September 1973.
Charges 9 and 12: conspiracy to murder in Spain between 1 January 1975 and 31 December 1976 and in Italy on 6 October 1975.
Charges 10 and 11: attempted murder in Italy on 6 October 1975.
Charges 13–29; and 31–32: torture on various occasions between 11 September 1973 and May 1977.
Charge 30: torture on 24 June 1989.

I turn then to consider which of those charges are extradition crimes.

Extradition crimes

As I understand the position, at the first hearing in the House of Lords the Crown Prosecution Service did not seek to rely on any conduct of Senator Pinochet occurring before 11 September 1973 (the date on which the coup occurred) or after 11 March 1990 (the date when Senator Pinochet retired as head of state). Accordingly, as the case was then presented, if Senator Pinochet was entitled to immunity such immunity covered the whole period of the alleged crimes. At the second hearing before your Lordships, however, the Crown Prosecution Service extended the period during which the crimes were said to have been committed: for example, see charges 1 and 4 where the conspiracies are said to have started on 1 January 1972, i.e. at a time before Senator Pinochet was head of state and therefore could be entitled to immunity. In consequence at the second hearing counsel for Senator Pinochet revived the submission that certain of the charges, in particular those relating to torture and conspiracy to torture, were not "extradition crimes" because at the time the acts were done the acts were not criminal under the law of the United Kingdom. Once raised, this point could not be confined simply to the period (if any) before Senator Pinochet became head of state. If the double criminality rule requires it to be shown that at the date of the conduct such conduct would have been criminal under the law of the United Kingdom, any charge based on torture or conspiracy to torture occurring before 29 September 1988 (when section 134 of the Criminal Justice Act came into force) could not be an "extradition crime" and therefore could not in any event found an extradition order against Senator Pinochet.

Under section 1(1) of the Act of 1989 a person who is accused of an "extradition crime" may be arrested and returned to the state which has requested extradition. Section 2 defines "extradition crime" so far as relevant as follows:

"(1) In this Act, except in Schedule 1, 'extradition crime' means:
(a) conduct in the territory of a foreign state, a designated Commonwealth country or a colony which, if it occurred in the United Kingdom, would constitute an offence punishable with imprisonment for a term of 12 months, or any greater punishment, and which, however described in the law of the foreign state, Commonwealth country or colony, is so punishable under that law;
(b) an extra-territorial offence against the law of a foreign state, designated Commonwealth country or colony which is punishable under that law with imprisonment for a term of 12 months, or any greater punishment, and which satisfies:
(i) the condition specified in subsection (2) below; or
(ii) all the conditions specified in subsection (3) below.

"(2) The condition mentioned in subsection (1)(b)(i) above is that in corresponding circumstances equivalent conduct would constitute an extra-territorial offence against the law of the United Kingdom punishable with imprisonment for a term of 12 months, or any greater punishment.

"(3) The conditions mentioned in subsection (1)(b)(ii) above are:
(a) that the foreign state, Commonwealth country or colony bases its jurisdiction on the nationality of the offender;
(b) that the conduct constituting the offence occurred outside the United Kingdom; and
(c) that, if it occurred in the United Kingdom, it would constitute an offence under the law of the United Kingdom punishable with imprisonment for a term of 12 months, or any greater punishment."

The question is whether the references to conduct "which, if it occurred in the United Kingdom, would constitute an offence" in section 2(1)(a) and (3)(c) refer to a hypothetical occurrence which took place at the date of the request for extradition ("the request date") or the date of the actual conduct ("the conduct date"). In the Divisional Court, the Lord Chief Justice (at p. 20 of the Transcript) held that the words required the acts to be criminal only at the request date. He said:

"I would however add on the retrospectivity point that the conduct alleged against the subject of the request need not in my judgment have been criminal here at the time the alleged crime was committed abroad. There is nothing in section 2 which so provides. What is necessary is that at the time of the extradition request the offence should be a criminal offence here and that it should then be punishable with 12 months imprisonment or more. Otherwise section 2(1)(a) would have referred to conduct which would at the relevant time 'have constituted' an offence and section 2(3)(c) would have said 'would have constituted'. I therefore reject this argument."

Lord Lloyd (who was the only member of the Committee to express a view on this point at the first hearing) took the same view. He said at p. 1481:

"But I agree with the Divisional Court that this argument is bad. It involves a misunderstanding of section 2 of the Extradition Act 1989. Section 2(1)(a) refers to conduct which would constitute an offence in the United Kingdom now. It does not refer to conduct which would have constituted an offence then."

My Lords, if the words of section 2 are construed in isolation there is room for two possible views. I agree with the Lord Chief Justice and Lord Lloyd that, if read in isolation, the words "if it occurred . . . would constitute" read more easily as a reference to a hypothetical event happening now, i.e. at the request date, than to a past hypothetical event, i.e. at the conduct date. But in my judgment the right construction is not clear. The word "it" in the phrase "if it occurred . . ." is a reference back to the actual conduct of the individual abroad which, by definition, is a past event. The question then would be "would that past event (including the date of its occurrence) constitute an offence under the law of the United Kingdom." The answer to that question would depend upon the United Kingdom law at that date.

But of course it is not correct to construe these words in isolation and your Lordships had the advantage of submissions which strongly indicate that the relevant date is the conduct date. The starting point is that the Act of 1989 regulates at least three types of extradition.

First, extradition to a Commonwealth country, to a colony or to a foreign country which is not a party to the European Convention on Extradition. In this class of case (which is not the present one) the procedure under Part III of the Act of 1989 requires the extradition request to be accompanied by evidence sufficient to justify arrest under the Act: section 7(2)(b). The Secretary of State then issues his authority to proceed which has to specify the offences under U.K. law which "would be constituted by equivalent conduct in the United Kingdom": section 7(5). Under section 8 the magistrate is given power to issue a warrant of arrest if he is supplied with such evidence "as would in his opinion justify the issue of a warrant for the arrest of a person accused": section 8(3). The committal court then has to consider, amongst other things, whether "the evidence would be sufficient to warrant his trial if the extradition crime had taken place within jurisdiction of the court" (emphasis added): section 9(8). In my judgment these provisions clearly indicate that the conduct must be criminal under the law of the United Kingdom at the conduct date and not only at the request date. The whole process of arrest and committal leads to a position where under section 9(8) the magistrate has to be satisfied that, under the law of the United Kingdom, if the conduct "had occurred" the evidence was sufficient to warrant his trial. This is a clear reference to the position at the date when the conduct in fact occurred. Moreover, it is in my judgment compelling that the evidence which the magistrate has to consider has to be sufficient "to warrant his trial". Here what is under consideration is not an abstract concept whether a hypothetical case is criminal but of a hard practical matter—would this case in relation to this defendant be properly committed for trial if the conduct in question had happened in the United Kingdom? The answer to that question must be "no" unless at that date the conduct was criminal under the law of the United Kingdom.

The second class of case dealt with by the Act of 1989 is where extradition is sought by a foreign state which, like Spain, is a party to the European Extradition Convention. The requirements applicable in such a case are the same as those I have dealt with above in relation to the first class of case save that the requesting state does not have to present evidence to provide the basis on which the magistrate can make his order to commit. The requesting state merely supplies the information. But this provides no ground for distinguishing Convention cases from the first class of case. The double criminality requirement must be the same in both classes of case.

Finally, the third class of case consists of those cases where there is an Order in Council in force under the Extradition Act 1870. In such cases, the procedure is not regulated by Part III of the Act of 1989 but by Schedule I to the Act of 1989: see section 1(3). Schedule I contains, in effect, the relevant provisions of the Act of 1870, which subject to substantial amendments had been in force down to the passing of the Act of 1989. The scheme of the Act of 1870 was to define "extradition crime" as meaning "a crime which, if committed in England . . . would be one of the crimes described in the first schedule to this Act": section 26. The first schedule to the Act of 1870 contains a list of crimes and is headed:

> "The following list of crimes is to be construed according to the law existing in England . . . at the date of the alleged crime, whether by common law or by statute made before or after the passing of this Act." (emphasis added)

It is therefore quite clear from the words I have emphasised that under the Act of 1870 the double criminality rule required the conduct to be criminal under English law at the conduct date not at the request date. Paragraph 20 of Schedule 1 to the Act of 1989 provides:

> " 'extradition crime', in relation to any foreign state, is to be construed by reference to the Order in Council under section 2 of the Extradition Act 1870 applying to that state as it had effect immediately before the coming into force of this Act and to any amendments thereafter made to that Order;"

Therefore in this class of case regulated by Schedule 1 to the Act of 1989 the same position applies as it formerly did under the Act of 1870, i.e. the conduct has to be a crime under English law at the conduct date. It would be extraordinary if the same Act required criminality under English law to be shown at one date for one form of extradition and at another date for another. But the case is stronger than that. We were taken through a trawl of the travaux preparatoires relating to the Extradition Convention and the departmental papers leading to the Act of 1989. They were singularly silent as to the relevant date. But they did disclose that there was no discussion as to changing the date on which the criminality under English law was to be demonstrated. It seems to me impossible that the legislature can have intended to change that date from the one which had applied for over a hundred years under the Act of 1870 (i.e. the conduct date) by a side wind and without investigation.

The charges which allege extradition crimes

The consequences of requiring torture to be a crime under U.K. law at the date the torture was committed are considered in Lord Hope's speech. As he demonstrates, the charges of torture and conspiracy to torture relating to conduct before 29 September 1988 (the date on which section 134 came into effect) are not extraditable, i.e. only those parts of the conspiracy to torture alleged in charge 2 and of torture and conspiracy to torture alleged in charge 4 which relate to the period after that date and the single act of torture alleged in charge 30 are extradition crimes relating to torture.

Lord Hope also considers, and I agree, that the only charge relating to hostage-taking (charge 3) does not disclose any offence under the Taking of Hostages Act 1982. The statutory offence consists of taking and detaining a person (the hostage), so as to compel someone who is not the hostage to do or abstain from doing some act: section 1. But the only conduct relating to hostages which is charged alleges that the person detained (the so-called hostage) was to be forced to do something by reason of threats to injure other non-hostages which is the exact converse of the offence. The hostage charges therefore are bad and do not constitute extradition crimes.

Finally, Lord Hope's analysis shows that the charge of conspiracy in Spain to murder in Spain (charge 9) and such conspiracies in Spain to commit murder in Spain, and such conspiracies in Spain prior to 29 September 1988 to commit acts of torture in Spain, as can be shown to form part of the allegations in charge 4 are extradition crimes.

I must therefore consider whether, in relation to these two surviving categories of charge, Senator Pinochet enjoys sovereign immunity. But first it is necessary to consider the modern law of torture.

Torture

Apart from the law of piracy, the concept of personal liability under international law for international crimes is of comparatively modern growth. The traditional subjects of international law are states not human beings. But consequent upon the war crime trials after the 1939–45 World War, the international community came to recognise that there could be criminal liability under international law for a class of crimes such as war crimes and crimes against humanity. Although there may be legitimate doubts as to the legality of the Charter of the Nuremberg Tribunal, in my judgment those doubts were stilled by the Affirmation of the Principles of International Law recognised by the Charter of Nuremberg Tribunal adopted by the United Nations General Assembly on 11 December 1946. That Affirmation affirmed the principles of international law recognised by the Charter of the Nuremberg Tribunal and the judgment of the Tribunal and directed the Committee on the codification of international law to treat as a matter of primary importance plans for the formulation of the principles recognised in the Charter of the Nuremberg Tribunal. At least from that date onwards the concept of personal liability for a crime in international law must have been part of international law. In the early years state torture was one of the elements of a war crime. In consequence torture, and various other crimes against humanity, were linked to war or at least to hostilities of some kind. But in the course of time this linkage with war fell away and torture, divorced from war or hostilities, became an international crime on its own: see Oppenheim's International Law (Jennings and Watts edition) vol. 1, 996; note 6 to Article 18 of the I.L.C. Draft Code of Crimes Against Peace; Prosecutor v. Furundzija Tribunal for Former Yugoslavia, Case No. 17–95–17/1–T. Ever since 1945, torture on a large scale has featured as one of the crimes against humanity: see, for example, U.N. General Assembly Resolutions 3059, 3452 and 3453 passed in 1973 and 1975; Statutes of the International Criminal Tribunals for former Yugoslavia (Article 5) and Rwanda (Article 3).

Moreover, the Republic of Chile accepted before your Lordships that the international law prohibiting torture has the character of jus cogens or a peremptory norm, i.e. one of those rules of international law which have a particular status. In Furundzija (supra) at para. 153, the Tribunal said:

"Because of the importance of the values it protects, [the prohibition of torture] has evolved into a peremptory norm or jus cogens, that is, a norm that enjoys a higher rank in the international hierarchy than treaty law and even 'ordinary' customary rules. The most conspicuous consequence of this higher rank is that the principle at issue cannot be derogated from by states through international treaties or local or special customs or even general customary rules not endowed with the same normative force. . . . Clearly, the jus cogens nature of the prohibition against torture articulates the notion that the prohibition has now become one of the most fundamental standards of the international community. Furthermore, this prohibition is designed to produce a deterrent effect, in that it signals to all members of the international community and the individuals over whom they wield authority that the prohibition of torture is an absolute value from which nobody must deviate." (See also the cases cited in Note 170 to the Furundzija case.)

The jus cogens nature of the international crime of torture justifies states in taking universal jurisdiction over torture wherever committed. International law provides that offences jus cogens may be punished by any state because the offenders are "common enemies of all mankind and all nations have an equal interest in their apprehension and prosecution": Demjanjuk v. Petrovsky (1985) 603 F. Supp. 1468; 776 F. 2d. 571.

It was suggested by Miss Montgomery, for Senator Pinochet, that although torture was contrary to international law it was not strictly an international crime in the highest sense. In the light of the authorities to which I have referred (and there are many others) I have no doubt that long before the Torture Convention of 1984 state torture was an international crime in the highest sense.

But there was no tribunal or court to punish international crimes of torture. Local courts could take jurisdiction: see Demjanjuk (supra); Attorney-General of Israel v. Eichmann (1962) 36 I.L.R.S. But the objective was to ensure a general jurisdiction so that the torturer was not safe wherever he went. For example, in this case it is alleged that during the Pinochet regime torture was an official, although unacknowledged, weapon of government and that, when the regime was about to end, it passed legislation designed to afford an amnesty to those who had engaged in institutionalised torture. If these allegations are true, the fact that the local court had jurisdiction to deal with the international crime of torture was nothing to the point so long as the totalitarian regime remained in power: a totalitarian regime will not permit adjudication by its own courts on its own shortcomings. Hence the demand for some international machinery to repress state torture which is not dependent upon the local courts where the torture was committed. In the event, over 110 states (including Chile, Spain and the United Kingdom) became state parties to the Torture Convention. But it is far from clear that none of them practised state torture. What was needed therefore was an international system which could punish those who were guilty of torture and which did not permit the evasion of punishment by the torturer moving from one state to another. The Torture Convention was agreed not in order to create an international crime which had not previously existed but to provide an international system under which the international criminal—the torturer—could find no safe haven. Burgers and Danelius (respectively the chairman of the United Nations Working Group on the 1984 Torture Convention and the draftsmen of its first draft) say, at p. 131, that it was "an essential purpose [of the Convention] to ensure that a torturer does not escape the consequences of his act by going to another country."

The Torture Convention

Article 1 of the Convention defines torture as the intentional infliction of severe pain and of suffering with a view to achieving a wide range of purposes "when such pain or suffering is inflicted by or at the instigation of or with the consent or acquiesence of a public official or other person acting in an official capacity." Article 2(1) requires each state party to prohibit torture on territory within its own jurisdiction and Article 4 requires each state party to ensure that "all" acts of torture are offences under its criminal law. Article 2(3) outlaws any defence of superior orders. Under Article 5(1) each state party has to establish its jurisdiction over torture (a) when committed within territory under its jurisdiction (b) when the alleged offender is a national of that state, and (c) in certain circumstances, when the victim is a national of that state. Under Article 5(2) a state party has to take jurisdiction over any alleged offender who is found within its territory. Article

6 contains provisions for a state in whose territory an alleged torturer is found to detain him, inquire into the position and notify the states referred to in Article 5(1) and to indicate whether it intends to exercise jurisdiction. Under Article 7 the state in whose territory the alleged torturer is found shall, if he is not extradited to any of the states mentioned in Article 5(1), submit him to its authorities for the purpose of prosecution. Under Article 8(1) torture is to be treated as an extraditable offence and under Article 8(4) torture shall, for the purposes of extradition, be treated as having been committed not only in the place where it occurred but also in the state mentioned in Article 5(1).

Who is an "official" for the purposes of the Torture Convention?

The first question on the Convention is to decide whether acts done by a head of state are done by "a public official or a person acting in an official capacity" within the meaning of Article 1. The same question arises under section 134 of the Criminal Justice Act 1988. The answer to both questions must be the same. In his judgment at the first hearing (at pp. 1476G-1477E) Lord Slynn held that a head of state was neither a public official nor a person acting in an official capacity within the meaning of Article 1: he pointed out that there are a number of international conventions (for example the Yugoslav War Crimes Statute and the Rwanda War Crimes Statute) which refer specifically to heads of state when they intend to render them liable. Lord Lloyd apparently did not agree with Lord Slynn on this point since he thought that a head of state who was a torturer could be prosecuted in his own country, a view which could not be correct unless such head of state had conducted himself as a public official or in an official capacity.

It became clear during the argument that both the Republic of Chile and Senator Pinochet accepted that the acts alleged against Senator Pinochet, if proved, were acts done by a public official or person acting in an official capacity within the meaning of Article 1. In my judgment these concessions were correctly made. Unless a head of state authorising or promoting torture is an official or acting in an official capacity within Article 1, then he would not be guilty of the international crime of torture even within his own state. That plainly cannot have been the intention. In my judgment it would run completely contrary to the intention of the Convention if there was anybody who could be exempt from guilt. The crucial question is not whether Senator Pinochet falls within the definition in Article 1: he plainly does. The question is whether, even so, he is procedurally immune from process. To my mind the fact that a head of state can be guilty of the crime casts little, if any, light on the question whether he is immune from prosecution for that crime in a foreign state.

Universal jurisdiction

There was considerable argument before your Lordships concerning the extent of the jurisdiction to prosecute torturers conferred on states other than those mentioned in Article 5(1). I do not find it necessary to seek an answer to all the points raised. It is enough that it is clear that in all circumstances, if the Article 5(1) states do not choose to seek extradition or to prosecute the offender, other states must do so. The purpose of the Convention was to introduce the principle aut dedere aut punire—either you extradite or you punish: Burgers and Danelius p. 131. Throughout the negotiation of the Convention certain countries wished to make the exercise of jurisdiction under Article 5(2) dependent upon the state assuming jurisdiction having refused extradition to an Article 5(1) state.

However, at a session in 1984 all objections to the principle of aut dedere aut punire were withdrawn. "The inclusion of universal jurisdiction in the draft Convention was no longer opposed by any delegation": Working Group on the Draft Convention U.N. Doc. E/CN. 4/1984/72, para. 26. If there is no prosecution by, or extradition to, an Article 5(1) state, the state where the alleged offender is found (which will have already taken him into custody under Article 6) must exercise the jurisdiction under Article 5(2) by prosecuting him under Article 7(1).

I gather the following important points from the Torture Convention:

1) Torture within the meaning of the Convention can only be committed by "a public official or other person acting in an official capacity", but these words include a head of state. A single act of official torture is "torture" within the Convention;

2) Superior orders provide no defence;

3) If the states with the most obvious jurisdiction (the Article 5(1) states) do not seek to extradite, the state where the alleged torturer is found must prosecute or, apparently, extradite to another country, i.e. there is universal jurisdiction.

4) There is no express provision dealing with state immunity of heads of state, ambassadors or other officials.

5) Since Chile, Spain and the United Kingdom are all parties to the Convention, they are bound under treaty by its provisions whether or not such provisions would apply in the absence of treaty obligation. Chile ratified the Convention with effect from 30 October 1988 and the United Kingdom with effect from 8 December 1988.

State immunity

This is the point around which most of the argument turned. It is of considerable general importance internationally since, if Senator Pinochet is not entitled to immunity in relation to the acts of torture alleged to have occurred after 29 September 1988, it will be the first time so far as counsel have discovered when a local domestic court has refused to afford immunity to a head of state or former head of state on the grounds that there can be no immunity against prosecution for certain international crimes.

Given the importance of the point, it is surprising how narrow is the area of dispute. There is general agreement between the parties as to the rules of statutory immunity and the rationale which underlies them. The issue is whether international law grants state immunity in relation to the international crime of torture and, if so, whether the Republic of Chile is entitled to claim such immunity even though Chile, Spain and the United Kingdom are all parties to the Torture Convention and therefore "contractually" bound to give effect to its provisions from 8 December 1988 at the latest.

It is a basic principle of international law that one sovereign state (the forum state) does not adjudicate on the conduct of a foreign state. The foreign state is entitled to procedural immunity from the processes of the forum state. This immunity extends to both criminal and civil liability. State immunity probably grew from the historical immunity of the person of the monarch. In any event, such personal immunity of the head of state persists to the present day: the head of state is entitled to the same immunity as the state itself. The diplomatic representative of the foreign state in the forum state is also afforded the same immunity in recognition of the dignity of the state which he represents. This immunity enjoyed by a head of state in power and an ambassador in post is a complete immunity attaching to the person of the head of state or ambassador and rendering him immune from all actions or prosecutions whether or not they relate to matters done for the benefit of the state. Such immunity is said to be granted ratione personae.

What then when the ambassador leaves his post or the head of state is deposed? The position of the ambassador is covered by the Vienna Convention on Diplomatic Relations, 1961. After providing for immunity from arrest (Article 29) and from criminal and civil jurisdiction (Article 31), Article 39(1) provides that the ambassador's privileges shall be enjoyed from the moment he takes up post; and subsection (2) provides:

> "(2) When the functions of a person enjoying privileges and immunities have come to an end, such privileges and immunities shall normally cease at the moment when he leaves the country, or on expiry of a reasonable period in which to do so, but shall subsist until that time, even in case of armed conflict. However, with respect to acts performed by such a person in the exercise of his functions as a member of the mission, immunity shall continue to subsist."

The continuing partial immunity of the ambassador after leaving post is of a different kind from that enjoyed ratione personae while he was in post. Since he is no longer the representative of the foreign state he merits no particular privileges or immunities as a person. However in order to preserve the integrity of the activities of the foreign state during the period when he was ambassador, it is necessary to provide that immunity is afforded to his official acts during his tenure in post. If this were not done the sovereign immunity of the state could be evaded by calling in question acts done during the previous ambassador's time. Accordingly under Article 39(2) the ambassador, like any other official of the state, enjoys immunity in relation to his official acts done while he was an official. This limited immunity, ratione materiae, is to be contrasted with the former immunity ratione personae which gave complete immunity to all activities whether public or private.

In my judgment at common law a former head of state enjoys similar immunities, ratione materiae, once he ceases to be head of state. He too loses immunity ratione personae on ceasing to be head of state: see Watts The Legal Position in International Law of Heads of States, Heads of Government and Foreign Ministers p. 88 and the cases there cited. He can be sued on his private obligations: Ex-King Farouk of Egypt v. Christian Dior (1957) 24 I.L.R. 228; Jimenez v. Aristeguieta (1962) 311 F. 2d 547. As ex head of state he cannot be sued in respect of acts performed whilst head of state in his public capacity: Hatch v. Baez [1876] 7 Hun. 596. Thus, at common law, the position of the former ambassador and the former head of state appears to be much the same: both enjoy immunity for acts done in performance of their respective functions whilst in office.

I have belaboured this point because there is a strange feature of the United Kingdom law which I must mention shortly. The State Immunity Act 1978 modifies the traditional complete immunity normally afforded by the common law in claims for damages against foreign states. Such modifications are contained in Part I of the Act. Section 16(1) provides that nothing in Part I of the Act is to apply to criminal proceedings. Therefore Part I has no direct application to the present case. However, Part III of the Act contains section 20(1) which provides:

> "Subject to the provisions of this section and to any necessary modifications, the Diplomatic Privileges Act 1964 shall apply to:
> (a) a sovereign or other head of state;
> (b) . . .
> (c) . . .
> as it applies to a head of a diplomatic mission . . ."

The correct way in which to apply Article 39(2) of the Vienna Convention to a former head of state is baffling. To what "functions" is one to have regard? When do they cease since the former head of state almost certainly never arrives in this country let alone leaves it? Is a former head of state's immunity limited to the exercise of the functions of a member of the mission, or is that again something which is subject to "necessary modification"? It is hard to resist the suspicion that something has gone wrong. A search was done on the parliamentary history of the section. From this it emerged that the original section 20(1)(a) read "a sovereign or other head of state who is in the United Kingdom at the invitation or with the consent of the Government of the United Kingdom." On that basis the section would have been intelligible. However it was changed by a Government amendment the mover of which said that the clause as introduced "leaves an unsatisfactory doubt about the position of heads of state who are not in the United Kingdom"; he said that the amendment was to ensure that heads of state would be treated like heads of diplomatic missions "irrespective of presence in the United Kingdom." The parliamentary history, therefore, discloses no clear indication of what was intended. However, in my judgment it does not matter unduly since Parliament cannot have intended to give heads of state and former heads of state greater rights than they already enjoyed under international law. Accordingly, "the necessary modifications" which need to be made will produce the result that a former head of state has immunity in relation to acts done as part of his official functions when head of state. Accordingly, in my judgment, Senator Pinochet as former head of state enjoys immunity ratione materiae in relation to acts done by him as head of state as part of his official functions as head of state.

The question then which has to be answered is whether the alleged organisation of state torture by Senator Pinochet (if proved) would constitute an act committed by Senator Pinochet as part of his official functions as head of state. It is not enough to say that it cannot be part of the functions of the head of state to commit a crime. Actions which are criminal under the local law can still have been done officially and therefore give rise to immunity ratione materiae. The case needs to be analysed more closely.

Can it be said that the commission of a crime which is an international crime against humanity and jus cogens is an act done in an official capacity on behalf of the state? I believe there to be strong ground for saying that the implementation of torture as defined by the Torture Convention cannot be a state function. This is the view taken by Sir Arthur Watts (supra) who said (at p. 82):

> "While generally international law . . . does not directly involve obligations on individuals personally, that is not always appropriate, particularly for acts of such seriousness that they constitute not merely international wrongs (in the broad sense of a civil wrong) but rather international crimes which offend against the public order of the international community. States are artificial legal persons: they can only act through the institutions and agencies of the state, which means, ultimately through its officials and other individuals acting on behalf of the state. For international conduct which is so serious as to be tainted with criminality to be regarded as attributable only to the impersonal state and not to the individuals who ordered or perpetrated it is both unrealistic and offensive to common notions of justice.
>
> "The idea that individuals who commit international crimes are internationally accountable for them has now become an accepted part of international law. Problems in this area—such as the non-existence of any standing international tribunal to have jurisdiction over such crimes, and the lack of agreement as to what acts are internationally criminal for this purpose—have not affected the general acceptance of the principle of individual responsibility for international criminal conduct."

Later, at p. 84, he said:

> "It can no longer be doubted that as a matter of general customary international law a head of state will personally be liable to be called to account if there is sufficient evidence that he authorised or perpetrated such serious international crimes."

It can be objected that Sir Arthur was looking at those cases where the international community has established an international tribunal in relation to which the regulating document expressly makes the head of state subject to the tribunal's jurisdiction: see, for example, the Nuremberg Charter Article 7; the Statute of the International Tribunal for former Yugoslavia; the Statute of the International Tribunal for Rwanda and the Statute of the International Criminal Court. It is true that in these cases it is expressly said that the head of state or former head of state is subject to the court's jurisdiction. But those are cases in which a new court with no existing jurisdiction is being established. The jurisdiction being established by the Torture Convention and the Hostages Convention is one where existing domestic courts of all the countries are being authorised and required to take jurisdiction internationally. The question is whether, in this new type of jurisdiction, the only possible view is that those made subject to the jurisdiction of each of the state courts of the world in relation to torture are not entitled to claim immunity.

I have doubts whether, before the coming into force of the Torture Convention, the existence of the international crime of torture as jus cogens was enough to justify the conclusion that the organisation of state torture could not rank for immunity purposes as performance of an official function. At that stage there was no international tribunal to punish torture and no general jurisdiction to permit or require its punishment in domestic courts. Not until there was some form of universal jurisdiction for the punishment of the crime of torture could it really be talked about as a fully constituted international crime. But in my judgment the Torture Convention did provide what was missing: a worldwide universal jurisdiction. Further, it required all member states to ban and outlaw torture: Article 2. How can it be for international law purposes an official function to do something which international law itself prohibits and criminalises? Thirdly, an essential feature of the international crime of torture is that it must be committed "by or with the acquiesence of a public official or other person acting in an official capacity." As a result all defendants in torture cases will be state officials. Yet, if the former head of state has immunity, the man most responsible will escape liability while his inferiors (the chiefs of police, junior army officers) who carried out his orders will be liable. I find it impossible to accept that this was the intention.

Finally, and to my mind decisively, if the implementation of a torture regime is a public function giving rise to immunity ratione materiae, this produces bizarre results. Immunity ratione materiae applies not only to ex-heads of state and ex-ambassadors but to all state officials who have been involved in carrying out the functions of the state. Such immunity is necessary in order to prevent state immunity being circumvented by prosecuting or suing the official who, for example, actually carried out the torture when a claim against the head of state would be precluded by the doctrine of immunity. If that applied to the present case, and if the implementation of the torture regime is to be treated as official business sufficient to found an immunity for the former head of state, it must also be official business sufficient to justify immunity for his inferiors who actually did the torturing. Under the Convention the international crime of torture can only be committed by an official or someone in an official capacity. They would all be entitled to immunity. It would follow that there can be no case outside Chile in which a successful prosecution for torture can be brought unless the State of Chile is prepared to waive its right to its officials immunity. Therefore the whole elaborate structure of universal jurisdiction over torture committed by officials is rendered abortive and one of the main objectives of the Torture Convention—to provide a system under which there is no safe haven for torturers—will have been frustrated. In my judgment all these factors together demonstrate that the notion of continued immunity for ex-heads of state is inconsistent with the provisions of the Torture Convention.

For these reasons in my judgment if, as alleged, Senator Pinochet organised and authorised torture after 8 December 1988, he was not acting in any capacity which gives rise to immunity ratione materiae because such actions were contrary to international law, Chile had agreed to outlaw such conduct and Chile had agreed with the other parties to the Torture Convention that all signatory states should have jurisdiction to try official torture (as defined in the Convention) even if such torture were committed in Chile.

As to the charges of murder and conspiracy to murder, no one has advanced any reason why the ordinary rules of immunity should not apply and Senator Pinochet is entitled to such immunity.

For these reasons, I would allow the appeal so as to permit the extradition proceedings to proceed on the allegation that torture in pursuance of a conspiracy to commit torture, including the single act of torture which is alleged in charge 30, was being committed by Senator Pinochet after 8 December 1988 when he lost his immunity.

In issuing to the magistrate an authority to proceed under section 7 of the Extradition Act 1989, the Secretary of State proceeded on the basis that the whole range of torture charges and murder charges against Senator Pinochet would be the subject matter of the extradition proceedings. Your Lordships' decision excluding from consideration a very large number of those charges constitutes a substantial change in the circumstances. This will obviously require the Secretary of State to reconsider his decision under section 7 in the light of the changed circumstances.

LORD GOFF OF CHIEVELEY

My Lords,

I. Introduction

The background to the present appeal is set out, with economy and lucidity, in the opinion of my noble and learned friend Lord Browne-Wilkinson, which I have had the opportunity of reading in draft. I gratefully adopt his account and, to keep my own opinion as short as reasonably possible, I do not propose to repeat it. The central question in the appeal is whether Senator Pinochet is entitled as former head of state to the benefit of state immunity ratione materiae in respect of the charges advanced against him, as set out in the schedule of charges prepared by Mr. Alun Jones Q.C. on behalf of the Government of Spain.

II. The principal issue argued on the appeal

Before the Divisional Court, and again before the first Appellate Committee, it was argued on behalf of the Government of Spain that Senator Pinochet was not entitled to the benefit of state immunity basically on two grounds, viz. first, that the crimes alleged against Senator Pinochet are so horrific that an exception must be made to the international law principle of state immunity; and second, that the crimes with which he is charged are crimes against international law, in respect of which state immunity is not available. Both arguments were rejected by the Divisional Court, but a majority of the first Appellate Committee accepted the second argument. The leading opinion was delivered by Lord Nicholls of Birkenhead, whose reasoning was of great simplicity. He said (see [1998] 3 W.L.R. 1456 at p. 1500C-F):

"In my view, article 39(2) of the Vienna Convention, as modified and applied to former heads of state by section 20 of the Act of 1978, is apt to confer immunity in respect of functions which international law recognises as functions of a head of state, irrespective of the terms of his domestic constitution. This formulation, and this test for determining what are the functions of a head of state for this purpose, are sound in principle and were not the subject of controversy before your Lordships. International law does not require the grant of any wider immunity. And it hardly needs saying that torture of his own subjects, or of aliens, would not be regarded by international law as a function of a head of state. All states disavow the use of torture as abhorrent, although from time to time some still resort to it. Similarly, the taking of hostages, as much as torture, has been outlawed by the international community as an offence. International law recognises, of course, that the functions of a head of state may include activities which are wrongful, even illegal, by the law of his own state or by the laws of other states. But international law has made plain that certain types of conduct, including torture and hostage-taking, are not acceptable conduct on the part of anyone. This applies as much to heads of state, or even more so, as it does to everyone else; the contrary conclusion would make a mockery of international law."

Lord Hoffmann agreed, and Lord Steyn delivered a concurring opinion to the same effect.

Lord Slynn of Hadley and Lord Lloyd of Berwick, however, delivered substantial dissenting opinions. In particular, Lord Slynn (see [1998] 3 W.L.R. 1456 at pp. 1471F-1475G) considered in detail "the developments in international law relating to what are called international crimes." On the basis of the material so reviewed by him, he concluded (at p. 1473C):

"It does not seem to me that it has been shown that there is any state practice or general consensus let alone a widely supported convention that all crimes against international law should be justiciable in national courts on the basis of the universality of jurisdiction. Nor is there any jus cogens in respect of such breaches of international law which requires that a claim of state or head of state immunity, itself a well-established principle of international law, should be overridden."

He went on to consider whether international law now recognises that some crimes, and in particular crimes against humanity, are outwith the protection of head of state immunity. He referred to the relevant material, and observed at p. 1474H:

". . . except in regard to crimes in particular situations before international tribunals these measures did not in general deal with the question as to whether otherwise existing immunities were taken away. Nor did they always specifically recognise the jurisdiction of, or confer jurisdiction on, national courts to try such crimes."

He then proceeded to examine the Torture Convention of 1984, the Genocide Convention of 1948 and the Taking of Hostages Convention of 1983, and concluded that none of them had removed the long established immunity of former heads of state.

I have no doubt that, in order to consider the validity of the argument advanced on behalf of the Government of Spain on this point, it was necessary to carry out the exercise so performed by Lord Slynn; and I am therefore unable, with all respect, to accept the simple approach of the majority of the first Appellate Committee. Furthermore, I wish to record my respectful agreement with the analysis, and conclusions, of Lord Slynn set out in the passages from his opinion to which I have referred. I intend no disrespect to the detailed arguments advanced before your Lordships on behalf of the appellants in this matter, when I say that in my opinion they did not succeed in shaking the reasoning, or conclusions, of Lord Slynn which I have set out above. However, having regard to (1) the extraordinary impact on this case of the double criminality rule, to which I will refer in a moment, and (2) the fact that a majority of your Lordships have formed the view that, in respect of the very few charges (of torture or conspiracy to torture) which survive the impact of the double criminality rule, the effect of the Torture Convention is that in any event Senator Pinochet is not entitled to the benefit of state immunity, the present issue has ceased to have any direct bearing on the outcome of the case. In these circumstances, I do not consider it necessary or appropriate to burden this opinion with a detailed consideration of the arguments addressed to the Appellate Committee on this issue. However, I shall return to the point when I come to consider the topic of state immunity later in this opinion.

III. The double criminality rule

During the course of the hearing before your Lordships, two new issues emerged or acquired an importance which they had not previously enjoyed. The first of these is the issue of double criminality, to which I now turn.

At the hearing before your Lordships Mr. Alun Jones Q.C., for the appellants, sought to extend backwards the period during which the crimes charged were alleged to have been committed, with the effect that some of those crimes could be said to have taken place before the coup following which Senator Pinochet came into power. The purpose was obviously to enable the appellants to assert that, in respect of these crimes, no immunity as former head of state was available to him. As a result Miss Clare Montgomery Q.C., for Senator Pinochet, revived the submission that certain of the charges related to crimes which were not extradition crimes because they were not, at the time they were alleged to have been committed, criminal under the law of this country, thus offending against the double criminality rule. Mr. Alun Jones Q.C. replied to this argument but, for the reasons given by my noble and learned friend Lord Browne-Wilkinson, with which I am respectfully in complete agreement, I too am satisfied that Miss Montgomery's submission was well-founded.

The appellants did not, however, analyse the consequences of this argument, if successful, in order to identify the charges against Senator Pinochet which would survive the application of the double criminality rule. That substantial task has, however, been undertaken by my noble and learned friend, Lord Hope of Craighead, to whom your Lordships owe a debt of gratitude. His analysis I respectfully accept. As he truly says, the impact upon the present case is profound. The great mass of the offences with which Senator Pinochet is charged must be excluded, as must also be the charge of hostage-taking which does not disclose an offence under the Taking of Hostages Act 1982. The principal charges which survive are those which relate to acts of torture alleged to have been committed, or conspiracies to torture which are alleged to have been active, after 29 September 1988, the date on which section 134 of the Criminal Justice Act 1988 (which gave effect to the Torture Convention in this country) came into effect. These are: charge

30, which relates to a single act of torture alleged to have been committed on 24 June 1989; and charges 2 and 4, which allege conspiracies to torture between 1 August 1973 and 1 January 1972 respectively, and 1 January 1990, in so far as they relate to the relatively brief period between 29 September 1988 and 1 January 1990. In addition, however, the charge of conspiracy to commit murder in Spain (charge 9), and such conspiracies to commit murder in Spain as can be shown to form part of the allegations in charge 4, also survive.

IV. State immunity

Like my noble and learned friend Lord Browne-Wilkinson, I regard the principles of state immunity applicable in the case of heads of state and former heads of state as being relatively non-controversial, though the legislation on which they are now based, the State Immunity Act 1978, is in a strange form which can only be explained by the legislative history of the Act.

There can be no doubt, in my opinion, that the Act is intended to provide the sole source of English law on this topic. This is because the long title to the Act provides (inter alia) that the Act is "to make new provision with regard to the immunities and privileges of heads of state." Since in the present case we are concerned with immunity from criminal process, we can ignore Part I (which does not apply to criminal proceedings) and turn straight to Part III, and in particular to section 20. Section 20(1) provides as follows:

> "Subject to the provisions of this section and to any necessary modifications, the Diplomatic Privileges Act 1964 shall apply to—(a) a sovereign or other head of state . . . as it applies to the head of a diplomatic mission."

The function of the Diplomatic Privileges Act 1964 is to give effect to the Vienna Convention on Diplomatic Relations in this country, the relevant articles of which are scheduled to the Act. The problem is, of course, how to identify the "necessary modifications" when applying the Vienna Convention to heads of state. The nature of the problem is apparent when we turn to Article 39 of the Convention, which provides:

> "1. Every person entitled to privileges and immunities shall enjoy them from the moment he enters the territory of the receiving state on proceeding to take up his post or, if already in its territory, from the moment when his appointment is notified to the Ministry for Foreign Affairs or such other ministry as may be agreed.
> "2. When the functions of a person enjoying privileges and immunities have come to an end, such privileges and immunities shall normally cease at the moment when he leaves the country, or on expiry of a reasonable period in which to do so, but shall subsist until that time, even in case of armed conflict. However, with respect to acts performed by such a person in the exercise of his functions as a member of the mission, immunity shall continue to subsist."

At first this seems very strange, when applied to a head of state. However, the scales fall from our eyes when we discover from the legislative history of the Act that it was originally intended to apply only to a sovereign or other head of state in this country at the invitation or with the consent of the government of this country, but was amended to provide also for the position of a head of state who was not in this country—hence the form of the long title, which was amended to apply simply to heads of state. We have, therefore, to be robust in applying the Vienna Convention to heads of state "with the necessary modifications". In the case of a head of state, there can be no question of tying Article 39(1) or (2) to the territory of the receiving state, as was suggested on behalf of the appellants. Once that is realised, there seems to be no reason why the immunity of a head of state under the Act should not be construed as far as possible to accord with his immunity at customary international law, which provides the background against which this statute is set: see Alcom Ltd. v. Republic of Colombia [1984] 1 A.C. 580, 597G, per Lord Diplock. The effect is that a head of state will, under the statute as at international law, enjoy state immunity ratione personae so long as he is in office, and after he ceases to hold office will enjoy the concomitant immunity ratione materiae "in respect of acts performed [by him] in the exercise of his functions [as head of state]", the critical question being "whether the conduct was engaged in under colour of or in ostensible exercise of the head of state's public authority" (see The Legal Position in International Law of Heads of States, Heads of Governments and Foreign Ministers by Sir Arthur Watts, Recueil des Cours, vol. 247 (1994–III), at p. 56). In this context, the contrast is drawn between governmental acts, which are functions of the head of state, and private acts, which are not.

There can be no doubt that the immunity of a head of state, whether ratione personae or ratione materiae, applies to both civil and criminal proceedings. This is because the immunity applies to any form of legal process. The principle of state immunity is expressed in the Latin maxim par in parem non habet imperium, the effect of which is that one sovereign state does not adjudicate on the conduct of another. This principle applies as between states, and the head of a state is entitled to the same immunity as the state itself, as are the diplomatic representatives of the state. That the principle applies in criminal proceedings is reflected in the Act of 1978, in that there is no equivalent provision in Part III of the Act to section 16(4) which provides that Part I does not apply to criminal proceedings.

However, a question arises whether any limit is placed on the immunity in respect of criminal offences. Obviously the mere fact that the conduct is criminal does not of itself exclude the immunity, otherwise there would be little point in the immunity from criminal process; and this is so even where the crime is of a serious character. It follows, in my opinion, that the mere fact that the crime in question is torture does not exclude state immunity. It has however been stated by Sir Arthur Watts (op. cit. at pp. 81–84) that a head of state may be personally responsible:

"for acts of such seriousness that they constitute not merely international wrongs (in the broad sense of a civil wrong) but rather international crimes which offend against the public order of the international community."

He then referred to a number of instruments, including the Charter of the Nuremberg Tribunal (1946), the Charter of the Tokyo Tribunal (1948), the International Law Commission's Draft Code of Crimes Against the Peace and Security of Mankind (provisionally adopted in 1988), and the Statute of the War Crimes Tribunal for former Yugoslavia (1993), all of which expressly provide for the responsibility of heads of state, apart from the Charter of the Tokyo Tribunal which contains a similar provision regarding the official position of the accused. He concluded, at p. 84, that:

"It can no longer be doubted that as a matter of general customary international law a head of state will personally be liable to be called to account if there is sufficient evidence that he authorised or perpetrated such serious international crimes."

So far as torture is concerned, however, there are two points to be made. The first is that it is evident from this passage that Sir Arthur is referring not just to a specific crime as such, but to a crime which offends against the public order of the international community, for which a head of state may be internationally (his emphasis) accountable. The instruments cited by him show that he is concerned here with crimes against peace, war crimes and crimes against humanity. Originally these were limited to crimes committed in the context of armed conflict, as in the case of the Nuremberg and Tokyo Charters, and still in the case of the Yugoslavia Statute, though there it is provided that the conflict can be international or internal in character. Subsequently, the context has been widened to include (inter alia) torture "when committed as part of a widespread or systematic attack against a civilian population" on specified grounds. A provision to this effect appeared in the International Law Commission's Draft Code of Crimes of 1996 (which was, I understand, provisionally adopted in 1988), and also appeared in the Statute of the International Tribunal for Rwanda (1994), and in the Rome Statute of the International Court (adopted in 1998); and see also the view expressed obiter by the U.S. Court of Appeals in Siderman de Blake v. Republic of Argentina (1992) 965 F. 2d 699 at p. 716. I should add that these developments were foreshadowed in the International Law Commission's Draft Code of Crimes of 1954; but this was not adopted, and there followed a long gap of about 35 years before the developments in the 1990s to which I have referred. It follows that these provisions are not capable of evidencing any settled practice in respect of torture outside the context of armed conflict until well after 1989 which is the latest date with which we are concerned in the present case. The second point is that these instruments are all concerned with international responsibility before international tribunals, and not with the exclusion of state immunity in criminal proceedings before national courts. This supports the conclusion of Lord Slynn ([1998] 3 W.L.R. 1456 at p. 1474H) that "except in regard to crimes in particular situations before international tribunals these measures did not in general deal with the question whether otherwise existing immunities were taken away", with which I have already expressed my respectful agreement.

It follows that, if state immunity in respect of crimes of torture has been excluded at all in the present case, this can only have been done by the Torture Convention itself.

V. The Torture Convention

I turn now to the Torture Convention of 1984, which lies at the heart of the present case. This is concerned with the jurisdiction of national courts, but its "essential purpose" is to ensure that a torturer does not escape the consequences of his act by going to another country: see the Handbook on the Convention by Burgers (the Chairman-Rapporteur of the Convention) and Danelius at p. 131. The Articles of the Convention proceed in a logical order. Article 1 contains a very broad definition of torture. For present purposes, it is important that torture has to be "inflicted by or at the instigation of or with the consent or acquiescence of a public official or other person acting in an official capacity." Article 2 imposes an obligation on each state party to take effective measures to prevent acts of torture in any territory under its jurisdiction. Article 3 precludes refoulement of persons to another state where there are substantial grounds for believing that he would be in danger of being subjected to torture. Article 4 provides for the criminalisation of torture by each state party. Article 5 is concerned with jurisdiction. Each state party is required to establish its jurisdiction over the offences referred to in Article 4 in the following cases:

"(a) when the offences are committed in any territory under its jurisdiction . . .;

(b) when the alleged offender is a national of that state;

(c) when the victim is a national of that state if that state considers it appropriate"

and also "over such offences in cases where the alleged offender is present in any territory under its jurisdiction and it does not extradite him. . . ."

Article 7 is concerned with the exercise of jurisdiction. Article 7(1) provides:

> "The state party in territory under whose jurisdiction a person alleged to have committed any offence referred to in Article 4 is found, shall in the cases contemplated in Article 5, if it does not extradite him, submit the case to its competent authorities for the purpose of prosecution."

This provision reflects the principle aut dedere aut punire, designed to ensure that torturers do not escape by going to another country.

I wish at this stage to consider briefly the question whether a head of state, if not a public official, is at least a "person acting in a public capacity" within Article 1(1) of the Torture Convention. It was my first reaction that he is not, on the ground that no one would ordinarily describe a head of state such as a monarch or the president of a republic as a "public official", and the subsidiary words "other person acting in a public capacity" appeared to be intended to catch a person who, while not a public official, has fulfilled the role of a public official, for example, on a temporary or ad hoc basis. Miss Montgomery, for Senator Pinochet, submitted that the words were not apt to include a head of state relying in particular on the fact that in a number of earlier conventions heads of state are expressly mentioned in this context in addition to responsible government officials. However, Dr. Collins for the Republic of Chile conceded that, in the Torture Convention, heads of state must be regarded as falling within the category of "other person acting in a public capacity"; and in these circumstances I am content to proceed on that basis. The effect of Dr. Collins' concession is that a head of state could be held responsible for torture committed during his term of office, although (as Dr. Collins submitted) the state of which he was head would be able to invoke the principle of state immunity, ratione personae or materiae, in proceedings brought against him in another national jurisdiction if it thought right to do so. Accordingly, on the argument now under consideration, the crucial question relates to the availability of state immunity.

It is to be observed that no mention is made of state immunity in the Convention. Had it been intended to exclude state immunity, it is reasonable to assume that this would have been the subject either of a separate article, or of a separate paragraph in Article 7, introduced to provide for that particular matter. This would have been consistent with the logical framework of the Convention, under which separate provision is made for each topic, introduced in logical order.

VI. The issue whether immunity ratione materiae has been excluded under the Torture Convention

(a) *The argument*

I now come to the second of the two issues which were raised during the hearing of the appeal, viz. whether the Torture Convention has the effect that state parties to the Convention have agreed to exclude reliance on state immunity ratione materiae in relation to proceedings brought against their public officials, or other persons acting in an official capacity, in respect of torture contrary to the Convention. In broad terms I understand the argument to be that, since torture contrary to the Convention can only be committed by a public official or other person acting in an official capacity, and since it is in respect of the acts of these very persons that states can assert state immunity ratione materiae, it would be inconsistent with the obligations of state parties under the Convention for them to be able to invoke state immunity ratione materiae in cases of torture contrary to the Convention. In the case of heads of state this objective could be achieved on the basis that torture contrary to the Convention would not be regarded as falling within the functions of a head of state while in office, so that although he would be protected by immunity ratione personae while in office as head of state, no immunity ratione materiae would protect him in respect of allegations of such torture after he ceased to hold office. There can, however, be no doubt that, before the Torture Convention, torture by public officials could be the subject of state immunity. Since therefore exclusion of immunity is said to result from the Torture Convention and there is no express term of the Convention to this effect, the argument has, in my opinion, to be formulated as dependent upon an implied term in the Convention. It is a matter of comment that, for reasons which will appear in a moment, the proposed implied term has not been precisely formulated; it has not therefore been exposed to that valuable discipline which is always required in the case of terms alleged to be implied in ordinary contracts. In any event, this is a different argument from that which was advanced to your Lordships by the appellants and those supporting them, which was that both torture contrary to the Torture Convention, and hostage-taking contrary to the Taking of Hostages Convention, constituted crimes under international law, and that such crimes cannot be part of the functions of a head of state as a matter of international law.

The argument now under consideration was not advanced before the Divisional Court; nor can it have been advanced before the first Appellate Committee, or it would have been considered by both Lord Slynn of Hadley and Lord Lloyd of Berwick in their dissenting opinions. It was not advanced before your Lordships by the appellants and those supporting them, either in their written cases, or in their opening submissions. In fact, it was introduced into the present case as a result of interventions by members of the Appellate Committee in the course of the argument. This they were, of course, fully entitled to do; and subsequently the point was very fairly put both to Miss Montgomery for Senator Pinochet and to Dr. Collins for the Government of Chile. It was subsequently adopted by Mr. Lloyd Jones, the amicus curiae, in his oral submissions to the Committee. The appellants, in their written submissions in reply, restricted themselves to submitting that "The conduct alleged in the present case is not conduct which amounts to official acts performed by the respondent in the exercise of his functions as head of state . . .": see paragraph 11 of their written submissions. They did not at that stage go so far as to submit that any torture contrary to the Torture Convention would not amount to such an official act. However, when he came to make his final oral submissions on behalf of the appellants, Professor Greenwood, following the lead of Mr. Lloyd Jones, and perhaps prompted by observations from the Committee to the effect that this was the main point in the case, went beyond his clients' written submissions in reply and submitted that, when an offence of torture is committed by an official within the meaning of section 134 of the Criminal Justice Act and Article 1 of the Torture Convention, no immunity ratione materiae can attach in respect of that act.

It is surprising that an important argument of this character, if valid, should previously have been overlooked by the fourteen counsel (including three distinguished Professors of International Law) acting for the appellants, and for Amnesty International and

Human Rights Watch which are supporting the appellants in this litigation. The concern thereby induced as to the validity of the argument is reinforced by the fact that it receives no support from the literature on the subject and, on the material before your Lordships, appears never to have been advanced before. At all events, having given the matter the most careful consideration, I am satisfied that it must be rejected as contrary to principle and authority, and indeed contrary to common sense.

(b) *Waiver of immunity by treaty must be express*

On behalf of the Government of Chile Dr. Collins' first submission was that a state's waiver of its immunity by treaty must always be express. With that submission, I agree.

I turn first to Oppenheim's International Law. The question of waiver of state immunity is considered at pp. 351–355 of the 9th edition, from which I quote the following passage:

> "A state, although in principle entitled to immunity, may waive its immunity. It may do so by expressly submitting to the jurisdiction of the court before which it is sued, either by express consent given in the context of a particular dispute which has already arisen, or by consent given in advance in a contract or an international agreement . . . A state may also be considered to have waived its immunity by implication, as by instituting or intervening in proceedings, or taking any steps in the proceedings relating to the merits of the case . . ."

It is significant that, in this passage, the only examples given of implied waiver of immunity relate to actual submission by a state to the jurisdiction of a court or tribunal by instituting or intervening in proceedings, or by taking a step in proceedings.

A similar approach is to be found in the Report of the International Law Commission on the Jurisdictional Immunities of States and their Property reported in 1991 Yb.I.L.C., vol. II, Part 2, in which a fuller exposition of the subject is to be found. Article 7 of the Commission's Draft Articles on this subject is entitled Express consent to exercise of jurisdiction. Article 7(1) provides as follows:

> "1. A state cannot invoke immunity from jurisdiction in a proceeding before a court of another state with regard to a matter or case if it has expressly consented to the exercise of jurisdiction by the court with regard to the matter or case:
>   (a) by international agreement;
>   (b) in a written contract; or
>   (c) by a declaration before the court or by a written communication in a specific proceeding."

I turn to the commentary on Article 7(1), from which I quote paragraph (8) in full:

> "In the circumstances under consideration, that is, in the context of the state against which legal proceedings have been brought, there appear to be several recognisable methods of expressing or signifying consent. In this particular connection, the consent should not be taken for granted, nor readily implied. Any theory of 'implied consent' as a possible exception to the general principles of state immunities outlined in this part should be viewed not as an exception in itself, but rather as an added explanation or justification for an otherwise valid and generally recognised exception. There is therefore no room for implying the consent of an unwilling state which has not expressed its consent in a clear and recognisable manner, including by the means provided in Article 8 [which is concerned with the effect of participation in a proceeding before a court]. It remains to be seen how consent would be given or expressed so as to remove the obligation of the court of another state to refrain from the exercise of its jurisdiction against an equally sovereign state."

The two examples then provided of how such consent would be given or expressed are (i) Consent given in a written contract, or by a declaration or a written communication in a specific proceeding, and (ii) Consent given in advance by international agreement. In respect of the latter, reference is made (in paragraph (10) to such consent being expressed in a provision of a treaty concluded by states; there is no reference to such consent being implied.

The general effect of these passages is that, in a treaty concluded between states, consent by a state party to the exercise of jurisdiction against it must, as Dr. Collins submitted, be express. In general, moreover, implied consent to the exercise of such jurisdiction is to be regarded only as an added explanation or justification for an otherwise valid and recognised exception, of which the only example given is actual submission to the jurisdiction of the courts of another state.

The decision of the Supreme Court of the United States in Argentine Republic v. Amerada Hess Shipping Corporation (1989) 109 S.Ct. 683 is consistent with the foregoing approach. In an action brought by a shipowner against the Argentine Republic for the loss of a ship through an attack by aircraft of the Argentine Air Force, the defendant relied upon state immunity. Among other arguments the plaintiff suggested that the defendant had waived its immunity under certain international agreements to which the United States was party. For this purpose, the plaintiff invoked para. 1605(a)(1) of the Foreign Sovereign Immunities Act 1976, which specifies, as one of a number of exceptions to immunity of foreign states, a case in which the foreign state has waived its immunity either explicitly or by implication. It was the plaintiff's contention that there was an implicit waiver in the relevant international agreements. This submission was tersely rejected by Rehnquist C.J., who delivered the judgment of the court, in the following words, at p. 693:

> "Nor do we see how a foreign state can waive its immunity under para. 1605(a)(1) by signing an international agreement that contains no mention of a waiver of immunity to suit in United States courts . . ."

Once again, the emphasis is on the need for an express waiver of immunity in an international agreement. This cannot be explained away as due to the provisions of the United States Act. On the contrary, the Act contemplates the possibility of waiver by implication; but in the context of a treaty the Supreme Court was only prepared to contemplate express waiver.

I turn next to the State Immunity Act 1978, the provisions of which are also consistent with the principles which I have already described. In Part I of the Act (which does not apply to criminal proceedings—see section 16(4)), it is provided by section 1(1) that "A state is immune from the jurisdiction of the courts of the United Kingdom except as provided in the following provisions of this Part of this Act." For the present purposes, the two relevant provisions are section 2, concerned with submission to the jurisdiction, and section 9, concerned with submissions to arbitration by an agreement in writing. Section 2(2) recognises that a state may submit to the jurisdiction by a prior written agreement, which I read as referring to an express agreement to submit. There is no suggestion in the Act that an implied agreement to submit would be sufficient, except in so far as an actual submission to the jurisdiction of a court of this country, may be regarded as an implied waiver of immunity; but my reading of the Act leads me to understand that such a submission to the jurisdiction is here regarded as an express rather than an implied waiver of immunity or agreement to submit to the jurisdiction. This is consistent with Part III of the Act, which by section 20 provides that, subject to the provisions of that section and to any necessary modifications, the Diplomatic Privileges Act 1964 shall apply to a sovereign or other head of state. Among the Articles of the Vienna Convention on Diplomatic Relations so rendered applicable by section 2 of the Act of 1964 is Article 32 concerned with waiver of immunity, paragraph 2 of which provides that such waiver must always be express, which I read as including an actual submission to the jurisdiction, as well as an express agreement in advance to submit. Once again, there is no provision for an implied agreement.

In the light of the foregoing it appears to me to be clear that, in accordance both with international law, and with the law of this country which on this point reflects international law, a state's waiver of its immunity by treaty must, as Dr. Collins submitted, always be express. Indeed, if this was not so, there could well be international chaos as the courts of different state parties to a treaty reach different conclusions on the question whether a waiver of immunity was to be implied.

(c)   *The functions of public officials and others acting in an official capacity*

However it is, as I understand it, suggested that this well-established principle can be circumvented in the present case on the basis that it is not proposed that state parties to the Torture Convention have agreed to waive their state immunity in proceedings brought in the states of other parties in respect of allegations of torture within the Convention. It is rather that, for the purposes of the Convention, such torture does not form part of the functions of public officials or others acting in an official capacity including, in particular, a head of state. Moreover since state immunity ratione materiae can only be claimed in respect of acts done by an official in the exercise of his functions as such, it would follow, for example, that the effect is that a former head of state does not enjoy the benefit of immunity ratione materiae in respect of such torture after he has ceased to hold office.

In my opinion, the principle which I have described cannot be circumvented in this way. I observe first that the meaning of the word "functions" as used in this context is well established. The functions of, for example, a head of state are governmental functions, as opposed to private acts; and the fact that the head of state performs an act, other than a private act, which is criminal does not deprive it of its governmental character. This is as true of a serious crime, such as murder or torture, as it is of a lesser crime. As the Lord Chief Justice said in the Divisional Court:

> ". . . a former head of state is clearly entitled to immunity in relation to criminal acts performed in the course of exercising public functions. One cannot therefore hold that any deviation from good democratic practice is outside the pale of immunity. If the former sovereign is immune from process in respect of some crimes, where does one draw the line?"

It was in answer to that question that the appellants advanced the theory that one draws the line at crimes which may be called "international crimes". If, however, a limit is to be placed on governmental functions so as to exclude from them acts of torture within the Torture Convention, this can only be done by means of an implication arising from the Convention itself. Moreover, as I understand it, the only purpose of the proposed implied limitation upon the functions of public officials is to deprive them, or as in the present case a former head of state, of the benefit of state immunity; and in my opinion the policy which requires that such a result can only be achieved in a treaty by express agreement, with the effect that it cannot be so achieved by implication, renders it equally unacceptable that it should be achieved indirectly by means of an implication such as that now proposed.

(d) *An implication must in any event be rejected*

In any event, however, even if it were possible for such a result to be achieved by means of an implied term, there are, in my opinion, strong reasons why any such implication should be rejected.

I recognise that a term may be implied into a treaty, if the circumstances are such that "the parties must have intended to contract on the basis of the inclusion in the treaty of a provision whose effect can be stated with reasonable precision"; see Oppenheim's International Law, 9th ed., p. 1271, n.4. It would, however, be wrong to assume that a term may be implied into a treaty on the same basis as a term may be implied into an ordinary commercial contract, for example to give the contract business efficacy (as to which see Treitel on Contract, 9th ed., pp. 185 et seq.). This is because treaties are different in origin, and serve a different purpose. Treaties are the fruit of long negotiation, the purpose being to produce a draft which is acceptable to a number, often a substantial number, of state parties. The negotiation of a treaty may well take a long time, running into years. Draft after draft is produced of individual articles, which are considered in depth by national representatives, and are the subject of detailed comment and consideration. The agreed terms may well be the fruit of "horse-trading" in order to achieve general agreement, and proposed articles may be amended, or even omitted in whole or in part, to accommodate the wishes or anxieties of some of the negotiating parties. In circumstances such as these, it is the text of the treaty itself which provides the only safe guide to its terms, though reference may be made, where appropriate, to the travaux preparatoires. But implied terms cannot, except in the most obvious cases, be relied on as binding the state parties who ultimately sign the treaty, who will in all probability include those who were not involved in the preliminary negotiations.

In this connection, however, I wish first to observe that the assumption underlying the present argument, viz. that the continued availability of state immunity is inconsistent with the obligations of state parties to the Convention, is in my opinion not justified. I have already summarised the principal articles of the Convention; and at this stage I need only refer to Article 7 which requires that a state party under whose jurisdiction a person alleged to have committed torture is found shall, in the cases contemplated in Article 5, if it does not extradite him, submit the case to its competent authorities for the purpose of prosecution. I wish to make certain observations on these provisions. First of all, in the majority of cases which may arise under the Convention, no question of state immunity will arise at all, because the public official concerned is likely to be present in his own country. Even when such a question does arise, there is no reason to assume that state immunity will be asserted by the state of which the alleged torturer is a public official; on the contrary, it is only in unusual cases, such as the present, that this is likely to be done. In any event, however, not only is there no mention of state immunity in the Convention, but in my opinion it is not inconsistent with its express provisions that, if steps are taken to extradite him or to submit his case to the authorities for the purpose of prosecution, the appropriate state should be entitled to assert state immunity. In this connection, I comment that it is not suggested that it is inconsistent with the Convention that immunity ratione personae should be asserted; if so, I find it difficult to see why it should be inconsistent to assert immunity ratione materiae.

The danger of introducing the proposed implied term in the present case is underlined by the fact that there is, as Dr. Collins stressed to your Lordships, nothing in the negotiating history of the Torture Convention which throws any light on the proposed implied term. Certainly the travaux preparatoires shown to your Lordships reveal no trace of any consideration being given to waiver of state immunity. They do however show that work on the draft Convention was on foot as long ago as 1979, five years before the date of the Convention itself. It is surely most unlikely that during the years in which the draft was under consideration no thought was given to the possibility of the state parties to the Convention waiving state immunity. Furthermore, if agreement had been reached that there should be such a waiver, express provision would inevitably have been made in the Convention to that effect. Plainly, however, no such agreement was reached. There may have been recognition at an early stage that so many states would not be prepared to waive their immunity that the matter was not worth pursuing; if so, this could explain why the topic does not surface in the travaux preparatoires. In this connection it must not be overlooked that there are many reasons why states, although recognising that in certain circumstances jurisdiction should be vested in another national court in respect of acts of torture committed by public officials within their own jurisdiction, may nevertheless have considered it imperative that they should be able, if necessary, to assert state immunity. The Torture Convention applies not only to a series of acts of systematic torture, but to the commission of, even acquiescence in, a single act of physical or mental torture. Extradition can nowadays be sought, in some parts of the world, on the basis of a simple allegation unsupported by prima facie evidence. In certain circumstances torture may, for compelling political reasons, be the subject of an amnesty, or some other form of settlement, in the state where it has been, or is alleged to have been, committed.

Furthermore, if immunity ratione materiae was excluded, former heads of state and senior public officials would have to think twice about travelling abroad, for fear of being the subject of unfounded allegations emanating from states of a different political persuasion. In this connection, it is a mistake to assume that state parties to the Convention would only wish to preserve state immunity in cases of torture in order to shield public officials guilty of torture from prosecution elsewhere in the world. Such an assumption is based on a misunderstanding of the nature and function of state immunity, which is a rule of international law restraining one sovereign state from sitting in judgment on the sovereign behaviour of another. As Lord Wilbeforce said in I Congreso del Partido [1983] 1 A.C. 244, 272, "The whole purpose of the doctrine of state immunity is to prevent such issues being canvassed in the courts of one state as to the acts of another." State immunity ratione materiae operates therefore to protect former heads of state, and (where immunity is asserted) public officials, even minor public officials, from legal process in foreign countries in respect of acts done in the exercise of their functions as such, including accusation and arrest in respect of alleged crimes. It can therefore be effective to preclude any such process in respect of alleged crimes, including allegations which are misguided or even malicious—a matter which can be of great significance where, for example, a former head of state is concerned and political passions are aroused. Preservation of state immunity is therefore a matter of particular importance to powerful countries whose heads of state perform an executive role, and who may therefore be regarded as possible targets by governments of states which, for deeply felt political reasons, deplore their actions while in office. But, to bring the matter nearer home, we must not overlook the fact that it is not only in the United States of America that a substantial body of opinion supports the campaign of the I.R.A. to overthrow the democratic government of Northern Ireland. It is not beyond the bounds of possibility that a state whose government is imbued with this opinion might seek to extradite from a third country, where he or she happens to be, a responsible Minister of the Crown, or even a more humble public official such as a police inspector, on the ground that he or she has acquiesced in a single act of physical or mental torture in Northern Ireland. The well-known case of The Republic of Ireland v. The United Kingdom (1978) 2 E.H.R.R. 25 provides an indication of circumstances in which this might come about.

Reasons such as these may well have persuaded possible state parties to the Torture Convention that it would be unwise to give up the valuable protection afforded by state immunity. Indeed, it would be strange if state parties had given up the immunity ratione materiae of a head of state which is regarded as an essential support for his immunity ratione personae. In the result, the subject of waiver of state immunity could well not have been pursued, on the basis that to press for its adoption would only imperil the very substantial advantages which could be achieved by the Convention even if no waiver of state immunity was included in it. As I have already explained, in cases arising under the Convention, state immunity can only be relevant in a limited number of cases. This is because the offence is normally committed in the state to which the official belongs. There he is unprotected by immunity, and under the Convention the state has simply to submit the case to the competent authorities. In practice state immunity is relevant in only two cases—where the offender is present in a third state, or where the offender is present in a state one of whose nationals was the victim, that state being different from the state where the offence was committed. A case such as the present must be regarded as most unusual. Having regard to considerations such as these, not to press for exclusion of state immunity as a provision of the Convention must have appeared to be a relatively small price to pay for the major achievement of widespread agreement among states (your Lordships were informed that 116 states had signed the Convention) in respect of all the other benefits which the Convention conferred. After all, even where it was possible for a state to assert state immunity, in many cases it would not wish to expose itself to the opprobrium which such a course would provoke; and in such cases considerable diplomatic or moral pressure could be exerted upon it to desist.

I wish to stress the implications of the fact that there is no trace in the travaux preparatoires of any intention in the Convention to exclude state immunity. It must follow, if the present argument is correct, first that it was so obvious that it was the intention that immunity should be excluded that a term could be implied in the Convention to that effect, and second that, despite that fact, during the negotiating process none of the states involved thought it right to raise the matter for discussion. This is remarkable. Moreover, it would have been the duty of the responsible senior civil servants in the various states concerned to draw the attention of their Governments to the consequences of this obvious implication, so that they could decide whether to sign a Convention in this form. Yet nothing appears to have happened. There is no evidence of any question being raised, still less of any protest being made, by a single state party. The conclusion follows either that every state party was content without question that state immunity should be excluded sub silentio, or that the responsible civil servants in all these states, including the United Kingdom, failed in their duty to draw this very important matter to the attention of their Governments. It is difficult to imagine that either of these propositions can be correct. In particular it cannot, I suspect, have crossed the minds of the responsible civil servants that state immunity was excluded sub silentio in the Convention.

The cumulative effect of all these considerations is, in my opinion, to demonstrate the grave difficulty of recognising an implied term, whatever its form, on the basis that it must have been agreed by all the state parties to the Convention that state immunity should be excluded. In this connection it is particularly striking that, in the Handbook on the Torture Convention by Burgers and Danelius, it is recognised that the obligation of a state party, under Article 5(1) of the Convention, to establish jurisdiction over offences of torture committed within its territory, is subject to an exception in the case of those benefiting from special immunities, including foreign diplomats. It is true that this statement could in theory be read as limited to immunity ratione personae; but in the absence of explanation it should surely be read in the ordinary way as applicable both to immunity ratione personae and its concomitant immunity ratione materiae, and in any event the total silence in this passage on the subject of waiver makes it highly improbable that there was any intention that immunity ratione materiae should be regarded as having been implicitly excluded by the Convention. Had there been such an intention, the authors would have been bound to refer to it. They do not do so.

The background against which the Torture Convention is set adds to the improbability of the proposition that the state parties to the Convention must have intended, directly or indirectly, to exclude state immunity ratione materiae. Earlier Conventions made provision for an international tribunal. In the case of such Conventions, no question of par in parem non habet imperium arose; but heads of state were expressly mentioned, so ensuring that they are subject to the jurisdiction of the international tribunal. In the case of the Taking of Hostages Convention and the Torture Convention, jurisdiction was vested in the national courts of state parties to the Convention. Here, therefore, for the first time the question of waiver of state immunity arose in an acute form. Curiously, the suggestion appears to be that state immunity was waived only in the case of the Torture Convention. Apart from that curiosity, however, for state parties to exclude state immunity in a Convention of this kind would be a remarkable surrender of the basic protection afforded by international law to all sovereign states, which underlines the necessity for immunity to be waived in a treaty, if at all, by express provision; and, having regard in particular to the express reference to heads of state in earlier Conventions, state parties would have expected to find an express provision in the Torture Convention if it had been agreed that state immunity was excluded. That it should be done by implication in the Torture Convention seems, in these circumstances, to be most improbable.

I add that the fact that 116 states have become party to the Torture Convention reinforces the strong impression that none of them appreciated that, by signing the Convention, each of them would silently agree to the exclusion of state immunity ratione materiae. Had it been appreciated that this was so, I strongly suspect that the number of signatories would have been far smaller. It should not be forgotten that national representatives involved in the preliminary discussions would have had to report back to their governments about the negotiation of an important international convention of this kind. Had such a representative, or indeed a senior civil servant in a country whose government was considering whether the country should become a party to the Convention, been asked by his Secretary of State the question whether state immunity would be preserved, it is unlikely that a point would have occurred to him which had been overlooked by all the fourteen counsel (including, as I have said, three distinguished professors of international law) appearing for the appellants and their supporters in the present case. It is far more probable that he would have had in mind the clear and simple words of the Chief Justice of the United States in the Amerada Hess and have answered that, since there was no mention of state immunity in the Convention, it could not have been affected. This demonstrates how extraordinary it would be, and indeed what a trap would be created for the unwary, if state immunity could be waived in a treaty sub silentio. Common sense therefore supports the conclusion reached by principle and authority that this cannot be done.

(e) *Conclusion*

For these reasons I am of the opinion that the proposed implication must be rejected not only as contrary to principle and authority, but also as contrary to common sense.

VII. The conclusion of Lord Hope of Craighead

My noble and learned friend Lord Hope of Craighead, having concluded that, so far as torture is concerned, only charges 2 and 4 (insofar as they apply to the period after 29 September 1988) and charge 30 survive the application of the double criminality point, has nevertheless concluded that the benefit of state immunity is not available to Senator Pinochet in respect of these three charges. He has reached this conclusion on the basis that (1) the two conspiracy charges, having regard to paragraph 9(3) of the Extradition Request, reveal charges that Senator Pinochet was party to a conspiracy to carry out a systematic, if not a widespread, attack on a section of the civil population, i.e. to torture those who opposed or might oppose his government, which would constitute a crime against humanity (see, e.g., Article 7(1) of the Rome Convention of 1998); and (2) the single act of torture alleged in charge 30 shows that an alleged earlier conspiracy to carry out such torture, constituting a crime against humanity, was still alive when that act was perpetrated after 29 September 1988. Furthermore, although he is (as I understand the position) in general agreement with Lord Slynn of Hadley's analysis, he considers that such a crime against humanity, or a conspiracy to commit such a crime, cannot be the subject of a claim to state immunity in a national court, even where it is alleged to have taken place before 1 January 1990.

I must first point out that, apart from the single act of torture alleged in charge 30, the only other cases of torture alleged to have occurred since 29 September 1988 are two cases, referred to in the Extradition Request but not made the subject of charges, which are alleged to have taken place in October 1988. Before that, there is one case alleged in 1984, before which it is necessary to go as far back as 1977. In these circumstances I find it very difficult to see how, after 29 September 1988, it could be said that there was any systematic or widespread campaign of torture, constituting an attack on the civilian population, so as to amount to a crime against humanity. Furthermore, insofar as it is suggested that the single act of torture alleged in charge 30 represents the last remnant of a campaign which existed in the 1970s, there is, quite apart from the factual difficulty of relating the single act to a campaign which is alleged to have been in existence so long ago, the question whether it would be permissible, in the context of extradition, to have regard to the earlier charges of torture, excluded under the double criminality rule, in order to establish that the single act of torture was part of a campaign of systematic torture which was still continuing in June 1989. This raises a question under section 6(4)(b) and (5) of the Extradition Act 1989, provisions which are by no means clear in themselves or easy to apply in the unusual circumstances of the present case.

In truth, however, the real problem is that, since the appellants did not consider the position which would arise if they lost the argument on the double criminality point, they did not address questions of this kind. If they had done so, the matter would have been argued out before the Appellate Committee, and Miss Montgomery and Dr. Collins, would have had an opportunity to reply and would no doubt have had a good deal to say on the subject. This is after all a criminal matter, and it is no part of the function of the court to help the prosecution to improve their case. In these circumstances it would not, in my opinion, be right to assist the prosecution by now taking such a point as this, when they have failed to do so at the hearing, in order to decide whether or not this is a case in which it would be lawful for extradition to take place.

I wish to add that, in any event, for the reasons given by Lord Slynn of Hadley to which I have already referred, I am of the opinion that in 1989 there was no settled practice that state immunity ratione materiae was not available in criminal proceedings before a national court concerned with an alleged crime against humanity, or indeed as to what constituted a crime against humanity (see [1998] 3 W.L.R. 1456 at pp. 1473C-D and 1474C-1475B). This is a matter which I have already considered in Part IV of this opinion.

For all these reasons I am, with great respect, unable to accompany the reasoning of my noble and learned friend on these particular points.

VIII. Conclusion

For the above reasons, I am of the opinion that by far the greater part of the charges against Senator Pinochet must be excluded as offending against the double criminality rule; and that, in respect of the surviving charges—charge 9, charge 30 and charges 2 and 4 (insofar as they can be said to survive the double criminality rule)—Senator Pinochet is entitled to the benefit of state immunity ratione materiae as a former head of state. I would therefore dismiss the appeal of the Government of Spain from the decision of the Divisional Court.

Lord Hope of Craighead

My Lords,

This is an appeal against the decision of the Divisional Court to quash the provisional warrants of 16 and 22 October 1998 which were issued by the metropolitan stipendiary magistrate under section 8(1)(b) of the Extradition Act 1989. The application to quash had been made on two grounds. The first was that Senator Pinochet as a former head of state of the Republic of Chile was entitled to immunity from arrest and extradition proceedings in the United Kingdom in respect of acts committed when he was head of state. The second was that the charges which had been made against him specified conduct which would not have been punishable in England when the acts were done, with the result that these were not extradition crimes for which it would be lawful for him to be extradited.

The Divisional Court quashed the first warrant, in which it was alleged that Senator Pinochet had murdered Spanish citizens in Chile, on the ground that it did not disclose any offence for which he could be extradited to Spain. Its decision on that point has not been challenged in this appeal. It also quashed the second warrant, in which it was alleged that Senator Pinochet was guilty of torture, hostage-taking, conspiracy to take hostages and conspiracy to commit murder. It did so on the ground that Senator Pinochet was entitled to immunity as a former head of state from the process of the English courts. The court held that the question whether these were offences for which, if he had no immunity, it would be lawful for him to be extradited was not a matter to be considered in that court at that stage. But Lord Bingham of Cornhill C.J. said that it was not necessary for this purpose that the conduct alleged constituted a crime which would have been punishable in this country at the time when it was alleged to have been committed abroad.

When this appeal was first heard in your Lordships' House the argument was directed almost entirely to the question whether Senator Pinochet was entitled as a former head of state to claim sovereign immunity in respect of the charges alleged against him in the second provisional warrant. It was also argued that the offences of torture and hostage-taking were not offences for which he could be extradited until these became offences for which a person could be prosecuted extra-territorially in the United Kingdom. But the second argument appears to have been regarded as no more than a side issue at that stage. This is not surprising in view of the terms of the second provisional warrant. The offences which it specified extended over periods lasting well beyond the date when the conduct became extra-territorial offences in this country. Only Lord Lloyd of Berwick dealt with this argument in his speech, and he confined himself to one brief comment. He said that it involved a misunderstanding of section 2 of the Extradition Act 1989, as in his view section 2(1)(a) referred to conduct which would constitute an offence in the United Kingdom now, not to conduct which would have constituted an offence then: [1998] 3 W.L.R. 1456, 1481F-G.

The offences alleged against Senator Pinochet

Four offences were set out in the second provisional warrant of 22 October 1998. These were:

(1) torture between 1 January 1988 and December 1992;
(2) conspiracy to torture between 1 January 1988 and 31 December 1992;
(3) (a) hostage-taking and (b) conspiracy to take hostages between 1 January 1982 and 31 January 1992; and
(4) conspiracy to commit murder between January 1976 and December 1992.

These dates must be compared with the date of the coup which brought Senator Pinochet to power in Chile, which was 11 September 1973, and the date when he ceased to be head of state, which was 11 March 1990. Taking the dates in the second provisional warrant at their face value, it appears (a) that he was not being charged with any acts of torture prior to 1 January 1988, (b) that he was not being charged with any acts of hostage-taking or conspiracy to take hostages prior to I January 1982 and (c) that he was not being charged with any conspiracy to commit murder prior to January 1976. On the other hand he was being charged with having committed these offences up to December 1992, well after the date when he ceased to be head of state in Chile.

The second appellant has taken the opportunity of the interval between the end of the first hearing of this appeal and the second hearing to obtain further details from the Spanish judicial authorities. He has explained that the provisional warrant was issued under circumstances of urgency and that the facts are more developed and complex than first appeared. And a number of things have happened since the date of the first hearing which, it is submitted, mean that the provisional warrant no longer has any life or effect. On 9 December 1998 the Secretary of State issued an authority to proceed under section 7(4) of the Act of 1989. On 10 December 1998 the Spanish indictment was preferred in Madrid, and on 24 December 1998 further particulars were drafted in accordance with

Article 13 of the European Convention on Extradition for furnishing with the extradition request.

Mr. Alun Jones Q.C. for the appellants said that it would be inappropriate for your Lordships in these circumstances to confine an examination of the facts to those set out in the provisional warrant and that it would be unfair to deprive him of the ability to rely on material which has been served within the usual time limits imposed in the extradition process. He invited your Lordships to examine all the material which was before the Secretary of State in December, including the formal request which was signed at Madrid on 3 November 1998 and the further material which has now been submitted by the Spanish Government. Draft charges have been prepared, of the kind which are submitted in extradition proceedings as a case is presented to the magistrate at the beginning of the main hearing under section 9(8) of the Act. This has been done to demonstrate how the charges which are being brought by the Spanish judicial authorities may be expressed in terms of English criminal law, to show the offences which he would have committed by his conduct against the law of this country.

The crimes which are alleged in the Spanish request are murder on such a scale as to amount to genocide and terrorism, including torture and hostage-taking. The Secretary of State has already stated in his authority to proceed that Senator Pinochet is not to be extradited to Spain for genocide. So that part of the request must now be left out of account. But my impression is that the omission of the allegation of genocide is of little consequence in view of the scope which is given in Spanish law to the allegations of murder and terrorism.

It is not our function to investigate the allegations which have been made against Senator Pinochet, and it is right to place on record the fact that his counsel, Miss Montgomery Q.C., told your Lordships that they are all strenuously denied by him. It is necessary to set out the nature and some of the content of these allegations, on the assumption that they are supported by the information which the Spanish judicial authorities have made available. This is because they form an essential part of the background to the issues of law which have been raised in this appeal. But the following summary must not be taken as a statement that the allegations have been shown to be true by the evidence, because your Lordships have not considered the evidence.

The material which has been gathered together in the extradition request by the Spanish judicial authorities alleges that Senator Pinochet was party to a conspiracy to commit the crimes of murder, torture and hostage-taking, and that this conspiracy was formed before the coup. He is said to have agreed with other military figures that they would take over the functions of government and subdue all opposition to their control of it by capturing and torturing those who opposed them, who might oppose them or who might be thought by others to be likely to oppose them. The purpose of this campaign of torture was not just to inflict pain. Some of those who were to be tortured were to be released, to spread words of the steps that would be taken against those who opposed the conspirators. Many of those who were to be tortured were be subjected to various other forms of atrocity, and some of them were be killed. The plan was to be executed in Chile and in several other counties outside Chile.

When the plan was put into effect victims are said to have been abducted, tortured and murdered pursuant to the conspiracy. This was done first in Chile, and then in other countries in South America, in the United States and in Europe. Many of the acts evidencing the conspiracy are said to have been committed in Chile before 11 September 1973. Some people were tortured at a naval base in August 1973. Large numbers of persons were abducted, tortured and murdered on 11 September 1973 in the course of the coup before the junta took control and Senator Pinochet was appointed its President. These acts continued during the days and weeks after the coup. A period of repression ensued, which is said to have been at its most intense in 1973 and 1974. The conspiracy is said to have continued for several years thereafter, but to have declined in intensity during the decade before Senator Pinochet retired as head of state on 11 March 1990. It is said that the acts committed in other countries outside Chile are evidence of the primary conspiracies and of a variety of sub-conspiracies within those states.

The draft charges which have been prepared in order to translate these broad accusations into terms of English law may be summarised as follows:

(1) conspiracy to torture between 1 January 1972 and 10 September 1973 and between 1 August 1973 and 1 January 1990—charges 1, 2 and 5;
(2) conspiracy to take hostages between 1 August 1973 and 1 January 1990—charge 3;
(3) conspiracy to torture in furtherance of which murder was committed in various countries including Italy, France, Spain and Portugal between 1 January 1972 and 1 January 1990—charge 4; (4) torture between 1 August 1973 and 8 August 1973 and on 11 September 1973—charges 6 and 8 [there is no charge 7];
(5) conspiracy to murder in Spain between 1 January 1975 and 31 December 1976 and in Italy on 6 October 1975—charges 9 and 12;
(6) attempted murder in Italy on 6 October 1975—charges 10 and 11;
(7) torture on various occasions between 11 September 1973 and May 1977—charges 13 to 29 and 31 to 32; and
(8) torture on 24 June 1989—charge 30.

This summary shows that some of the alleged conduct relates to the period before the coup when Senator Pinochet was not yet head of state. Charges 1 and 5 (conspiracy to torture) and charge 6 (torture) relate exclusively to that period. Charges 2 and 4 (conspiracy to torture) and charge 3 (conspiracy to take hostages) relate to conduct over many years including the period before the coup. None of the conduct now alleged extends beyond the period when Senator Pinochet ceased to be head of state.

Only one charge (charge 30—torture on 24 June 1989) relates exclusively to the period after 29 September 1988 when section 134 of the Criminal Justice Act 1988, to which I refer later, was brought into effect. But charges 2 and 4 (conspiracy to torture) and charge 3 (conspiracy to take hostages) which relate to conduct over many years extend over this period also. Two acts of torture which are said to have occurred between 21 and 28 October 1988 are mentioned in the extradition request. They have not been included as separate counts in the list of draft charges, but it is important not to lose sight of the fact that the case which is being made against Senator Pinochet by the Spanish judicial authorities is that each act of torture has to be seen in the context of a continuing conspiracy to commit torture. As a whole, the picture which is presented is of a conspiracy to commit widespread and systematic torture and murder in order to obtain control of the government and, having done so, to maintain control of government by those means for as long as might be necessary.

Against that background it is necessary first to consider whether the relevant offences for the purposes of this appeal are those which were set out in the second provisional warrant or those which are set out in the draft charges which have been prepared in the light of the further information which has been obtained from the Spanish judicial authorities.

On one view it might be said that, as the appeal is against the decision of the Divisional Court to quash the second provisional warrant, your Lordships should be concerned only with the charges which were set out in that document. If that warrant was bad on the ground that the charges which it sets out are charges in respect of which Senator Pinochet has immunity, everything else that has taken place in reliance upon that warrant must be bad also. If he was entitled to immunity, no order should have been made against him in the committal proceedings and the Secretary of State should not have issued an authority to proceed. But Article 13 of the European Convention on Extradition which, following the enactment of the Extradition Act 1989, the United Kingdom has now ratified (see the European Convention on Extradition Order 1990, S.I. 1990 No. 1507), provides that if the information communicated by the requesting party is found to be insufficient to allow the requested party to make a decision in pursuance of the Convention the requested party may ask for the necessary supplementary information to be provided to it by the requesting party.

It is clear that the first provisional warrant was prepared in circumstances of some urgency, as it was believed that Senator Pinochet was about to leave the United Kingdom in order to return to Chile. Once begun, the procedure was then subject to various time limits. There was also the problem of translating the Spanish accusations, which cover so many acts over so long a period, into the terms of English criminal law. I do not think that it is surprising that the full extent of the allegations which were being made was not at first appreciated. In my opinion the Spanish judicial authorities were entitled to supplement the information which was originally provided in order to define more clearly the charges which were the subject of the request. On this view it would be right to regard the material which is now available as explanatory of the charges which the second provisional warrant was intended to comprise. Mr. Clive Nicholls Q.C. for Senator Pinochet said that he was content with this approach in the interests of finality.

Are the alleged offences "extradition crimes"?

If your Lordships are willing, as I suggest we should be, to examine this material it is necessary to subject it to further analysis. The starting point is section 1(1) of the Extradition Act 1989, which provides that a person who is accused in a foreign state of the commission of an extradition crime may be arrested and returned to that state in accordance with the extradition procedures in Part III of the Act. The expression "extradition crime" is defined in section 2 of the Act under two headings. The first, which is set out in section 2(1)(a), refers to

"conduct in the territory of a foreign state . . . which, if it occurred in the United Kingdom, would constitute an offence punishable with imprisonment for a term of twelve months, or any greater punishment, and which, however described in the law of the foreign state&!!;is so punishable under that law."

The second, which is set out in section 2(1)(b) read with section 2(2), refers to an extra-territorial offence against the law of a foreign state which is punishable under that law with imprisonment for a term of 12 months or any greater punishment, and which in corresponding circumstances would constitute an extra-territorial offence against the law of the United Kingdom punishable with imprisonment for a term of 12 months or any greater punishment.

For reasons which have been explained by my noble and learned friend Lord Browne-Wilkinson, the critical issue on the question of sovereign immunity relates to the effect of the United Nations Convention against Torture and other Cruel, Inhuman or Degrading Treatment or Punishment of 10 December 1984 ("the Torture Convention") and the offences which allege torture. As to those alleged offences which do not fall within the scope of the Torture Convention and which could not be prosecuted here under section 134 of the Criminal Justice Act 1988, any loss of immunity would have to be decided on other grounds. But there is no need to examine this question in the case of those alleged offences for which Senator Pinochet could not in any event be extradited. The purpose of the following analysis is to remove from the list of draft charges those charges which fall into that category either because they are not extradition crimes as defined by section 2 of the Extradition Act 1989 or because for any other reason other than on grounds of immunity they are charges on which Senator Pinochet could not be extradited.

This analysis proceeds on the basis that the definition of the expression "extradition crime" in section 2 of the Act of 1989 requires the conduct which is referred to in section 2(1)(a) to have been an offence which was punishable in the United Kingdom when that conduct took place. It also proceeds on the basis that it requires the extra-territorial offence which is referred to in section 2(1)(b) to have been an extra-territorial offence in the United Kingdom on the date when the offence took place. The principle of double criminality would suggest that this was the right approach, in the absence of an express provision to the contrary. The tenses used in section 2 seem to me to be equivocal on this point. They leave it open to examination in the light of the provisions of the Act as a whole. The argument in favour of the date when the conduct took place has particular force in the case of those offences listed in section 22(4) of the Act. These have been made extra-territorial offences in order to give effect to international conventions, but neither the conventions nor the provisions which gave effect to them were intended to operate retrospectively.

I respectfully agree with the reasons which my noble and learned friend Lord Browne-Wilkinson has given for construing the definition as requiring that the conduct must have been punishable in the United Kingdom when it took place, and that it is not sufficient for the appellants to show that it would be punishable here were it to take place now.

Hostage-taking

An offence under the Taking of Hostages Act 1982 is one of those offences, wherever the act takes place, which is deemed by section 22(6) of the Extradition Act 1989 to be an offence committed within the territory of any other state against whose law it is an offence. This provision gives effect to the International Convention against the Taking of Hostages of 18 December 1979 ("the Hostage Convention"). Under section 1 of the Act of 1982 hostage-taking is an extra-territorial offence against the law of the United Kingdom. Section 1(1) of that Act defines the offence in these terms:

> "A person, whatever his nationality, who, in the United Kingdom or elsewhere,:
> (a) detains any other person ('the hostage'), and
> (b) in order to compel a State, international governmental organisation or person to do or to abstain from doing any act, threatens to kill, injure or continue to detain the hostage,
> commits an offence."

Mr. Jones accepted that he did not have particulars of any case of hostage-taking. He said that his case was that Senator Pinochet was involved in a conspiracy to take hostages for the purposes which were made unlawful by section 1 of the Act. Charge 3 of the draft charges, which is the only charge which alleges conspiracy to take hostages, states that the course of conduct which was to be pursued was to include the abduction and torture of persons as part of a campaign to terrify and subdue those who were disposed to criticise or oppose Senator Pinochet or his fellow conspirators. Those who were not detained were to be intimidated, through the accounts of survivors and by rumour, by fear that they might suffer the same fate. Those who had been detained were to be compelled to divulge information to the conspirators by the threatened injury and detention of others known to the abducted persons by the conspirators.

But there is no allegation that the conspiracy was to threaten to kill, injure or detain those who were being detained in order to compel others to do or to abstain from doing any act. The narrative shows that the alleged conspiracy was to subject persons already detained to threats that others would be taken and that they also would be tortured. This does not seem to me to amount to a conspiracy to take hostages within the meaning of section 1 of the Act of 1982. The purpose of the proposed conduct, as regards the detained persons, was to subject them to what can best be described as a form of mental torture.

One of the achievements of the Torture Convention was to provide an internationally agreed definition of torture which includes both physical and mental torture in the terms set out in Article 1:

> "For the purposes of this convention, torture means any act by which severe pain or suffering, whether physical or mental, is intentionally inflicted on a person for such purposes as obtaining from him or a third person information or a confession, punishing him for an act he or a third person has committed or is suspected of having committed, or intimidating or coercing him or a third person, or for any reason based on discrimination of any kind . . . "

The offence of torture under English law is constituted by section 134(1) of the Criminal Justice Act 1988, which provides:

> "A public official or person acting in an official capacity, whatever his nationality, commits the offence of torture if in the United Kingdom or elsewhere he intentionally inflicts severe pain or suffering on another in the performance or purported performance of his official duties."

Section 134(3) provides that it is immaterial whether the pain or suffering is physical or mental and whether it is caused by an act or an omission. So, in conformity with the Convention, the offence includes mental as well as physical torture. It seems to me that the conspiracy which charge 3 alleges against Senator Pinochet was a conspiracy to inflict mental torture, and not a conspiracy to take hostages.

I would hold therefore that it is not necessary for your Lordships to examine the Hostage Convention in order to see whether its terms were such as to deprive a former head of state of any immunity from a charge that he was guilty of hostage-taking. In my opinion Senator Pinochet is not charged with the offence of hostage-taking within the meaning of section 1 (1) of the Taking of Hostages Act 1982.

Conspiracy to murder and attempted murder

The charges of conspiracy to torture include allegations that it was part of the conspiracy that some of those who were abducted and tortured would thereafter be murdered. Charge 4 alleges that in furtherance of that agreement about four thousand persons of many nationalities were murdered in Chile and in various other countries outside Chile. Two other charges, charges 9 and 12, allege conspiracy to murder—in one case of a man in Spain and in the other of two people in Italy. Charge 9 states that Senator Pinochet agreed in Spain with others who were in Spain, Chile and France that the proposed victim would be murdered in Spain. Charge 12 does not say that anything was done in Spain in furtherance of the alleged conspiracy to murder in Italy. There is no suggestion in either of these charges that the proposed victims were to be tortured. Two further charges, charges 10 and 11, allege the attempted murder of the two people in Italy who were the subject of the conspiracy to commit murder there. Here again there is no suggestion that they were to be tortured before they were murdered.

Murder is a common law crime which, before it became an extra-territorial offence if committed in a convention country under section 4 of the Suppression of Terrorism Act 1978, could not be prosecuted in the United Kingdom if it was committed abroad except in the case of a murder committed abroad by a British citizen: Offences against the Person Act 1861, section 9. A murder or attempted murder committed by a person in Spain, whatever his nationality, is an extradition crime for the purposes of his extradition to Spain from the United Kingdom under section 2(1)(a) of the Extradition Act 1989 as it is conduct which would be punishable here if it occurred in this country. But the allegation relating to murders in Spain and elsewhere which is made against Senator Pinochet is not that he himself murdered or attempted to murder anybody. It is that the murders were carried out, or were to be carried out, in Spain and elsewhere as part of a conspiracy and that he was one of the conspirators.

Section 1 of the Criminal Law Act 1977 created a new statutory offence of conspiracy to commit an offence triable in England and Wales. The offence of conspiracy which was previously available at common law was abolished by section 5. Although the principal offence was defined in the statute more narrowly, in other respects it codified the pre-existing law. It came into force on 1 December 1977: S.I. 1977 No. 1682. Subsection (4) of that section provides:

> "In this Part of this Act 'offence' means an offence triable in England and Wales, except that it includes murder notwithstanding that the murder in question would not be so triable if committed in accordance with the intention of the parties to the agreement."

The effect of that subsection is that a person, whatever his nationality, who agrees in England to a course of conduct which will involve the offence of murder abroad may be prosecuted here for the offence of conspiracy to murder even although the murder itself would not have been triable in this country. It re-enacted a provision to the same effect in section 4 of the Offences against the Person Act 1861, which it in part repealed: see Schedule 13 to the Act of 1977. Section 4 of the Act of 1861 was in these terms:

> "All persons who shall conspire, confederate, and agree to murder any person, whether he be a subject of Her Majesty or not, and whether he be within the Queen's Dominions or not, and whosoever shall solicit, encourage, persuade, or endeavour to persuade, or shall propose to any person, to murder any other person, whether he be a subject of Her Majesty or not, and whether he be within the Queen's Dominions or not, shall be guilty of a misdemeanour, and being convicted thereof shall be liable, at the discretion of the court, to be kept in penal servitude for any term not more than ten and not less than three years,—or to be imprisoned for any term not exceeding two years, with or without hard labour."

So the conduct which is alleged against Senator Pinochet in charge 9—that between 1 January 1975 and 31 December 1976 he was a party to a conspiracy in Spain to murder someone in Spain—is an offence for which he could, unless protected by immunity, be extradited to Spain under reference to section 4 of the Act of 1861, as it remained in force until the relevant part of it was repealed by the Act of 1977. This is because his partici-pation in the conspiracy in Spain was conduct by him in Spain for the purposes of section 2(1)(a) of the Extradition Act 1989.

The conduct which is alleged against him in charge 4 is that he was a party to a con-spiracy to murder, in furtherance of which about four thousand people were murdered in Chile and in various countries outside Chile including Spain. It is implied that this con-spiracy was in Chile, so I would hold that this is not conduct by him in Spain for the pur-poses of section 2(1)(a) of Act of 1989. The question then is whether it is an extra-territorial offence within the meaning of section section 2(1)(b) of that Act.

A conspiracy to commit a criminal offence in England is punishable here under the common law rules as to extra-territorial conspiracies even if the conspiracy was formed outside England and nothing was actually done in this country in furtherance of the con-spiracy: Somchai Liangsiriprasert v. Government of the United States of America [1991] 1 A.C. 225. In that case it was held by the Judicial Committee, applying the English com-mon law, that a conspiracy to traffic in a dangerous drug in Hong Kong entered into in Thailand could be tried in Hong Kong although no act pursuant to that conspiracy was done in Hong Kong. Lord Griffiths, delivering the judgment of the Board, said at p. 251C-D:

> "Their Lordships can find nothing in precedent, comity or good sense that should inhibit the com-mon law from regarding as justiciable in England inchoate crimes committed abroad which are intended to result in the commission of criminal offences in England."

In Regina v. Sansom [1991] 2 Q.B. 130 the appellants had been charged with conspiracy contrary to section 1 of the Criminal Law Act 1977, which does not in terms deal with extra-territorial conspiracies. The Court of Appeal rejected the argument that the prin-ciple laid down in Somchai referred only to the common law and that it could not be applied to conspiracies charged under the Act of 1977. Taylor L.J. said, at p. 138B that it should now be regarded as the law of England on this point.

As Lord Griffiths observed in Somchai at p. 244C, it is still true, as a broad general statement, that English criminal law is local in its effect and that the criminal law does not concern itself with crimes committed abroad. But I consider that the common law of England would, applying the rule laid down in Somchai, also regard as justiciable in England a conspiracy to commit an offence anywhere which was triable here as an extra-territorial offence in pursuance of an international convention, even although no act was done here in furtherance of the conspiracy. I do not think that this would be an unrea-sonable extension of the rule. It seems to me that on grounds of comity it would make good sense for the rule to be extended in this way in order to promote the aims of the con-vention.

Prior to the coming into force of the Suppression of Terrorism Act 1978, a conspiracy which was formed outside this country to commit murder in some country other than England in pursuance of which nothing was done in England to further that conspiracy would not be punishable in England, as it was not the intention that acts done in pur-suance of the conspiracy would result in the commission of a criminal offence in this country. The presumption against the extra-territorial application of the criminal law would have precluded such conduct from being prosecuted here. Section 4(1) of the Act of 1978 gives the courts of the United Kingdom jurisdiction over a person who does any act in a convention country which, if he had done that act in a part of the United Kingdom, would have made him guilty in that part of the United Kingdom of an offence mentioned in some, but not all, of the paragraphs of Schedule 1 to that Act. Murder is one of the offences to which that provision applies. But that Act, which was passed to give effect to the European Convention on the Suppression of Terrorism of 27 January 1977, did not come into force until 21 August 1978: S.I. 1978 No. 1063. And Chile is not a convention country for the purposes of that Act, nor is it one of the non-convention countries to which its provisions have been applied by section 5 of the Act of 1978. Only two non-convention countries have been so designated. These are the United States (S.I. 1986 No. 2146) and India (S.I. 1993 No. 2533).

Applying these principles, the only conduct alleged against Senator Pinochet as conspiracy to murder in charge 4 for which he could be extradited to Spain is that part of it which alleges that he was a party to a conspiracy in Spain to commit murder in Spain prior to 21 August 1978. As for the allegation that he was a party to a conspiracy in Spain or elsewhere to commit murder in a country which had been designated as a convention country after that date, the extradition request states that acts in furtherance of the conspiracy took place in France in 1975, in Spain in 1975 and 1976 and in the United States and Portugal in 1976. These countries have now been designated as countries to which the Suppression of Terrorism Act 1978 applies. But the acts which are alleged to have taken place there all pre-date the coming into force of that Act. So the extra-territorial jurisdiction cannot be applied to them.

The alleged offences of attempted murder in Italy are not, as such, offences for which Senator Pinochet could be extradited to Spain under reference to section 2(1)(a) of the Act of 1989 because the alleged conduct did not take place in Spain and because he is not of Spanish nationality. But for their date they would have been offences for which he could have been extradited from the United Kingdom to Spain under reference to section 2(1)(b), on the grounds, first, that murder is now an extra-territorial offence under section 4(1)(a) of the Suppression of Terrorism Act 1978 as it is an offence mentioned in paragraph 1 of Schedule 1 to that Act, Italy has been designated as a convention country (S.I. 1986 No. 1137) and, second, that an offence of attempting to commit that offence is an extra-territorial offence under section 4(1)(b) of the Act of 1978. But the attempted murders in Italy which are alleged against Senator Pinochet are said to have been committed on 6 October 1975. As the Act of 1978 was not in force on that date, these offences are not capable of being brought within the procedures laid down by that Act.

Finally, to complete the provisions which need to be reviewed under this heading, mention should be made of an amendment which was made to Schedule 1 to the Suppression of Terrorism Act 1978 by section 22 of the Criminal Justice Act 1988, which includes within the list of offences set out in that schedule the offence of conspiracy. That section appears in Part 1 of the Act of 1988, most of which was repealed before having been brought into force following the enactment of the Extradition Act 1989. But section 22 was not repealed. It was brought into force on 5 June 1990: S.I. 1990 No. 1145. It provides that there shall be added at the end of the schedule a new paragraph in these terms:

> "21. An offence of conspiring to commit any offence mentioned in a preceding paragraph of this Schedule."

At first sight it might seem that the effect of this amendment was to introduce a statutory extra-territorial jurisdiction in regard to the offence of conspiracy, wherever the agreement was made to participate in the conspiracy. But this offence does not appear in the list of offences in that Schedule in respect of which section 4(1) of the Suppression of Terrorism Act 1978 gives jurisdiction, if committed in a convention country, as extra-territorial offences. In any event section 22 was not brought into force until 5 June 1990: S.I. 1990 No. 1145. This was after the last date when Senator Pinochet is alleged to have committed the offence of conspiracy.

Torture and conspiracy to torture

Torture is another of those offences, wherever the act takes place, which is deemed by section 22(6) of the Extradition Act 1989 to be an offence committed within the territory of any other state against whose law it is an offence. This provision gives effect to the Torture Convention of 10 December 1984. But section 134 of the Criminal Justice Act 1988 also gave effect to the Torture Convention. It made it a crime under English law for a public official or a person acting in an official capacity to commit acts of both physical and mental torture: see subsection (3). And it made such acts of torture an extra-territorial offence wherever they were committed and whatever the nationality of the perpetrator: see subsection (1). Read with the broad definition which the expression "torture" has been given by Article 1 of the Convention and in accordance with ordinary principles, the offence which section 134 lays down must be taken to include the ancillary offences of counselling, procuring, commanding and aiding or abetting acts of torture and of being an accessory before or after the fact to such acts. All of these offences became extra-territorial offences against the law of the United Kingdom within the meaning of section 2(2) of the Extradition Act 1989 as soon as section 134 was brought into force on 29 September 1988.

Section 134 does not mention the offence of conspiracy to commit torture, nor does Article 1 of the Convention, nor does section 22(6) of the Extradition Act 1989. So, while the courts of the United Kingdom have extra-territorial jurisdiction under section 134 over offences of official torture wherever in the world they were committed, that section does not give them extra-territorial jurisdiction over a conspiracy to commit torture in any other country where the agreement was made outside the United Kingdom and no acts in furtherance of the conspiracy took place here. Nor is it conduct which can be deemed to take place in the territory of the requesting country under section 22(6) of the Act of 1989.

However, the general statutory offence of conspiracy under section 1 of the Criminal Law Act 1977 extends to a conspiracy to commit any offence which is triable in England and Wales. Among those offences are all the offences over which the courts in England and Wales have extra-territorial jurisdiction, including the offence under section 134 of the Act of 1988. And, for reasons already mentioned, I consider that the common law rule as to extra-territorial conspiracies laid down in Somchai Liangsiriprasert v. Government of the United States of America [1991] 1 A.C. 225 applies if a conspiracy which was entered into abroad was intended to result in the commission of an offence, wherever it was intended to be committed, which is an extra-territorial offence in this country. Accordingly the courts of this country could try Senator Pinochet for acts of torture in Chile and elsewhere after 29 September 1988, because they are extra-territorial offences under section 134 of the Act of 1988. They could also try him here for conspiring in Chile or elsewhere after that date to commit torture, wherever the torture was to be committed, because torture after that date is an extra-territorial offence and the courts in England have jurisdiction over such a conspiracy at common law.

Torture prior to 29 September 1989

Section 134 of the Criminal Law Act 1988 did not come into force until 29 September 1988. But acts of physical torture were already criminal under English law. Among the various offences against the person which would have been committed by torturing would have been the common law offence of assault occasioning actual bodily harm or causing injury and the statutory offence under section 18 of the Offences against the Person Act 1861 of wounding with intent to cause grievous bodily harm. A conspiracy which was entered into in England to commit these offences in England was an offence at common law until the common law offence was replaced on 1 December 1977 by the statutory offence of conspiracy in section 1 of the Criminal Law Act 1977 which remains in force and available. As I have said, I consider that a conspiracy which was entered into abroad to commit these offences in England would be triable in this country under the common law rule as to extra-territorial conspiracies which was laid down in Somchai Liangsiriprasert v. Government of the United States of America [1991] 1 A.C. 225 if they were extra-territorial offences at the time of the alleged conspiracy.

However none of these offences, if committed prior to the coming into force of section 134 of the Criminal Justice Act 1988, could be said to be extra-territorial offences against the law of the United Kingdom within the meaning of section 2(2) of the Extradition Act 1989 as there is no basis upon which they could have been tried extra-territorially in this country. The offences listed in Schedule 1 to the Suppression of Terrorism Act 1978 include the common law offence of assault and the statutory offences under the Offences against the Person Act 1861. But none of these offences are included in the list of offences which are made extra-territorial offences if committed in a convention country by section 4(1) of the Extradition Act 1989. So the rule laid down in Somchai cannot be applied to any conspiracy to commit these offences in any country outside England, as it would not be an extra-territorial conspiracy according to English law. Senator Pinochet could only be extradited to Spain for such offences under reference to section 2(1)(a) of the Act of 1989 if he was accused of conduct in Spain which, if it occurred in the United Kingdom, would constitute an offence which would be punishable in this country. Section 22(6) of the Act of 1989 is of no assistance, because torture contrary to the Torture Convention had not yet become an offence in this country.

None of the charges of conspiracy to torture and none of the various torture charges allege that Senator Pinochet did anything in Spain which might qualify under section 2(1)(a) of the Act of 1989 as conduct in that country. All one can say at this stage is that, if the information presented to the magistrate under section 9(8) of the Act of 1989 in regard to charge 4 were to demonstrate (i) that he did something in Spain prior to 29 September 1988 to commit acts of torture there, or (ii) that he was party to a conspiracy in Spain to commit acts of torture in Spain, that would be conduct in Spain which would meet the requirements of section 2(1)(a) of that Act.

Torture after 29 September 1989

The effect of section 134 of the Criminal Justice Act 1988 was to make acts of official torture, wherever they were committed and whatever the nationality of the offender, an extra-territorial offence in the United Kingdom. The section came into force two months after the passing of the Act on 29 September 1988, and it was not retrospective. As from that date official torture was an extradition crime within the meaning of section 2(1) of the Extradition Act 1989 because it was an extra-territorial offence against the law of the United Kingdom.

The general offence of conspiracy which was introduced by section 1 of the Criminal Law Act 1977 applies to any offence triable in England and Wales: section 1(4). So a conspiracy which took place here after 29 September 1988 to commit offences of official torture, wherever the torture was to be carried out and whatever the nationality of the alleged torturer, is an offence for which Senator Pinochet could be tried in this country if he has no immunity. This means that a conspiracy to torture which he entered into in Spain after that date is an offence for which he could be extradited to Spain, as it would be an extradition offence under section 2(1)(a) of the Act of 1989. But, as I have said, I consider that the common law of England would, applying the rule laid down in Somchai Liangsiriprasert v. Government of the United States of America [1991] 1 A.C. 225, also regard as justiciable in England a conspiracy to commit an offence which was triable here as an extra-territorial offence in pursuance of an international convention, even although no act was done here in furtherance of the conspiracy. This means that he could be extradited to Spain under reference to section 2(1)(b) of the Act of 1989 on charges of conspiracy to torture entered into anywhere which related to periods after that date. But, as section 134 of the Act of 1988 does not have retrospective effect, he could not be extradited to Spain for any conduct in Spain or elsewhere amounting to a conspiracy to commit torture, wherever the torture was to be carried out, which occurred before 29 September 1988.

The conduct which is alleged against Senator Pinochet under the heading of conspiracy in charge 4 is not confined to the allegation that he was a party to an agreement that people were to be tortured. Included in that charge is the allegation that many people in various countries were murdered after being tortured in furtherance of the conspiracy that they would be tortured and then killed. So this charge includes charges of torture as well as conspiracy to torture. And it is broad enough to include the ancillary offences of counselling, procuring, commanding, aiding or abetting, or of being accessory before or after the fact to, these acts of torture. Ill-defined as this charge is, I would regard it as including allegations of torture and of conspiracy to torture after 29 September 1988 for which, if he has no immunity, Senator Pinochet could be extradited to Spain on the ground that, as they were extra-territorial offences against the law of the United Kingdom, they were extradition crimes within the meaning of section 2(1) of the Act of 1989.

What is the effect of the qualification which I have just mentioned, as to the date on which these allegations of torture and conspiracy to torture first became offences for which, at the request of Spain, Senator Pinochet could be extradited? In the circumstances of this case its effect is a profound one. It is to remove from the proceedings the entire course of such conduct in which Senator Pinochet is said to have engaged from the moment he embarked on the alleged conspiracy to torture in January 1972 until 29 September 1988. The only offences of torture and conspiracy to torture which are punishable in this country as extra-territorial offences against the law of the United Kingdom within the meaning of section 2(2) of the Act of 1989 are those offences of torture and conspiracy to torture which he is alleged to have committed on or after 29 September 1988. But almost all the offences of torture and murder, of which there are alleged to have been about four thousand victims, were committed during the period of repression which was at its most intense in 1973 and 1974. The extradition request alleges that during the period from 1977 to 1990 only about 130 such offences were committed. Of that number only three have been identified in the extradition request as having taken place after 29 September 1988.

Of the various offences which are listed in the draft charges only charge 30, which refers to one act of official torture in Chile on 24 June 1989, relates exclusively to the period after 29 September 1988. Two of the charges of conspiracy to commit torture extend in part over the period after that date. Charge 2 alleges that Senator Pinochet committed this offence during the period from 1 August 1973 to 1 January 1990, but it does not allege that any acts of torture took place in furtherance of that conspiracy. Charge 4 alleges that he was party to a conspiracy to commit torture in furtherance of which acts of murder following torture were committed in various countries including Spain during the period from 1 January 1972 to 1 January 1990. The only conduct alleged in charges 2 and 4 for which Senator Pinochet could be extradited to Spain is that part of the alleged conduct which relates to the period after 29 September 1988.

Although the allegations of conspiracy to torture in charge 2 and of torture and conspiracy to torture in charge 4 must now be restricted to the period from 29 September 1988 to 1 January 1990, the fact that these allegations remain available for the remainder of the period is important because of the light which they cast on the single act of torture alleged in charge 30. For reasons which I shall explain later, I would find it very difficult to say that a former head of state of a country which is a party to the Torture Convention has no immunity against an allegation of torture committed in the course of governmental acts which related only to one isolated instance of alleged torture. But that is not the case which the Spanish judicial authorities are alleging against Senator Pinochet. Even when reduced to the period from 29 September 1988 until he left office as head of state, which the provisions for speciality protection in section 6(4) of the Extradition Act 1989 would ensure was the only period in respect of which the Spanish judicial authorities would be entitled to bring charges against him if he were to be extradited, the allegation is that he was a party to the use of torture as a systematic attack on all those who opposed or who might oppose his government.

The extradition request states that between August 1977, when the National Intelligence Directorate (DINA) was dissolved and replaced by the National Intelligence Bureau (CNI), the Directorate of Communications of the Militarised Police (DICOM-CAR) and the Avenging Martyrs Commando (COVERMA), while engaged in a policy of repression acting on orders emanating from Augusto Pinochet, systematically performed torture on detainees (Bound Record, vol. 2, pp. 314–315). Among the methods which are said to have been used was the application of electricity to sensitive parts of the body, and it is alleged that the torture sometimes led to the victim's death. Charge 30 alleges that the victim died after having been tortured by inflicting electric shock. The two victims of an incident in October 1988, which is mentioned in the extradition request but is not the subject of a separate count in the list of draft charges, are said to have shown signs of the application of electricity after autopsy. It appears that the evidence has revealed only these three instances after 29 September 1988 when acts of official torture were perpetrated in pursuance of this policy. Even so, this does not affect the true nature and quality of those acts. The significance of charges 2 and 4 may be said to lie in the fact that they show that a policy of systematic torture was being pursued when those acts were perpetrated.

I must emphasise that it is not our function to consider whether or not the evidence justifies this inference, and I am not to be taken as saying that it does. But it is plain that the information which is before us is capable of supporting the inference that the acts of torture which are alleged during the relevant period were of that character. I do not think that it would be right to approach the question of immunity on a basis which ignores the fact that this point is at least open to argument. So I consider that the argument that Senator Pinochet has no immunity for this reduced period is one which can properly be examined in the light of developments in customary international law regarding the use of widespread or systematic torture as an instrument of state policy.

Charges which are relevant to the question of immunity

The result of this analysis is that the only charges which allege extradition crimes for which Senator Pinochet could be extradited to Spain if he has no immunity are: (1) those charges of conspiracy to torture in charge 2, of torture and conspiracy to torture in charge 4 and of torture in charge 30 which, irrespective of where the conduct occurred, became extra-territorial offences as from 29 September 1988 under section 134 of the Criminal Justice Act 1988 and under the common law as to extra territorial conspiracies; (2) the conspiracy in Spain to murder in Spain which is alleged in charge 9; (3) such conspiracies in Spain to commit murder in Spain and such conspiracies in Spain prior to 29 September 1988 to commit acts of torture in Spain, as can be shown to form part of the allegations in charge 4.

So far as the law of the United Kingdom is concerned, the only country where Senator Pinochet could be put on trial for the full range of the offences which have been alleged against him by the Spanish judicial authorities is Chile.

State immunity

Section 20(1)(a) of the State Immunity Act 1978 provides that the Diplomatic Privileges Act 1964 applies, subject to "any necessary modifications", to a head of state as it applies to the head of a diplomatic mission. The generality of this provision is qualified by section 20(5), which restricts the immunity of the head of state in regard to civil proceedings in the same way as Part I of the Act does for diplomats. This reflects the fact that section 14 already provides that heads of state are subject to the restrictions in Part I. But there is nothing in section 20 to indicate that the immunity from criminal proceedings which Article 31.1 of the Vienna Convention as applied by the Act of 1964 gives to diplomats is restricted in any way for heads of state. Section 23(3), which provides that the provisions of Parts I and II of the Act do not operate retrospectively, makes no mention of Part III. I infer from this that it was not thought that Part III would give rise to the suggestion that it might operate in this way.

It seems to me to be clear therefore that what section 20(1) did was to give statutory force in the United Kingdom to customary international law as to the immunity which heads of state, and former heads of state in particular, enjoy from proceedings in foreign national courts. Marcos and Marcos v. Federal Department of Police [1990] 102 I.L.R 198, 203 supports this view, as it was held in that case that the Article 39.2 immunity was available under customary international law to the former head of state of the Republic of the Philippines.

The question then is to what extent does the immunity which Article 39.2 gives to former diplomats have to be modified in its application to former heads of state? The last sentence of Article 39.2 deals with the position after the functions of the diplomat have come to an end. It provides that "with respect to acts performed by such person in the exercise of his functions as a member of the mission, immunity shall continue to subsist." It is clear that this provision is dealing with the residual immunity of the former diplomat ratione materiae, and not with the immunity ratione personae which he enjoys when still serving as a diplomat. In its application to a former head of state this provision raises two further questions: (1) does it include functions which the head of state performed outside the receiving state from whose jurisdiction he claims immunity, and (2) does it include acts of the kind alleged in this case—which Mr. Alun Jones Q.C. accepts were not private acts but were acts done in the exercise of the state's authority?

As to the first of these two further questions, it is plain that the functions of the head of state will vary from state to state according to the acts which he is expected or required to perform under the constitution of that state. In some countries which adhere to the traditions of constitutional monarchy these will be confined largely to ceremonial or symbolic acts which do not involve any executive responsibility. In others the head of state is head of the executive, with all the resources of the state at his command to do with as he thinks fit within the sphere of action which the constitution has given to him. I have not found anything in customary international law which would require us to confine the expression "his functions" to the lowest common denominator. In my opinion the functions of the head of state are those which his own state enables or requires him to perform in the exercise of government. He performs these functions wherever he is for the time being as well as within his own state. These may include instructing or authorising acts to be done by those under his command at home or abroad in the interests of state security. It would not be right therefore to confine the immunity under Article 39.2 to acts done in the receiving state. I would not regard this as a "necessary modification" which has to be made to it under section 20(1) of the Act of 1978.

As to the second of those questions, I consider that the answer to it is well settled in customary international law. The test is whether they were private acts on the one hand or governmental acts done in the exercise of his authority as head of state on the other. It is whether the act was done to promote the state's interests—whether it was done for his own benefit or gratification or was done for the state: United States v. Noriega (1990) 746 F.Supp. 1506, 1519–1521. Sir Arthur Watts Q.C. in his Hague Lectures, The Legal Position in International Law of Heads of States, Heads of Governments and Foreign Ministers (1994–III) 247 Recueil des cours, p. 56, said : "The critical test would seem to be whether the conduct was engaged in under colour of or in ostensible exercise of the head of state's public authority." The sovereign or governmental acts of one state are not matters upon which the courts of other states will adjudicate: I Congreso del Partido [1983] A.C. 244, 262C per Lord Wilberforce. The fact that acts done for the state have involved conduct which is criminal does not remove the immunity. Indeed the whole purpose of the residual immunity ratione materiae is to protect the former head of state against allegations of such conduct after he has left office. A head of state needs to be free to promote his own state's interests during the entire period when he is in office without being subjected to the prospect of detention, arrest or embarrassment in the foreign legal system of the receiving state: see United States v. Noriega, p. 1519; Lafontant v. Aristide (1994) 844 F.Supp. 128, 132. The conduct does not have to be lawful to attract the immunity.

It may be said that it is not one of the functions of a head of state to commit acts which are criminal according to the laws and constitution of his own state or which customary international law regards as criminal. But I consider that this approach to the question is unsound in principle. The principle of immunity ratione materiae protects all acts which the head of state has performed in the exercise of the functions of government. The purpose for which they were performed protects these acts from any further analysis. There are only two exceptions to this approach which customary international law has recognised. The first relates to criminal acts which the head of state did under the colour of his authority as head of state but which were in reality for his own pleasure or benefit. The examples which Lord Steyn gave [1998] 3 W.L.R. 1456, 1506B-C of the head of state who kills his gardener in a fit of rage or who orders victims to be tortured so that he may observe them in agony seem to me plainly to fall into this category and, for this reason, to lie outside the scope of the immunity. The second relates to acts the prohibition of which has acquired the status under international law of jus cogens. This compels all states to refrain from such conduct under any circumstances and imposes an obligation erga omnes to punish such conduct. As Sir Arthur Watts Q.C. said in his Hague Lectures, page 89, note 198, in respect of conduct constituting an international crime, such as war crimes, special considerations apply.

But even in the field of such high crimes as have achieved the status of jus cogens under customary international law there is as yet no general agreement that they are outside the immunity to which former heads of state are entitled from the jurisdiction of foreign national courts. There is plenty of source material to show that war crimes and crimes against humanity have been separated out from the generality of conduct which customary international law has come to regard as criminal. These developments were described by Lord Slynn of Hadley [1998] 3 W.L.R. 1456, 1474D-H and I respectfully agree with his analysis. As he said, at p. 1474H, except in regard to crimes in particular situations where international tribunals have been set up to deal with them and it is part of the arrangement that heads of state should not have any immunity, there is no general recognition that there has been a loss of immunity from the jurisdiction of foreign national courts. This led him to sum the matter up in this way at p. 1475B-E:

> "So it is necessary to consider what is needed, in the absence of a general international convention defining or cutting down head of state immunity, to define or limit the former head of state immunity in particular cases. In my opinion it is necessary to find provision in an international convention to which the state asserting, and the state being asked to refuse, the immunity of a former head of state for an official act is a party; the convention must clearly define a crime against international law and require or empower a state to prevent or prosecute the crime, whether or not committed in its jurisdiction and whether or not committed by one of its nationals; it must make it clear that a national court has jurisdiction to try a crime alleged against a former head of state, or that having been a head of state is no defence and that expressly or impliedly the immunity is not to apply so as to bar proceedings against him. The convention must be given the force of law in the national courts of the state; in a dualist country like the United Kingdom that means by legislation, so that with the necessary procedures and machinery the crime may be prosecuted there in accordance with the procedures to be found in the convention."

That is the background against which I now turn to the Torture Convention. As all the requirements which Lord Slynn laid out in the passage at p. 1475B-E save one are met by it, when read with the provisions of sections 134 and 135 of the Criminal Justice Act 1988 which gave the force of law to the Convention in this country, I need deal only with the one issue which remains. Did it make it clear that a former head of state has no immunity in the courts of a state which has jurisdiction to try the crime?

The Torture Convention and Loss of Immunity

The Torture Convention is an international instrument. As such, it must be construed in accordance with customary international law and against the background of the subsisting residual former head of state immunity. Article 32.2 of the Vienna Convention, which forms part of the provisions in the Diplomatic Privileges Act 1964 which are extended to heads of state by section 20(1) of the Sovereign Immunity Act 1978, subject to "any necessary modifications", states that waiver of the immunity accorded to diplomats "must always be express". No modification of that provision is needed to enable it to apply to heads of state in the event of it being decided that there should be a waiver of their immunity. The Torture Convention does not contain any provision which deals expressly with the question whether heads of state or former heads of state are or are not to have immunity from allegations that they have committed torture.

But there remains the question whether the effect of the Torture Convention was to remove the immunity by necessary implication. Although Article 32.2 says that any waiver must be express, we are required nevertheless to consider whether the effect of the Convention was necessarily to remove the immunity. This is an exacting test. Section 1605(a)(1) of the United States Federal Sovereignty Immunity Act provides for an implied waiver, but this section has been narrowly construed: Siderman de Blake v. Republic of Argentina (1992) 965 F.2d 699, p. 720; Princz v. Federal Republic of Germany (1994) 26 F.3d 1166, p. 1174; Argentine Republic v. Amerada Hess Shipping Corporation (1989) 109 S.Ct. 683, p. 693. In international law the need for clarity in this matter is obvious. The general rule is that international treaties should, so far as possible, be construed uniformly by the national courts of all states.

The preamble to the Torture Convention explains its purpose. After referring to Article 5 of the Universal Declaration of Human Rights which provides that no one shall be subjected to torture or other cruel, inhuman or degrading treatment and to the United Nations Declaration of 9 December 1975 regarding torture and other cruel, inhuman or degrading treatment or punishment, it states that it was desired "to make more effective the struggle against torture and other cruel, inhuman or degrading treatment or punishment throughout the world". There then follows in Article 1 a definition of the term "torture" for the purposes of the Convention. It is expressed in the widest possible terms. It means "any act by which severe pain or suffering, whether physical or mental, is intentionally inflicted" for such purposes as obtaining information or a confession, punishment, intimidation or coercion or for any reason based on discrimination of any kind. It is confined however to official torture by its concluding words, which require such pain or suffering to have been "inflicted by or at the instigation of or with the consent or acquiescence of a public official or other person acting in an official capacity".

This definition is so broadly framed as to suggest on the one hand that heads of state must have been contemplated by its concluding words, but to raise the question on the other hand whether it was also contemplated that they would by necessary implication be deprived of their immunity. The words "public official" might be thought to refer to someone of lower rank than the head of state. Other international instruments suggest that where the intention is to include persons such as the head of state or diplomats they are mentioned expressly in the instrument: see Article 27 of the Rome Statute of the International Criminal Court which was adopted on 17 July 1998. But a head of state who resorted to conduct of the kind described in the exercise of his function would clearly be "acting in an official capacity". It would also be a strange result if the provisions of the Convention could not be applied to heads of state who, because they themselves inflicted torture or had instigated the carrying out of acts of torture by their officials, were the persons primarily responsible for the perpetration of these acts.

Yet the idea that the framing of the definition in these terms in itself was sufficient to remove the immunity from prosecution for all acts of torture is also not without difficulty. The jus cogens character of the immunity enjoyed by serving heads of state ratione personae suggests that, on any view, that immunity was not intended to be affected by the Convention. But once one immunity is conceded it becomes harder, in the absence of an express provision, to justify the removal of the other immunities. It may also be noted that Burgers and Danelius, in their Handbook on the Convention against Torture and Other Cruel, Inhuman or Degrading Treatment or Punishment, at p. 131, make this comment on Article 5.1 of the Convention, which sets out the measures which each state party is required to take to establish its jurisdiction over the offences of torture which it is required by Article 4 to make punishable under its own criminal law:

> "This means, first of all, that the state shall have jurisdiction over the offence when it has been committed in its territory. Under international or national law, there may be certain limited exceptions to this rule, e.g. in regard to foreign diplomats, foreign troops, parliament members or other categories benefiting from special immunities, and such immunities may be accepted insofar as they apply to criminal acts in general and are not unduly extensive."

These observations, although of undoubted weight as Jan Herman Burgers of the Netherlands was a Chairman/Rapporteur to the Convention, may be thought to be so cryptic as to defy close analysis. But two points are worth making about them. The first is that they recognise that the provisions of the Convention are not inconsistent with at least some of the immunities in customary international law. The second is that they make no mention of any exception which would deprive heads of state or former heads of state of their customary international law immunities. The absence of any reference to this matter suggests that the framers of the Convention did not consider it. The Reports of the Working Group on the Draft Convention to the Economic and Social Council of the Commission on Human Rights show that many meetings were held to complete its work. These extended over several years, and many issues were raised and discussed before the various delegations were content with its terms. If the issue of head of state and former head of state immunity was discussed at any of these meetings, it would without doubt have been mentioned in the reports. The issue would have been recognised as an important one on which the delegations would have to take instructions from their respective governments. But there is no sign of this in any of the reports which have been shown to us.

The absence of any discussion of the issue is not surprising, once it is appreciated that the purpose of the Convention was to put in place as widely as possible the machinery which was needed to make the struggle against torture more effective throughout the world. There was clearly much to be done, as the several years of discussion amply demonstrate. According to Burgers and Danelius, p. 1, the principal aim was to strengthen the existing position by a number of supportive measures. A basis had to be laid down for legislation to be enacted by the contracting states. An agreed definition of torture, including mental torture, had to be arrived at for the adoption by states into their own criminal law. Provisions had to be agreed for the taking of extra-territorial jurisdiction to deal with these offences and for the extradition of offenders to states which were seeking to prosecute them. As many states do not extradite their own citizens and the

Convention does not oblige states to extradite, they had to undertake to take such measures as might be necessary to establish jurisdiction over these offences in cases where the alleged offender was present within their territory but was not to be extradited. For many, if not all, states these arrangements were innovations upon their domestic law. Waiver of immunities was not mentioned. But, as Yoram Dinstein, Diplomatic Immunity from Jurisdiction Ratione Materiae (1966) International and Comparative Law Quarterly, 76, 80 had already pointed out, it would be entirely meaningless to waive the immunity unless local courts were able, as a consequence, to try the offender.

These considerations suggest strongly that it would be wrong to regard the Torture Convention as having by necessary implication removed the immunity ratione materiae from former heads of state in regard to every act of torture of any kind which might be alleged against him falling within the scope of Article 1. In Siderman de Blake v. Republic of Argentina (1992) 965 F.2d 699, 714–717 it was held that the alleged acts of official torture, which were committed in 1976 before the making of the Torture Convention, violated international law under which the prohibition of official torture had acquired the status of jus cogens. Cruel acts had been perpetrated over a period of seven days by men acting under the direction of the military governor. Argentina was being ruled by an anti-semitic military junta, and epithets were used by those who tortured him which indicated that Jose Siderman was being tortured because of his Jewish faith. But the definition in Article 1 is so wide that any act of official torture, so long as it involved "severe" pain or suffering, would be covered by it.

As Burgers and Danelius point out at p. 122, although the definition of torture in Article 1 may give the impression of being a very precise and detailed one, the concept of "severe pain and suffering" is in fact rather a vague concept, on the application of which to a specific case there may be very different views. There is no requirement that it should have been perpetrated on such a scale as to constitute an international crime in the sense described by Sir Arthur Watts in his Hague Lectures at p. 82, that is to say a crime which offends against the public order of the international community. A single act of torture by an official against a national of his state within that state's borders will do. The risks to which former heads of state would be exposed on leaving office of being detained in foreign states upon an allegation that they had acquiesced in an act of official torture would have been so obvious to governments that it is hard to believe that they would ever have agreed to this. Moreover, even if your Lordships were to hold that this was its effect, there are good reasons for doubting whether the courts of other states would take the same view. An express provision would have removed this uncertainty.

Nevertheless there remains the question whether the immunity can survive Chile's agreement to the Torture Convention if the torture which is alleged was of such a kind or on such a scale as to amount to an international crime. Sir Arthur Watts in his Hague Lectures, p. 82 states that the idea that individuals who commit international crimes are internationally accountable for them has now become an accepted part of international law. The international agreements to which states have been striving in order to deal with this problem in international criminal courts have been careful to set a threshold for such crimes below which the jurisdiction of those courts will not be available. The Statute of the International Tribunal for the Former Yugoslavia (1993) includes torture in article 5 as one of the crimes against humanity. In paragraph 48 of his Report to the United Nations the Secretary-General explained that crimes against humanity refer to inhuman acts of a very serious nature, such as wilful killing, torture or rape, committed as part of a widespread or systematic attack against any civilian population. Similar observations appear in paragraphs 131 to 135 of the Secretary-General's Report of 9 December 1994 on the Rwanda conflict. Article 3 of the Statute of the International Tribunal for Rwanda (1994) included torture as one of the crimes against humanity "when committed as part of a widespread or systematic attack against any civilian population" on national, political, ethnic or other grounds. Article 7 of the Rome Statute contains a similar limitation to acts of widespread or systematic torture.

The allegations which the Spanish judicial authorities have made against Senator Pinochet fall into that category. As I sought to make clear in my analysis of the draft charges, we are not dealing in this case—even upon the restricted basis of those charges on which Senator Pinochet could lawfully be extradited if he has no immunity—with isolated acts of official torture. We are dealing with the remnants of an allegation that he is guilty of what would now, without doubt, be regarded by customary international law as an international crime. This is because he is said to have been involved in acts of torture which were committed in pursuance of a policy to commit systematic torture within Chile and elsewhere as an instrument of government. On the other hand it is said that, for him to lose his immunity, it would have to be established that there was a settled practice for crime of this nature to be so regarded by customary international law at the time when they were committed. I would find it hard to say that it has been shown that any such settled practice had been established by 29 September 1988. But we must be careful not to attach too much importance to this point, as the opportunity for prosecuting such crimes seldom presents itself.

Despite the difficulties which I have mentioned, I think that there are sufficient signs that the necessary developments in international law were in place by that date. The careful discussion of the jus cogens and erga omnes rules in regard to allegations of official torture in Siderman de Blake v. Republic of Argentina (1992) 26 F.2d 1166, pp. 714–718, which I regard as persuasive on this point, shows that there was already widespread agreement that the prohibition against official torture had achieved the status of a jus cogens norm. Articles which were published in 1988 and 1989 are referred to at p. 717 in support of this view. So I think that we can take it that that was the position by 29 September 1988. Then there is the Torture Convention of 10 December 1984. Having secured a sufficient number of signatories, it entered into force on 26 June 1987. In my opinion, once the machinery which it provides was put in place to enable jurisdiction over such crimes to be exercised in the courts of a foreign state, it was no longer open to any state which was a signatory to the Convention to invoke the immunity ratione materiae in the event of allegations of systematic or widespread torture committed after that date being made in the courts of that state against its officials or any other person acting in an official capacity.

As Sir Arthur Watts, Q.C. has explained in his Hague Lectures (1994) at p. 82, the general principle in such cases is that of individual responsibility for international criminal conduct. After a review of various general international instruments relating mainly but not exclusively to war crimes, of which the most recent was the International Law Commission's draft Code of Crimes against the Peace and Security of Mankind of 1988, he concludes at p. 84 that it can no longer be doubted that as a matter of general customary international law a head of state will personally be liable to be called to account if there is sufficient evidence that he authorised or perpetrated such serious international crimes. A head of state is still protected while in office by the immunity ratione personae, but the immunity ratione materiae on which he would have to rely on leaving office must be denied to him.

I would not regard this as a case of waiver. Nor would I accept that it was an implied term of the Torture Convention that former heads of state were to be deprived of their immunity ratione materiae with respect to all acts of official torture as defined in article 1. It is just that the obligations which were recognised by customary international law in the case of such serious international crimes by the date when Chile ratified the Convention are so strong as to override any objection by it on the ground of immunity ratione materiae to the exercise of the jurisdiction over crimes committed after that date which the United Kingdom had made available.

I consider that the date as from which the immunity ratione materiae was lost was 30 October 1988, which was the date when Chile's ratification of the Torture Convention on 30 September 1988 took effect. Spain had already ratified the Convention. It did so on 21 October 1987. The Convention was ratified by the United Kingdom on 8 December 1988 following the coming into force of section 134 of the Criminal Justice Act 1988. On the approach which I would take to this question the immunity ratione materiae was lost when Chile, having ratified the Convention to which section 134 gave effect and which Spain had already ratified, was deprived of the right to object to the extra-territorial jurisdiction which the United Kingdom was able to assert over these offences when the section came into force. But I am content to accept the view of my noble and learned friend Lord Saville of Newdigate that Senator Pinochet continued to have immunity until 8 December 1988 when the United Kingdom ratified the Convention.

Conclusion

It follows that I would hold that, while Senator Pinochet has immunity ratione materiae from prosecution for the conspiracy in Spain to murder in Spain which is alleged in charge 9 and for such conspiracies in Spain to murder in Spain and such conspiracies in Spain prior to 8 December 1988 to commit acts of torture in Spain as could be shown to be part of the allegations in charge 4, he has no immunity from prosecution for the charges of torture and of conspiracy to torture which relate to the period after that date. None of the other charges which are made against him are extradition crimes for which, even if he had no immunity, he could be extradited. On this basis only I too would allow the appeal, to the extent necessary to permit the extradition to proceed on the charges of torture and conspiracy to torture relating to the period after 8 December 1988.

The profound change in the scope of the case which can now be made for the extradition to Spain of Senator Pinochet will require the Secretary of State to reconsider his decision to give authority to proceed with the extradition process under section 7(4) of the Extradition Act 1989 and, if he decides to renew that authority, with respect to which of the alleged crimes the extradition should be authorised. It will also make it necessary for the magistrate, if renewed authority to proceed is given, to pay very careful attention to the question whether the information which is laid before him under section 9(8) of the Act supports the allegation that torture in pursuance of a conspiracy to commit systematic torture, including the single act of torture which is alleged in charge 30, was being committed by Senator Pinochet after 8 December 1988 when he lost his immunity.

LORD HUTTON

My Lords,

The rehearing of this appeal has raised a number of separate issues which have been fully considered in the speech of my noble and learned friend Lord Browne-Wilkinson which I have had the benefit of reading in draft. I am in agreement with his reasoning and conclusion that the definition of an "extradition crime" in the Extradition Act 1989 requires the conduct to be criminal under United Kingdom law at the date of commission. I am also in agreement with the analysis and conclusions of my noble and learned friend Lord Hope of Craighead as to the alleged crimes in respect of which Senator Pinochet could be extradited apart from any issue of immunity. I further agree with the view of Lord Browne-Wilkinson that Senator Pinochet is entitled to immunity in respect of charges of murder and conspiracy to murder, but I wish to make some observations on the issue of immunity claimed by Senator Pinochet in respect of charges of torture and conspiracy to torture.

Senator Pinochet ceased to be head of state of Chile on 11 March 1990, and he claims immunity as a former head of state. The distinction between the immunity of a serving head of state and the immunity of a former head of state is discussed by Sir Arthur Watts K.C.M.G., Q.C. in his monograph, "The Legal Position in International Law of Heads of States, Heads of Governments and Foreign Ministers". He states at pp. 53, 88 and 89:

> "It is well established that, put broadly, a head of state enjoys a wide immunity from the criminal, civil and administrative jurisdiction of other states. This immunity—to the extent that it exists—becomes effective upon his assumption of office, even in respect of events occurring earlier. . .
>
> "A head of state's immunity is enjoyed in recognition of his very special status as a holder of his state's highest office . . .
>
> "A former head of state is entitled under international law to none of the facilities, immunities and privileges which international law accords to heads of states in office. . .
>
> "After his loss of office he may be sued in relation to his private activities, both those taking place while he was still head of state, as well as those occurring before becoming head of state or since ceasing to be head of state. . .
>
> "A head of state's official acts, performed in his public capacity as head of state, are however subject to different considerations. Such acts are acts of the state rather than the head of state's personal acts, and he cannot be sued for them even after he has ceased to be head of state. The position is similar to that of acts performed by an ambassador in the exercise of his functions for which immunity continues to subsist even after the ambassador's appointment has come to an end."

Section 20 in Part III of the State Immunity Act 1978 provides that, subject to any necessary modifications, the Diplomatic Privileges Act 1964 shall apply to a sovereign or other head of state, and section 2 of the Act of 1964 provides that the Articles of the Vienna Convention on Diplomatic Relations set out in Schedule 1 to the Act shall have the force of law in the United Kingdom. The Articles set out in Schedule 1 include Articles 29, 31 and 39. Article 29 provides:

> "The person of a diplomatic agent shall be inviolable. He shall not be liable to any form of arrest or detention."

Article 31 provides:

> "1. A diplomatic agent shall enjoy immunity from the criminal jurisdiction of the receiving state."

Article 39 provides:

> "1. Every person entitled to privileges and immunities shall enjoy them from the moment he enters the territory of the receiving state on proceedings to take up his post or, if already in its territory, from the moment when his appointment is notified to the Ministry for Foreign Affairs or such other ministry as may be agreed.
>
> "2. When the functions of a person enjoying privileges and immunities have come to an end, such privileges and immunities shall normally cease at the moment when he leaves the country, or on expiry of a reasonable period in which to do so, but shall subsist until that time, even in case of armed conflict. However, with respect to acts performed by such a person in the exercise of his functions as a member of the mission, immunity shall continue to subsist."

One of the issues raised before your Lordships is whether section 20 of the State Immunity Act relates only to the functions carried out by a foreign head of state when he is present within the United Kingdom, or whether it also applies to his actions in his own state or in another country. Section 20 is a difficult section to construe, but I am of opinion that, with the necessary modifications, the section applies the provisions of the Diplomatic Privileges Act, and therefore the Articles of the Vienna Convention, to the actions of a head of state in his own country or elsewhere, so that, adopting the formulation of Lord Nicholls of Birkenhead in the earlier hearing [1998] 3 W.L.R. 1456, 1499E, with the addition of seven words, the effect of section 20 of the Act of 1978, section 2 of the Diplomatic Privileges Act and of the Articles of the Vienna Convention is that:

> "a former head of state shall continue to enjoy immunity from the criminal jurisdiction of the United Kingdom with respect to acts performed by him, whether in his own country or elsewhere, in the exercise of his functions as a head of state."

I consider, however, that section 20 did not change the law in relation to the immunity from criminal jurisdiction to which a former head of state was entitled in the United Kingdom but gave statutory form to the relevant principle of international law which was part of the common law.

Therefore the crucial question for decision is whether, if committed, the acts of torture (in which term I include acts of torture and conspiracy to commit torture) alleged against Senator Pinochet were carried out by him in the performance of his functions as head of state. I say "if committed" because it is not the function of your Lordships in this appeal to decide whether there is evidence to substantiate the allegations and Senator Pinochet denies them. Your Lordships had the advantage of very learned and detailed submissions from counsel for the parties and the interveners and from the amicus curiae (to which submissions I would wish to pay tribute) and numerous authorities from many jurisdictions were cited.

It is clear that the acts of torture which Senator Pinochet is alleged to have committed were not acts carried out in his private capacity for his personal gratification. If that had been the case they would have been private acts and it is not disputed that Senator Pinochet, once he had ceased to be head of state, would not be entitled to claim immunity in respect of them. It was submitted on his behalf that the acts of torture were carried out for the purposes of protecting the state and advancing its interests, as Senator Pinochet saw them, and were therefore governmental functions and were accordingly performed as functions of the head of state. It was further submitted that the immunity which Senator Pinochet claimed was the immunity of the state of Chile itself. In the present proceedings Chile intervened on behalf of Senator Pinochet and in paragraph 10 of its written case Chile submitted:

" . . . the immunity of a head of state (or former head of state) is an aspect of state immunity . . . Immunity of a head of state in his public capacity is equated with state immunity in international law . . . Actions against representatives of a foreign government in respect of their governmental or official acts are in substance proceedings against the state which they represent, and the immunity is for the benefit of the state."

Moreover, it was submitted that a number of authorities established that the immunity which a state is entitled to claim in respect of the acts of its former head of state or other public officials applies to acts which are unlawful and criminal.

My Lords, in considering the authorities it is necessary to have regard to a number of matters. First, it is a principle of international law that a state may not be sued in the courts of another state without its consent (although this principle is now subject to exceptions—the exceptions in the law of the United Kingdom being set out in the State Immunity Act 1978). Halsbury's Laws of England 4th ed. published in 1977 vol. 18 para 1548 stated:

"An independent sovereign state may not be sued in the English courts against its will and without its consent. This immunity from the jurisdiction is derived from the rules of international law, which in this respect have become part of the law of England. It is accorded upon the grounds that the exercise of jurisdiction would be incompatible with the dignity and independence of any superior authority enjoyed by every sovereign state. The principle involved is not founded upon any technical rules of law, but upon broad considerations of public policy, international law and comity."

Secondly, many of the authorities cited by counsel were cases where an action in tort for damages was brought against a state. Thirdly, a state is responsible for the actions of its officials carried out in the ostensible performance of their official functions notwithstanding that the acts are performed in excess of their proper functions. Oppenheim's International Law, 9th ed., states at page 545:

"In addition to the international responsibility which a state clearly bears for the official and authorised acts of its administrative officials and members of its armed forces, a state also bears responsibility for internationally injurious acts committed by such persons in the ostensible exercise of their official functions but without that state's command or authorisation, or in excess of their competence according to the internal law of the state, or in mistaken, ill-judged or reckless execution of their official duties. A state's administrative officials and members of its armed forces are under its disciplinary control, and all acts of such persons in the apparent exercise of their official functions or invoking powers appropriate to their official character are prima facie attributable to the state. It is not always easy in practice to draw a clear distinction between unauthorised acts of officials and acts committed by them in their private capacity and for which the state is not directly responsible. With regard to members of armed forces the state will usually be held responsible for their acts if they have been committed in the line of duty, or in the presence of and under the orders of an official superior."

Fourthly, in respect of the jurisdiction of the courts of the United Kingdom, foreign states are now expressly given immunity in civil proceedings (subject to certain express exceptions) by statute. Part I of the State Immunity Act 1978 relating to civil proceedings provides in section 1(1):

"A state is immune from the jurisdiction of the courts of the United Kingdom except as provided in the following provisions of this part of this Act."

But Part I of the Act has no application to criminal jurisdiction and section 16(4) in Part I provides:

"This Part of this Act does not apply to criminal proceedings."

In the United States of America section 1604 of the Foreign Sovereign Immunities Act 1976 provides:

"Subject to existing international agreements to which the United States is a party at the time of enactment of this Act a foreign state shall be immune from the jurisdiction of the courts of the United States and of the states except as provided in sections 1605 to 1607 of this chapter."

Counsel for Senator Pinochet and for Chile relied on the decision of the Court of Appeal in Al-Adsani v. Government of Kuwait (1996) 107 I.L.R. 536 where the plaintiff brought an action for damages in tort against the government of Kuwait claiming that he had been tortured in Kuwait by officials of that government. The Court of Appeal upheld a claim by the government of Kuwait that it was entitled to immunity. Counsel for the plaintiff submitted that the rule of international law prohibiting torture is so fundamental that it is jus cogens which overrides all other principles of international law, including the principle of sovereign immunity. This submission was rejected by the Court of Appeal on the ground that immunity was given by section 1 of the State Immunity Act 1978 and that the immunity was not subject to an overriding qualification in respect of torture or other acts contrary to international law which did not fall within one of the express exceptions contained in the succeeding sections of the Act. Ward L.J. stated at p. 549:

"Unfortunately, the Act is as plain as plain can be. A foreign state enjoys no immunity for acts causing personal injury committed in the United Kingdom and if that is expressly provided for the conclusion is impossible to escape that state immunity is afforded in respect of acts of torture committed outside this jurisdiction."

A similar decision was given by the United States Court of Appeals, Ninth Circuit, in Siderman de Blake v. Republic of Argentina (1992) 965 F.2d 699 where an Argentine family brought an action for damages in tort against Argentina and one of its provinces for acts of torture by military officials. Argentina claimed that it was entitled to immunity under the Foreign Sovereign Immunities Act and the Court of Appeals, with reluctance, upheld this claim. The argument advanced on behalf of the plaintiffs was similar to that advanced in the Al-Adsani case, but the court ruled that it was obliged to reject it because of the express provisions of the Foreign Sovereign Immunities Act, stating at p. 718:

"The Sidermans argue that since sovereign immunity itself is a principle of international law, it is trumped by jus cogens. In short, they argue that when a state violates jus cogens, the cloak of immunity provided by international law falls away, leaving the state amenable to suit.

"As a matter of international law, the Sidermans' argument carries much force.

. . .

"Unfortunately, we do not write on a clean slate. We deal not only with customary international law, but with an affirmative Act of Congress, the FSIA. We must interpret the FSIA through the prism of Amerada Hess. Nothing in the text or legislative history of the FSIA explicitly addresses the effect violations of jus cogens might have on the FSIA's cloak of immunity. Argentina contends that the Supreme Court's statement in Amerada Hess that the FSIA grants immunity 'in those cases involving alleged violations of international law that do not come within one of the FSIA's exceptions', 488 U.S. at 436, 109 S.Ct. at 688, precludes the Sidermans' reliance on jus cogens in this case. Clearly, the FSIA does not specifically provide for an exception to sovereign immunity based on jus cogens. In Amerada Hess, the court had no occasion to consider acts of torture or other violations of the peremptory norms of international law, and such violations admittedly differ in kind from transgressions of jus dispositivum, the norms derived from international agreements or customary international law with which the Amerada Hess court dealt. However, the court was so emphatic in its pronouncement 'that immunity is granted in those cases involving alleged violations of international law that do not come within one of the FSIA's exceptions,' Amerada Hess, 488 U.S. at 436, 109 S. Ct. at 688, and so specific in its formulation and method of approach, id. at 439, 109 S.Ct. at 690 ('Having determined that the FSIA provides the sole basis for obtaining jurisdiction over a foreign state in federal court, we turn to whether any of the exceptions enumerated in the Act apply here'), we conclude that if violations of jus cogens committed outside the United States are to be exceptions to immunity, Congress must make them so. The fact that there has been a violation of jus cogens does not confer jurisdiction under the FSIA."

It has also been decided that where an action for damages in tort is brought against officials of a foreign state for actions carried out by them in ostensible exercise of their governmental functions, they can claim state immunity, notwithstanding that their actions were illegal. The state itself, if sued directly for damages in respect of their actions would be entitled to immunity and this immunity would be impaired if damages were awarded against the officials and then the state was obliged to indemnify them. In Jaffe v. Miller [1993] I.L.R. 446, government officials were sued in tort for laying false criminal charges and for conspiracy for kidnap, and it was held that they were entitled to claim immunity. Finlayson J.A., delivering the judgment of the Ontario Court of Appeal, stated at pp. 458–459:

> "I also agree with the reasoning on this issue put forward by counsel for the respondents. Counsel submitted that to confer immunity on a government department of a foreign state but to deny immunity to the functionaries, who in the course of their duties performed the acts, would render the State Immunity Act ineffective. To avoid having its action dismissed on the ground of state immunity, a plaintiff would have only to sue the functionaries who performed the acts. In the event that the plaintiff recovered judgment, the foreign state would have to respond to it by indemnifying its functionaries, thus, through this indirect route, losing the immunity conferred on it by the Act. Counsel submitted that when functionaries are acting within the scope of their official duties, as in the present case, they come within the definition of 'foreign state'."

In my opinion these authorities and similar authorities relating to claims for damages in tort against states and government officials do not support the claim of Senator Pinochet to immunity from criminal proceedings in the United Kingdom because the immunity given by Part I of the State Immunity Act 1978 does not apply to criminal proceedings.

Counsel for Senator Pinochet and for Chile further submitted that under the rules of international law courts recognise the immunity of a former head of state in respect of criminal acts committed by him in the purported exercise of governmental authority. In Marcos and Marcos v. Federal Department of Police (1989) 102 I.L.R. 198 the United States instituted criminal proceedings against Ferdinard Marcos, the former President of the Philippines, and his wife, who had been a Minister in the Philippine Government. They were accused of having abused their positions to acquire for themselves public funds and works of art. The United States authorities sought legal assistance from the Swiss authorities to obtain banking and other documents in order to clarify the nature of certain transactions which were the subject of investigation. Mr. Marcos and his wife claimed immunity as the former leaders of a foreign state. In its judgment the Swiss federal tribunal stated at p. 203:

> "The immunity in relation to their functions which the appellants enjoyed therefore subsisted for those criminal acts which were allegedly committed while they were still exercising their powers in the Republic of the Philippines. The proceedings brought against them before the United States

courts could therefore only be pursued pursuant to an express waiver by the State of the Philippines of the immunity which public international law grants them not as a personal advantage but for the benefit of the state over which they ruled."

The tribunal then held that the immunity could not be claimed by Mr. & Mrs Marcos in Switzerland because there had been an express waiver by the State of the Philippines. However I would observe that in that case Mr. and Mrs Marcos were not accused of violating a rule of international law which had achieved the status of jus cogens.

Counsel also relied on the decision of the Federal Constitutional Court of the Federal Republic of Germany In re Former Syrian Ambassador to the German Democratic Republic (unreported) 10 June 1997. In that case the former Syrian ambassador to the German Democratic Republic was alleged to have failed to prevent a terrorist group from removing a bag of explosives from the Syrian Embassy, and a few hours later the explosives were used in an attack which left one person dead and more than 20 persons seriously injured. Following German unification and the demise of the German Democratic Republic in 1990 a District Court in Berlin issued an arrest warrant against the former ambassador for complicity in murder and the causing of an explosion. The Provincial Court quashed the warrant but the Court of Appeal overruled the decision of the Provincial Court and restored the validity of the warrant, holding that "The complainant was held to have contributed to the attack by omission. He had done nothing to prevent the explosives stored at the embassy building from being removed." The former ambassador then lodged a constitutional complaint claiming that he was entitled to diplomatic immunity.

The Constitutional Court rejected the complaint and held that the obligation limited to the former German Democratic Republic to recognise the continuing immunity of the complainant, according to Article 39(2) of the Vienna Convention, was not transferred to the Federal Republic of Germany by the international law of state succession.

Counsel for Senator Pinochet and for Chile relied on the following passage in the judgment of the constitutional court:

"For the categorization as an official act, it is irrelevant whether the conduct is legal according to the legal order of the Federal Republic of Germany (see above B.II.2.a)bb)) and whether it fulfilled diplomatic functions in the sense of Article 3 of the VCDR (see also the position taken by the [Swiss] Federal Political Department on 12 May [82] 1961, Schweizerisches Jahrbuch für internationles Recht (SJIR) 21 [1964] p. 171; however, a different position was taken by the Federal Political Department on 31 January 1979, reproduced in SJIR 36 (1980), p. 210 at 211 f.). The commission of criminal acts does not simply concern the functions of the mission. If a criminal act was never considered as official, there would be no substance to continuing immunity.

"In addition, there is no relevant customary international law exception from diplomatic immunity here (see Preamble to the VCDR, 5th paragraph) . . .

"Diplomatic immunity from criminal prosecution basically knows no exception for particularly serious violations of law. The diplomat can in such situations only be declared persona non grata."

However, two further parts of the judgment are to be noted. First, it appears that the explosives were left in the embassy when the ambassador was absent, and his involvement began after the explosives had been left in the embassy. The report states:

"The investigation conducted by the Public Prosecutor's Office concluded that the bombing attack was planned and carried out by a terrorist group. The complainant's sending state had, in a telegram, instructed its embassy in East Berlin to provide every possible assistance to the group. In the middle of August 1983 a member of the terrorist group appeared in the embassy while the

260   *The Pinochet Case: A Legal and Constitutional Analysis*

complainant was absent and requested permission from the then third secretary to deposit a bag in the embassy. In view of the telegram, which was known to him, the third secretary granted that permission.

"Later, the member of the terrorist group returned to the embassy and asked the third secretary to transport the bag to West Berlin for him in an embassy car. At the same time, he revealed that there were explosives in the bag. The third secretary informed the complainant of the request. The complainant first ordered the third secretary to bring him the telegram, in order to read through the text carefully once again, and then decided that the third secretary could refuse to provide the transportation. After the third secretary had returned and informed the terrorist of this, the terrorist took the bag, left the embassy and conveyed the explosive in an unknown manner towards West Berlin."

It appears that these facts were taken into account by the constitutional court when it stated:

"The complainant acted in the exercise of his official functions as a member of the mission, within the meaning of Article 39(2)(2) of the VCDR, because he is charged with an omission that lay within the sphere of his responsibility as ambassador, and which is to that extent attributable to the sending state.

"The complainant was charged with having done nothing to prevent the return of the explosive. The Court of Appeal derived the relevant obligation of conduct out of the official responsibility of the complainant, as leader of the mission, for objects left in the embassy. After the explosive was left in the embassy and therefore in the complainant's sphere of control and responsibility, he was obligated, within the framework of his official duties, to decide how the explosive would then be dealt with. The complainant made such a decision, apparently on the basis of the telegraphed instruction from his sending state, so that private interests are not discernible (on the classification of activities on the basis of instructions see the Bingham Case in McNair, International Law Opinions, Vol. 1, 1956, p. 196 at 197; Denza, Diplomatic Law, 1976, p. 249 f.; Salmon Manuel de Droit Diplomatique, 1994, p. 458 ff.). Instead, the complainant responded to the third secretary directly, in his position as the superior official, and, according to the view of the Court of Appeal, sought the best solution for the embassy."

In addition the constitutional court stated that the rules of diplomatic law constitute a self-contained regime and drew a distinction between the immunity of a diplomat and the immunity of a head of state or governmental official and stated:

"Article 7 of the Charter of the International Military Tribunal of Nuremberg (UNTS. Vol. 82, p. 279) [7] and following it Article 7(2) of the Statute of the International Criminal Tribunal for Yugoslavia (ILM 32 (1993), p. 1192), as well as Article 6(2) of the Statute for the International Criminal Tribunal for Rwanda (ILM 33 (1994), p. 1602) state that the official position of an accused, whether as a leader of a state or as a responsible official in a Government department, does not serve to free him from responsibility or mitigate punishment. Exemptions from immunity for cases of war criminals, violations of international law and offences against jus cogens under international law have been discussed as developments of this rule. . . .However, as the wording of Article 7 of the Charter of the International Military Tribunal of Nuremberg makes clear, these exceptions are relevant only to the applicable law of state organs that flows directly from it, in particular for members of the Government, and not to diplomatic immunity.

"State immunity and diplomatic immunity represent two different institutions of international law, each with their own rules, so that no inference can be drawn from any restrictions in one sphere as to possible effects in the other."

Therefore I consider that the passage in the judgment relied on by counsel does not give support to the argument that acts of torture, although criminal, can be regarded as functions of a head of state.

In 1946 the General Assembly of the United Nations affirmed: "The principles of international law recognised by the Charter of the Nuremberg Tribunal and the judgment of the Tribunal" and gave the following directive to its International Law Commission:

"This Committee on the codification of international law established by the resolution of the General Assembly of 11 December 1946, to treat as a matter of primary importance plans for the formulation, in the context of a general codification of offences against the peace and security of mankind, or of an international criminal code, of the principles recognised in the Charter of the Nuremberg Tribunal and in the judgment of the Tribunal."

Pursuant to this directive the 1950 Report of the International Law Commission to the General Assembly set out the following principle followed by the commentary contained in paragraph 103:

"The fact that a person who committed an act which constitutes a crime under international law acted as head of state or responsible Government official does not relieve him from responsibility under international law.

"103. This principle is based on article 7 of the Charter of the Nürnberg Tribunal. According to the Charter and the judgment, the fact that an individual acted as head of state or responsible government official did not relieve him from international responsibility. 'The principle of international law which, under certain circumstances, protects the representatives of a state',said the Tribunal, 'cannot be applied to acts which are condemned as criminal by international law. The authors of these acts cannot shelter themselves behind their official position in order to be freed from punishment. . . .' The same idea was also expressed in the following passage of the findings: 'He who violates the laws of war cannot obtain immunity while acting in pursuance of the authority of the state if the state in authorising action moves outside its competence under international law."

The 1954 International Law Commission draft code of offences against the peace and security of mankind provided in Article III:

"The fact that a person acted as head of state or as responsible Government official does not relieve him of responsibility for committing any of the offences defined in the code."

The Statute of the International Tribunal for the former Yugoslavia established by the Security Council of the United Nations in 1993 for the prosecution of persons responsible for serious violations of international humanitarian law committed in the territory of the former Yugoslavia since 1991 provided in Article 7 paragraph 2:

"The official position of any accused person, whether as head of state or Government or as a responsible Government official, shall not relieve such person of criminal responsibility nor mitigate punishment."

The Statute of the International Tribunal for Rwanda established by the Security Council of the United Nations in 1994 for the prosecution of persons responsible for genocide and other serious violations of international humanitarian law committed in the territory of Rwanda in 1994 provided in Article 6 paragraph 2:

"The official position of any accused person, whether as head of state or Government or as a responsible Government official shall not relieve such person of criminal responsibility nor mitigate punishment."

The 1996 draft code of the International Law Commission of Crimes against the Peace and Security of Mankind provided in Article 7:

"The official position of an individual who commits a crime against the peace and security of mankind, even if he acted as head of state of Government, does not relieve him of criminal responsibility or mitigate punishment."

In July 1998 in Rome the United Nations Diplomatic Conference of Plenipotentiaries on the Establishment of an International Criminal Court adopted the Statute of the International Criminal Court. The Preamble to the Statute states (inter alia):

"Mindful that during this century millions of children, women and men have been victims of unimaginable atrocities that deeply shock the conscience of humanity,

"Recognizing that such grave crimes threaten the peace, security and well-being of the world,

"Affirming that the most serious crimes of concern to the international community as a whole must not go unpunished and that their effective prosecution must be ensured by taking measures at the national level and by enhancing international cooperation,

"Determined to put an end to impunity for the perpetrators of these crimes and thus to contribute to the prevention of such crimes,

"Determined to these ends and for the sake of present and future generations, to establish an independent permanent International Criminal Court in relationship with the United Nations system, with jurisdiction over the most serious crimes of concern to the international community as a whole.

"Emphasising that the International Criminal Court established under this Statute shall be complementary to national criminal jurisdictions.

"Resolved to guarantee lasting respect for the enforcement of international justice,

"Have agreed as follows:"

Article 5 of the Statute provides that jurisdiction of the court shall be limited to the most serious crimes of concern to the international community as a whole which include crimes against humanity. Article 7 states that "crime against humanity" means a number of acts including murder and torture when committed as part of a widespread or systematic attack directed against any civilian population, with knowledge of the attack.

Article 27 provides:

"1. This Statute shall apply equally to all persons without any distinction based on official capacity. In particular, official capacity as a head of state or Government, a member of a Government or parliament, an elected representative or a government official shall in no case exempt a person from criminal responsibility under this Statute, nor shall it, in and of itself, constitute a ground for reduction of sentence.

"2. Immunities or special procedural rules which may attach to the official capacity of a person, whether under national or international law, shall not bar the court from exercising its jurisdiction over such a person."

Therefore since the end of the second world war there has been a clear recognition by the international community that certain crimes are so grave and so inhuman that they constitute crimes against international law and that the international community is under a duty to bring to justice a person who commits such crimes. Torture has been recognised as such a crime. The preamble to the Convention against Torture and Other Cruel, Inhuman or Degrading Treatment or Punishment 1984 ("the Torture Convention), which has been signed by the United Kingdom, Spain and Chile and by over one hundred other nations, states:

"Considering that, in accordance with the principles proclaimed in the Charter of the United Nations, recognition of the equal and inalienable rights of all members of the human family is the foundation of freedom, justice and peace in the world,

"Recognizing that those rights derive from the inherent dignity of the human person,

"Considering the obligation of states under the Charter, in particular Article 55, to promote universal respect for, and observance of, human rights and fundamental freedoms,

"Having regard to article 5 of the Universal Declaration of Human Rights and article 7 of the International Covenant on Civil and Political Rights, both of which provide that no one shall be subjected to torture or to cruel, inhuman or degrading treatment or punishment,

"Having regard also to the Declaration on Protection of All Persons from Being Subjected to Torture and Other Cruel, Inhuman or Degrading Treatment or Punishment adopted by the General Assembly on 9 December 1975

"Desiring to make more effective the struggle against torture and other cruel, inhuman or degrading treatment or punishment throughout the world,

"Have agreed as follows:"

Article 1 defines "torture" as any act by which severe pain or suffering, whether physical or mental, is intentionally inflicted on a person for purposes specified in the Article such as punishment or intimidation or obtaining information or a confession, and such pain and suffering is inflicted "by or at the instigation of or with the consent or acquiescence of a public official or other person acting in an official capacity."

The Convention then contains a number of Articles designed to make the measures against public officials who commit acts of torture more effective. In their handbook on the Convention, Burgers and Danelius stated at p. 1:

"It is expedient to redress at the outset a widespread misunderstanding as to the objective of the Convention against Torture and other Cruel, Inhuman or Degrading Treatment or Punishment, adopted by the General Assembly of the United Nations in 1984. Many people assume that the Convention's principal aim is to outlaw torture and other cruel, inhuman or degrading treatment or punishment. This assumption is not correct insofar as it would imply that the prohibition of these practices is established under international law by the Convention only and that this prohibition will be binding as a rule of international law only for those states which have become parties to the Convention. On the contrary, the Convention is based upon the recognition that the above-mentioned practices are already outlawed under international law. The principal aim of the Convention is to strengthen the existing prohibition of such practices by a number of supportive measures."

As your Lordships hold that there is no jurisdiction to extradite Senator Pinochet for acts of torture prior to 29 September 1988, which was the date on which section 134 of the Criminal Justice Act 1988 came into operation, it is unnecessary to decide when torture became a crime against international law prior to that date, but I am of opinion that acts of torture were clearly crimes against international law and that the prohibition of torture had required the status of ius cogens by that date.

The appellants accepted that in English courts a serving head of state is entitled (ratione personae) to immunity in respect of acts of torture which he has committed. Burgers and Danelius, referring to the obligation of a state party to the convention to establish its jurisdiction over offences of torture, recognise that some special immunities may exist in respect of acts of torture and state at p. 131:

"under international or national law, there may be certain limited exceptions to this rule, e.g. in relation to foreign diplomats, foreign troops, parliament members or other categories benefiting from special immunities, and such immunities may be accepted insofar as they apply to criminal acts in general and are not unduly extensive."

It is also relevant to note that article 98 of the Rome Statute establishing the International Criminal Court provides:

"The court may not proceed with a request for surrender or assistance which would require the requested state to act inconsistently with its obligations under international law with respect to the state or diplomatic immunity of a person or property of a third state, unless the court can first obtain the cooperation of that third state for the waiver of the immunity."

But the issue in the present case is whether Senator Pinochet, as a former head of state, can claim immunity (ratione materiae) on the grounds that acts of torture committed by him when he was head of state were done by him in exercise of his functions as head of state. In my opinion he is not entitled to claim such immunity. The Torture Convention makes it clear that no state is to tolerate torture by its public officials or by persons acting in an official capacity and Article 2 requires that:

"1. Each state party shall take effective legislative, administrative, judicial or other measures to prevent acts of torture in any territory under its jurisdiction."

Article 2 further provides that:

"2. No exceptional circumstances whatsoever, whether a state of war or a threat of war, internal political instability or any other public emergency, may be invoked as a justification of torture."

Article 4 provides:

"1. Each state party shall ensure that all acts of torture are offences under its criminal law. The same shall apply to an attempt to commit torture and to an act by any person which constitutes complicity or participation in torture."
"2. Each state party shall make these offences punishable by appropriate penalties which take into account their grave nature."

Article 7 provides:

"1. The state party in the territory under whose jurisdiction a person alleged to have committed any offence referred to in article 4 is found, shall in the cases contemplated in article 5, if it does not extradite him, submit the case to its competent authorities for the purpose of prosecution."

I do not accept the argument advanced by counsel on behalf of Senator Pinochet that the provisions of the Convention were designed to give one state jurisdiction to prosecute a public official of another state in the event of that state deciding to waive state immunity. I consider that the clear intent of the provisions is that an official of one state who has committed torture should be prosecuted if he is present in another state.

Therefore having regard to the provisions of the Torture Convention, I do not consider that Senator Pinochet or Chile can claim that the commission of acts of torture after 29 September 1988 were functions of the head of state. The alleged acts of torture by Senator Pinochet were carried out under colour of his position as head of state, but they cannot be regarded as functions of a head of state under international law when international law expressly prohibits torture as a measure which a state can employ in any circumstances whatsoever and has made it an international crime. It is relevant to observe that in 1996 the military government of Chile informed a United Nations working group on human rights violations in Chile that torture was unconditionally prohibited in Chile, that the Constitutional prohibition against torture was fully enforced and that:

"It is therefore apparent that the practice of inflicting unlawful ill-treatment has not been instituted in our country as is implied by the resolution [a UN resolution critical of Chile] and that such ill-treatment is not tolerated; on the contrary, a serious, comprehensive and coherent body of provisions exist to prevent the occurrence of such ill-treatment and to punish those responsible for any type of abuse."

It is also relevant to note that in his opening oral submissions on behalf of Chile Dr. Lawrence Collins Q.C. stated:

"the Government of Chile, several of whose present members were in prison or exile during those years, deplores the fact that the governmental authorities of the period of the dictatorship committed major violations of human rights in Chile. It reaffirms its commitment to human rights, including the prohibition of torture."

In its written submissions (which were repeated by Dr. Collins in his oral submissions) Chile stated:

"The Republic intervenes to assert its own interest and right to have these matters dealt with in Chile. The purpose of the intervention is not to defend the actions of Senator Pinochet whilst he was head of state. Nor is the purpose to prevent him from being investigated and tried for any crime he is alleged to have committed whilst in office, provided that any investigation and trial takes place in the only appropriate courts, namely those of Chile. The democratically elected Government of the Republic of Chile upholds the commitment of the Republic under international conventions to the maintenance and promotion of human rights. The position of the Chilean Government on state immunity is not intended as a personal shield for Senator Pinochet, but is intended to defend Chilean national sovereignty, in accordance with generally accepted principles of international law. Its plea, therefore, does not absolve Senator Pinochet from responsibility in Chile if the acts alleged against him are proved."

My Lords, the position taken by the democratically elected Government of Chile that it desires to defend Chilean national sovereignty and considers that any investigation and trial of Senator Pinochet should take place in Chile is understandable. But in my opinion that is not the issue which is before your Lordships; the issue is whether the commission of acts of torture taking place after 29 September 1988 was a function of the head of state of Chile under international law. For the reasons which I have given I consider that it was not.

Article 32(2) of the Vienna Convention set out in Schedule 1 to the Diplomatic Privileges Act 1964 provides that: "waiver must always be express." I consider, with respect, that the conclusion that after 29 September 1988 the commission of acts of torture was not under international law a function of the head of state of Chile does not involve the view that Chile is to be taken as having impliedly waived the immunity of a former head of state. In my opinion there has been no waiver of the immunity of a former head of state in respect of his functions as head of state. My conclusion that Senator Pinochet is not entitled to immunity is based on the view that the commission of acts of torture is not a function of a head of state, and therefore in this case the immunity to which Senator Pinochet is entitled as a former head of state does not arise in relation to, and does not attach to, acts of torture.

A number of international instruments define a crime against humanity as one which is committed on a large scale. Article 18 of the Draft Code of Crimes against the Peace and Security of Mankind 1996 provides:

"A crime against humanity means any of the following acts, when committed in a systematic manner on a large scale or instigated or directed by a Government or any organisation or a group:
(a) Murder;
(b) Extermination;
(c) Torture . . ."

And article 7 of the 1998 Rome Statute of the International Criminal Court provides:

> "For the purposes of this Statute, 'crime against humanity' means any of the following acts when committed as part of a wide spread or systematic attack directed against any civilian population, with knowledge of the attack:
> (a) Murder;
> (b) Extermination;
> . . .
> (f) Torture
> . . ."

However, article 4 of the Torture Convention provides that:

> "Each state party shall ensure that all acts of torture are offences under its criminal law." (emphasis added)

Therefore I consider that a single act of torture carried out or instigated by a public official or other person acting in a official capacity constitutes a crime against international law, and that torture does not become an international crime only when it is committed or instigated on a large scale. Accordingly I am of opinion that Senator Pinochet cannot claim that a single act of torture or a small number of acts of torture carried out by him did not constitute international crimes and did not constitute acts committed outside the ambit of his functions as head of state.

For the reasons given by Oppenheim at p. 545, which I have cited in an earlier part of this judgment, I consider that under international law Chile is responsible for acts of torture carried out by Senator Pinochet, but could claim state immunity if sued for damages for such acts in a court in the United Kingdom. Senator Pinochet could also claim immunity if sued in civil proceedings for damages under the principle stated in Jaffe v. Miller. But I am of opinion that there is no inconsistency between Chile and Senator Pinochet's entitlement to claim immunity if sued in civil proceedings for damages and Senator Pinochet's lack of entitlement to claim immunity in criminal proceedings for torture brought against him personally. This distinction between the responsibility of the state for the improper and unauthorised acts of a state official outside the scope of his functions and the individual responsibility of that official in criminal proceedings for an international crime is recognised in Article 4 and the commentary thereon in the 1996 draft Report of the International Law Commission:

> "Responsibility of States
>   The fact that the present Code provides for the responsibility of individuals for crimes against the peace and security of mankind is without prejudice to any question of the responsibility of states under international law.
> "Commentary
> (1) Although, as made clear by article 2, the present Code addresses matters relating to the responsibility of individuals for the crimes set out in Part II, it is possible, indeed likely, as pointed out in the commentary to article 2, that an individual may commit a crime against the peace and security of mankind as an 'agent of the State', 'on behalf of the State', 'in the name of the State' or even in a de facto relationship with the state, without being vested with any legal power.
> (2) The 'without prejudice' clause contained in article 4 indicates that the present Code is without prejudice to any question of the responsibility of a state under international law for a crime committed by one of its agents. As the commission already emphasised in the commentary to article 19 of the draft articles on state responsibility, the punishment of individuals who are organs of the state 'certainly does not exhaust the prosecution of the international responsibility incumbent upon the state for internationally wrongful acts which are attributed to it in such cases by

reason of the conduct of its organs'. The state may thus remain responsible and be unable to exonerate itself from responsibility by invoking the prosecution or punishment of the individuals who committed the crime."

Therefore for the reasons which I have given I am of opinion that Senator Pinochet is not entitled to claim immunity in the extradition proceedings in respect of conspiracy to torture and acts of torture alleged to have been committed by him after 29 September 1988 and to that extent I would allow the appeal. However I am in agreement with the view of Lord Browne-Wilkinson that the Secretary of State should reconsider his decision under section 7 of the Extradition Act 1989 in the light of the changed circumstances arising from your Lordships' decision.

LORD SAVILLE OF NEWDIGATE

My Lords,

In this case the Government of Spain seeks the extradition of Senator Pinochet (the former head of state of Chile) to stand trial in Spain for a number of alleged crimes. On this appeal two questions of law arise.

Senator Pinochet can only be extradited for what in the Extradition Act 1989 is called an extradition crime. Thus the first question of law is whether any of the crimes of which he stands accused in Spain is an extradition crime within the meaning of that Act.

As to this, I am in agreement with the reasoning and conclusions in the speech of my noble and learned friend Lord Browne-Wilkinson. I am also in agreement with the reasons given by my noble and learned friend Lord Hope of Craighead in his speech for concluding that only those few allegations that he identifies amount to extradition crimes.

These extradition crimes all relate to what Senator Pinochet is said to have done while he was head of state of Chile. The second question of law is whether, in respect of these extradition crimes, Senator Pinochet can resist the extradition proceedings brought against him on the grounds that he enjoys immunity from these proceedings.

In general, under customary international law serving heads of state enjoy immunity from criminal proceedings in other countries by virtue of holding that office. This form of immunity is known as immunity ratione personae. It covers all conduct of the head of state while the person concerned holds that office and thus draws no distinction between what the head of state does in his official capacity (i.e. what he does as head of state for state purposes) and what he does in his private capacity.

Former heads of state do not enjoy this form of immunity. However, in general under customary international law a former head of state does enjoy immunity from criminal proceedings in other countries in respect of what he did in his official capacity as head of state. This form of immunity is known as immunity ratione materiae.

These immunities belong not to the individual but to the state in question. They exist in order to protect the sovereignty of that state from interference by other states. They can, of course, be modified or removed by agreement between states or waived by the state in question.

In my judgment the effect of Section 20(1)(a) of the State Immunity Act 1978 is to give statutory force to these international law immunities.

The relevant allegations against Senator Pinochet concern not his private activities but what he is said to have done in his official capacity when he was head of state of Chile. It is accepted that the extradition proceedings against him are criminal proceedings. It follows that unless there exists, by agreement or otherwise, any relevant qualification or exception to the general rule of immunity ratione materiae, Senator Pinochet is immune from this extradition process.

The only possible relevant qualification or exception in the circumstances of this case relates to torture.

I am not persuaded that before the Torture Convention there was any such qualification or exception. Although the systematic or widespread use of torture became universally condemned as an international crime, it does not follow that a former head of state, who as head of state used torture for state purposes, could under international law be prosecuted for torture in other countries where previously under that law he would have enjoyed immunity ratione materiae.

The Torture Convention set up a scheme under which each state becoming a party was in effect obliged either to extradite alleged torturers found within its jurisdiction or to refer the case to its appropriate authorities for the purpose of prosecution. Thus as between the states who are parties to the Convention, there is now an agreement that each state party will establish and have this jurisdiction over alleged torturers from other state parties.

This country has established this jurisdiction through a combination of Section 134 of the Administration of Justice Act 1988 and the Extradition Act 1989. It ratified the Torture Convention on 8 December 1988. Chile's ratification of the Convention took effect on 30 October 1988 and that of Spain just over a year earlier.

It is important to bear in mind that the Convention applies (and only applies) to any act of torture "inflicted by or at the instigation of or with the consent or acquiescence of a public official or other person acting in an official capacity." It thus covers what can be described as official torture and must therefore include torture carried out for state purposes. The words used are wide enough to cover not only the public officials or persons acting in an official capacity who themselves inflict torture but also (where torture results) those who order others to torture or who conspire with others to torture.

To my mind it must follow in turn that a head of state, who for state purposes resorts to torture, would be a person acting in an official capacity within the meaning of this Convention. He would indeed to my mind be a prime example of an official torturer.

It does not follow from this that the immunity enjoyed by a serving head of state, which is entirely unrelated to whether or not he was acting in an official capacity, is thereby removed in cases of torture. In my view it is not, since immunity ratione personae attaches to the office and not to any particular conduct of the office holder.

On the other hand, the immunity of a former head of state does attach to his conduct whilst in office and is wholly related to what he did in his official capacity.

So far as the states that are parties to the Convention are concerned, I cannot see how, so far as torture is concerned, this immunity can exist consistently with the terms of that Convention. Each state party has agreed that the other state parties can exercise jurisdiction over alleged official torturers found within their territories, by extraditing them or referring them to their own appropriate authorities for prosecution; and thus to my mind can hardly simultaneously claim an immunity from extradition or prosecution that is necessarily based on the official nature of the alleged torture.

Since 8 December 1988 Chile, Spain and this country have all been parties to the Torture Convention. So far as these countries at least are concerned it seems to me that from that date these state parties are in agreement with each other that the immunity ratione materiae of their former heads of state cannot be claimed in cases of alleged official torture. In other words, so far as the allegations of official torture against Senator Pinochet are concerned, there is now by this agreement an exception or qualification to the general rule of immunity ratione materiae.

I do not reach this conclusion by implying terms into the Torture Convention, but simply by applying its express terms. A former head of state who it is alleged resorted to torture for state purposes falls in my view fairly and squarely within those terms and on the face of it should be dealt with in accordance with them. Indeed it seems to me that it is those who would seek to remove such alleged official torturers from the machinery of the Convention who in truth have to assert that by some process of implication or otherwise the clear words of the Convention should be treated as inapplicable to a former head of state, notwithstanding he is properly described as a person who was "acting in an official capacity".

I can see no valid basis for such an assertion. It is said that if it had been intended to remove immunity for alleged official torture from former heads of state there would inevitably have been some discussion of the point in the negotiations leading to the treaty. I am not persuaded that the apparent absence of any such discussions takes the matter any further. If there were states that wished to preserve such immunity in the face of universal condemnation of official torture, it is perhaps not surprising that they kept quiet about it.

It is also said that any waiver by states of immunities must be express, or at least unequivocal. I would not dissent from this as a general proposition, but it seems to me that the express and unequivocal terms of the Torture Convention fulfil any such requirement. To my mind these terms demonstrate that the states who have become parties have clearly and unambiguously agreed that official torture should now be dealt with in a way which would otherwise amount to an interference in their sovereignty.

For the same reasons it seems to me that the wider arguments based on Act of State or non-justiciability must also fail, since they are equally inconsistent with the terms of the Convention agreed by these state parties.

I would accordingly allow this appeal to the extent necessary to permit the extradition proceedings to continue in respect of the crimes of torture and (where it is alleged that torture resulted) of conspiracy to torture, allegedly committed by Senator Pinochet after 8 December 1988. I would add that I agree with what my noble and learned friend Lord Hope of Craighead has said at the end of his speech with regard to the need for the Secretary of State to reconsider his decision and (if renewed authority to proceed is given) the very careful attention the magistrate must pay to the information laid before him.

LORD MILLETT

My Lords,

I have had the advantage of reading in draft the speech of my noble and learned friend, Lord Browne-Wilkinson. Save in one respect, I agree with his reasoning and conclusions. Since the one respect in which I differ is of profound importance to the outcome of this appeal, I propose to set out my own process of reasoning at rather more length than I might otherwise have done.

State immunity is not a personal right. It is an attribute of the sovereignty of the state. The immunity which is in question in the present case, therefore, belongs to the Republic of Chile, not to Senator Pinochet. It may be asserted or waived by the state, but where it is waived by treaty or convention the waiver must be express. So much is not in dispute.

The doctrine of state immunity is the product of the classical theory of international law. This taught that states were the only actors on the international plane; the rights of individuals were not the subject of international law. States were sovereign and equal: it followed that one state could not be impleaded in the national courts of another; par in parem non habet imperium. States were obliged to abstain from interfering in the internal affairs of one another. International law was not concerned with the way in which a sovereign state treated its own nationals in its own territory. It is a cliche of modern international law that the classical theory no longer prevails in its unadulterated form. The idea that individuals who commit crimes recognised as such by international law may be held internationally accountable for their actions is now an accepted doctrine of international law. The adoption by most major jurisdictions of the restrictive theory of state immunity, enacted into English law by Part 1 of the State Immunity Act 1978, has made major inroads into the doctrine as a bar to the jurisdiction of national courts to entertain civil proceedings against foreign states. The question before your Lordships is whether a parallel, though in some respects opposite, development has taken place so as to restrict the availability of state immunity as a bar to the criminal jurisdiction of national courts.

Two overlapping immunities are recognised by international law; immunity ratione personae and immunity ratione materiae. They are quite different and have different rationales.

Immunity ratione personae is a status immunity. An individual who enjoys its protection does so because of his official status. It enures for his benefit only so long as he holds office. While he does so he enjoys absolute immunity from the civil and criminal jurisdiction of the national courts of foreign states. But it is only narrowly available. It is confined to serving heads of state and heads of diplomatic missions, their families and servants. It is not available to serving heads of government who are not also heads of state, military commanders and those in charge of the security forces, or their subordinates. It would have been available to Hitler but not to Mussolini or Tojo. It is reflected in English law by section 20(1) of the State Immunity Act 1978, enacting customary international law and the Vienna Convention on Diplomatic Relations (1961).

The immunity of a serving head of state is enjoyed by reason of his special status as the holder of his state's highest office. He is regarded as the personal embodiment of the state itself. It would be an affront to the dignity and sovereignty of the state which he personifies and a denial of the equality of sovereign states to subject him to the jurisdiction of the municipal courts of another state, whether in respect of his public acts or private affairs. His person is inviolable; he is not liable to be arrested or detained on any ground whatever. The head of a diplomatic mission represents his head of state and thus embodies the sending state in the territory of the receiving state. While he remains in office he is entitled to the same absolute immunity as his head of state in relation both to his public and private acts.

This immunity is not in issue in the present case. Senator Pinochet is not a serving head of state. If he were, he could not be extradited. It would be an intolerable affront to the Republic of Chile to arrest him or detain him.

Immunity ratione materiae is very different. This is a subject-matter immunity. It operates to prevent the official and governmental acts of one state from being called into question in proceedings before the courts of another, and only incidentally confers immunity on the individual. It is therefore a narrower immunity but it is more widely available. It is available to former heads of state and heads of diplomatic missions, and any one whose conduct in the exercise of the authority of the state is afterwards called into question, whether he acted as head of government, government minister, military commander or chief of police, or subordinate public official. The immunity is the same whatever the rank of the office-holder. This too is common ground. It is an immunity from the civil and criminal jurisdiction of foreign national courts but only in respect of governmental or official acts. The exercise of authority by the military and security forces of the state is the paradigm example of such conduct. The immunity finds its rationale in the equality of sovereign states and the doctrine of non-interference in the internal affairs of other states: see Duke of Brunswick v. King of Hanover (1848) 2 H.L.Cas. 1; Hatch v. Baez (1876) 7 Hun. 596 U.S.; Underhill v. Hernandez (1897) 168 U.S. 456. These hold that the courts of one state cannot sit in judgment on the sovereign acts of another. The immunity is sometimes also justified by the need to prevent the serving head of state or diplomat from being inhibited in the performance of his official duties by fear of the consequences after he has ceased to hold office. This last basis can hardly be prayed in aid to support the availability of the immunity in respect of criminal activities prohibited by international law.

Given its scope and rationale, it is closely similar to and may be indistinguishable from aspects of the Anglo-American Act of State doctrine. As I understand the difference between them, state immunity is a creature of international law and operates as a plea in bar to the jurisdiction of the national court, whereas the Act of State doctrine is a rule of domestic law which holds the national court incompetent to adjudicate upon the lawfulness of the sovereign acts of a foreign state.

Immunity ratione materiae is given statutory form in English law by the combined effect of section 20(1) of the State Immunity Act 1978 the Diplomatic Privileges Act 1964 and Article 39.2 of the Vienna Convention. The Act of 1978 is not without its difficulties. The former head of state is given the same immunity "subject to all necessary modifications" as a former diplomat, who continues to enjoy immunity in respect of acts committed by him "in the exercise of his functions." The functions of a diplomat are limited to diplomatic activities, ie. acts performed in his representative role in the receiving state. He has no broader immunity in respect of official or governmental acts not performed in exercise of his diplomatic functions: see Dinstein on Diplomatic Immunity from Jurisdiction Ratione Materiae (1966) 15 International and Comparative Law Quarterly 76 at 82. There is therefore a powerful argument for holding that, by a parity of reasoning, the statutory immunity conferred on a former head of state by the Act of 1978 is confined to acts performed in his capacity as head of state, ie. in his representative role. If so, the statutory immunity would not protect him in respect of official or governmental acts which are not distinctive of a head of state, but which he performed in some other official capacity, whether as head of government, commander-in-chief or party leader. It is, however, not necessary to decide whether this is the case, for any narrow statutory immunity is subsumed in the wider immunity in respect of other official or governmental acts under customary international law.

The charges brought against Senator Pinochet are concerned with his public and official acts, first as Commander-in-Chief of the Chilean army and later as head of state. He is accused of having embarked on a widespread and systematic reign of terror in order to obtain power and then to maintain it. If the allegations against him are true, he deliberately employed torture as an instrument of state policy. As international law stood on the eve of the Second World War, his conduct as head of state after he seized power would probably have attracted immunity ratione materiae. If so, I am of opinion that it would have been equally true of his conduct during the period before the coup was successful.

He was not then, of course, head of state. But he took advantage of his position as Commander-in-Chief of the army and made use of the existing military chain of command to deploy the armed forces of the state against its constitutional government. These were not private acts. They were official and governmental or sovereign acts by any standard.

The immunity is available whether the acts in question are illegal or unconstitutional or otherwise unauthorised under the internal law of the state, since the whole purpose of state immunity is to prevent the legality of such acts from being adjudicated upon in the municipal courts of a foreign state. A sovereign state has the exclusive right to determine what is and is not illegal or unconstitutional under its own domestic law. Even before the end of the Second World War, however, it was questionable whether the doctrine of state immunity accorded protection in respect of conduct which was prohibited by international law. As early as 1841, according to Quincy Wright (see (1947) 41 A.J.I.L at p. 71), many commentators held the view that:

> "the Government's authority could not confer immunity upon its agents for acts beyond its powers under international law."

Thus state immunity did not provide a defence to a crime against the rules of war: see Sir Hirsch Lauterpacht (1947) 63 L.Q.R. pp. 442–3. Writing in (1946) 59 Harvard Law Journal 396 before the Nuremberg Tribunal delivered its judgment and commenting on the seminal judgment of Chief Justice Marshall in Schooner Exchange v. McFaddon (1812) 11 U.S. (7 Cranch) 116, Sheldon Glueck observed at p. 426:

> "As Marshall implied, even in an age when the doctrine of sovereignty had a strong hold, the non-liability of agents of a state for 'acts of state' must rationally be based on the assumption that no member of the Family of Nations will order its agents to commit flagrant violations of international and criminal law."

Glueck added (at p. 427) that:

> "In modern times a state is—ex hypothesi—incapable of ordering or ratifying acts which are not only criminal according to generally accepted principles of domestic penal law but also contrary to that international law to which all states are perforce subject. Its agents, in performing such acts, are therefore acting outside their legitimate scope; and must, in consequence be held personally liable for their wrongful conduct."

It seems likely that Glueck was contemplating trial before municipal courts, for more than half a century was to pass before the establishment of a truly international criminal tribunal. This would also be consistent with the tenor of his argument that the concept of sovereignty was of relatively recent origin and had been mistakenly raised to what he described as the "status of some holy fetish."

Whether conduct contrary to the peremptory norms of international law attracted state immunity from the jurisdiction of national courts, however, was largely academic in 1946, since the criminal jurisdiction of such courts was generally restricted to offences committed within the territory of the forum state or elsewhere by the nationals of that state. In this connection it is important to appreciate that the International Military Tribunal (the Nuremberg Tribunal) which was established by the four Allied Powers at the conclusion of the Second World War to try the major war criminals was not, strictly speaking, an international court or tribunal. As Sir Hersch Lauterpacht explained in Oppenheim's International Law vol. II 7th ed. (1952) pp. 580–1, the Tribunal was:

"... the joint exercise by the four states which established the Tribunal, of a right which each of them was entitled to exercise separately on its own responsibility in accordance with international law."

In its judgment the Tribunal described the making of the Charter as an exercise of sovereign legislative power by the countries to which the German Reich had unconditionally surrendered, and of the undoubted right of those countries to legislate for the occupied territories which had been recognised by the whole civilised world.

Article 7 of the Charter of the Tribunal provided:

"The official position of defendants, whether as heads of state or responsible officials in government departments, shall not be considered as freeing them from responsibility or mitigating punishment." (my emphasis)

In its judgment the Tribunal ruled that:

"... the very essence of the Charter is that individuals have international duties which transcend the national obligations of obedience imposed by the individual state. He who violates the rules of war cannot obtain immunity while acting in pursuance of the authority of the state if the state in authorising action moves outside its competence under international law ... The principle of international law, which under certain circumstances protects the representatives of a state, cannot be applied to acts which are condemned as criminal by international law" (my emphasis).

The great majority of war criminals were tried in the territories where the crimes were committed. As in the case of the major war criminals tried at Nuremberg, they were generally (though not always) tried by national courts or by courts established by the occupying powers. The jurisdiction of these courts has never been questioned and could be said to be territorial. But everywhere the plea of state immunity was rejected in respect of atrocities committed in the furtherance of state policy in the course of the Second World War; and nowhere was this justified on the narrow (though available) ground that there is no immunity in respect of crimes committed in the territory of the forum state.

The principles of the Charter of the International Military Tribunal and the Judgment of the Tribunal were unanimously affirmed by Resolution 95 of the General Assembly of the United Nations in 1946. Thereafter it was no longer possible to deny that individuals could be held criminally responsibility for war crimes and crimes against peace and were not protected by state immunity from the jurisdiction of national courts. Moreover, while it was assumed that the trial would normally take place in the territory where the crimes were committed, it was not suggested that this was the only place where the trial could take place.

The Nuremberg Tribunal ruled that crimes against humanity fell within its jurisdiction only if they were committed in the execution of or in connection with war crimes or crimes against peace. But this appears to have been a jurisdictional restriction based on the language of the Charter. There is no reason to suppose that it was considered to be a substantive requirement of international law. The need to establish such a connection was natural in the immediate aftermath of the Second World War. As memory of the war receded, it was abandoned.

In 1946 the General Assembly had entrusted the formulation of the principles of international law recognised in the Charter of the Nuremberg Tribunal and the Judgment of the Tribunal to the International Law Commission. It reported in 1954. It rejected the principle that international criminal responsibility for crimes against humanity should be limited to crimes committed in connection with war crimes or crimes against peace. It was, however, necessary to distinguish international crimes from ordinary domestic offences. For this purpose, the Commission proposed that acts would constitute international crimes only if they were committed at the instigation or the toleration of state authorities. This is the distinction which was later adopted in the Convention against Torture (1984). In my judgment it is of critical importance in relation to the concept of immunity ratione materiae. The very official or governmental character of the acts which is necessary to found a claim to immunity ratione materiae, and which still operates as a bar to the civil jurisdiction of national courts, was now to be the essential element which made the acts an international crime. It was, no doubt, for this reason that the Commission's draft code provided that: "The fact that a person acted as head of state or as a responsible Government official does not relieve him of responsibility for committing any of the offences defined in the code."

The landmark decision of the Supreme Court of Israel in Attorney-General of Israel v. Eichmann (1962) 36 I.L.R. 5 is also of great significance. Eichmann had been a very senior official of the Third Reich. He was in charge of Department IV D-4 of the Reich Main Security Office, the Department charged with the implementation of the Final Solution, and subordinate only to Heydrich and Himmler. He was abducted from Argentina and brought to Israel, where he was tried in the District Court for Tel Aviv. His appeal against conviction was dismissed by the Supreme Court. The means by which he was brought to Israel to face trial has been criticised by academic writers, but Israel's right to assert jurisdiction over the offences has never been questioned.

The court dealt separately with the questions of jurisdiction and Act of State. Israel was not a belligerent in the Second World War, which ended three years before the state was founded. Nor were the offences committed within its territory. The District Court found support for its jurisdiction in the historic link between the State of Israel and the Jewish people. The Supreme Court preferred to concentrate on the international and universal character of the crimes of which the accused had been convicted, not least because some of them were directed against non-Jewish groups (Poles, Slovenes, Czechs and gipsies).

As a matter of domestic Israeli law, the jurisdiction of the court was derived from an Act of 1950. Following the English doctrine of Parliamentary supremacy, the court held that it was bound to give effect to a law of the Knesset even if it conflicted with the principles of international law. But it went on to hold that the law did not conflict with any principle of international law. Following a detailed examination of the authorities, including the judgment of the Permanent Court of International Justice in the Lotus case, 7 September 1927, it concluded that there was no rule of international law which prohibited a state from trying a foreign national for an act committed outside its borders. There seems no reason to doubt this conclusion. The limiting factor that prevents the exercise of extra-territorial criminal jurisdiction from amounting to an unwarranted interference with the internal affairs of another state is that, for the trial to be fully effective, the accused must be present in the forum state.

Significantly, however, the court also held that the scale and international character of the atrocities of which the accused had been convicted fully justified the application of the doctrine of universal jurisdiction. It approved the general consensus of jurists that war crimes attracted universal jurisdiction: see, for example, Greenspan's The Modern Law of Land Warfare (1959) where he writes at p. 420 that:

"Since each sovereign power stands in the position of a guardian of international law, and is equally interested in upholding it, any state has the legal right to try war crimes, even though the crimes have been committed against the nationals of another power and in a conflict to which that state is not a party."

This seems to have been an independent source of jurisdiction derived from customary international law, which formed part of the unwritten law of Israel, and which did not depend on the statute. The court explained that the limitation often imposed on the exercise of universal jurisdiction, that the state which apprehended the offender must first offer to extradite him to the state in which the offence was committed, was not intended to prevent the violation of the latter's territorial sovereignty. Its basis was purely practical. The great majority of the witnesses and the greater part of the evidence would normally be concentrated in that state, and it was therefore the most convenient forum for the trial.

Having disposed of the objections to its jurisdiction, the court rejected the defence of Act of State. As formulated, this did not differ in any material respect from a plea of immunity ratione materiae. It was based on the fact that in committing the offences of which he had been convicted the accused had acted as an organ of the state, "whether as head of the state or a responsible official acting on the government's orders." The court applied Article 7 of the Nuremberg Charter (which it will be remembered expressly referred to the head of state) and which it regarded as having become part of the law of nations.

The case is authority for three propositions:

(1) There is no rule of international law which prohibits a state from exercising extraterritorial criminal jurisdiction in respect of crimes committed by foreign nationals abroad.
(2) War crimes and atrocities of the scale and international character of the Holocaust are crimes of universal jurisdiction under customary international law.
(3) The fact that the accused committed the crimes in question in the course of his official duties as a responsible officer of the state and in the exercise of his authority as an organ of the state is no bar to the exercise of the jurisdiction of a national court.

The case was followed in the United States in Demjanjuk v. Petrovsky (1985) 603 F. Supp. 1468 aff'd. 776 F. 2d. 571. In the context of an extradition request by the State of Israel the court accepted Israel's right to try a person charged with murder in the concentration camps of Eastern Europe. It held that the crimes were crimes of universal jurisdiction, observing:

"International law provides that certain offences may be punished by any state because the offenders are enemies of all mankind and all nations have an equal interest in their apprehension and punishment."

The difficulty is to know precisely what is the ambit of the expression "certain offences".

Article 5 of the Universal Declaration of Human Rights of 1948 and Article 7 of the International Covenant on Civil and Political Rights of 1966 both provided that no one shall be subjected to torture or to cruel, inhuman or degrading treatment or punishment. A resolution of the General Assembly in 1973 proclaimed the need for international co-operation in the detection, arrest, extradition and punishment of persons guilty of war crimes and crimes against humanity. A further resolution of the General Assembly in 1975 proclaimed the desire to make the struggle against torture more effective throughout the world. The fundamental human rights of individuals, deriving from the inherent dignity of the human person, had become a commonplace of international law. Article 55 of the Charter of the United Nations was taken to impose an obligation on all states to promote universal respect for and observance of human rights and fundamental freedoms.

The trend was clear. War crimes had been replaced by crimes against humanity. The way in which a state treated its own citizens within its own borders had become a matter of legitimate concern to the international community. The most serious crimes against humanity were genocide and torture. Large scale and systematic use of torture and murder by state authorities for political ends had come to be regarded as an attack upon the international order. Genocide was made an international crime by the Genocide Convention in 1948. By the time Senator Pinochet seized power, the international community had renounced the use of torture as an instrument of state policy. The Republic of Chile accepts that by 1973 the use of torture by state authorities was prohibited by international law, and that the prohibition had the character of jus cogens or obligation erga omnes. But it insists that this does not confer universal jurisdiction or affect the immunity of a former head of state ratione materiae from the jurisdiction of foreign national courts.

In my opinion, crimes prohibited by international law attract universal jurisdiction under customary international law if two criteria are satisfied. First, they must be contrary to a peremptory norm of international law so as to infringe a jus cogens. Secondly, they must be so serious and on such a scale that they can justly be regarded as an attack on the international legal order. Isolated offences, even if committed by public officials, would not satisfy these criteria. The first criterion is well attested in the authorities and text books: for a recent example, see the judgment of the international tribunal for the territory of the former Yugoslavia in Prosecutor v. Anto Furundzija (unreported) given on 10 December 1998, where the court stated:

> "At the individual level, that is, of criminal liability, it would seem that one of the consequences of the jus cogens character bestowed by the international community upon the prohibition of torture is that every state is entitled to investigate, prosecute, and punish or extradite individuals accused of torture who are present in a territory under its jurisdiction."

The second requirement is implicit in the original restriction to war crimes and crimes against peace, the reasoning of the court in Eichmann, and the definitions used in the more recent Conventions establishing ad hoc international tribunals for the former Yugoslavia and Rwanda.

Every state has jurisdiction under customary international law to exercise extra-territorial jurisdiction in respect of international crimes which satisfy the relevant criteria. Whether its courts have extra-territorial jurisdiction under its internal domestic law depends, of course, on its constitutional arrangements and the relationship between customary international law and the jurisdiction of its criminal courts. The jurisdiction of the English criminal courts is usually statutory, but it is supplemented by the common law. Customary international law is part of the common law, and accordingly I consider that the English courts have and always have had extra-territorial criminal jurisdiction in respect of crimes of universal jurisdiction under customary international law.

In their handbook on the Convention against Torture (1984), Burgers and Danelius wrote at p. 1:

> "Many people assume that the Convention's principal aim is to outlaw torture and other cruel, inhuman or degrading treatment or punishment. This assumption is not correct insofar as it

would imply that the prohibition of these practices is established under international law by the Convention only and that the prohibition will be binding as a rule of international law only for those states which have become parties to the Convention. On the contrary, the Convention is based upon the recognition that the above-mentioned practices are already outlawed under international law. The principal aim of the Convention is to strengthen the existing prohibition of such practices by a number of supportive measures."

In my opinion, the systematic use of torture on a large scale and as an instrument of state policy had joined piracy, war crimes and crimes against peace as an international crime of universal jurisdiction well before 1984. I consider that it had done so by 1973. For my own part, therefore, I would hold that the courts of this country already possessed extra-territorial jurisdiction in respect of torture and conspiracy to torture on the scale of the charges in the present case and did not require the authority of statute to exercise it. I understand, however, that your Lordships take a different view, and consider that statutory authority is require before our courts can exercise extra-territorial criminal jurisdiction even in respect of crimes of universal jurisdiction. Such authority was conferred for the first time by section 134 of the Criminal Justice Act 1988, but the section was not retrospective. I shall accordingly proceed to consider the case on the footing that Senator Pinochet cannot be extradited for any acts of torture committed prior to the coming into force of the section.

The Convention against Torture (1984) did not create a new international crime. But it redefined it. Whereas the international community had condemned the widespread and systematic use of torture as an instrument of state policy, the Convention extended the offence to cover isolated and individual instances of torture provided that they were committed by a public official. I do not consider that offences of this kind were previously regarded as international crimes attracting universal jurisdiction. The charges against Senator Pinochet, however, are plainly of the requisite character. The Convention thus affirmed and extended an existing international crime and imposed obligations on the parties to the Convention to take measures to prevent it and to punish those guilty of it. As Burgers and Danielus explained, its main purpose was to introduce an institutional mechanism to enable this to be achieved. Whereas previously states were entitled to take jurisdiction in respect of the offence wherever it was committed, they were now placed under an obligation to do so. Any state party in whose territory a person alleged to have committed the offence was found was bound to offer to extradite him or to initiate proceedings to prosecute him. The obligation imposed by the Convention resulted in the passing of section 134 of the Criminal Justice Act 1988.

I agree, therefore, that our courts have statutory extra-territorial jurisdiction in respect of the charges of torture and conspiracy to torture committed after the section had come into force and (for the reasons explained by my noble and learned friend, Lord Hope of Craighead) the charges of conspiracty to murder where the conspiracy took place in Spain.

I turn finally to the plea of immunity ratione materiae in relation to the remaining allegations of torture, conspiracy to torture and conspiracy to murder. I can deal with the charges of conspiracy to murder quite shortly. The offences are alleged to have taken place in the requesting state. The plea of immunity ratione materiae is not available in respect of an offence committed in the forum state, whether this be England or Spain.

The definition of torture, both in the Convention and section 134, is in my opinion entirely inconsistent with the existence of a plea of immunity ratione materiae. The offence can be committed only by or at the instigation of or with the consent or acquiescence of a public official or other person acting in an official capacity. The official or governmental nature of the act, which forms the basis of the immunity, is an essential ingredient of the offence. No rational system of criminal justice can allow an immunity which is co-extensive with the offence.

In my view a serving head of state or diplomat could still claim immunity ratione personae if charged with an offence under section 134. He does not have to rely on the character of the conduct of which he is accused. The nature of the charge is irrelevant; his immunity is personal and absolute. But the former head of state and the former diplomat are in no different position from anyone else claiming to have acted in the exercise of state authority. If the respondent's arguments were accepted, section 134 would be a dead letter. Either the accused was acting in a private capacity, in which case he cannot be charged with an offence under the section; or he was acting in an official capacity, in which case he would enjoy immunity from prosecution. Perceiving this weakness in her argument, counsel for Senator Pinochet submitted that the United Kingdom took jurisdiction so that it would be available if, but only if, the offending state waived its immunity. I reject this explanation out of hand. It is not merely far-fetched; it is entirely inconsistent with the aims and object of the Convention. The evidence shows that other states were to be placed under an obligation to take action precisely because the offending state could not be relied upon to do so.

My Lords, the Republic of Chile was a party to the Torture Convention, and must be taken to have assented to the imposition of an obligation on foreign national courts to take and exercise criminal jurisdiction in respect of the official use of torture. I do not regard it as having thereby waived its immunity. In my opinion there was no immunity to be waived. The offence is one which could only be committed in circumstances which would normally give rise to the immunity. The international community had created an offence for which immunity ratione materiae could not possibly be available. International law cannot be supposed to have established a crime having the character of a jus cogens and at the same time to have provided an immunity which is co-extensive with the obligation it seeks to impose.

In my opinion, acts which attract state immunity in civil proceedings because they are characterised as acts of sovereign power may, for the very same reason, attract individual criminal liability. The respondents relied on a number of cases which show that acts committed in the exercise of sovereign power do not engage the civil liability of the state even if they are contrary to international law. I do not find those decisions determinative of the present issue or even relevant. In England and the United States they depend on the terms of domestic legislation; though I do not doubt that they correctly represent the position in international law. I see nothing illogical or contrary to public policy in denying the victims of state sponsored torture the right to sue the offending state in a foreign court while at the same time permitting (and indeed requiring) other states to convict and punish the individuals responsible if the offending state declines to take action. This was the very object of the Torture Convention. It is important to emphasise that Senator Pinochet is not alleged to be criminally liable because he was head of state when other responsible officials employed torture to maintain him in power. He is not alleged to be vicariously liable for the wrongdoing of his subordinates. He is alleged to have incurred direct criminal responsibility for his own acts in ordering and directing a campaign of terror involving the use of torture. Chile insists on the exclusive right to prosecute him. The Torture Convention, however, gives it only the primary right. If it does not seek his extradition (and it does not) then the United Kingdom is obliged to extradite him to another requesting state or prosecute him itself.

My Lords, we have come a long way from what I earlier described as the classical theory of international law—a long way in a relatively short time. But as the Privy Council pointed out in In re Piracy Jure Gentium [1934] A.C. 586 at p. 597, international law has not become a crystallised code at any time, but is a living and expanding branch of the law. Glueck observed (op.cit. at p. 398) that:

> "unless we are prepared to abandon every principle of growth for international law, we cannot deny that our own day has its right to institute customs."

In a footnote to this passage he added:

> "Much of the law of nations has its roots in custom. Custom must have a beginning; and customary usages of states in the matter of national and personal liability for resort to prohibited methods of warfare and to wholesale criminalism have not been petrified for all time."

The law has developed still further since 1984, and continues to develop in the same direction. Further international crimes have been created. Ad hoc international criminal tribunals have been established. A permanent international criminal court is in the process of being set up. These developments could not have been foreseen by Glueck and the other jurists who proclaimed that individuals could be held individually liable for international crimes. They envisaged prosecution before national courts, and this will necessarily remain the norm even after a permanent international tribunal is established. In future those who commit atrocities against civilian populations must expect to be called to account if fundamental human rights are to be properly protected. In this context, the exalted rank of the accused can afford no defence.

For my own part, I would allow the appeal in respect of the charges relating to the offences in Spain and to torture and conspiracy to torture wherever and whenever carried out. But the majority of your Lordships think otherwise, and consider that Senator Pinochet can be extradited only in respect of a very limited number of charges. This will transform the position from that which the Secretary of State considered last December. I agree with my noble and learned friend Lord Browne-Wilkinson that it will be incumbent on the Secretary of State to reconsider the matter in the light of the very different circumstances which now prevail.

LORD PHILLIPS OF WORTH MATRAVERS

My Lords,
The Spanish government seeks extradition of Senator Pinochet to stand trial for crimes committed in a course of conduct spanning a lengthy period. My noble and learned friend Lord Browne-Wilkinson has described how, before your Lordships' House, the Spanish Government contended for the first time that the relevant conduct extended back to 1 January 1972, and now covered a significant period before Senator Pinochet became head of state and thus before acts done in that capacity could result in any immunity. This change in the Spanish Government's case rendered critical issues that have hitherto barely been touched on. What is the precise nature of the double criminality rule that governs whether conduct amounts to an extradition crime and what parts of Senator Pinochet's alleged conduct satisfy that rule? On the first issue I agree with the conclusion reached by Lord Browne-Wilkinson and on the second I agree with the analysis of my noble and learned friend, Lord Hope of Craighead.

These conclusions greatly reduce the conduct that can properly form the subject of a request for extradition under our law. They leave untouched the question of whether the English court can assert any criminal jurisdiction over acts committed by Senator Pinochet in his capacity of head of state. It is on that issue, the issue of immunity, that I would wish to add some comments of my own.

State immunity

There is an issue as to whether the applicable law of immunity is to be found in the State Immunity Act 1978 or in principles of public international law, which form part of our common law. If the statute governs it must be interpreted, so far as possible, in a manner which accords with public international law. Accordingly I propose to start by considering the position at public international law.

The nature of the claim to immunity

These proceedings have arisen because Senator Pinochet chose to visit the United Kingdom. By so doing he became subject to the authority that this state enjoys over all within its territory. He has been arrested and is threatened with being removed against his will to Spain to answer criminal charges which are there pending. That has occurred pursuant to our extradition procedures. Both the executive and the court has a role to play in the extradition process. It is for the court to decide whether the legal requirements which are a precondition to extradition are satisfied. If they are, it is for the Home Secretary to decide whether to exercise his power to order that Senator Pinochet be extradited to Spain.

If Senator Pinochet were still the head of state of Chile, he and Chile would be in a position to complain that the entire extradition process was a violation of the duties owed under international law to a person of his status. A head of state on a visit to another country is inviolable. He cannot be arrested or detained, let alone removed against his will to another country, and he is not subject to the judicial processes, whether civil or criminal, of the courts of the state that he is visiting. But Senator Pinochet is no longer head of state of Chile. While as a matter of courtesy a state may accord a visitor of Senator Pinochet's distinction certain privileges, it is under no legal obligation to do so. He accepts, and Chile accepts, that this country no longer owes him any duty under international law by reason of his status ratione personae. Immunity is claimed, ratione materiae, on the ground that the subject matter of the extradition process is the conduct by Senator Pinochet of his official functions when he was head of state. The claim is put thus in his written case:

> "There is no distinction to be made between a head of state, a former head of state, a state official or a former state official in respect of official acts performed under colour of their office. Immunity will attach to all official acts which are imputable or attributable to the state. It is therefore the nature of the conduct and the capacity of the Respondent at the time of the conduct alleged, not the capacity of the Respondent at the time of any suit, that is relevant."

We are not, of course, here concerned with a civil suit but with proceedings that are criminal in nature. Principles of the law of immunity that apply in relation to civil litigation will not necessarily apply to a criminal prosecution. The nature of the process with which this appeal is concerned is not a prosecution but extradition. The critical issue that the court has to address in that process is, however, whether the conduct of Senator Pinochet which forms the subject of the extradition request constituted a crime or crimes under English law. The argument in relation to extradition has proceeded on the premise that the same principles apply that would apply if Senator Pinochet were being prosecuted in this country for the conduct in question. It seems to me that that is an appropriate premise on which to proceed.

Why is it said to be contrary to international law to prosecute someone who was once head of state, or a state official, in respect of acts committed in his official capacity? It is common ground that the basis of the immunity claimed is an obligation owed to Chile, not to Senator Pinochet. The immunity asserted is Chile's. Were these civil proceedings in which damages were claimed in respect of acts committed by Senator Pinochet in the government of Chile, Chile could argue that it was itself indirectly impleaded. That argument does not run where the proceedings are criminal and where the issue is Senator Pinochet's personal responsibility, not that of Chile. The following general principles are advanced in Chile's written case as supporting the immunity claimed:

> "(a) the sovereign equality of states and the maintenance of international relations require that the courts of one state will not adjudicate on the governmental acts of another state;
> (b) intervention in the internal affairs of other states is prohibited by international law;
> (c) conflict in international relations will be caused by such adjudication or intervention."

These principles are illustrated by the following passage from Hatch v. Baez (1876) 7 Hun. 596, 5 Am. Int. L. Cas. 434, a case in which the former President of the Dominican Republic was sued in New York for injuries allegedly sustained at his hands in San Domingo.

> "The counsel for the plaintiff relies on the general principle, that all persons, of whatever rank or condition, whether in or out of office, are liable to be sued by them in violation of law. Conceding the truth and universality of that principle, it does not establish the jurisdiction of our tribunals to take cognizance of the official acts of foreign governments. We think that, by the universal comity of nations and the established rules of international law, the courts of one country are bound to abstain from sitting in judgement on the acts of another government done within its own territory. Each state is sovereign throughout its domain. The acts of the defendant for which he is sued were done by him in the exercise of that part of the sovereignty of St. Domingo which belongs to the executive department of that government. To make him amenable to a foreign jurisdiction for such acts, would be a direct assault upon the sovereignty and independence of his country. The only remedy for such wrongs must be sought through the intervention of the government of the person injured.
> "The fact that the defendant has ceased to be president of St. Domingo does not destroy his immunity. That springs from the capacity in which the acts were done, and protects the individual who did them, because they emanated from a foreign and friendly government."

This statement was made in the context of civil proceedings. I propose to turn to the sources of international law to see whether they establish that those principles have given rise to a rule of immunity in relation to criminal proceedings.

The sources of immunity

Many rules of public international law are founded upon or reflected in Conventions. This is true of those rules of state immunity which relate to civil suit—see the European Convention on State Immunity 1972. It is not, however, true of state immunity in relation to criminal proceedings. The primary source of international law is custom, that is "a clear and continuous habit of doing certain actions which has grown up under the conviction that these actions are, according to international law, obligatory or right"—Oppenheim's International Law, 9th ed. p. 27. Other sources of international law are judicial decisions, the writing of authors and "the general principles of law recognised by all civilised nations"—see Article 38 of the Statute of the International Court of Justice. To what extent can the immunity asserted in this appeal be traced to such sources?

Custom

In what circumstances might a head of state or other state official commit a criminal offence under the law of a foreign state in the course of the performance of his official duties?

Prior to the developments in international law which have taken place in the last fifty years, the answer is very few. Had the events with which this appeal is concerned occurred in the 19th century, there could have been no question of Senator Pinochet being subjected to criminal proceedings in this country in respect of acts, however heinous, committed in Chile. This would not have been because he would have been entitled to immunity from process, but for a more fundamental reason. He would have committed no crime under the law of England and the courts of England would not have purported to exercise a criminal jurisdiction in respect of the conduct in Chile of any national of that state. I have no doubt that the same would have been true of the courts of Spain. Under international practice criminal law was territorial. This accorded with the fundamental principle of international law that one state must not intervene in the internal affairs of another. For one state to have legislated to make criminal acts committed within the territory of another state by the nationals of the latter would have infringed this principle. So it would to have exercised jurisdiction in respect of such acts. An official of one state could only commit a crime under the law of another state by going to that state and committing a criminal act there. It is certainly possible to envisage a diplomat committing a crime within the territory to which he was accredited, and even to envisage his doing so in the performance of his official functions—though this is less easy. Well established international law makes provision for the diplomat. The Vienna Convention on Diplomatic Relations 1961 provides for immunity from civil and criminal process while the diplomat is in post and, thereafter, in respect of conduct which he committed in the performance of his official functions while in post. Customary international law provided a head of state with immunity from any form of process while visiting a foreign state. It is possible to envisage a visiting head of state committing a criminal offence in the course of performing his official functions while on a visit and when clothed with status immunity. What seems inherently unlikely is that a foreign head of state should commit a criminal offence in the performance of his official functions while on a visit and subsequently return after ceasing to be head of state. Certainly this cannot have happened with sufficient frequency for any custom to have developed in relation to it. Nor am I aware of any custom which would have protected from criminal process a visiting official of a foreign state who was not a member of a special mission had he had the temerity to commit a criminal offence in the pursuance of some official function. For these reasons I do not believe that custom can provide any foundation for a rule that a former head of state is entitled to immunity from criminal process in respect of crimes committed in the exercise of his official functions.

Judicial decisions

In the light of the considerations to which I have just referred, it is not surprising that Senator Pinochet and the Republic of Chile have been unable to point to any body of judicial precedent which supports the proposition that a former head of state or other government official can establish immunity from criminal process on the ground that the crime was committed in the course of performing official functions. The best that counsel for Chile has been able to do is to draw attention to the following obiter opinion of the Swiss Federal Tribunal in Marcos and Marcos v. Federal Department of Police (1989) 102 I.L.R. 198 at pp. 202–3.

> "The privilege of the immunity from criminal jurisdiction of heads of state . . . has not been fully codified in the Vienna Convention [on Diplomatic Relations]. . . . But it cannot be concluded that the texts of conventions drafted under the aegis of the United Nations grant a lesser protection to heads of foreign states than to the diplomatic representatives of the state which those heads of state lead or universally represent. . . . Articles 32 and 39 of the Vienna Convention must therefore apply by analogy to heads of state."

Writings of authors

We have been referred to the writings of a number of learned authors in support of the immunity asserted on behalf of Senator Pinochet. Oppenheim comments at para. 456:

> "All privileges mentioned must be granted to a head of state only so long as he holds that position. Therefore, after he has been deposed or has abdicated, he may be sued, at least in respect of obligations of a private character entered into while head of state. For his official acts as head of state he will, like any other agent of a state, enjoy continuing immunity."

This comment plainly relates to civil proceedings.

Satow's Guide to Diplomatic Practice 5th Edition deals in Chapter 2 with the position of a visiting head of state. The authors deal largely with immunity from civil proceedings but state (at p. 10) that under customary international law "he is entitled to immunity—probably without exception—from criminal and civil jurisdiction". After a further passage dealing with civil proceedings, the authors state:

> "A head of state who has been deposed or replaced or has abdicated or resigned is of course no longer entitled to privileges or immunities as a head of state. He will be entitled to continuing immunity in regard to acts which he performed while head of state, provided that the acts were performed in his official capacity; in this his position is no different from that of any agent of the state."

Sir Arthur Watts in his monologue on The Legal Position in International Law of Heads of State, Heads of Government and Foreign Ministers, Recueil des cours, volume 247 (1994—III) deals with the loss of immunity of a head of state who is deposed on a foreign visit. He then adds at p. 89:

> "A head of state's official acts, performed in his public capacity as head of state, are however subject to different considerations. Such acts are acts of the state rather than the head of state's personal acts, and he cannot be sued for them even after he has ceased to be head of state. The position is similar to that of acts performed by an ambassador in the exercise of his functions, for which immunity continues to subsist even after the ambassador's appointment has come to an end."

My Lords, I do not find these writings, unsupported as they are by any reference to precedent or practice, a compelling foundation for the immunity in respect of criminal proceedings that is asserted.

General principles of law recognised by all civilised nations

The claim for immunity raised in this case is asserted in relation to a novel type of extraterritorial criminal jurisdiction. The nature of that jurisdiction I shall consider shortly. If immunity from that jurisdiction is to be established it seems to me that this can only be on the basis of applying the established general principles of international law relied upon by Chile to which I have already referred, rather than any specific rule of law relating to immunity from criminal process.

These principles underlie some of the rules of immunity that are clearly established in relation to civil proceedings. It is time to take a closer look at these rules, and at the status immunity that is enjoyed by a head of state ratione personae.

Immunity from civil suit of the State itself

It was originally an absolute rule that the court of one state would not entertain a civil suit brought against another state. All states are equal and this was said to explain why one state could not sit in judgment on another. This rule was not viable once states began to involve themselves in commerce on a large scale and state practice developed an alternative restrictive rule of state immunity under which immunity subsisted in respect of the public acts of the state but not for its commercial acts. A distinction was drawn between acts done jure imperii and acts done jure gestionis. This refinement of public international law was described by Lord Denning, M.R. in Trendtex Trading Corporation v. Central Bank of Nigeria [1977] 1 Q.B. 529. In that case the majority of the Court of Appeal held that the common law of England, of which international law forms part, had also changed to embrace the restrictive theory of state immunity from civil process. That change was about to be embodied in statute, the State Immunity Act 1978, which gave effect to the European Convention on State Immunity of 1972.

Part I of the Act starts by providing:

> "1. General immunity from jurisdiction
> (1) A state is immune from the jurisdiction of the courts of the United Kingdom except as provided in the following provisions of this Part of this Act."

Part I goes on to make provision for a number of exceptions from immunity, the most notable of which is, by Section 3, that in relation to a commercial transaction entered into by the state.

Part I does not apply to criminal proceedings—Section 16 (4).

The immunity of a head of state ratione personae

An acting head of state enjoyed by reason of his status absolute immunity from all legal process. This had its origin in the times when the head of state truly personified the state. It mirrored the absolute immunity from civil process in respect of civil proceedings and reflected the fact that an action against a head of state in respect of his public acts was, in effect, an action against the state itself. There were, however, other reasons for the immunity. It would have been contrary to the dignity of a head of state that he should be subjected to judicial process and this would have been likely to interfere with the exercise of his duties as a head of state. Accordingly the immunity applied to both criminal and civil proceedings and, insofar as civil proceedings were concerned, to transactions entered into by the head of state in his private as well as his public capacity.

When the immunity of the state in respect of civil proceedings was restricted to exclude commercial transactions, the immunity of the head of state in respect of transactions entered into on behalf of the state in his public capacity was similarly restricted, although the remainder of his immunity remained—see Sections 14 (1) (a) and 20 (5) of the Act of 1978.

Immunity ratione materiae

This is an immunity of the state which applies to preclude the courts of another state from asserting jurisdiction in relation to a suit brought against an official or other agent of the state, present or past, in relation to the conduct of the business of the state while in office. While a head of state is serving, his status ensures him immunity. Once he is out of office, he is in the same position as any other state official and any immunity will be based upon the nature of the subject matter of the litigation. We were referred to a number of examples of civil proceedings against a former head of state where the validity of a claim to immunity turned, in whole or in part, on whether the transaction in question was one in which the defendant had acted in a public or a private capacity: Ex King Farouk of Egypt v. Christian Dior, S.A.R.L. (1957) 24 I.L.R. 228; Soc. Jean Desses v. Prince Farouk (1963) 65 I.L.R. 37; Jiminez v. Aristeguieta 311 F. 2d. 547; U.S. v. Noriega (1997) 117 F. 3rd. 1206.

There would seem to be two explanations for immunity ratione materiae. The first is that to sue an individual in respect of the conduct of the state's business is, indirectly, to sue the state. The state would be obliged to meet any award of damage made against the individual. This reasoning has no application to criminal proceedings. The second explanation for the immunity is the principle that it is contrary to international law for one state to adjudicate upon the internal affairs of another state. Where a state or a state official is impleaded, this principle applies as part of the explanation for immunity. Where a state is not directly or indirectly impleaded in the litigation, so that no issue of state immunity as such arises, the English and American courts have nonetheless, as a matter of judicial restraint, held themselves not competent to entertain litigation that turns on the validity of the public acts of a foreign state, applying what has become known as the act of state doctrine. Two citations well illustrate the principle:

1. Underhill v. Hernandez (1897) 168 U.S. 456 at p. 457 (per Fuller C.J.):

    "Every sovereign state is bound to respect the independence of every other sovereign state, and the courts of one country will not sit in judgment on the acts of the government of another done within its own territory. Redress of grievances by reason of such acts must be obtained through the means open to be availed of by sovereign powers as between themselves . . . The immunity of individuals from suits brought in foreign tribunals for acts done within their own states, in the exercise of governmental authority, whether as civil officers or as military commanders, must necessarily extend to the agents of governments ruling by paramount force as matter of fact."

2. Buck v. Att. Gen. [1965] Ch. 475, 770, per Diplock L.J.:

    "As a member of the family of nations, the Government of the United Kingdom (of which this court forms part of the judicial branch) observes the rules of comity, videlicet, the accepted rules of mutual conduct as between state and state which each state adopts in relation to other states to adopt in relation to itself. One of those rules is that it does not purport to exercise jurisdiction over the internal affairs of any other independent state, or to apply measures of coercion to it or to its property, except in accordance with the rules of public international law. One of the commonest applications of this rule by the judicial branch of the United Kingdom Government is the well-known doctrine of sovereign immunity. A foreign state cannot be impleaded in the English courts without its consent: see Duff Development Co. v. Kelantan Government. As was made clear in Rahimtoola v. Nizam of Hyderabad, the application of the doctrine of sovereign immunity does not depend upon the persons between whom the issue is joined, but upon the subject-matter of the issue. For the English court to pronounce upon the validity of a law of a foreign sovereign state within its own territory so that the validity of that law became the res of the res judicata in the suit, would be to assert jurisdiction over the internal affairs of that state. That would be a breach of the rules of comity"

It is contended on behalf of the respondent that the question of whether an official is acting in a public capacity does not depend upon whether he is acting within the law of the state on whose behalf he purports to act, or even within the limits of international law. His conduct in an official capacity will, whether lawful or unlawful, be conduct of the state and the state will be entitled to assert immunity in respect of it. In the field of civil litigation these propositions are supported by authority. There are a number of instances where plaintiffs have impleaded states claiming damages for injuries inflicted by criminal conduct on the part of state officials which allegedly violated international law. In those proceedings it was of the essence of the plaintiffs' case that the allegedly criminal conduct was conduct of the state and this was not generally in issue. What was in issue was whether the criminality of the conduct deprived the state of immunity and on that issue the plaintiffs failed. Counsel for the Respondent provided us with an impressive, and depressing, list of such case:

Saltany v. Reagan (1988) 702 F. Supp. 319 (claims of assassination and terrorism); Siderman de Blake v. Republic of Argentine (1992) 965 F.2d 699 (claim of torture); Princz v. Federal Republic of Germany (1994) 26 F. 3d 1166 (D.C. Cir. 1994) (claim in respect of the holocaust); Al-Adsani v. Government of Kuwait (1996) 107 I.L.R. 536 (claim of torture); Sampson v. Federal Republic of Germany 975 F. Supp. 1108 (N.D. Ill. 1997) (claim in respect of the holocaust); Smith v. Libya, 886 F. Supp. 406 (EDNY, 1995) 101 F. 3d 239 (2d Cir. 1996) (claim in respect of Lockerbie bombing); Persinger v. Islamic Republic of Iran 729 F.2d 835, (D.C. Cir. 1984) (claim in relation to hostage taking at the U.S. Embassy).

It is to be observed that all but one of those cases involved decisions of courts exercising the federal jurisdiction of the United States, Al-Adsani v. Government of Kuwait being a decision of the Court of Appeal of this country. In each case immunity from civil suit was afforded by statute—in America, the Foreign Sovereign Immunities Act and, in England, the State Immunity Act 1978. In each case the court felt itself precluded by the clear words of the statute from acceding to the submission that state immunity would not protect against liability for conduct which infringed international law.

The vital issue

The submission advanced on behalf of the respondent in respect of the effect of public international law can, I believe, be summarised as follows:

1. One state will not entertain judicial proceedings against a former head of state or other state official of another state in relation to conduct performed in his official capacity.

2. This rule applies even if the conduct amounts to a crime against international law.
3. This rule applies in relation to both civil and criminal proceedings.

For the reasons that I have given and if one proceeds on the premise that Part I of the State Immunity Act correctly reflects current international law, I believe that the first two propositions are made out in relation to civil proceedings. The vital issue is the extent to which they apply to the exercise of criminal jurisdiction in relation to the conduct that forms the basis of the request for extradition. This issue requires consideration of the nature of that jurisdiction.

The development of international criminal law

In the latter part of this century there has been developing a recognition among states that some types of criminal conduct cannot be treated as a matter for the exclusive competence of the state in which they occur. In the 9th edition of Oppenheim, published in 1992, the authors commented at p. 998:

> "While no general rule of positive international law can as yet be asserted which gives to states the right to punish foreign nationals for crimes against humanity in the same way as they are, for instance, entitled to punish acts of piracy, there are clear indications pointing to the gradual evolution of a significant principle of international law to that effect. That principle consists both in the adoption of the rule of universality of jurisdiction and in the recognition of the supremacy of the law of humanity over the law of the sovereign state when enacted or applied in violation of elementary human rights in a manner which may justly be held to shock the conscience of mankind."

The appellants, and those who have on this appeal been given leave to support them, contend that this passage, which appears verbatim in earlier editions, is out of date. They contend that international law now recognises a category of criminal conduct with the following characteristics:

1) It is so serious as to be of concern to all nations and not just to the state in which it occurs.
2) Individuals guilty of it incur criminal responsibility under international law.
3) There is universal jurisdiction in respect of it. This means that international law recognises the right of any state to prosecute an offender for it, regardless of where the criminal conduct took place.
4) No state immunity attaches in respect of any such prosecution.

My Lords, this is an area where international law is on the move and the move has been effected by express consensus recorded in or reflected by a considerable number of international instruments. Since the Second World War states have recognised that not all criminal conduct can be left to be dealt with as a domestic matter by the laws and the courts of the territories in which such conduct occurs. There are some categories of crime of such gravity that they shock the consciousness of mankind and cannot be tolerated by the international community. Any individual who commits such a crime offends against international law. The nature of these crimes is such that they are likely to involve the concerted conduct of many and liable to involve the complicity of the officials of the state in which they occur, if not of the state itself. In these circumstances it is desirable that jurisdiction should exist to prosecute individuals for such conduct outside the territory in which such conduct occurs.

I believe that it is still an open question whether international law recognises universal jurisdiction in respect of international crimes—that is the right, under international law, of the courts of any state to prosecute for such crimes wherever they occur. In relation to war crimes, such a jurisdiction has been asserted by the State of Israel, notably in the prosecution of Adolf Eichmann, but this assertion of jurisdiction does not reflect any general state practice in relation to international crimes. Rather, states have tended to agree, or to attempt to agree, on the creation of international tribunals to try international crimes. They have however, on occasion, agreed by conventions, that their national courts should enjoy jurisdiction to prosecute for a particular category of international crime wherever occurring.

The principle of state immunity provides no bar to the exercise of criminal jurisdiction by an international tribunal, but the instruments creating such tribunals have tended, nonetheless, to make it plain that no exception from responsibility or immunity from process is to be enjoyed by a head of state or other state official. Thus the Charter of the Nuremberg Tribunal 1945 provides by Article 7:

> "The official position of defendants, whether as head of state or responsible officials in Government Departments shall not be considered as freeing them from responsibility or mitigating punishment"

The Tokyo Charter of 1946, the Statute of the International Criminal Tribunal for the former Yugoslavia of 1993, the Statute of the International Criminal Tribunal for Rwanda 1994 and the Statute of the International Criminal Court 1998 all have provisions to like effect.

Where states, by convention, agree that their national courts shall have jurisdiction on a universal basis in respect of an international crime, such agreement cannot implicitly remove immunities ratione personae that exist under international law. Such immunities can only be removed by express agreement or waiver. Such an agreement was incorporated in the Convention on the Prevention and Suppression of the Crime of Genocide 1984, which provides:

> "Persons committing genocide or any of the other acts enumerated in Article III shall be punished, whether they are constitutionally responsible rulers, public officials, or private individuals."

Had the Genocide Convention not contained this provision, an issue could have been raised as to whether the jurisdiction conferred by the Convention was subject to state immunity ratione materiae. Would international law have required a court to grant immunity to a defendant upon his demonstrating that he was acting in an official capacity? In my view it plainly would not. I do not reach that conclusion on the ground that assisting in genocide can never be a function of a state official. I reach that conclusion on the simple basis that no established rule of international law requires state immunity ratione materiae to be accorded in respect of prosecution for an international crime. International crimes and extra-territorial jurisdiction in relation to them are both new arrivals in the field of public international law. I do not believe that state immunity ratione materiae can co-exist with them. The exercise of extra-territorial jurisdiction overrides the principle that one state will not intervene in the internal affairs of another. It does so because, where international crime is concerned, that principle cannot prevail. An international crime is as offensive, if not more offensive, to the international community when committed under colour of office. Once extra-territorial jurisdiction is established, it makes no sense to exclude from it acts done in an official capacity.

There can be no doubt that the conduct of which Senator Pinochet stands accused by Spain is criminal under international law. The Republic of Chile has accepted that torture is prohibited by international law and that the prohibition of torture has the character of jus cogens and or obligation erga omnes. It is further accepted that officially sanctioned torture is forbidden by international law. The information provided by Spain accuses Senator Pinochet not merely of having abused his powers as head of state by committing torture, but of subduing political opposition by a campaign of abduction, torture and murder that extended beyond the boundaries of Chile. When considering what is alleged, I do not believe that it is correct to attempt to analyse individual elements of this campaign and to identify some as being criminal under international law and others as not constituting international crimes. If Senator Pinochet behaved as Spain alleged, then the entirety of his conduct was a violation of the norms of international law. He can have no immunity against prosecution for any crime that formed part of that campaign.

It is only recently that the criminal courts of this country acquired jurisdiction, pursuant to Section 134 of the Criminal Justice Act 1984, to prosecute Senator Pinochet for torture committed outside the territorial jurisdiction, provided that it was committed in the performance, or purported performance, of his official duties. Section 134 was passed to give effect to the rights and obligations of this country under the Convention against Torture and Other Cruel, Inhuman or Degrading Treatment or Punishment of 1984, to which the United Kingdom, Spain and Chile are all signatories. That Convention outlaws the infliction of torture "by or at the instigation of or with the consent or acquiescence of a public official or other person acting in an official capacity". Each state party is required to make such conduct criminal under its law, wherever committed. More pertinently, each state party is required to prosecute any person found within its jurisdiction who has committed such an offence, unless it extradites that person for trial for the offence in another state. The only conduct covered by this Convention is conduct which would be subject to immunity ratione materiae, if such immunity were applicable. The Convention is thus incompatible with the applicability of immunity ratione materiae. There are only two possibilities. One is that the States Parties to the Convention proceeded on the premise that no immunity could exist ratione materiae in respect of torture, a crime contrary to international law. The other is that the States Parties to the Convention expressly agreed that immunity ratione materiae should not apply in the case of torture. I believe that the first of these alternatives is the correct one, but either must be fatal to the assertion by Chile and Senator Pinochet of immunity in respect of extradition proceedings based on torture.

The State Immunity Act 1978

I have referred earlier to Part I of the State Immunity Act 1978, which does not apply to criminal proceedings. Part III of the Act, which is of general application is headed "Miscellaneous and Supplementary". Under this Part, Section 20 provides:

"(1) Subject to the provisions of this section and to any necessary modifications, the Diplomatic Privileges Act 1964 shall apply to-
   (a) a sovereign or other head of state;
   (b) members of his family forming part of his household; and
   (c) his private servants,
as it applies to the head of a diplomatic mission, to members of his family forming part of his household and to his private servants."

The Diplomatic Privileges Act 1964 was passed to give effect to the Vienna Convention on Diplomatic Relations of 1961. The preamble to the Convention records that "peoples of all nations from ancient times have recognised the status of diplomatic agents". The Convention codifies long standing rules of public international law as to the privileges and immunities to be enjoyed by a diplomatic mission. The Act of 1964 makes applicable those Articles of the Convention that are scheduled to the Act. These include Article 29, which makes the person of a diplomatic agent immune from any form of detention and arrest, Article 31 which confers on a diplomatic agent immunity from the criminal and civil jurisdiction of the receiving state and Article 39, which includes the following provisions:

> "1. Every person entitled to privileges and immunities shall enjoy them from the moment he enters the territory of the receiving state on proceedings to take up his post or, if already in its territory, from the moment when his appointment is notified to the Ministry for Foreign Affairs or such other ministry as may be agreed.
> "2. When the functions of a person enjoying privileges and immunities have come to an end, such privileges and immunities shall normally cease at the moment when he leaves the country, or on expiry of a reasonable period in which to do so, but shall subsist until that time, even in case of armed conflict. However, with respect to acts performed by such a person in the exercise of his functions as a member of the mission, immunity shall continue to subsist."

The question arises of how, after the "necessary modifications", these provisions should be applied to a head of state. All who have so far in these proceedings given judicial consideration to this problem have concluded that the provisions apply so as to confer the immunities enjoyed by a diplomat upon a head of state in relation to his actions wherever in the world they take place. This leads to the further conclusion that a former head of state continues to enjoy immunity in respect of acts committed "in the exercise of his functions" as head of state, wherever those acts occurred.

For myself, I would not accord Section 20 of the Act of 1978 such broad effect. It seems to me that it does no more than to equate the position of a head of state and his entourage visiting this country with that of a diplomatic mission within this country. Thus interpreted, Section 20 accords with established principles of international law, is readily applicable and can appropriately be described as supplementary to the other Parts of the Act. As Lord Browne-Wilkinson has demonstrated, reference to the parliamentary history of the Section discloses that this was precisely the original intention of Section 20, for the section expressly provided that it applied to a head of state who was "in the United Kingdom at the invitation or with the consent of the Government of the United Kingdom". Those words were deleted by amendment. The mover of the amendment explained that the object of the amendment was to ensure that heads of state would be treated like heads of diplomatic missions "irrespective of presence in the United Kingdom".

Senator Pinochet and Chile have contended that the effect of Section 20, as amended, is to entitle Senator Pinochet to immunity in respect of any acts committed in the performance of his functions as head of state anywhere in the world, and that the conduct which forms the subject matter of the extradition proceedings, insofar as it occurred when Senator Pinochet was head of state, consisted of acts committed by him in performance of his functions as head of state.

If these submissions are correct, the Act of 1978 requires the English court to produce a result which is in conflict with international law and with our obligations under the Torture Convention. I do not believe that the submissions are correct, for the following reasons:

As I have explained, I do not consider that Section 20 of the Act of 1978 has any application to conduct of a head of state outside the United Kingdom. Such conduct remains governed by the rules of public international law. Reference to the parliamentary history of the section, which I do not consider appropriate, serves merely to confuse what appears to me to be relatively clear.

If I am mistaken in this view and we are bound by the Act of 1978 to accord to Senator Pinochet immunity in respect of all acts committed "in performance of his functions as head of state", I would not hold that the course of conduct alleged by Spain falls within that description. Article 3 of the Vienna Convention, which strangely is not one of those scheduled to the Act of 1964, defines the functions of a diplomatic mission as including "protecting in the receiving state the interests of the sending state and of its nationals, within the limits permitted by international law" [the emphasis is mine].

Insofar as Part III of the Act of 1978 entitles a former head of state to immunity in respect of the performance of his official functions I do not believe that those functions can, as a matter of statutory interpretation, extend to actions that are prohibited as criminal under international law. In this way one can reconcile, as one must seek to do, the provisions of the Act of 1978 with the requirements of public international law.

For these reasons, I would allow the appeal in respect of so much of the conduct alleged against Senator Pinochet as constitutes extradition crimes. I agree with Lord Hope as to the consequences which will follow as a result of the change in the scope of the case.

Prepared 24 March 1999

Index